THE LEFT BANK

THE LEFT BANK

Writers, Artists, and Politics from
the Popular Front to the Cold War

Herbert R. Lottman

Halo Books   San Francisco, CA

Published by:

HALO BOOKS
Post Office Box 2529, San Francisco, CA 94126

Copyright © 1991 by Halo Books

Typography by BookPrep
Manufactured in the United States of America
Originally Published by Houghton-Mifflin 1981

Library of Congress Catalog Card Number
91-28879

Library of Congress Cataloging-in-Publication Data
Lottman, Herbert R.
    The Left Bank : writers, artists, and politics from the popular front to the
cold war / Herbert Lottman.
        p.   cm.
    Includes bibliographical references and indexes.
    ISBN 0-9622874-4-X : $14.95
    1. Rive gauche (Paris, France)—Intellectual life—20th century.
2. Paris (France)—Intellectual life—20th century.
3. Intellectuals—France—Paris—Political activity.   4. Politics and
literature—France—Paris—History—20th century. I. Title.
DC752.L43L67   1991
944'.360815—dc20

Thanks to this "right of inspection" [of one's neighbor's territory] the idea of international justice begins to override that of "local interest" justice so convenient to various nationalisms. Thanks to this right, to the pressure of inspection, the Reichstag trial acquitted the innocent . . .
— ANDRÉ GIDE (1934)

Writers — our comrades — who have traveled to the United States, or across Latin America, have been telling us how closely those peoples are following current events in France. On the success or failure of the French Popular Front may depend, they assure us, the political orientation of the world for the next fifty years.
— JEAN GUÉHENNO (1936)

I never shouted from public platforms . . . No! No! No! I never miked or pimped at meetings. I love you, my Stalin! My adorable Litvinov! My Comintern! . . . I've never voted in my life! . . . I never signed a manifesto . . . for the martyrs of this . . . the tortured of that . . . You can rest assured . . . It's always a matter of Jews . . . of a yid or a Masonic committee . . .
— LOUIS-FERDINAND CÉLINE (1937)

Contents

Acknowledgments

MANY OF THE LEADING actors of the period covered in this book are no longer alive, and I have had to rely on their written record: memoirs and correspondence, but also on the memories of their companions. Others with whom I should have liked to talk were not available for objective interviewing, and their biographies are being written by their sympathizers. Fortunately, many of their secrets, by which I mean the historically significant acts they may prefer to keep us from remembering, are contained in old newspapers and magazines, and in the musty books and documents of the period, to be discovered not so much in libraries as in the second-hand bookshops of today's Left Bank.

I did obtain help from many who witnessed these years. They include, and I am grateful to each of them, Jorge Amado, Henri Amouroux, Raymond Aron, André Bay, Mme Julien Benda, François Bondy, Claude Bourdet, Christian Bourgois, Jean Cassou, André and Lucie Chamson, Edmond Charlot, Pierre Daix, Marguerite Duras, Max-Pol Fouchet, Eugène Guillevic, Gerhard Heller, Jean Lescure, Yves Lévy, Clara Malraux, Dionys Mascolo, Claude Morgan, Jacqueline Paulhan, Charles Ronsac, Pierre Schaeffer, Lucien Scheler, Gilbert Sigaux, Manès Sperber, Roger Stéphane, René Tavernier, and Jean Bruller ("Vercors").

Useful work was done in Paris at the Bibliothèque Sainte-Geneviève, and in the archives to which it gives shelter: the Bibliothèque Jacques Doucet. And in the Centre de Documentation Juive Contemporaine, the libraries of La Documentation Française and the Assemblée Nationale, the Communist Party's Institut Maurice Thorez (now Institut de Recherches Marxistes), the research library of the French book trade's Cercle de la Librairie. My gratitude goes to Suzanne Berger, who kindly read the manuscript with a critical pencil poised over it.

Introduction

THIS STORY BEGINS in the Paris of the 1930s, when a comparatively small group of men and women, not all of them French, most of them writers (or journalists and teachers who were occasional writers), appeared to stand at the center of the world stage. For not only France, but much of what was then the literate universe, was concerned by what was being said and done on the Left Bank — that narrow strip of old houses and older streets along the Seine where writers and artists lived and worked. Their manifestos echoed throughout Europe, and as far away as Stalinist Russia and capitalist America. More than one member of the group was actually invited to bear witness far from home — in the United States or the Soviet Union. A few traveled to Germany to challenge Hitler on his home ground (or to praise him); many fought in the Spanish Civil War. The story ends only after two major confrontations shook the group: during the German occupation of France in the Second World War, when they sometimes fought on opposing sides, and again in liberated France, when the divisions were along equally rigid ideological lines.

By then a large cloud was to cover the Left Bank of Paris, something of a nuclear cloud — the fallout of the struggle between East and West. This cloud had the curious ancillary effect of reducing the apparent dimensions, and influence, of the Left Bank. It no longer mattered as much, to the rest of the literate universe, what that small group of French and foreign intellectuals was likely to do or to say. Therefore the years 1930 on one side, 1950 on the other, roughly delimit the period. They encompass the rise and fall of the committed intellectual. When the smoke cleared, most of the best of them had ceased to be publicly concerned with the world beyond France. When we hear about them afterward, they are involved in strictly national issues such as the

Algerian war, the Gaullist regime, the May 1968 rebellion.

Two things become apparent early in this story. One is that the international impact of many of the actors in these events is disproportionate to their artistic achievement. Surely no one had greater prestige among "engaged" intellectuals in the first years than André Malraux, and yet the literary value of what he published at the peak of his political activity has been vigorously questioned. He himself admitted that his most consciously engaged book, the anti-Fascist novel *Le Temps du mépris* ("Days of Wrath"), was a failure, and many would say the same for his Spanish war novel *L'Espoir* ("Man's Hope"), and for his unfinished occupation novel. André Gide was to confess that he had ceased to write when he began to involve himself in politics; his engaged work is not his best. Similarly, some truly minor talents, such as that of Pierre Drieu La Rochelle, carried their authors a long way thanks to the provocative nature of their politics. Since this is more of a political history than a literary one, the books most cited of an admired author may not be those most admired, but rather some less successful works that define an activity or a commitment, or describe a milieu. It would seem that to produce enduring literature, one had to be a loner, like Céline when he wrote *Voyage au bout de la nuit* ("Journey to the End of the Night") and *Mort à crédit* ("Death on the Installment Plan"), Sartre at the time of *La Nausée* ("Nausea"), or Camus of *L'Etranger* ("The Stranger").

The other thing — a curious one to observers born far from the Left Bank — is the remarkable loyalty between men and women whom opinions and sometimes wars should have separated once and for all. They went to the same schools and then taught in the same universities, or they worked on the same magazines and in the same publishing houses, took coffee in the same salons, sat side by side in restaurants and cafés. They may even have fought together on the far right, say, until one of their number moved to the far left, without ever quite breaking ties with the friends left behind. The resulting confusion in the order of battle is sometimes enough to make the head spin. It may even suggest that commitments were not always taken seriously, especially when the committed wore the fancy dress of the dilettantes of *La Nouvelle Revue Française*. Indeed, at times the engagement was not serious, but at other times it certainly was. Thus Jean Paulhan of *La Nouvelle Revue Française*, a man who confounds analysis by seeming disengaged when most engaged, was arrested by the Nazis for perilous acts of resistance, but was not shot as others in the network were, thanks to the intervention of a pro-Fascist collaborator who had taken over his office. We shall also see old friends denouncing each other in circumstances that could lead to arrest, torture, death. At the height of Left Bank Stalinism, one old friend might condemn another to loss of career or social banishment over a difference of opinion — even an opinion on such a subject as the way to portray Stalin's mustache (in the controversial portrait by Picasso).

While this book is concerned with cultural and not economic history, the politico-literary wars of the Left Bank were played out against an exceptional background — that of the long depression that affected every aspect of France's economic and social life from the beginning of the 1930s — and in a context of international crisis that opened no window to hope anywhere, certainly not in the nontotalitarian world. A crisis that a well-meaning ruling party and class was helpless to confront or resolve. This situation encouraged curiosity about — sympathy for — the Soviet experiment, strengthened the domestic Communist Party, and led to a new economic deal in the form of Léon Blum's Popular Front. But first France was to go through the agonies of a deliberate policy of deflation. In 1935 it had two million unemployed, in a work force of 12.5 million. From depression to military defeat and enemy occupation, from occupation to grim postwar recovery: the years described in this history were far from idyllic. If material considerations rarely appear in the memoirs and memories of that time, it may be because writers and artists and other intellectuals lived on the fringes of society.

Contrary to Left Bank mythology, there are few Americans or British on the stage. The heroic period of the Lost Generation following World War I had come to a close some time before the main events of this book. Those of the Lost Generation who continued to live in Paris, or to visit it with any regularity, such as F. Scott Fitzgerald or Ernest Hemingway, saw the city as a moveable feast, and they usually took from it more than they put in. A few like Gertrude Stein and Sylvia Beach contributed to the artistic and literary wealth of their adopted city, and certainly should have their place in a strictly cultural account of the Left Bank. But they were hardly engaged in history in the same sense as the protagonists of this book — committed to a politics, prepared to defend it in the marketplace of ideas. For Henry Miller, indeed, the political drama of the 1930s was a nuisance that interfered with his living and working in Paris. The few Anglo-Americans who did contribute to political history — a Waldo Frank or an E.M. Forster in the 1930s, a Richard Wright in the 1940s — are dealt with in the appropriate places.

When the story begins, in an earlier but not necessarily a more innocent time, it is as though the men and women who are to play leading roles are sitting for a group portrait, similar to the *Hommage à Delacroix* of Fantin-Latour, in which we can identify Manet, Whistler, Baudelaire, and other eminent contemporaries. Such group portraits of the protagonists actually exist, in the photographs of the eminences of French literature and politics taken during summer seminars at the Abbey of Pontigny. Before the gathering storm.

The Left Bank

Curtain Raiser

IN THOSE YEARS one could never be certain where Ilya Grigoryevich Ehrenburg might be found — perhaps in Moscow, more likely in Paris. And did anyone know where he really stood, he who had written satirical novels such as *The Extraordinary Adventures of Julio Jurenito and His Disciples*, which in the darker days of Stalinism could not be seen in a Soviet bookstore or library (nor probably in anyone's home, either)? Ehrenburg himself later recollected that in the 1930s in Montparnasse his behavior was more that of a young poet than of a serious writer. But when the last guest had left his ground-floor apartment facing the railroad tracks behind the Gare Montparnasse, the same Ehrenburg would turn to his writing table, among the disorder of piled books and paintings and favorite pipes, to prepare another hard-line article for *Izvestia*, the Moscow daily newspaper for which he was a correspondent. A *bon vivant* and familiar figure at the bar of La Coupole on the Boulevard du Montparnasse, Ehrenburg was also an astute political operator, one of the few Soviet writers of his reputation, one of the only Jewish writers, to survive the Moscow purge years at the end of the 1930s. When his peers were in detention camps, he was receiving Stalin Prizes, and he was still alive when the time came to chronicle that unbelievable era.

Ehrenburg's sincerity may be believed when he expressed concern about the rise of Fascism; the man-about-Montparnasse would have been as alarmed about that as the Soviet journalist. He accompanied André Malraux on a journey from Paris to Moscow in 1934, and the two attended a congress of Soviet writers. Back in Paris that autumn, he attended a meeting where André Gide joined Malraux on the speakers' platform to listen to firsthand accounts of the Moscow congress. As

Ehrenburg later told it, then and there a woman friend whispered to him that Soviet and French writers ought to cooperate in the anti-Fascist movement. Did Ehrenburg need convincing? Whatever the answer to that, he reported the suggestion to Moscow, concluding with a proposal for the creation of an anti-Fascist writers' organization.

Moscow's reply came quickly, in a telephone call from the Soviet ambassador to France: Stalin himself wished to talk to Ehrenburg. So he packed his bags again and was back in Moscow in November. On December 1, still waiting for the summons to the Kremlin, he dropped in to see his editor-in-chief at *Izvestia*. The man appeared thunderstruck. Sergei Kirov, the popular secretary of the Communist Party of Leningrad, had just been murdered. The death of this Politburo member set off one of history's bloodiest massacres — purge trials, deportations, executions — and nearly two decades of fear. It took some time before survivors dared consider that Stalin himself had probably ordered the assassination of his potential rival.

Ehrenburg did not see Stalin on that visit; Stalin had taken charge of the investigation of the murder. Instead, Ehrenburg received his instructions from the Party's central committee: he was to submit a precise plan for an international writers' organization. On his return to Paris, he made the appropriate contacts. With Malraux, of course, and with Gide, both of whom could be counted on; with Paul Nizan, the young Communist intellectual par excellence; with Paul Vaillant-Couturier, the Party's chief liaison with writers and intellectuals; and with eminent friends of the Soviet Union such as Jean Guéhenno, the liberal and pacifist editor-in-chief of *Europe*.

In March 1935, a group of writers met to draw up a program. Thus it came about that an International Writers Congress for the Defense of Culture was organized, to be held in Paris from June 21 to 25. Every significant writer with a social conscience was invited. Apart from the French, the delegation from across the Channel was probably the most prestigious, with the novelists Aldous Huxley and E. M. Forster, and John Strachey, the gentleman Marxist. From the United States the organizers drew a lesser-known group of Communists and fellow thinkers, among them Waldo Frank, who had just helped found a League of American Writers in New York, and Michael Gold, columnist for the American Communist Party's *Daily Worker*. The German émigrés Heinrich Mann, Ernst Toller, Bertolt Brecht, Anna Seghers, and Lion Feuchtwanger, and Robert Musil of Austria were scheduled speakers. The Soviet Union was to send its best-known living author,

Maxim Gorki, Alexei Tolstoi (no relation to Leo, the French would discover to their disappointment), and Ehrenburg, of course.

The French home team was also impressive. It included Gide, Malraux, Guéhenno, the Communists Louis Aragon and Henri Barbusse, and also Tristan Tzara of the old Dada movement, the Surrealist René Crevel, and André Chamson, a novelist of provincial life, who was an aide to Edouard Daladier, the Radical Socialist political leader.

Shortly before the official opening of the congress, André Breton came upon Ilya Ehrenburg crossing the Boulevard du Montparnasse — in search of tobacco for his pipe, as it happened. Breton was the leader of the politically active Surrealists, who had embraced Communism and the October Revolution until they became discouraged by the increasingly police-state orientation of the Stalinist system and by the official doctrine of Socialist Realism, which seemed to exclude artistic experiment. Ehrenburg's sudden appearance reminded Breton of the attacks on his friends and himself in a book Ehrenburg had published the previous year. In it Ehrenburg had mocked the Surrealists, who he said were involved only with "pederasty and dreams," while living on inherited wealth or a wife's dowry. Women, wrote Ehrenburg, represented conformity to Surrealists; they really preferred "onanism, pederasty, fetichism, exhibitionism, and even sodomy." As for their politics: "The Soviet Union disgusts them because people work in that country."

So Breton announced himself in the tobacco shop and began slapping Ehrenburg on the face, while his victim, making no effort to defend himself, asked what it was all about. He soon informed Breton that he had offended an official Soviet delegate to the International Writers Congress and would be banned from its proceedings — Ehrenburg insisting that those who use fists to decide arguments were Fascists. Breton replied that by offending Ehrenburg he had not offended the Soviet delegation any more than it had offended him when Ehrenburg's book was published.

Malraux and Gide, among others, assumed that Breton would retaliate. The Surrealists were known for scandalous tracts, provocative speeches; many outside the movement thought that was what Surrealism was all about. In the spirit of revolt, the Surrealists had become Communists in the 1920s. One of the most provocative of the band, Louis Aragon, had moved especially close to the Communists, so close that he was even persuaded to disavow his Surrealist comrades. When

Breton, Paul Eluard, and René Crevel were excluded from the French Communist Party, Aragon became its brightest literary light.

But René Crevel continued to enjoy good relations with the Communists. He even wrote for the Communist-controlled *Commune*, of which Aragon was an editor. So it was Crevel, whom everyone admired for his spontaneity and earnest good will, who took on the task, despite fragile health, of reconciling his two cherished loyalties, Communism and Surrealism. The Surrealists, in any case, represented an insignificant minority to the Communists; offending them mattered little even in the narrowest circles of intellectual Paris. The main thing was to keep provocateurs out of the International Writers Congress.

Crevel asked Malraux and Jean Cassou — an art critic sympathetic to Surrealism and other contemporary movements, and a fervent advocate of working with the Communists against Fascism — to intervene with Aragon so that Breton could take part in the congress. Aragon replied that the matter was in the hands of the Soviet delegates, since they threatened to withdraw if Breton were allowed to participate. Crevel then persuaded Cassou, who was an imposing thirty-eight years old and a respectable civil servant, to use his authority on the adamant Russians. The occasion would be a gathering of delegates at that favorite café, the venerable Closerie des Lilas on the Boulevard du Montparnasse.

When Cassou entered the café, Crevel nodded in the direction of Ilya Ehrenburg. While Crevel watched with manifest anguish, Cassou approached the Russian writer and told him, "At an anti-Fascist meeting you can't ban the man who represents the Surrealists." Ehrenburg grunted, "Breton acted like a cop. If he is allowed to speak, the Soviet delegation will walk out." Cassou went to Crevel and whispered, "It's hopeless." Visibly upset, Crevel joined Cassou and Tristan Tzara to hail a taxi in the rain. They dropped Tzara off near the Boulevard Saint-Germain, Cassou got out at Saint-Germain-des-Prés, and Crevel kept the cab to go up to Montmartre. That night he killed himself. *L'Humanité*, the Communist newspaper, treated the event with respect; its story appeared on the opening day of the congress:

REVOLUTIONARY WRITER
RENÉ CREVEL IS DEAD

"He had been ill for a number of years," the story explained. "In the last two weeks the disease had reappeared with distressing symptoms. René Crevel was unable to bear it."

PART I

The
Setting

1   Moving In

THERE WAS A TIME, if a Frenchman had the right qualifications, had gone to the right schools, and possessed proper introductions, when certain neighborhoods of the Left Bank could serve as a virtual extension of his living room. Or his living room, suitably located, could occasionally replace café tables, book and magazine editorial offices, even meeting halls. At one time, the privileged places were a few streets in Montparnasse, particularly a group of cafés on the boulevard of that name. But by the middle of the 1930s, the cluster of narrow lanes surrounding the church and square of Saint-Germain-des-Prés, with its unsurpassed density of bookstores and publishing houses, galleries and outdoor cafés, began to claim the position it would hold for at least the next twenty years. Farther east along the Left Bank, one had gone to school, had taught, or was teaching. In times of crisis, there was a choice of meeting halls; the newest and largest, the Palais de la Mutualité, would become the preferred assembly point for this and successive generations. There was a further feature of the Left Bank — one's creative life, one's friendships and affections, were played out on a stage that would soon have the whole world as an audience.

Several of the actors on this stage considered 1935 as the year when Saint-Germain-des-Prés came into its own. That was when André Breton and his band of Surrealists began to favor the subdued Café des Deux Magots, opposite the Romanesque church of Place Saint-Germain-des-Prés. It was also then that a new generation of writers and poets took possession of the neighboring Café de Flore. Many were migrating only a few hundred yards north from the traditional crossroads of cafés and artists' studios of Montparnasse, which itself had followed Montmartre as the preferred quarter of painters and poets, providing

solace and shelter and entertainment to much of the creative elite of the
first decades of the century, among them Picasso, Apollinaire, Max
Jacob, Modigliani, Braque, Vlaminck, Cocteau.

It was apparently also in 1935 that Picasso moved his entourage from
Montparnasse to what was still felt to be the provincial calm of Saint-
Germain-des-Prés; they settled first at the Deux Magots, then at the
Flore. The German art student Arno Breker, who returned to Paris a
few years later as a successful sculptor to escort a surprise tourist, the
conqueror Adolf Hitler, through his favorite haunts, also remembered
the Flore and the Deux Magots as "oases of silence" where "the
assiduous writer found the right conditions for concentration." For
Breker, "These establishments have always been able to anchor in this
neighborhood the vagabond heart of the world's nomads."

It was in 1935 that Léon-Paul Fargue, the quintessential café-goer and
poet, moved to the Boulevard Saint-Germain, bringing his legend with
him from Montparnasse. He became the Baedeker of the neighborhood, summing up his observations in his book Le Piéton de Paris:

> If during the day there is a meeting of the French Cabinet, a boxing match
> in New Jersey, a grand prize for conformists, a literary splash, a celebrity
> contest on the Right Bank or a shouting match, the café-goers of Place
> Saint-Germain-des-Prés are the first to hear the results of these
> encounters and competitions.

For Fargue, this square was the place where "one feels the most up to
date, the closest to real events, to the people who know the real truths
about the nation, the world, and art." He continued with a description
of each of the cafés that had become "as famous today as national
institutions": the Deux Magots, with successful writers like Jean
Giraudoux, snobs, and well-to-do American ladies; the Flore, with its
political and literary traditions; and then his beloved Lipp, whose turn-
of-the-century ceramic decorations happened to be the work of his own
father and uncle. The Brasserie Lipp, remarks Fargue (citing the critic
Albert Thibaudet), owed much of its attractiveness to the proximity of
the Nouvelle Revue Française, a couple of publishers, the fine old
bookshop called the Divan, the literary and cultural press, the nearby
Théâtre du Vieux-Colombier (then a center of the experimental stage),
the upper house of the French parliament, and also "to the Popular
Front, the booksellers, the second-hand book dealers and intellectual
hotel managers of this unique quarter . . ."

If one had the good fortune to live in this village, as did Jean Cassou, the writer and critic, one might feel that one owned a window on the world.   Indeed, Cassou's window overlooked the cafés of Saint-Germain-des-Prés. His wife had only to glance out of the window to tell her husband that a certain writer of their acquaintance was entering the Deux Magots, and then leaving it to go into the Flore. Once downstairs, seated among friends at the Deux Magots, Cassou himself could observe, and meet, friends at other cafés nearby. In that era before the automobile made street-watching uncomfortable, table-hopping was normal here, as well as on the Boulevard du Montparnasse, from the Rotonde Café to the Dôme across the wide avenue, from the Dôme to the Select. Needless to say, Cassou's publishers (Emile-Paul, Grasset, Gallimard) were all located within a ten-minute walk from his home.

★ ★ ★

It was generally agreed, in those between-the-wars years, that France was the center of the literary and artistic world, and of course Paris was the center of that center. Not only had it gathered the best of the current generation from distant provinces and neighboring nations, but it was training the best of the next. Just before World War II, 45.7 percent of France's university students were enrolled in Parisian schools, and 91 percent of the university-level schools were in Paris. Is there a need to add that they were concentrated in a few streets of the Left Bank?

"The Left Bank is Paris's countryside," wrote Albert Thibaudet, in the aptly titled La République des professeurs:

> Young provincials arrive in Paris . . . by the Montagne Sainte-Geneviève [in the Latin Quarter], its high schools, its institutions of higher learning, its Sorbonne. They bring to it . . . reserves of provincial energy, the salt of the earth, French endurance . . .

Jean Guéhenno, who was to play a leading role in the political wars of the Left Bank, described another republic, not of professors but of "of letters," "that in which ideas are unmade and remade," and "which is not much greater in area than it was two hundred years ago at the time our masters, the philosophers of enlightenment, founded it." He went on with as suitable an introduction to the topography of the Left Bank as can be found anywhere:

> It [the Republic of Letters] is wholly contained in a few Parisian houses, some cramped magazine or publishing offices, some drawing rooms, some cafés,

some artists' studios, some attic rooms. It is not easy to penetrate this
world. The real dialogue takes place between a few dozen writers who
acknowledge each other, and that is all . . .

Even schoolchildren knew this. At least one manual for classroom use
published between the World Wars provided maps to illustrate the
concentration of schools of higher learning, and the book world, on the
Left Bank.

Of course, the university tradition of the Latin Quarter dated back to
the Middle Ages, and a well-documented literary life went on there in
the seventeenth century with Racine, Molière, and Madame de La
Fayette, and in the following century with Voltaire and Sainte-Beuve.
Perhaps the intellectual Left Bank acquired its true vocation in the
nineteenth century, symbolized by, if not limited to, the promiscuous
café life there. One name keeps coming up in the social history of the
neighborhood: Café Procope on the Rue de l'Ancienne-Comédie,
frequented by the makers of the *Encyclopédie*, Diderot, Voltaire,
Rousseau, Beaumarchais, Danton, and Marat, then in the Romantic
years by Balzac, George Sand, Musset, and still later by Zola, Huysmans,
Maupassant, and Cézanne. Or the Café Voltaire in the Place de
l'Odéon, later transformed into an American library; it was host to
Verlaine and Mallarmé in the era of the Symbolists, and to Paul Bourget
and Maurice Barrès at the turn of the century.

By the end of the nineteenth century, the fifth, sixth, and seventh
districts or *arrondissements*, comprising the heart of the Left Bank, were
among the preferred residential neighborhoods of thinkers, although not
necessarily of successful authors, for they followed the upper classes into
more desirable Right Bank sections. But the literary magazines were on
the Left Bank, particularly the avant-garde reviews, and so were their
contributors and their readers. When a journal became prosperous, it
deserted the bohemian districts to migrate to the Right Bank, along with
its leading writers and editors.

There was also an American Left Bank, superimposed on the French
one, utilizing the same streets and cafés and coffee cups, but not quite
(or not necessarily) at the same times or in the same ways. This Left
Bank centered on the famous Dôme-Rotonde-Select and Coupole
crossroads of Montparnasse, extending northward to the Deux Magots
and the Flore at Saint-Germain-des-Prés. "No matter what café in
Montparnasse you ask a taxi-driver to bring you to from the right bank of

the river," Ernest Hemingway's Jake Barnes observes in *The Sun Also
Rises*, "they always take you to La Rotonde. Ten years from now it will
probably be Le Dôme." The Americans of Montparnasse were already
something of a legend in 1925, when Gustave Fuss-Amoré and Maurice
des Ombiaux wrote a magazine-style account of the Montparnasse they
knew. "Montparnasse is the center of the world!" is their opening line.
The authors pay particular homage to the young American women they
encountered there:

> After dinner, when the young American girls stroll in Montparnasse on
> summer evenings in their light dresses, it's a youth festival! They have
> adopted the habit of going out without hats, informal and carefree,
> stressing their carefree attitudes by a twig held in the hand or a cigarette
> stuck between the lips . . .
>   At times the sidewalk tables at the Dôme give the impression of being a
> recreation yard for these young Yankees. In the evening they are willing
> partners in a one-step or a shimmy; the afternoon, they play little girls'
> games . . .

It had not always been that bad, the authors suggested:

> There was a Left Bank spirit, very clearly opposed to that of the Right
> Bank. Let us say it frankly: the existence of a powerful foreign colony in
> Montparnasse, the respect which it manifested for the great moments of
> French thought and art, contributed to strengthen this antagonism.

But now — this is 1925 — the authors fear that the American colony,
thanks to a highly favorable currency exchange, may have grown more in
quantity than in quality. One can no longer feel quite at home. Yet the
Left Bank of the young American girls dancing the shimmy was also the
Left Bank of Hemingway and Fitzgerald, and in *A Moveable Feast*
Hemingway provides a walking tour of the area, from his rooms in the
Rue Cardinal-Lemoine at the eastern limits of the Latin Quarter, along
the riverbank lined with bookstalls, in and out of the bistros, to Brasserie
Lipp, then to the Dôme, Rotonde, and Select. "In the three principal
cafés I saw people that I knew by sight and others that I knew to speak
to," he wrote. "But there were always much nicer-looking people that I
did not know that, in the evening with the lights just coming on, were
hurrying to some place to drink together, to eat together and then to
make love." Hemingway might wind up his walk at an American cultural
landmark, the Shakespeare & Company bookshop at 12, Rue de

l'Odéon, run by Sylvia Beach. Miss Beach had been inspired by an earlier, French landmark at number 7 of the same street — La Maison des Amis des Livres, a small bookshop and lending library owned by Adrienne Monnier, whose customers included some of the most prestigious names in contemporary letters, and others who were to become known.

Sylvia Beach went on to establish a bookshop and lending library of her own, but hers was for books in English. It quickly became a home away from home for American and British visitors — tourists and longer-term residents. They might even receive their mail there, and a few enjoyed banking privileges as well; Miss Beach sometimes punned it by calling her bookshop "The Left Bank." She also became the original publisher in English of James Joyce's controversial *Ulysses*, which made her a semiofficial channel to Joyce while he lived in Paris. In a similarly informal fashion she began to represent American writers and amateur publishers. Then her polyvalent activity and her association with Adrienne Monnier brought her into touch not only with Americans such as Gertrude Stein, Ezra Pound, Hemingway, and Fitzgerald, but with French writers curious about the Anglo-Americans and their new literature: André Gide, Paul Valéry, Jean Paulhan, Jules Romains, Georges Duhamel, André Chamson, Jean Schlumberger. Adrienne Monnier's Amis des Livres served as an occasional literary salon, with readings of new works by a Valéry or an André Breton, recitals of new music by Erik Satie, Darius Milhaud. Joyce found a French public there. Many French authors at the beginning of their careers met for the first time at the Monnier or Beach bookshops, and many received encouragement from these bookseller ladies.

★   ★   ★

There was a definite Left Bank mentality: a special sort of patriotism, when it was not ideology. The Right Bank, it has been noted, claimed André Maurois, Sacha Guitry, Marcel Pagnol, *Le Roi des Resquilleurs* (a popular film of the early 1930s), Ginger Rogers, and Fred Astaire. Left Bank culture encompassed Jean Giraudoux, Luis Buñuel, *Drôle de drame* (the Marcel Carné-Jacques Prévert burlesque film), Gaston Baty, William Powell, and Myrna Loy. In a work with the expressive title *Saint-Germain-des-Prés, mon village*, Léo Larguier expressed scorn for the cafés of the Right Bank, "gigantic hotel lobbies, extravagant palaces, without a quiet corner, and where the people of our neighborhood could not survive." Emmanuel Berl, evoking the contempt of the Left Bank's *Nouvelle Revue Française* for the popular actor Sacha Guitry, was quoted: "There was always this prejudice, at the *Nouvelle Revue Française*, that when one didn't live on the Left Bank, somewhere around the Rue Vaneau, in other words in a neighborhood as dull as a small town, there was something wrong with you . . . and you weren't a real writer."

When Berl informed Roger Martin du Gard, that *Nouvelle Revue Française* eminence, that he was going to move to the Right Bank, Martin du Gard expressed horror. "Couldn't you find anything around here?" For such people, the Right Bank was the domain of the mindless middle classes, and the life of the mind couldn't cross the Seine.

One might draw a political map of the Left Bank. From the point of view of a militant student of the 1930s, the university quarter, from the Place du Panthéon as far west as the Odéon intersection, was in the hands of the right-wing students of Action Française. The left would take it over during the years of the Popular Front. Farther west, and south to Montparnasse, the neighborhood belonged to writers and artists who in principle stood outside the political arena. These writers and artists also had, in Simone de Beauvoir's expression, an ideology, but without political consequences. The habitués of the Café de Flore, for example, took Jacques Prévert as their idol. "Their anticonformist attitude served above all to justify their inertia," Beauvoir, the young teacher, observed. "They spent the day expressing their distaste in bored little phrases interrupted by yawning."

If the veterans of France's political wars — of the Dreyfus affair, notably — seemed to be pursuing the combat at these sidewalk café tables, so the émigrés were planning the wars to come. Before the Russian Revolution, Leon Trotski and Lenin's companion, the critic and playwright Anatoli Lunacharsky — who as Soviet commissar of education would continue to represent a bridge between east and west — were customers at the Left Bank cafés; so for a time was Lenin himself. In the 1930s there was a Soviet corner at La Coupole whenever Ilya Ehrenburg was in town. But by that time politics had grown to become the principal concern of the best representatives of the Left Bank.

2 Making Friends

AMONG THE SCHOOLS of higher education of the Latin Quarter, the Ecole Normale Supérieure enjoyed special status. Its selection process was such (arduous training in a preparatory year known as the *khâgne*), its program so conceived, its atmosphere so much like that of an American college fraternity house, that graduates of ENS seemed a race apart. Many of them went on from the teaching career to which they were pledged to politics and the creative arts. They became government officials, sometimes even heads of government, and one was elected President of the Republic. They became political chieftains, or distinguished themselves in journalism, fiction, or poetry, and then, whatever the chosen field, frequently ended their careers in the Académie Française. Socialist leaders Jean Jaurès, Léon Blum, the Catholic essayist and poet Charles Péguy, authors Romain Rolland and Jules Romains, and playwright Jean Giraudoux all graduated from the Normale. The *normaliens* are among the protagonists of this book because of the part they played in the crisis years of the 1930s and beyond. At times they played their parts on opposing sides, although their behavior was often determined by the years spent at the Ecole Normale Supérieure.

In *La République des professeurs*, Albert Thibaudet, himself a *normalien*, pointed to another characteristic of the school: its role as a melting pot. If the cost of education for degrees in medicine and law exceeded the means of working and rural classes, schoolteachers could come up from the ranks because scholarships were available to allow them to pursue their studies. Writing in the 1920s, Thibaudet found that eight or nine out of ten students of the Normale had won such scholarships. So one could have been born and raised in a distant province, and still be accepted at the Normale; indeed, during one's time at the preparatory *khâgne* and then at ENS, one might make connections that would serve throughout a lifetime. It was as effective a way to enter society as to grow up in a good Paris neighborhood.

The best-known examples of lasting friendships between Ecole Normale comrades in the generation that concerns us are those between Jean-Paul Sartre and Raymond Aron, Sartre and Paul Nizan, Sartre and Maurice Merleau-Ponty (who later became the editor of *Sartre's magazine Les Temps Modernes*), and Sartre and Simone de Beauvoir (for she was working for an advanced teaching degree at more or less the same time and places). Before joining his life to Beauvoir's, Sartre had been closest to his fellow student philosophers. With Raymond Aron, he fought battles of ideas with all the passion of a scholar. But once she entered the picture, no one else was as close to him again. The later careers of Aron — teaching, writing, political science, and political action — and Sartre — philosophy teacher, then engaged writer — kept them apart, just as teaching assignments had separated them after graduation. But in the euphoria of post-World War II Paris, Aron joined the first editorial board of *Les Temps Modernes*, although it should have been clear that Sartre and he were worlds apart politically. The Ecole Normale was the common denominator.

Sartre has written with tenderness of his school years with Paul Nizan. Both knew that they wanted to be writers. Nizan achieved early fame, although his real talents and energy went into politics. The two men resembled each other physically, each wearing glasses, each afflicted with the squinting that accompanies strabismus. Other students (Raymond Aron recalled) spoke of them as if they were Corneille and Racine. During the 1930s, while Nizan was moving up in the Communist Party hierarchy, making his presence felt throughout France and as far from France as the USSR, Sartre was by his own confession apolitical, even if "a left-winger at heart, of course, like everyone else." Nizan's rapid rise flattered Sartre; it seemed to give the passive member of this couple a sort of revolutionary grace. "Our friendship was so precious and we were taken for each other so often that it was I as much as he who wrote his lead articles in [the Communist Party daily] *Ce Soir*," Sartre later recalled. Sartre and Aron were witnesses at Nizan's marriage in 1927.

And then, after Nizan's dramatic break with the Communist Party in August 1939, when it endorsed the Soviet pact of nonaggression with Nazi Germany (Nizan died soon after on a battlefield in northern

France), the Communist whispering campaign against him stirred
Sartre's dormant friendship into life. Despite the euphoric Popular
Front atmosphere of postliberation Paris, Sartre challenged .the
Communists to prove the allegation that Nizan had been a secret
government informer, or put an end to their slander. It was as if a time
bomb set in the classrooms of the Ecole Normale Supérieure had gone
off a quarter of a century later.*

★   ★   ★

The very special life of a *normalien* has been described by the Breton
novelist Henri Queffélec, who migrated from his native Brittany to
enroll in a Paris lycée to prepare for the entrance examinations to ENS.
Queffélec became a product of that melting pot, in which provincials
like him were integrated with sophisticated young Parisians who were
better dressed and more relaxed in their manners. He studied for his
exams alongside a brilliant Far-Eastern-scholar-to-be, René Etiemble
(another who later joined Sartre at *Les Temps Modernes*); Robert
Brasillach, a budding Fascist; and Roger Vailland, who was a right-wing
ideologist before turning to the extreme left. (In his memoirs Queffélec
remarks that when Brasillach was executed for wartime collaboration
with the Nazis, the man who wrote most movingly about him was
Vailland, by then better known as an apologist for the Communists, but
an old school comrade all the same.)

Others in Queffélec's class were Jacques Talagrand, who became an
Action Française polemicist, and who used the name Thierry Maulnier
in his career as a critic even then; Louis Poirier, who would sign his
much-admired literary works Julien Gracq; the militant leftist and
subsequent Christian mystic, Simone Weil; and Georges Pompidou,
Charles de Gaulle's prime minister and successor as President of the
Republic (another who came to the Latin Quarter from the rural and
remote provinces). "One is a *normalien*," Pompidou would recall, "as
one is a prince of the blood. The entrance exam is only the dubbing.
The ceremony has its ritual, the vigil of arms taking place in appropriate
retreats, under the protection of our kings."

The school itself, as Thierry Maulnier wrote of it later, "was a secret
society, with a coded language, recognition signals, and that solidarity
among members which seems stronger than religious or political differ-

---

* See Chapter 28, "New Faces and Old."

ences . . . " Students were assigned to small monks' cells called *turnes*, and were expected to attend courses at the nearby Sorbonne for their university degrees. *Normaliens* were likely to be left-leaning or liberal in their politics; the school has been called the breeding ground of the dominant political group of its time, and members of the student body were conspicuous at Popular Front and anti-Fascist meetings of the 1930s.

And yet a significant element of the ENS in these years was a hard right-wing clique, of which Robert Brasillach was the best-known member. Born in southern France, raised there and in Burgundy, Brasillach was yet another who came up to Paris at the age of sixteen to study for the ENS entrance exams at the Louis-le-Grand lycée. With Thierry Maulnier and Roger Vailland, his circle included Maurice Bardèche, who married Brasillach's sister. As a student, Brasillach became involved with Action Française, the movement started by Charles Maurras, who had a lively core of followers in the universities, many of whom went on to leadership positions in the Fascist movements of the 1930s and of the German occupation years. Brasillach contributed articles to the Action Française student newspaper and then to the popular daily *L'Action Française* and the political weeklies *Candide* and *Je Suis Partout*. He even brought his political friends back to the school compound on the Rue d'Ulm, just south of the Place du Panthéon, for parties. Did that constitute a Fascist cell at the ENS? Probably not. There are few *normaliens* on the list of signatories of the (unsuccessful) petition to General de Gaulle in 1945 requesting a pardon for Brasillach after his death sentence for collusion with the German occupying forces.

So in the end the "*normalien* spirit" hardly determined the politics of the individual *normalien*. Another graduate, the historian and Action Française polemicist Pierre Gaxotte, suggested that it was more a matter of the *way* questions were dealt with than of their substance — "a certain taste for erudite clowning combined with a keen requirement of independence. Emile Henriot expressed much the same thought when he denied that the ENS was simply "the seminary of the French Republic," for Charles Péguy's Catholicism had been reinforced there, and so were Edouard Herriot's democratic convictions. Henriot (writing in a French newspaper in 1935) went on to cite what was then the youngest generation of ENS graduates, whose beliefs ranged from Christian and royalist to Socialist. Ironically, the Socialist he offered in evidence, Marcel Déat, later became the leader of a pro-Fascist movement. To the *normalien* and Communist Paul Nizan, the corps of professors to which the students of his school were exposed were nothing but valets of the upper classes.

It should be evident that if not all graduates of the Ecole Normale Supérieure became writers, at the very least they were intellectuals. In France, as in the USSR, it is frequent practice to consider all members of the teaching profession as part of the intelligentsia. If one accepts this practice, one must also accept the statistic that in 1936, the year the Popular Front government was voted into office, there were 450,000 intellectuals in France, or 2 percent of the active population; of these, 186,000 were state school teachers.

3   At Home

A YOUNG REFUGEE from Hitler's Germany, Ernst Erich Noth, noted in his memoirs the importance of the literary salon for first encounters in Paris. "Only a writer with an established reputation . . . could offer himself the luxury of refusing such invitations regularly." Then, even more than later, a French interior was a very private place, and one was less likely to be invited home than in New York, London, or apparently Berlin.

In those days there were still some drawing rooms in the great tradition, presided over by the Polignacs, the Rochefoucaulds, the Noailles — aristocratic families, patrons of the arts. If the protagonists of the political struggles of the 1930s often met in somewhat more workaday surroundings, such as the speakers' platforms or committee rooms of the new intellectual-political movements, or in one or another of the Left Bank's prestigious publishing houses, magazines, or bookshops, they also found time for the most formal meeting places of all, the "at homes" of the patrons, and of certain distinguished men and women of letters. These formal meeting places are among the most difficult for us to recreate today because they are the most removed from contemporary behavior.

In the absence of a history of the influence of Daniel Halévy as a master of ceremonies of intellectual Paris, some elements for such a history must be given here. It was in the Halévy salon that young André Malraux met his lifelong friend and political enemy Pierre Drieu La Rochelle (according to witnesses, either of them was capable of dominating a roomful of his elders). André Chamson met Malraux here. For Jean Guéhenno, the young teacher who was to become an influential editor and essayist, Halévy's drawing room was an introduction to "the Republic of Letters." After reading an essay by

Guéhenno, Halévy had invited him to call, encouraged him to go on writing, published him, introduced him to his contemporaries. (Guéhenno had lost his own best friends in the First World War, which contributed to making him the visceral pacifist he was.)

In Halévy's living room, in "an old and dark house, on the edge of the old Seine river, before a curtain of rustling poplars," Guéhenno discovered "culture itself." He met Malraux and Drieu La Rochelle there, and Chamson (who was later to be his partner on the Popular Front weekly *Vendredi*); also Emmanuel Berl, who published Gallimard's weekly *Marianne*. The novelist Louis Guilloux often met the philosopher Julien Benda at Halévy's, but (Guilloux confided to his diary) that did not stop the sharp-tongued Benda from saying nasty things about Halévy to everyone else. (Lucie Mazauric, André Chamson's wife and work companion, saw Benda as the guest invited for the day but who stays for years, and then goes away angry.) Besides Benda, guests of Halévy's own generation included the Catholic philosopher Gabriel Marcel, the novelist François Mauriac, the author and journalist Abel Bonnard, the painter and art critic Jacques-Emile Blanche.

Daniel Halévy was the great-grandson of a German Jew who had been the cantor at the principal synagogue in Paris, and co-author with one of his sons of the first French-Hebrew dictionary (the other son became famous as a composer). Daniel's own father was a critic, playwright, author of popular operettas, a contributor to *La Vie Parisienne*, the illustrated weekly of entertainment and fashion, and a familiar face in literary drawing rooms. By that time the Halévys had traveled a considerable distance from their ancestral faith, identifying themselves rather with the Catholic and Protestant upper classes. Daniel Halévy was a historian and biographer of Nietzsche, a collaborator of Charles Péguy on his *Cahiers de la Quinzaine*. He was an outspoken defender of Dreyfus, which led to breaking with an anti-Semitic friend, the painter Degas, in that feverish time. Later his conservative instincts took charge, and he was even to regret the intensity of his youthful commitment. At a distance and in today's political terms, this man who was both a humanitarian Socialist and a friend of the nationalist Maurice Barrès poses an enigma. In the 1930s Guéhenno acknowledged that he was a *grand bourgeois conservateur*, yet ready to give a hearing to all points of view. "A peasant of Paris," Lucie Mazauric described him, with his sober, even somber clothing worn with "nonchalant elegance," delicate features framed by a trim beard. And "he led the conversation without raising his voice."

In 1897 Halévy and his parents moved to a town house on the Quai de l'Horloge just off the Pont Neuf, Paris's oldest stone bridge — not quite the Left Bank, but only a short walk across the bridge away. In the 1920s, Halévy became responsible for a series of books called Cahiers Verts at the publishing house of Bernard Grasset, and he made it a vehicle for new writers. Many leading literary and political figures of the time were published in this series, when they were not actually introduced by it. In the 1920s alone Cahiers Verts published Julien Benda, Emmanuel Berl, André Chamson, Pierre Drieu La Rochelle, Jean Giono, Jean Giraudoux, Jean Guéhenno, André Malraux, Gabriel Marcel, François Mauriac, Charles Maurras, Henry de Montherlant, Paul Morand, and Albert Thibaudet, to mention only those who will appear here and there in this book. Although he could sponsor a Malraux or a Chamson, in his own work Halévy showed himself to be anti-Popular Front, even anti-Republic; and then, when he went so far as to approve the Vichy regime during the German occupation of France, he ceased to be the mentor of the Left Bank young. André Chamson recalled that as early as 1934, the year of the right-wing riots and the left-wing response, Halévy no longer seemed an appropriate host for those thinking as Chamson did.

Halévy received his guests in a Second Empire parlor enhanced by paintings by Degas, a floor above the quay. It has been said that these were meetings of men; that Madame Halévy served the tea and then bowed out of the assembly. But Lucie Mazauric Chamson was a regular participant, and in the decade (1925-1934) when she and her husband frequented the salon, she was not the only woman in the room: Halévy's wife was there, his mother too, and sometimes his daughter. Clara Malraux accompanied her husband. The Chamsons met the Malrauxs for the first time at the Halévy salon, on the couple's return from Indochina, where André had been arrested for the theft of priceless Khmer statuary, to be saved from prison by an outcry of protest from the French literary establishment. "Halévy was rather pleased," Chamson's wife remembered, "to set this black diamond in the middle of the motley group of stars who decorated his drawing room." At his "at homes," Halévy received not only Parisians but visiting provincials and foreigners too, and not all the guests were of the literary world. Robert Aron recalled an afternoon in the 1930s when a Colonel Charles de Gaulle explained his military theories to the assembled guests.

★   ★   ★

No other stage on which the actors of our drama appeared was quite as formal as the Halévy salon. A more typical scene from the 1930s is the crowded living room or office of a harried young writer, still a young husband or father and very much preoccupied by the struggle for survival as well as the class struggle. So it was for Malraux, receiving in his home at 44, Rue du Bac, just opposite the offices of his publisher, Gallimard, and of Gallimard's flagship journal, La Nouvelle Revue Française — familiarly, the N.R.F. Conveniently between office and apartment stood the Pont Royal Hotel, whose basement bar was a favorite of the N.R.F. staff.

A remarkable novelist of ideas, Malraux had fought the Chinese Revolution so convincingly in his novels that others assumed, and he played along with the assumption, that he had witnessed, even acted in the events. He spoke equally convincingly on the psychology of art, often to the confounding of his audience. He was far from being a parlor intellectual; the awarding of the coveted Goncourt Prize to La Condition humaine ("Man's Fate") in 1933 gave him national stature. "In bookstore windows they are showing the twenty-fifth printing of the book," Ilya Ehrenburg reported to his Russian readers, "and the critics are raving about him in the press." Even the exiled Leon Trotski engaged in a dialogue with Malraux, taking him for a peer, if a misguided one.

The newly arrived anti-Nazi refugee Manès Sperber saw Malraux as "tall, svelte, with light brown hair and a lock of it hiding his forehead... A long face with mobile features, deformed now and then by a nervous contraction which made him seem to grow older or younger in the course of a conversation." He had "the eloquence of the intellectual fully in control of his means of expression and who, with a sharp eye, measures their effects with precision." "Malraux has the thin face of a young girl," Ehrenburg reported home. "He is extremely nervous. He doesn't know how to listen." But Ehrenburg admired the versatility of the man. "He lives surrounded by Buddhas, but this doesn't stop him from being deeply concerned by the economic problems of the world."

An actor, his detractors grunted. Much later Malraux would tell an interviewer that intellectuals had experienced the Popular Front through their feelings, while for the Communist International, anti-Fascist unity of action had been a strategy carefully worked out (though by that time he was denying that he himself had ever been a revolutionary internationalist). Whatever his private feelings about Marxism and the Communist Party, Malraux was an enthusiastic participant in anti-Fascist unity of action.

The Malraux apartment was comfortably large, but inconveniently laid out. To enter the living room, which was also the dining room and bedroom, visitors had to walk through their host's office. The Malrauxs seldom received large groups, but there always seemed to be *someone* around. Five or six couples could be considered regular visitors. One was Bernard Groethuysen, the essayist, philosopher, and literary critic, with his politically active wife. Raymond Aron might be a guest, or Léo Lagrange of the Popular Front government, or editor Emmanuel Berl. There were even times there when one felt on the political front lines without leaving home: through her windows Clara Malraux could hear the extreme rightists shouting slogans as they marched down their favorite parade route, the Boulevard Saint-Germain.

During the early years of Fascism and anti-Fascism, the Malrauxs were in almost constant conference with their friends, at the Rue du Bac apartment or at someone else's apartment, in cafés, on the streets. "Revolution," decided Clara Malraux, "is seeing each other a lot."

And there were the foreigners: the Soviet journalist Ehrenburg, the refugees from Hitler's Germany, the Italian anti-Fascists like Nicola Chiaromonte, later the fugitives from defeated Republican Spain. Thus Ernst Erich Noth had been recommended to Malraux, notably by Malraux's intimate friend Eddy du Perron, the Dutch writer, as an authority on Nazism who could provide information that would be useful to Malraux in the writing of his anti-Nazi novel *Le Temps du mépris* ("Days of Wrath" in the American edition, "Days of Contempt" in the British). But Malraux quickly forgot the reason Noth had come to him, and during frequent visits to the Rue du Bac in the following weeks Noth was asked no questions. (He found Malraux passionate in politics, but lacking in human warmth.)

Manès Sperber, who had already been in a Nazi prison before arriving in Paris in the spring of 1934 to work in an anti-Fascist organization alongside other refugees, met Bernard Groethuysen while signing a book contract at Gallimard. Groethuysen told him that Malraux would like to meet him, and soon he was seated in the Malrauxs' all-purpose living room, with Clara interpreting his German. It must have been difficult to translate "percussive phrases that [Malraux] set off like rockets: abridged conclusions of his thought, of which his listener could only presume the content, because instead of summing up his ideas Malraux hurried along to formulate new ones." One had to pay attention, "because Malraux spoke too much and indiscriminately, with a rapidity which took your breath away." This visitor imagined a long-distance runner who tried to overtake himself. But Sperber returned again and again. At the time he felt that Malraux was "the Saint-just of anti-Fascism." Young intellectuals saw in him their "exemplary representative, their spokesman and champion."

Later, when Sperber was down and out in Paris, freezing in his hotel room and unable to afford more than one meal a day, he was asked to the Rue du Bac after lunch, on a day when the Malraux had invited André Gide and Paul Nizan to their table. The hungry Sperber was offered a glass of brandy, and then the alcohol and the warmth of the apartment caused him to doze while Gide was talking. "That someone could fall asleep during his first meeting with André Gide . . . was, at the time, unimaginable." Such was the fate of an émigré intellectual. Sperber hastened to add that André and Clara happened to be the most generous hosts he knew.

★   ★   ★

At that time, André Gide was probably the best-known representative of French letters at home or abroad. He had been a published writer since 1911, with two dozen or more books in print, and although many of them propounded aesthetics that could only be described as introspective, he was doing what he could to remain in touch with the youngest and most avant-garde of his readers. In his early work, he had seemed the image of traditional French Protestantism, austere and unbending, but his themes soon expanded to embrace the most sensuous of hedonisms, and he was an early advocate of a very literary homosexuality. He was known to inhabit a refined, somewhat bookish environment while at the same time reaching out to other cultures and literatures. When he finally admitted social concerns to his writing table, it was as if he had begun a second career. But even after his travels in French Africa and his subsequent condemnation of colonialism, the image of dilettantism persisted. "As a destroyer, Gide pierces upper-

class ideologies with a spear," a critic noted in Henri Barbusse's pro-
Communist newspaper *Monde* in 1929. "But after that he washes his
hands, abstains from action, offering us nothing but further reasons for
concern."

Then his critics on the left stopped criticizing. In the July 1932 issue of
La Nouvelle Revue Française Gide offered a section of his private journal
up for public scrutiny. "But above all I should like to live long enough to
see the plans of Russia succeed," he had written. "All my heart applauds
this gigantic and still so human enterprise." In September of that year
another section of his journal was published. "I should like to cry out my
sympathy for the USSR; and I should like my cry to be heard." (These
journal entries were written in 1931.) Then the N.R.F. published, from
Gide's journal of April 1931, this confidence: "If my life were necessary
to assure the success of the USSR, I should sacrifice it at once." It was the
year of his sixty-third birthday.

Considering Gide's reputation, his position in the literary establishment, these declarations were newsworthy, and the press did not fail to
pick them up, although the conversion was treated with sarcasm by those
who took it for passing fashion. But the Communist paper *L'Humanité*
saw Gide's confessions as "typical of the attraction which the magnificent
Soviet experiment exercises, even on bourgeois intellectuals." Ilya
Ehrenburg reported the news to his Russian readers with even greater
enthusiasm: "There is no need to speak here of the courage of André
Gide — all his past life dispenses us of the need for such praise. Paul
Claudel ended up in the Church, Paul Valéry in the French Academy,
André Gide in life."

With his declaration of love for Soviet Communism, Gide was to be
drawn into history. Soon after the first sensational pages of his journal
appeared in print, he was asked to endorse a World Congress Against
War which Henri Barbusse and Romain Rolland were promoting. This
meeting, to become known as the Amsterdam Congress, was the first
large-scale international rally of its kind. Gide also accepted the
chairmanship of a meeting called to denounce Hitlerism in March 1933,
sponsored by the Association of Revolutionary Writers and Artists, in
the company of Malraux, Guéhenno, and Vaillant-Couturier. There
Gide stated that even if the USSR *also* restricts freedom, it was "to make
it possible at long last to establish a new society."

We should have to read the complete published *Journal* of Gide to
understand the basic ambiguities of his position. The writer who

revealed anti-Semitism in his remarks on his lycée classmate Léon Blum, who had at one time sympathized with Charles Maurras and Action Française, and who was still attracted by the personality of Adolf Hitler, confessed to his journal: "I don't understand anything about politics. If it interests me, it is in the manner of a Balzac novel." He refused to put his name to political manifestos and petitions, he wrote, not to set himself apart, "but I don't believe that I have encountered a single proclamation of this kind the contents of which I could approve entirely, and which did not distort my position on some point."

Yet despite himself he now belonged to a cause. He was even becoming a familiar name to those who would never read a line of his work. The *N.R.F.* critic Ramon Fernandez recounts an authentic story: that on February 12, 1934, during the general strike following the portentous right-wing rioting of February 6, a construction worker was heard to exclaim: "What we need is rifles, to march into the rich neighborhoods. That's the only place that serious things can be done. And then we need someone to lead us, a chief, a real man . . . say a guy like Gide."

Yet, a month before the February 6 riots, Gide had accompanied André Malraux into the dragon's lair, to Hitler's capital, in an attempt to persuade Nazi propaganda minister Joseph Goebbels to release Georgi Dimitrov and his fellow defendants, who had been acquitted of the charge of setting fire to the Reichstag, the German parliament building, but not yet freed. Goebbels did not receive them, but Gide and Malraux left their request on his desk, and the Dimitrov group was out of jail by the end of February. In March 1934 Gide affirmed in a letter to a journalist the "right of inspection" that every man possessed concerning his neighbor, thanks to which international justice was taking precedence over local versions easier to manipulate. "Thanks to this right, to the pressure of inspection, the Reichstag trial acquitted the innocent; thanks to it the defendants were released at last." By then Gide was an expected presence on the speakers' platforms at meetings, and a name — despite himself — at the bottom of petitions. He confessed, at a debate on his work at the Union pour la Vérité in January 1935: "Since I became involved in political concerns four years ago, I have stopped writing."

★   ★   ★

To reach the Gide apartment one had only to cross the Boulevard Saint-Germain from the Malrauxs' Rue du Bac, taking a right turn to the Rue

Vaneau; on his way to the Gallimard offices, Gide routinely passed the Malrauxs' door. Even a slow walker could bridge the distance in ten minutes, and Gide and Malraux exchanged visits often in those years.

In the mid-1930s, apart from the Halévy "at homes," Gide's was probably the most traditional literary salon that writers of the youngest generation could experience. Gide's best biographer, the faithful Maria Van Rysselberghe, who was at once his unofficial hostess, confidante, and the mother of the woman with whom he had a child out of wedlock, possessed an apartment of her own next door to Gide's, on the top floor of that solid middle-class apartment building at 1 bis, Rue Vaneau. She considered her neighbor's apartment a "crossroads"; it seemed to her that everyone who had a problem, everyone who was about to set forth on a journey, or who was returning from one, felt it necessary to stop in here. The visitors she registers in her extraordinary diary make up a who's who of thinking Paris. For the young couple André Chamson and Lucie Mazauric, the Gide apartment was more of a collective experience. With the other guests they sat in a circle, each speaking in turn. Gide solicited the advice of his visitors, young or old, on matters of concern to him, subtly turning the conversation around to his subject, for there always was a subject of the day. They might talk about literature, but more often, in those turbulent years, about politics.

★   ★   ★

There were other poles of attraction. The Surrealists, for example, who lived and worked and fought each other on a now demolished stretch of the Rue du Château behind the Gare Montparnasse — about as far as one could be, spiritually and geographically, from André Breton's headquarters in the Rue Fontaine below Montmartre. A sad little pavilion in a sad little neighborhood, set back from the street behind a wall; it had fallen into the hands of ragpickers, until even they abandoned it. Marcel Duhamel rented and transformed it, Yves Tanguy decorated it lugubriously. The young Surrealists who didn't live at 54, Rue du Château, regularly nevertheless used it as a meeting place.

According to André Thirion, the member of the community who best described it, the essential difference between the Right Bank group around Breton and the Rue du Château was the freer atmosphere of the latter. Breton ruled his group with a whip, while the younger crowd in Montparnasse was less hampered by doctrine. To the "purity" of Breton's Rue Fontaine, Thirion opposed the more eclectic working environment of his Montparnasse den. When Georges Sadoul, the movie critic and companion of Louis Aragon, took over the lease, the atmosphere became increasingly political, and for a time they even had as a temporary lodger one Alfred Kurella, an agent of the Communist International responsible for cultural affairs.

Not far from the Rue du Château was the large artist's studio of Louis Aragon, hugging the Boulevard du Montparnasse at 5, Rue Campagne-Première. (Aragon had decorated the toilet at 54, Rue du Château, but he didn't live there.) Another short walk in that dim nether-Montparnasse and one was *chez* Ilya Ehrenburg, on the graceless Rue du Cotentin. Nino Frank, who remembered that Ehrenburg's key was always in the door, as if to signal that all callers were welcome, recounted an evening gathering there in honor of the visiting Evgeny Zamiatin, author of *We* and still in the good graces of his country's regime. André and Clara Malraux were also present, she again serving as an interpreter, for Zamiatin spoke German but no French. André and Lucie Chamson remembered the apartment as impersonal, typical of a furnished flat, to which Ehrenburg's chief contribution was a pet dog. And Ehrenburg himself told of a visit from Gide, who picked up a cookie and used it to gesticulate as he spoke, until the dog (a mixture of Scottish terrier and spaniel) leaped up to grab it. Without paying attention, Gide took another cookie and waved it until it too was snatched by the dog, and so on and on.

When the Chamsons still lived in Paris, in the Rue Thouin behind the Place du Panthéon, they invited friends after dinner, for they couldn't afford to feed their eminent guests. Gide met some of the younger generation there, and once he was invited with Edouard Daladier; the two men had wanted to meet. Another time, there was a knock at the door and Chamson opened it to three students from the Ecole Normale Supérieure who told him that they admired his work and had wanted to shake his hand. They turned out to be Robert Brasillach, Jean-Paul Maxence, and Jacques Talagrand ("Thierry Maulnier"), all of them on the extreme right wing and proud to be there; until that time, Chamson had not written or said anything that would have shocked them. (Brasillach's later attack on Chamson in *L'Action Française*, the racist, royalist, and reactionary organ of Charles Maurras, ended their relations.)

After the Chamsons moved to Versailles, where André was curator of the palace, they could receive more elegantly, if less conveniently for their guests, and some of the Left Bank transferred itself there for the

Chamsons' Sunday receptions — notably Gide and Roger Martin du Gard, Guéhenno, Aragon, Ehrenburg, Nizan, sometimes Antoine de Saint-Exupéry, Jean Schlumberger and Jean Paulhan of the *N.R.F.*

In that *N.R.F.* circle, Bernard Groethuysen was something of an *éminence grise*. Once more, we are indebted to Gide's confidante, Maria Van Rysselberghe, whom he called his *petite dame*, for an impression of the Groethuysen home on the Rue Campagne-Première. "What a pleasant atmosphere surrounds them!" she exclaims. "His fertile imagination, his impartiality allow the airing of all points of view." "Groeth — which is how they called him, with respect and sympathy, at the *N.R.F.*," recalled Manès Sperber, "was a man of noble bearing, attuned to the calm and steady tone of his speech and to the gestures which accompanied it." He wore a beard, he was a nonstop smoker. Of Dutch and Russian parentage, he was a specialist in German culture and had taught at the University of Berlin. His wife was of Russian origin, and both had Communist sympathies. *Eminence grise?* All concur that he had an influence, occult perhaps, on Gide, Malraux, and other leading figures of the Gallimard and *Nouvelle Revue Française* group. He introduced many of them to the work of Marx as well as to that of Kafka.

And then Roger Martin du Gard would receive at his quaintly charming house on the Rue du Cherche-Midi, connecting Saint-Germain-des-Prés to Montparnasse. As the Chamsons recalled it, discussions here were less political, less passionate; as at the Rue Vaneau, dainty sandwiches were served. Another *N.R.F.* regular, Jean Schlumberger, lived on nearby Rue d'Assas. While waiting to be served, the Chamsons and their fellow guests, the booksellers Adrienne Monnier and Sylvia Beach, were led by a maître d'hôtel into a library filled with paintings.

The Rue de l'Odéon bookshops, already mentioned, were important as meeting places for those without a salon to go to, but above all as places where the book of the moment, the guest of the moment, the poem to be read aloud, always had the center of the floor. On her own arrival in Paris, Lucie Mazauric signed up at the lending library of Adrienne Monnier, and so joined a roster that included Gide, Jules Romains, André Maurois, Valery Larbaud, and Léon-Paul Fargue.

Both Monnier and Beach seemed to hold nonstop open house. "Ostentatious and simple at once, without money and without complexes about money, they always had a good reason to invite a group of friends," recalled Lucie Mazauric. "They were gay, amusing, not a bit women-of-letters, sympathetic to living literature, harsh on conformists." Throughout their apprentice years, for Lucie and André Chamson "the main headquarters" of their friends was Adrienne Monnier's Maison des Amis des Livres, with Adrienne and Sylvia Beach acting as hostesses while the young hopes of French letters were exposed to the approving gaze of their seniors — Paul Valéry, Paul Claudel, Gide and Martin du Gard of course, and sometimes, thanks to Sylvia Beach, James Joyce too.

4 Place of Work, Place of Play

OBSERVING FROM THIS DISTANCE the ferment of the 1930s, we cannot help being impressed by the extent to which the activity was collective — the product of organizations, of committees open or closed, or meetings, small and informal or large and public. The most remarkable product of the gregarious actors of this story was political rhetoric, and one is reminded again and again that no great literary work was produced in France during these political years. André Malraux, for one, did his best writing before he began appearing on speakers' platforms, as did his elder, André Gide. When significant work appeared, it was done by solitary souls who rejected organizations and causes: by Louis-Ferdinand Céline, for example, or even by Jean-Paul Sartre, although he too reduced his creative output when finally he joined the political world. Later, the same would be said of Albert Camus, who virtually had to become an interior exile before he was able to return to creative work. What will last of those prewar years, besides the products of the solitary souls and the misanthropes, is precisely the literary and political criticism, the exalted discourse of the weekly newspapers and monthly reviews. Against the energy created by the urgency of those years, pure literature had little or no chance.

The common ground of Left Bank intellectuals was the offices of their publishing houses, as well as those of the daily, weekly, or monthly periodicals to which they contributed. For those without a letter of introduction to an influential man or woman of letters, a publishing house could be the great equalizer. One didn't even have to have money for coffee or drinks, for someone in the company would be sure to invite the visitor to a neighborhood bar. Then, as later, most publishers in France were clustered in the three Left Bank *arrondissements* along the Seine. Most of the prestigious literary houses were within a few streets of the old church at Saint-Germain-des-Prés: Gallimard, along with the monthly *Nouvelle Revue Française,* on the Rue Sébastien-Bottin; Grasset on the Rue des Saints-Pères; Emile-Paul Frères on the Rue de l'Abbaye; Flammarion on the Rue Racine; Plon on the Rue Garancière; Mercure de France (with the magazine of that name) on the Rue de Condé; Rieder on the Boulevard Saint-Germain; Fasquelle on the Rue de Grenelle.

Gallimard was at the top of the heap. Gallimard and *La Nouvelle Revue Française:* Could anyone have unraveled the web of publishing house, monthly magazine, the editors and writers of one or the other or both, in that rabbit hutch? Gallimard liked to be known as "Editions de la Nouvelle Revue Française," and the colophon *nrf* appeared on every book published. Certainly there was a merry mixing of book publishing and magazine staffs, and most contributors to the monthly had their books published by Gallimard; sometimes the books were serialized first in the magazine. One of the founders of *La Nouvelle Revue Française* (with Jean Schlumberger and businessman Gaston Gallimard) was André Gide, who in his curiosity about new literature of whatever origin, about new politics wherever they might lead him, seemed a personification of the spirit of N.R.F. One of the first books published by Editions de la Nouvelle Revue Française, back in 1911, was Gide's, and in the following decades this prolific author became one of the most dependable producers for both publishing house and magazine. At first the monthly was published from Schlumberger's home on the Rue d'Assas; later on, it became part of the rabbit hutch on the Rue Sébastien-Bottin (then called the Rue de Beaune), and let no one put asunder what had been joined together so well.

Curious about new literature, but not about all of it: it is almost a cliché that the finicky classicists of the *N.R.F.* group missed out on Marcel Proust, and on others of the promising young, who could sometimes find a sympathetic ear across the Boulevard Saint-Germain in competitor Bernard Grasset. Gide confessed to his *Journal* as early as 1923 that there was a group of N.R.F. "rejectees"; at least eight authors had been "blackballed." About the N.R.F. spirit it might also be said that it involved a considerable amount of log-rolling. One wrote for one's friends, but could one receive useful criticism from friends? If

André Malraux, an editor at the Gallimard publishing house and a member of the reading committee, reviewed a new book by Gide for *La Nouvelle Revue Française,* Gide would know about it in advance. In fact, a faithful *N.R.F.* supporter might read criticism of his work, written by a friend, in proofs. By the time our story opens, the principal tastemaker at Gallimard, and on the magazine, was no longer Gide but Jean Paulhan, his junior by some fifteen years, who replaced one of the original *N.R.F.* team, Jacques Rivière, who had died in 1925. If Paulhan resembled Gide in any way, it was in the catholicity of his taste, allied with self-assurance concerning his own literary judgment, and a deceptive — and disarming — air of naïveté. But unlike the politically adventurous Gide, who was becoming increasingly outspoken in his commitments, Paulhan rejected doctrines. His political attitude prior to the Second World War was summed up as "Don't Count on Us," as he titled an editorial he contributed to *La Nouvelle Revue Française* after the signing of the Munich pact in 1938. Paulhan refused to allow literature to be placed in the service of politics. "I don't know whether Baudelaire is healthy or unhealthy," he wrote at that time. "I don't know whether he can be recommended for family reading, or to generals... But if there is one absurd attitude the government can take, it is to ask Baudelaire to write his poems to the glory of family values."

There was room for many points of view in the *Nouvelle Revue Française,* just as there was room at Gallimard for Drieu La Rochelle's book *Socialisme fasciste* in 1934, sandwiched between Malraux's *La Condition humaine* ("Man's Fate") in 1933 and *Le Temps du mépris* in 1935. Gallimard's pre–World War II catalogue could almost be taken for a bibliography of contemporary literature, with only a few names missing. And a Gallimard author could live out a literary career with reviews by fellow Gallimard authors, with prizes from Gallimard jurors. Of the formal Gallimard receptions that brought together the elite of French letters, Gide's *petite dame,* Maria Van Rysselberghe, said: "It's the occasion to meet people who had been lost from sight, or to match a face to a name at last."

Inside the hutch on the Rue Sébastien-Bottin, literature could be seen in the making, for the editors who occupied offices there also wrote most of the essays and the books published there. Literary history might be made in an office no larger than six feet square — Malraux's was not much larger — or in the railroad station of an entrance lobby, one of the crossroads of civilization in those years. Casual encounters spilled out to the street, to the dim little neighborhood cafés, or the posh basement bar of the Pont Royal. Upstairs in the Gallimard building, in one or another tiny office, the Malrauxs and Paulhans and Raymond Queneaus were reading manuscripts and writing reports about them, planning book series, anthologies.

The literary and social life of the hutch was pursued each summer in Burgundy, where the ancient Cistercian abbey of Pontigny had been converted into a center for symposia that brought Gide and the other N.R.F. pioneers together with the rising generation, during serious day-time discussions, evening walks, and parlor games. Here a young Malraux, a young Sartre, made useful contacts, and met not only their elders but others of their own age, in propitious surroundings. During the rest of the year the founder of the Pontigny symposia, Paul Desjardins, organized literary-political afternoons under the aegis of the Union pour la Vérité on Rue Visconti near Saint-Germain-des-Prés. Here a new book and its author, young or old, would face an audience of men and women of letters, not all of them sympathetic to the guest of honor.

★　★　★

There were other such clusters, one of them in the Bernard Grasset building on the Rue des Saints-Pères. There were also the offices of the cultural and political weeklies (which were called newspapers; we would call them magazines). It was in the offices of Marianne, a large, newspaper-format weekly sponsored by Gallimard and directed by Emmanuel Berl, that André Malraux first noticed the young woman who became his companion and the mother of his sons. Josette Clotis was then Berl's secretary, and Malraux met her again at a Sunday luncheon at the Gallimard home. On Saturday nights, when the magazine was ready to go to press, the wives and friends of Marianne contributors would join them at the printers. A Gide, a Jean Cassou, a famous writer such as André Maurois or Joseph Kessel, might be present, along with members of the Malraux generation, and they would all go off to a restaurant with the Gallimards.

And there was Jean Guéhenno's Europe, edited in the offices of the book publisher Rieder on Place Saint-Sulpice, and then at 108, Boulevard Saint-Germain, more precisely in a single, poorly lit room stacked with books and manuscripts. Here the visitor came face to face with the humanist, pacifist lycée professor Guéhenno, and possibly with one or another of the contributors, either by chance or thanks to Guéhenno's matchmaking. When Guéhenno resigned in protest against the Communist Party takeover of *Europe*, his successor, Jean Cassou, continued to receive authors in new quarters on the Boulevard Saint-Michel, then on Place de la Sorbonne.

The history of the Left Bank meeting halls also waits to be written. By the time our story begins the favored gathering place was the Palais de la Mutualité, in a smartly designed building serving as headquarters of a social insurance association, just off Place Maubert in the Latin Quarter. Its large auditorium at basement level, in the style known as *arts décoratifs* fashionable at the time of its conception in 1931, could seat 2200, while a smaller auditorium one floor above street level could take 900 more. From this distance it seems that the Mutualité was never without a conference or congress or protest rally during the 1930s. For less ambitious meetings one had a choice of the Sociétés Savantes, with its quaint cupola in the Rue Danton, the Salle de Géographie, near the Café de Flore on Boulevard Saint-Germain, or the all-purpose building at 44, Rue de Rennes, alongside the Café des Deux Magots, where one could hold a public rally or a secret cell meeting. In Montparnasse the old Salle Bullier at the Observatoire intersection, the traditional site of student balls, was a favorite hall for mass meetings in the first half of the decade.

Nor should it be forgotten that the most formal literary institution of all was located in the heart of the Left Bank: the Académie Française, with its ceremonial meetings of honored writers, professors, scientists. In those years the Académie included among its forty elected members many of the leaders of the intellectual right wing: Abel Bonnard, Abel Hermant, André Bellessort, Jacques Bainville, Jérôme Tharaud, and Charles Maurras.

And then we come to the most democratic of meeting places: the cafés. To understand their role, one must first understand how much of a Frenchman's interchange with his fellows took place outside the home. One could not only meet friends in a café but conduct business there, spend half a day writing letters, or even a book. One needed no invitation to strike up a conversation with a stranger at a neighboring table, and an appointment in a café often replaced an invitation home. It kept home inviolate, and if home was a garret, all the more reason for receiving in style in a brassy beer hall.

Few memoirs of the period fail to refer to the traditional literary and art salons that were the cafés of Montparnasse and Saint-Germain-des-Prés. Some cafés were associated with particular political groups or ideologies. The Flore, opened in the Second Empire, was in a sense the true headquarters of Action Française in the early years of the century. The movement's first manifestos, bristling with royalism, were composed on its tables, and Charles Maurras actually called one of his books *Au Signe de Flore* —"At the Sign of Flore." (Maurras lived just a short walk away at 60, Rue de Verneuil.) Apollinaire, who lived a few hundred feet farther along the boulevard, met his friends at the Flore, where they founded a review called *Les Soirées de Paris*.

In opposition to the traditional, sometimes fashionable, and relatively expensive Flore and Deux Magots, the younger generation would choose a less pretentious café, usually within eyesight of the more famous ones: the Bonaparte at the corner of the Place Saint-Germain-des-Prés, Le Mabillon on the boulevard. Meanwhile at the Flore, at Deux Magots, an already established poet or painter, André Breton or Pablo Picasso, might be seated in the center of a group. Sometimes there was an air of pomp about it: Picasso arrives on the square, he stops in at the Brasserie Lipp to greet friends, looks for familiar faces at the Deux Magots, then makes a longer stop at a table at the Flore with the Paul Eluards, the Georges Braques. (It was at the Deux Magots that Eluard introduced Picasso to Dora Maar, who was the chief feminine presence in his life during the years of concern to us.) And when it is time to dine, Picasso crosses the street to Lipp again, to be seated beside members of parliament, perhaps a cabinet minister, leading members of the bar, of the Académie Française, stars of theater and film, his peers in art and literature.

In *Le Piéton de Paris*, Léon-Paul Fargue evokes the atmosphere of Lipp on the eve of World War II: "One couldn't write thirty lines in a newspaper in Paris, paint a painting, or hold strong political opinions," he declares with pardonable exaggeration, "without devoting at least one evening a week to this café-restaurant . . . Lipp is certainly one of the places, the only one perhaps, where for the price of a draft beer one can have a faithful and complete summing-up of a political or intellectual day in France." The right-wing Fargue could not resist the pleasure of describing the evening when the Socialist leader Léon Blum and his wife were insulted by political enemies at their table at Lipp, the incident degenerating into a free-for-all. Fargue himself was felled by a "reactionary carafe," to be treated by a couple of doctors who happened to be sharing his table. The owners of Lipp opened another café in a similar Alsatian beer-hall style next door to the Sorbonne at the beginning of the 1930s. This place, called Balzar, never attained the senior café's sparkle, which may be why it was preferred by those seeking seclusion — Jean-Paul Sartre, for example. When too much celebrity drove him from Saint-Germain-des-Prés in the years following the liberation of Paris, Sartre also took shelter at the Pont Royal basement bar near Gallimard. Malraux's time at the Pont Royal was in the decade preceding World War II; once he became famous, he could never be led into a bar again.

South and west of Saint-Germain-des-Prés, at the strategic joining of the Boulevard du Montparnasse and the Boulevard Saint-Michel or Boul' Mich,' stood La Closerie des Lilas, hospitable to poets from the time of Baudelaire and Verlaine, and a favorite of the young Gide, of Apollinaire, Max Jacob. By the 1930s it was a quiet place where Hemingway could sit with a *café crème* and his writing pad without risking interruption. Farther along the Boulevard du Montparnasse one ran into everybody. As Fargue described it in prewar Paris: "The poet or the painter who wishes to succeed in Bucharest or in Seville must necessarily, in the present state of affairs in old Europe, do a tour of duty at the Rotonde or the Coupole, two sidewalk academies where one learns Bohemian life, scorn for the middle classes, humor, and how to hold a glass." The cafés could also serve as listening posts, as outdoor parlors, for the intensely serious young teachers and writers Sartre and Simone de Beauvoir. In the middle of the 1930s decade, whenever they were in Paris (for both then had teaching assignments outside the city), their headquarters was Le Dôme, a landmark café at the intersection of Boulevards Raspail and Montparnasse since the early years of the century.

Beauvoir was actually able to work at Le Dôme starting at breakfast, sitting in a rear booth surrounded by German refugees who passed the time reading newspapers or playing chess. Fargue's sort of foreigner was represented as well: Bohemian artists and writers exchanging passionate ideas passionately. She was grateful for all this movement; it was encouraging to raise one's eyes from a blank page to find that people still existed. She could identify famous painters among the café customers, with lesser-known artists such as Alberto Giacometti, Ilya Ehrenburg "with heavy features under a mass of hair." In the evening, "big American girls tippled majestically." Later, when she and Sartre moved to a hotel near the Montparnasse cemetery, a few hundred yards south —Baudelaire was buried in the cemetery, and in 1980 Sartre himself—

she was able to work in her room. But serious discussions, even with Sartre, continued to take place in a booth at the rear of Le Dôme. Beauvoir's weighty memoirs are sprinkled with the names of cafés.

La Coupole was certainly the largest café-restaurant in town. When it opened its doors for the first time, just before Christmas, 1927, it became the forum of Montparnasse almost at once, and it had the right dimensions for the role. Hundreds could be seated at once between the pillars decorated by painters, French or foreign, who were familiar faces to café customers of Montparnasse in those years. At the left side of the café a swinging door opened to a bar, which became the meeting place of political figures, journalists, painters, sculptors.

One could usually find Ilya Ehrenburg at a large table in the Coupole bar, sometimes in the company of the Surrealists (before he attacked them, and they counterattacked, in the middle of the 1930s) or with a visitor from his home country. The ambivalent Ehrenburg, free man among free men, a Stalinist in Russia, stood out boldly in the Paris of the 1930s. As we will see, he was one of the Soviet Union's most effective political agents in France, although his friend Nino Frank concluded that he lived not in France but in Montparnasse, "where he had the leisure to construct a portable, docile USSR, set up in a Paris that he had also built for himself." One of his soirées at the Coupole was, for better or for worse, a contribution to literary and political history. Elsa Triolet, the sister of Vladimir Mayakovski's Lili Brik, was sitting at the Ehrenburg table when Louis Aragon walked up to say hello. "She attacked at once, almost without shame," recalled Aragon's Surrealist friend André Thirion. "At the beginning this worried Aragon. With his taste for mystery, the Surrealist obsession with the police, he thought that he detected a trap. 'She's probably a spy,' he said, when he told us about his first meeting with her." When Aragon did not appear at their regular haunts, Elsa continued her pursuit through his friends — such as Thirion. Thus began the romantic liaison of this politico-literary couple, which would span the 1930s and their lives.

5   Smaller Worlds

THERE COULD NOT have been a more select club than that of the political émigrés, but they had no choice about that. The largest group in the 1930s was quite expectedly composed of refugees, or voluntary exiles, from Nazi Germany and from other Nazi- or Fascist-controlled countries; by the nature of their plight, they were politically concerned even when not politically active. In the avant-garde were those who were not refugees so much as emissaries: Communist operatives assigned to anti-Fascist action. The most extraordinary among them was Willy Münzenberg, but he deserves and will receive greater attention later. In his memoirs Arthur Koestler tells how a Communist "caucus" controlled the Association of German Writers in Exile, which served as a cultural base for the Paris émigrés, principally through meetings where German and French writers might read from their works, or lecture on literature. Among those in the caucus was Anna Seghers, who already enjoyed an international reputation through her books. And there were Egon Erwin Kisch, a journalist from Czechoslovakia; Bodo Uhse, who later joined the Republican side in the Spanish Civil War, and returned to East Germany after World War II to edit a magazine; Gustav Regler, about whom more will be heard. There was also the eminent critic and sociologist Walter Benjamin, a solitary figure, although he participated dutifully in the Association of German Writers. Manès Sperber, psychologist and author, joined this circle on his own arrival in Paris.

Some of the refugees were as active in the Communist Party as in literature. Alfred Kantorovicz, for one, although he was to become a refugee a second time when he abandoned the East German Communist paradise in 1957 for the West. Ilya Ehrenburg in his Paris years met Bertolt Brecht and Ernst Toller. One writer not in the caucus, for he was a sympathizer and not a member of the Party, was the popular Jewish novelist and playwright Lion Feuchtwanger.

With few exceptions the exiles lived badly, and found Paris society shut off to them. A Hemingway, who didn't need it, might be invited to a Frenchman's home for dinner, but a refugee, hardly ever. They might be accepted as writers by other writers, and usually their political convictions would assure them a welcome by local Communists. Often these encounters took place in cafés or at home at the coffee hour. When the refugee writers met in the cafés of the Left Bank, their conversation usually concerned money and the lack of it, an anguish made more acute because French authorities required each to prove that he had funds enough to live on. Irmgard Keun, then a young novelist forced to flee Hitler's Germany because of the allegedly anti-German image projected by her books, later recalled that forty-odd refugees used a single thousand-franc note for this purpose, passing it from one to another when it was time to visit police headquarters. When it was her turn to show the tattered note to the *commissaire* he grunted, "Seems to me that I've seen that bill before." She remembered something else the refugees had in common: the problem of writing when one has been cut off from one's roots, and yet does not know enough about one's adopted country to write about that, either.

Arthur Koestler was a man used to living by his wits. His parents were Hungarians, he had lived in Palestine, and in his eclectic career he had worked for the Ullstein periodicals in pre-Nazi Berlin, until he abandoned journalism for Communism, to travel and write in the Soviet Union. While still with the Ullsteins, he was sent to Paris as a correspondent in the 1920s, at which time he was a regular customer of the Montparnasse cafés. But when he returned to Paris in 1933 it was as an exile without means, for his possessions in Berlin had been confiscated. His memoirs tell a painful story of life as an exile — living in a cheap hotel, depending on charity. At one point Koestler sealed the edges of his doors and windows and turned on the gas. But as he lowered himself to an insect-stained mattress to wait for death, a book fell on his head. He got up and turned off the gas.

Even when he worked for the Comintern agent Willy Münzenberg in a Communist-front organization, Koestler found that French intellectuals, for all the encouragement and material assistance they offered, kept their distance. Neither he nor any of his friends was ever invited to a French home. He was aware that this reserve was normal French behavior, and when he had lived in Paris as a foreign correspondent it hardly bothered him. But poverty and exile made him sensitive; he dearly missed the hospitality of a home. Instead, he felt, a Frenchman would embrace you and then leave you "shivering in the street, condemned to remain forever a permanent tourist or permanent exile, as the case may be." Thus the majority of refugees lived in a kind of ghetto, reading their own press, frequenting their own clubs and cafés. During Koestler's seven years as a refugee in France he lived exclusively in the company of fellow refugees, who continued to write and to think in German.

It did not help Koestler's opinion of France that at the outbreak of war he was arrested by French police and sent to a detention camp; after his release he spent three months under police harassment while finishing *Darkness at Noon.*

Manès Sperber had first met Koestler in Vienna, and got to know him better in Berlin. Now in Paris they found themselves working side by side in the Communist-controlled Institute for the Study of Fascism. And Sperber, a disciple and biographer of the Viennese psychoanalyst Alfred Adler, became a link between the German exiles and André Malraux, and through Malraux met other French intellectuals. Sperber also became familiar with the Left Bank's café life. One particular place on the Boulevard Saint-Michel was of special interest to him: Le Mahieu. Lenin had been a regular customer there in his time of exile, and in Sperber's years the Communists still favored it with their patronage. But when he had the choice, Sperber chose the Luxembourg Gardens just across the street.

Gustav Regler lived close to the Luxembourg Gardens, in rooms on the Rue du Tournon where Koestler had also resided. In another neighborhood farther south, Koestler had shared quarters with another writer, Johannes Becher, and later they moved to a furnished room. Then, when Koestler was interned at the outbreak of World War II, the police searched the room and found plans for the antiaircraft defense of Paris hidden in the flush tank. Apparently Becher's mistress, a Soviet agent, had abandoned them there when she accompanied Becher to Moscow at the outbreak of war. Such was the social life of the refugees. (Becher, author of a "Hymn to Stalin," became Minister of Education in post-war East Germany.)

As for Regler, he had abandoned a comfortable existence as a businessman in Berlin because, inspired by reading Gide's *Retour de*

l'Enfant prodigue while he sat in Le Dôme, he wanted to write. Settled in
Paris with the woman he loved, he reacted to the rise of Hitler by joining
the Communist Party, and soon was part of the Münzenberg apparatus
along with Koestler and Sperber. Whenever he felt discouraged by
official Communist doctrine, a visit to Malraux soothed him. "The talks
in his apartment in the Rue du Bac were the best antidote to the official
formulae," Regler later recalled. "We strove to pierce through the
tangle of reality . . . There was the incorruptible Guéhenno, the
brilliantly clear-headed [Nicola] Chiaromonte, and there was Clara
Malraux, logical, proud, and rebellious . . ."

On a visit to the Writers Club in Leningrad in that period, Regler was
asked whether he thought that Malraux would reject the Communist
cause because of the crudeness of Party leaders in Paris. Regler replied
with a laugh, "I don't suppose the lion in the zoo worries very much
because there are ordinary wildcats in the next cage." Nor did he think
that Malraux himself would ever enter the next cage — that is, join the
Party. Regler himself, after serving as a political commissar in the
International Brigade in the Spanish Civil War, became disillusioned
with Communism. By the time he escaped from France in May 1940, his
old comrades considered him an enemy.

Nicola Chiaromonte was only one of the Italian anti-Fascist refugees
in Paris in those years. He had company in the members of the Giustizia
e Libertà resistance movement founded in Paris in 1929, although two of
the founders, Carlo and Nello Rosselli, were murdered by French right-
wing extremists in 1937. Chiaromonte himself, who was in Paris from
1934 to 1940, his stay interrupted only by engagement in the Spanish
war, had a friend in Malraux. He attended one of the summer seminars
at the Abbey of Pontigny, and a meeting of the International Writers
Association in June 1936 where Malraux was one of the speakers.

★   ★   ★

One group of foreigners remained sheltered from the commotion of
France in crisis: the young Americans who had come there to enjoy the
cityscape and an atmosphere conducive to creation. Henry Miller was
particularly creative in that pre-World War II decade. He and his friends
lived in a little world of their own, a world lovingly described by Anaïs
Nin. In the beginning Miller scorned his fellow countrymen in
Montparnasse, refusing to associate with "the insufferable idiots at the
Dôme and the Coupole," although later he decided that it was not a sin

to sit down with Americans at sidewalk cafés. He had little contact with the French until the publication of *Tropic of Cancer*, and even after that most of the callers at his Villa Seurat apartment south of Montparnasse were resident or visiting foreigners. Not only was Miller unconcerned by the deepening European crisis at the end of the 1930s, he thought of it as an interference with his work, and worried that external forces over which he had no control would trouble his peace of mind. "I saw Henry trembling and groaning," Nin told her diary, "Henry in an agony of egoistic concern, raging because peace and security were torn from him by greater exterior forces."

Some Americans lacked shelter: the newspaper correspondents who by the nature of their work had to know what was going on. One of the most sensitive — and the closest to the French in many ways, although not to the politically oriented writers who are the principal subject of this book — was Elliot Paul, an editor of the Paris edition of the *New York Herald*, and with Eugene Jolas a founder of the little magazine that first published selections of James Joyce's enigmatic *Finnegans Wake*. Elliot Paul lived on a humble Latin Quarter street he would abandon only to the German invaders, and then immortalized the street in *The Last Time I Saw Paris*. More than one American of a later generation was drawn to Paris by this book of mourning for a dead city.

PART II

The Thirties

6   Founding Fathers

ONE OF THE QUALITIES that distinguished writers and artists of the 1930s from those who preceded them in political involvement was the internationalization of the concern — the conviction, in Gide's phrase, that each of them had a "right to inspect his neighbor's territory." Of course artists, writers, poets, teachers had been involved in the events of their times before, and the French had made heroes of Victor Hugo, exiled republican, and Emile Zola, the defender of Dreyfus and of justice.   But they had usually been engaged in contesting their own government's acts, or a set of abuses blamed on the ruling class.   In the 1930s a new state of mind developed.   Henceforth the chief concern of committed individuals and their organizations was external.   In France, that meant reacting to the rise of Fascism, the danger of war, the Spanish Civil War and its clash of ideologies, defending the Soviet Union — or attacking its leadership.

During the 1930s in France many were allied with their government rather than against it, just as members of the Soviet literary establishment were allied with theirs.   The dominant ideology of the decade could even be said to be Radical Socialist, after the political party that ruled or participated in most of the cabinets, while the most respected writers were also considered "Radical Socialist" in their orientation — Gide, for example, Jean Giraudoux, Jules Romains.   Historian Jean Touchard remarked of Gide that he was the very image of the free man, "free against families, against convention, against judges, against the churches and conspicuous converts, against parties and prejudices, against nationalism in the style of [Maurice] Barrès, against dogmatism, against authority, against fanaticism."   Such Radical Socialism was not a doctrine, but a list of minimal demands anyone could accept.   The democratic tradition that it nurtured helped the French to resist the temptations of Fascism.

Certainly the International Writers Congress of 1935 differed from most earlier events of the kind in that the "defense of culture" was to be waged against Fascism and Nazism, first of all in the foreign countries that had given birth to them. "Our entire history is a series of Dreyfus affairs," Jean Cassou said in retrospect. "The [World War II] Resistance was a Dreyfus affair. The Spanish war... was a Dreyfus affair for French opinion..." If justice was a universal concept, Cassou and his comrades could shift their focus from domestic to foreign Dreyfus affairs, and deal as eagerly with their neighbors' crises as with their own. It became clearer and clearer, as the decade drew to a close, that foreign troubles would become French ones.

French dictionaries attribute the phrase *écrivain engagé* ("committed writer") to Jean-Paul Sartre, and date it at the end of World War II. In fact, Jean Guéhenno had spoken of the writer's *engagement* as early as 1933, and there may be earlier references still. Julien Benda's *La Trahison des clercs* ("The Treason of the Intellectuals"), published in 1927, was taken as an attack on such involvement in the political arena. Benda's intellectuals were philosophers, religious leaders, writers, artists, scientists; what he objected to was the *partisan* nature of their commitment, for in the better old days (he said), intellectuals had remained aloof from mundane political passions.

Romain Rolland and Henri Barbusse might be called the founding fathers of *engagement*. They were born in 1866 and 1873 respectively, and each made a mark in literature at least a full generation before any other of our protagonists except Gide. Rolland is best remembered for his roman-fleuve *Jean-Christophe*, published before the First World War, and Barbusse for *Le Feu* ("Under Fire"), a stark account of trench life published during that war.

Rolland had taught music and art, and wrote a great deal about music and musicians. His Jean-Christophe is a composer in the mold of Beethoven, whose biography Rolland also wrote. During World War I he became a voluntary exile in Switzerland, abandoning forever an apartment on the Boulevard du Montparnasse just opposite the old Closerie des Lilas; his pamphlet *Au-dessus de la mêlée* — literally "Above the Crowd" — which called for an end to the war, was denounced in France as pro-German and subversive. He turned over the money he received for the Nobel Prize for Literature to the International Red

Cross, welcomed the Russian Revolution of 1917, and from then on supported both Communist and pacifist causes. A naïve and effusive idealist, a frequent contributor to the Communist and Communist-inspired press, Rolland was the guiding spirit behind the monthly magazine *Europe*, founded in 1923, and whose editor-in-chief in the first half of the 1930s was Jean Guéhenno. Barbusse, who had lived in the Soviet Union, published the weekly *Monde* until his death in 1935. After that, Rolland lamented to Guéhenno that it was "shameful that all the Communist and anti-Fascist organizations . . . must always depend on old men, ill and in their seventies, like Barbusse and myself, to run them, preside over them, whip them up!" What about the younger ones: Jean-Richard Bloch, André Malraux, Paul Nizan, Guéhenno himself? Guéhenno replied that a solid reputation based on accomplished work gave one the necessary credit, and none of the younger writers had that. "All this means," concluded Guéhenno, "that we need you very badly."

Rolland and Barbusse were among the first to see the crisis of their time as universal, to attempt to extend the concerns of French intellectuals beyond the French border, and to elicit the cooperation of their foreign counterparts in these causes. In the 1930s both men had to deal with another problem: to reconcile their sincere pacifism with the increasing likelihood that Fascism, particularly in the form of Hitler's Nazism, could not be stopped without recourse to war. Certainly the Soviet Union, to the defense of which both men had dedicated their careers and their lives, could not be saved by words alone.

There was no ambiguity about Henri Barbusse's choices. He had been the literary editor of *L'Humanité*, the Communist daily, and at the end of his life published a laudatory book about Stalin. His *Monde* was founded in the wake of an international conference of so-called revolutionary writers in Moscow in 1927, although its board of sponsors suggested a broader base: Maxim Gorki of the Soviet Union, yes, but also Albert Einstein, Upton Sinclair, Manuel Ugarte of Argentina, Miguel de Unamuno of Spain. The words that were virtually his last appeared in Barbusse's popular 1935 biography of Stalin: "If Stalin has faith in the masses, the opposite is also true. The new Russia has a veritable cult for Stalin, but this cult based on confidence springs forth from the people." Barbusse died in Moscow two months after the close of the International Writers Congress in Paris.

★   ★   ★

The movement that became known as "Amsterdam-Pleyel" was a rallying cry in the 1930s, inevitably linked with that other combination, "Rolland-Barbusse." The reference was to two conferences with somewhat contradictory purposes, somewhat obscure origins, and built-in rivalries that would never quite disappear.

The first priority for Romain Rolland, lifelong pacifist, was to prevent the outbreak of a new war. Fascism was a new threat, but Fascism also signified war; somehow, by challenging one of them, the other could be defeated too. As late as 1935, Rolland published a warning in Barbusse's *Monde* that war would serve only Hitler, while *peace* would be fatal to him. So that back in 1932, when Mussolini's less threatening form of Fascism had been in power ten years and Hitler's was only a potential menace, it was easier for a member of the generation traumatized by the First World War to see peace as the most cherished goal, the most threatened by the new face of evil.

The initiative came from Rolland and from Barbusse, who in the spring of 1932, set up a committee to prepare an international conference against war. The immediate pretext was the threat of an attack on the Soviet Union by Japan, then extending its occupation of Manchuria on the eastern frontier of the USSR, and by smaller Eastern European nations incited (so the Soviets and their French friends claimed) by Western imperialism. Rolland's May Day appeal in L'Humanité, repeated in Moscow by *Pravda*, began explicitly:

> The Fatherland is in danger! Our international Fatherland... The USSR is threatened.
> And in reaction, the entire world is on the eve of collapse . . .

Europe was being handed over to Fascism, his message explained, while the Western democracies, betrayed by their parliamentary leaders, were too weak to react. War could come at any moment. The original plan was to hold the conference in Geneva on June 28, 1932, the anniversary of the assassination of Archduke Franz Ferdinand in Sarajevo, the first shot of the First World War. Problems of organization, and of finding a hospitable site after the Canton of Geneva banned the meeting, caused its postponement until August, and the changing of the site to Amsterdam.

The first act of the Barbusse-Rolland committee was to invite support from well-known international figures, such as Albert Einstein, Heinrich Mann, John Dos Passos, Theodore Dreiser, Upton Sinclair, George

Bernard Shaw, H.G. Wells, and Madame Sun Yat-sen. National sponsoring committees were formed, with Roger Baldwin, Malcolm Cowley, Theodore Dreiser, John Dos Passos, Michael Gold, and Upton Sinclair in the United States; Bertrand Russell and the popular psychologist Havelock Ellis in Great Britain; Eugène Dabit, Georges Duhamel, André Gide, Jean Guéhenno, Bernard Lecache (of the League Against Anti-Semitism), and Paul Vaillant-Couturier of *L'Humanité* among the French. The Surrealists, led by André Breton, and then including Roger Caillois, René Char, René Crevel, and Paul Eluard, announced their support of the Amsterdam congress, but with their habitual rhetoric attacked "the evil and deeply counterrevolutionary role" of Barbusse and Rolland, along with their "humanitarian mysticism, which is really more pernicious than any abstract theology."

And if the Communists of France and everywhere else guaranteed full support, the Socialists, particularly through the Socialist (or Second) International, rejected the Barbusse-Rolland initiative as Communist-inspired. The result of this Communist campaign and this Socialist boycott was to assemble under the auspices of international Communism a representative grouping of committed intellectuals who were either Communist sympathizers to begin with, or sufficiently removed from the political arena to be unaffected by the attacks on the Amsterdam meeting. Later the Communists spoke of the event as the first where they had been involved with like-minded persons not committed to their movement — the first example of a united front and prototype of the Popular Front.

If we accept Romain Rolland's own report, the meeting "was the most powerful mass demonstration from all over the world, against imperialism from all over the world . . . since the war [World War I]." Over five thousand delegates had received mandates from their respective movements, and nearly 2200 were actually present, the others prevented from coming by material difficulties such as the cost of travel, or because of governmental bans. Officially these delegates represented over thirty thousand organizations, with thirty million members. The following week, a follow-up meeting in a Left Bank hall — the Bullier, now vanished — brought together twenty thousand people, who spilled out to the adjacent Place de l'Observatoire, where they became the target, so Rolland claimed in *Europe*, of "savage charges" by police forces led by Prefect Jean Chiappe, who was one of the chief villains in the eyes of the French left in that decade.

The Amsterdam meeting was held in a hall used for that city's automobile show. It opened with the singing of the "Internationale." On the speakers' platform Henri Barbusse was flanked by Marcel Cachin, the general manager of *L'Humanité*, by the American novelist Sherwood Anderson, whose *Winesburg, Ohio* had appeared in French five years earlier (Anderson, then fifty-five, was editor of a small-town American newspaper), and by a personality even less well known than Anderson, a German émigré named Willy Münzenberg. There was a rousing message from the absent Romain Rolland calling for a *front unique*, a concept he admitted was frightening to many. He contrasted the Western nations beset with imperialism against the proletarian USSR, "whose existence alone is a challenge to the old world of exploiters." The congress concluded by issuing a manifesto in the name of "intellectual and manual workers" against war and Fascism, against the imperialist nations favoring war, in defense of the USSR. A permanent organization was established; in its leadership the names of Gorki, Cachin, Einstein, Heinrich Mann, Dreiser, Dos Passos, Anderson, and Münzenberg were joined once more.

Münzenberg — "this great artist in revolutions" is the way Rolland described him, evoking in *Europe* his "incendiary eloquence" during the Amsterdam congress. We shall see him less often as a platform speaker than as a discreet agent of the Communist International — the Comintern — in Paris, responsible for setting up Communist-front movements. In fact the Socialist International, in the person of its secretary, Friedrich Adler, and the French Socialist daily *Le Populaire*, were already denouncing Münzenberg as the "occult power" behind Amsterdam. To the charge of Communist domination of the congress and its governing bodies, and of the permanent organization set up to pursue its goals, Henri Barbusse offered these statistics: the 2196 delegates included 1041 independents, Radical Socialists, and others from the center-left of the political spectrum; 830 Communists; and 291 Socialists, in addition to 24 independent Socialists and 10 dissident Socialists.

★ ★ ★

Less than a year later, in June 1933, shortly after the coming to power of Adolf Hitler in Germany, a second international meeting was held in Paris. The European Anti-Fascist Congress was booked into the Salle Pleyel, a Right Bank concert hall built to hold three thousand, and the hall was packed. The meeting was summed up in *L'Humanité*'s front-page headline: NOUVELLE VICTOIRE DU FRONT UNIQUE.

Once more, leading French personalities (including André Gide this time) were among the sponsors. And once more the Socialist International and *Le Populaire* boycotted it. Of course, the Pleyel meeting shared another characteristic with the Amsterdam congress: it had the benefit of the organizing talent of Willy Münzenberg.

Ten days later, the French sponsors of the Amsterdam and the Pleyel congresses met to unite their forces in a single Committee of Struggle Against War and Fascism, combining the themes of the two events as well as the personae. Soon after, the international organizations also merged; the new secretariat included the name of Münzenberg as well as Barbusse. The new movement, most of whose activity was to take place in France, became known as Amsterdam-Pleyel. Its structure allowed the Communists to reach heretofore uncommitted people who desired to participate in the fight for peace, against the rising menace of Fascism. As far away as French Algeria, for example, the student Albert Camus served his political apprenticeship in the ranks of the Amsterdam-Pleyel movement, under a local leader who was a Communist, and who later brought Camus into the Party itself.

7   Engagement with Moscow

NO MATTER WHERE one begins a history, there is always an earlier period. Deciding where the story of intellectual commitment should begin raises at least one question. But this does not deal with the matter of causes: was it because the Soviet Union, acting through the Comintern, had devised a strategy for enlisting support from individuals and groups beyond Soviet borders that the anti-Fascist movements of the 1930s developed as they did? Or was it because sincere men and women, Communist sympathizers or not, threw themselves into the anti-Fascist struggle, seeing it as a legitimate effort regardless of its origins? Nor does this address the question of whether the Communist initiative left a permanent blotch on the movement, compromising it irretrievably. Such matters would become relevant at the time of the Spanish Civil War, when anti-Fascists who were Communists murdered anti-Fascists who were Trotskyists, and again later when the Soviet-German pact of August 1939 forced loyal Communists to sabotage what had until then been a united front against Fascism. Summoned to the presence of Charles de Gaulle in 1944, André Malraux evoked the situation of intellectuals. "French politics has always had its writers on call, from Voltaire to Victor Hugo," he told de Gaulle. "They played an important role in the Dreyfus affair. They thought they had rediscovered that role at the time of the Popular Front. But already they were being used. This utilization, on the Communist side, was worked out with considerable cleverness by Willy Münzenberg . . ."

A strong case can be made that intellectual involvement in the archetypical form it assumed in France in the years before World War II was Münzenberg's creation. This is certainly an exaggeration, but with our hindsight it seems astounding that Romain Rolland could describe him publicly as "this great artist in revolutions" as early as 1932. Münzenberg did not invent the Communist fellow traveler; what he did was to devise organizational instruments that could make a fellow traveler most effective. Nor was he really an occult influence, with the rabble-rousing talent he possessed. But did his fellow speakers and sponsors know that he was acting as an agent of the Comintern? Clara Malraux remembered Münzenberg's role in the small, informal gatherings on the Rue de Bac when anti-Fascist organizational strategy was hammered out. It was clear that Münzenberg took the initiative, and that after the discussion he would do the summing up. Apparently it did not bother the others that he was calling the shots — he was not a writer, he was Moscow's man, but weren't they all sympathizers with the Moscow line?

Münzenberg did not frequent the literary and political cafés; he avoided that kind of public life. His Left Bank was a narrow alley at 83, Boulevard du Montparnasse, in a small room at the back of a small building, where he sat at a desk piled high with papers. "He had the calm and intensity of a chess master walking from board to board, playing twenty games at once," remembered Gustav Regler.

We know more about the inner workings of the Münzenberg organization thanks to Arthur Koestler, who described Münzenberg as nothing less than the "Western Propaganda Chief" for the Communist International, "the grey eminence and invisible organizer of the anti-Fascist world crusade." When Koestler arrived in Paris in 1933 to work for this Western Propaganda Chief, Münzenberg was pitting his wits against the Nazis, who had indicted another Comintern operative, Georgi Dimitrov, who was accused with four others of having set fire to the Reichstag, the German parliament building in Berlin. Münzenberg's tactic was to set up anti-Fascist organizations with non-Communist sponsorship, although effective control of these organizations was in the hands of a Communist caucus. In fact it was Münzenberg's World Committee for the Relief of the Victims of German Fascism that was headquartered on that narrow alley off the Boulevard du Montparnasse, although his presence would not be perceived by the casual visitor, who was expected to consider the Committee as a philanthropic activity backed by a prestigious sponsoring group. Münzenberg also set up a company to publish propaganda material such as *The Brown Book of the Hitler Terror and the Burning of the Reichstag*, a landmark in anti-Nazi literature. And the World Committee gave birth to a Committee of

Inquiry into the Origins of the Reichstag Trial. The voyage of Gide and Malraux to seek the liberation of Dimitrov and his fellow defendants — who were kept in detention even after their acquittal — was part of this campaign, making skillful use of the prestige of French writers. Indeed, few international activities of this kind in those years — including the International Writers Congress Of 1935 took place without Münzenberg's talents and funds.

Münzenberg was born into a German working-class family, and as a young man did factory work. During World War I he lived in Switzerland, where he met Lenin and other exiled revolutionaries. He was one of the founders of the German Communist Party, which he represented in the Reichstag, and in 1920 he was president of the Communist Youth International in Moscow. A year later he founded International Workers Aid, an organization directed from Moscow, ostensibly to supply assistance to the famine-stricken Soviet Union, and an excellent instrument for recruiting sympathizers. IWA became known as the "Münzenberg Trust," operating publishing enterprises, newspapers, magazines, book clubs; in Germany alone, in pre-Hitler days, it controlled two daily newspapers and an illustrated weekly magazine with a circulation said to be in the millions. Its activity extended as far as Japan. The film production department was responsible for some of Sergei Eisenstein's classic motion pictures.

After the collapse of the Weimar Republic, IWA operated from its Paris base to become a center of underground resistance to the Nazi regime. When Arthur Koestler met Willy Münzenberg, he was forty-four years of age, "a shortish, square, squat, heavy-boned man with powerful shoulders, who gave the impression that bumping against him would be like colliding with a stream-roller. His face had the forceful simplicity of a woodcut," remembered Koestler in his autobiography, "but there was a basic friendliness about it... Though without a trace of pomposity or arrogance, his person emanated such authority that I have seen Socialist cabinet ministers, hard-boiled bankers, and Austrian dukes behave like schoolboys in his presence."

During the Stalin purge years of the late 1930s, Münzenberg removed himself from Comintern discipline — and from the grasp of the Soviet secret police. He remained in Paris and founded a German-language weekly newspaper, *Die Zukunft* ("The Future"), working with other disillusioned Communist functionaries such as Koestler and Sperber (himself a former employee of another Left Bank Comintern front, the

Institute for the Study of Fascism). Münzenberg being Münzenberg, he had soon won the support of international personalities such as Thomas Mann, Sigmund Freud, E.M. Forster, and Aldous Huxley.

★ ★ ★

And consider the case of Eugen Fried, a somewhat lonelier man, fated to wield the power of the Comintern in less overt circumstances. Few of the artists and writers who worked in the Communist movements of the 1930s would have met him, or even heard his name; in fact, he was known by a pseudonym, "Clément." It is now believed that the decision of the French Communist Party to abandon its hostility to cooperation with other left-wing parties (including the Socialists) was whispered to Communist Party secretary Maurice Thorez by "Clément," acting as the chief Comintern agent in France in liaison with the Party. Thorez's oldest son, Maurice, Jr., later credited "Clément" with the conception not only of the Popular Front but of similar overtures to Catholics and other groups. "If the French knew all that he did for them," the elder Thorez told his son following the Second World War, "they would erect a statue to him." A Communist leader of the time later said that Thorez never made a political decision that was not dictated or inspired, or at least verified and approved, by "Clément."

Eugen Fried was born in 1900 in Trnava, Slovakia. A member of the central committee of the Communist Party of Czechoslovakia, at the end of the 1920s he joined the Comintern's Orgburo, or Organization Bureau, which controlled Communist leadership around the world. Although attacked as a left-wing deviationist within his own Czechoslovak party, he was given a full-time assignment with the Comintern in 1931 and sent to Paris, where he lived as "Clément" until 1939. According to a former Party official, "Clément" shared women as well as ideas with Maurice Thorez. One of the women was Thorez's first wife; another was Ana Pauker, also a Comintern agent at the time, who in the years following World War II became secretary general of the Rumanian Communist Party and that country's Minister of Foreign Affairs before being purged by Stalin. At the start of the Second World War "Clément" moved on to Belgium to run the French Communist Party there with Thorez and Jacques Duclos. One day he was shot down in his own apartment. The official story is that German occupation forces murdered him, but the Germans were more likely to have wanted him alive so as to be able to interrogate him. So it is now believed that he was another victim of the Soviet secret police. Much later, during the Slansky purge trial in postwar Czechoslovakia, it became obvious that the legend of "Clément" was still a fearful one, for the secret police of Communist Czechoslovakia sought to prove that he had been a Trotskyist all the while he was employed by the Comintern.

Not only had "Clément" planned strategy with Maurice Thorez, but he also advised the writer and poet Louis Aragon and Jean-Richard Bloch when they published the Communist daily Ce Soir in the years leading up to World War II. Aragon later confessed to having met frequently with "Clément" to obtain his advice. If we believe Aragon, "Clément" stood with him against critics of Ce Soir within the Party itself. Such was the power, and the omnipresence, of Eugen Fried.

It is not to be suggested that Aragon himself was another Münzenberg or another "Clément," or even an Ilya Ehrenburg. But as the best-known creative artist in the French Communist Party, and (with nearly four decades of Party loyalty) the longest-lasting, Aragon is a key to much of the interplay between Communist and non-Communist intellectuals in the period that concerns us. As a young man, Aragon was a pure poet, under the star of Apollinaire. With André Breton, his companion during military service, he participated in the capers of Dada. With Breton, Philippe Soupault, and other young Parisians, he carved out a free-swinging territory called Surrealism, which moved easily from automatic writing and iconoclastic poetry and painting to provocative politics. To embrace Soviet Communism at a time when that system seemed the avant-garde response to bourgeois society appeared a logical next step. At the end of the 1920s, the Surrealists joined the French Communist Party virtually en bloc. In the spring of 1930, Aragon and Breton pledged to fight on the Soviet side if the imperialists declared war.

Later that same year, Aragon traveled to the Soviet Union with Georges Sadoul, the first of the Surrealists to do so. They attended a conference of revolutionary writers in Kharkov, a university city in the northeast Ukraine, from November 6 to 15. They were quickly caught up in internal Soviet polemics and a more rigid orthodoxy than they had bargained for — one that required, for example, that they join in denouncing their Surrealist comrades back home. Soon Breton, Paul Eluard, and René Crevel were expelled from the Communist Party, while Aragon's star became even brighter.

Louis Aragon managed to reconcile his own tastes in art and literature with the restrictive and hardly credible doctrine of Socialist Realism. There seemed to be two Aragons, a poet and an apologist, and he enjoyed keeping the two in balance. As the party's apostle to the artists and writers of the Left Bank, Aragon may also have seen himself as a commissar with the power to send dissenters off to symbolic Siberias. Yet to many independent left-wing writers and artists he seemed more of a spoiled child, with decidedly worldly ambitions; for example, he enjoyed exchanging witticisms with countesses in their literary salons.

Communist organizational activity in artistic and literary circles only became what it became after the Kharkov congress, thanks to a Soviet-inspired International Union of Revolutionary Writers, based in Moscow, which produced and sent out to the world a magazine called *Literature of the World Revolution* in four separate language editions. Its first issue contained Aragon's poem "Front Rouge" ("Red Front"), whose subversive tone led to the magazine's confiscation by the French police and to Aragon's indictment for "incitement to murder."

★   ★   ★

In France the International Union of Revolutionary Writers soon had an affiliate in the Association of Revolutionary Writers and Artists (AEAR), whose own magazine was *Commune*. Its first issue was dated July 1933. After a year of activity, Paul Vaillant-Couturier (who until his death in 1937 outranked even Aragon among Communist Party intellectuals) was able to report that AEAR had enrolled 550 members from the fields of literature, the plastic arts, architecture, music, theater, film, and photography —"nonconformist writers and artists who wish to struggle alongside the proletariat." The sponsoring group included Aragon, Barbusse, Breton, Luis Buñuel, René Crevel, Paul Eluard, the American Surrealist photographer and painter Man Ray, art historian Elie Faure, Romain Rolland. Among its guiding principles:

> There is no neutral art, no neutral literature . . .
> A proletarian literature and art are about to be born . . .
> The economic crisis, the Fascist threat, the danger of war, the example of cultural development of the Soviet masses in the face of the regression of Western civilization, at present offer objective conditions favorable to the development of a proletarian and revolutionary literary and artistic activity in France.

On March 21, 1933, AEAR put on a rally that would be the model of unity-of-action events of this decade. In *L'Humanité* that day Vaillant-Couturier declared that AEAR was proving that it had rid itself of sectarian tendencies. Citing Marx to the effect that part of the ruling class breaks off to join the revolutionary movement whenever the class struggle reaches a decisive moment, he said that it would be absurd to criticize the origins of those who demonstrate that they are prepared to fight for the revolutionary class.

Perhaps a theoretical lesson of this kind was necessary to introduce André Gide to the working class. For he was the star that night, as chairman and principal speaker. Seated at the center of the speakers' table, he was accompanied by Malraux, Eugène Dabit, Jean Guéhenno, Vaillant-Couturier; nothing about this arrangement suggested that the Communists were the true initiators of the event. Gide apologized to his audience: "I am hardly an orator, and I feel as unqualified as one can be presiding at any kind of affair at all." He spoke of the anguish caused by the events in Germany — Hitler had been in power for two months now, Nazi repression was beginning to be felt — but he also evoked the lack of civil liberties in the Soviet Union, agreeing, however, that this was a different case, since the goal of that country was the creation of a new society.

Guéhenno spoke with more force. "The duty of writers is commitment. If Fascism has come to Germany, it is perhaps because time was allowed to go by. For my part, I believe that the duty of all artists and all writers is to announce right away which side they are on." "In the event of war," cried Malraux, "our thoughts will turn toward Moscow, we shall turn toward the Red Army!"

It was this Association of Revolutionary Writers and Artists that sponsored the Maisons de la Culture (Houses of Culture), the first of which opened in Paris in April 1934, offering music and poetry, lectures (on literature, motion pictures, foreign cultures), and a heavy dose of politics. By 1936 the total membership of this movement was claimed as 96,000. The extent to which the network of the Houses of Culture took root is suggested by the fact that as far away as Algeria, young Albert Camus set up a branch to which lecturers could be sent from the Paris headquarters. Camus and his friends also founded an amateur theatrical group to present politically significant plays, the counterpart of the People's Theater sponsored by the House of Culture movement in mainland France.

8 Engagement in Moscow

UNTIL THE 1970s the Soviet Union belonged to no international copyright convention, and its government-controlled publishing houses translated foreign literature without permission and without payment. But whenever it was in the interest of the Soviet state, payment was made all the same. Considering the size of the Soviet Union and the number of languages spoken by its peoples, the sums of money owed to authors in the West for translation rights to their books could be considerable. There might even be a movie version of a novel, and an adaptation for the stage. When a foreign writer was tapped for favored treatment, either with a cash payment or an account in Soviet currency that could be used during a visit to the USSR, it was as if he or she had won a lottery.

And so a number of Western European writers in the 1930s were able to travel through Soviet territory in grand style. "Several among you have had books translated into the languages of our Soviet Union," Ilya Ehrenburg reminded an audience at the International Writers Congress in Paris in June 1935. "Don't think that these are simply translations, just a few more books . . . They are acts." It was almost as if he were evoking royalty fees when he concluded: "There are hundreds of thousands, millions of people who respond to your books with their lives."

But note how a skeptic, Roland Dorgelès, reported the use of royalty payments as bait, after a visit to the Soviet Union in 1936: "Those who go to Moscow go as one picks up a check. Those who leave the USSR leave with contracts." Another visitor who could not be accused of Communist sympathies was Georges Duhamel, but he did not criticize the USSR on his return. As early as 1928, in *Le Voyage de Moscou*, he explained how the government publishing house had "spontaneously" offered him a fee for his books already published in the Soviet Union, as well as a contract for future works.

Or take Malraux. During the early period of his political activity, when the Soviets were giving the highest priority to unity of action between Communists and writers with left-wing sympathies, he was tempted by the possibility that his ambitious novel *La Condition humaine* ("Man's Fate") would be produced as a motion picture by a director of the caliber of Sergei Eisenstein, already famous for *Potemkin*. Ilya Ehrenburg communicated an offer along these lines to Malraux on the eve of the Soviet Writers Congress, which Malraux was to attend in the summer of 1934. Nothing came of the project, and Clara Malraux guessed it was because Eisenstein was already in the bad graces of Stalin; he and his films would soon enter a long period of purgatory.

Or Gide. The Soviets offered, more or less in the same period, to adapt his novel *Les Caves du Vatican* for the movies. This time the offer was relayed through Louis Aragon, who also indicated changes the Soviets wanted to make in the scenario so that the story would be useful as antireligious propaganda. Nothing came of this project, either, but in those crucial early months of anti-Fascist unity, Paul Vaillant-Couturier informed Gide of the plan to publish *Les Caves du Vatican* in installments in *L'Humanité*.' Even as the author was refusing the project *L'Humanité* was announcing it, and Gide let it happen. There could not have been any urgency; the original book had been published in 1914.

The bait could be withdrawn as readily. Gide's only politically committed work, the play *Robert ou l'Intérêt Général*, was translated into Russian by Aragon's companion, Elsa Triolet, for production in Moscow. Then Gide made his journey to the Soviet Union, which led to his critical *Retour de l'U.R.S.S.*,* making him an enemy of the people in the Soviet view and depriving him of a sure triumph in the Soviet theater.

Gide later recorded his astonishment at the deluxe treatment he had been given, as a valuable friend of the Soviet Union. "Without there having been an attempt at corruption," he said, he could see how it benefited his hosts to favor writers and others who could speak well of the country, and how advantageous it could be to the writer, too. "The disproportionate profits that I am offered over there frighten me." Gide explained: "The Moscow press informed me that in the space of a few months over 400,000 copies of my books were sold. I shall leave the

* See Part II, Chapter 13, "Gide's Return."

royalty payments to the imagination. And the articles so richly paid! If I had written a book of praise to the USSR and to Stalin, what a fortune I'd have made!"

Two of his traveling companions, Gide added, "scoured the antique shops, the junk shops, the second-hand dealers, not knowing how to spend the thousands of rubles of advance royalties they had been given and knew they couldn't take out of the country." Gide himself couldn't begin to use up the enormous sum at his disposal, since every centime they spent, from expenses of the trip itself down to cigarettes, was paid for by their hosts.

The iconoclast Céline, standing alone in the 1930s, nearly as far from the ideological right as from the left, denied in one of his books (*Bagatelles pour un massacre*) that his visit to the Soviet Union in 1936 had been paid for by his hosts. "I paid everything with my own pennies . . . with my own little dough earned honestly: hotel, taxis, trips, interpreter, chow . . ." Indeed, he said, the Soviets still owed him money. But by confessing that he had spent money he had *earned*, Céline was unknowingly revealing that he too had benefited from the special treatment given those the Soviets wished to seduce. For under the situation then prevailing, they owed nothing and paid nothing for translation rights unless they wished to win over an author. Indeed, Céline had gone to the Soviet Union at the government's invitation, to spend his nonexportable royalties there. The Soviets simply guessed wrong in his case.

There were group tours, too. The meeting known as the First Congress of Soviet Writers, held in Moscow in August 1934, was one, in a sense. From the point of view of public relations, this congress was handled more adroitly than the Kharkov meeting four years earlier, with its atmosphere of Ivan the Terrible against background music by Prokofiev. If priority was still given to internal Soviet politics and to the doctrine of Socialist Realism, this time it was possible for Soviet sympathizers who were not card-carrying members of the Communist Party to feel more at ease. And so that great standard bearer of the "fellow-traveling" left, André Malraux, was all but carried to Moscow by Ilya Ehrenburg. The Ehrenburgs and the Malrauxs took the train and Channel ferry to London, where they boarded a Soviet ship, the *Dzershinski* (named after the founder of the secret police).

In all, the Malrauxs spent about three months in the USSR. A considerable portion of this time was given over to visiting factories, a favorite occupation of guests of the Soviet Union. They could also see the Paul Nizans, for Nizan was then based in Moscow, working for a French-language periodical; the Louis Fischers; and Gustav Regler. Clara Malraux later recalled that she and André first became close to Nizan and Regler in Moscow; both later became familiar faces at their Rue du Bac evenings. Louis Aragon and Elsa Triolet were also there, but they were not particularly close to the Malrauxs — or to anyone else — in Moscow. Malraux had long sessions with Sergei Eisenstein planning the scenario of La Condition humaine, which would never be filmed. Although the Malrauxs paid their own way, they lived nicely on Soviet royalties from that book — so nicely that Clara was able to buy a fur coat.

Nizan introduced Malraux to the Soviet public shortly before his arrival, through an article in Literaturnaya Gazeta. He warned Russian readers that Malraux did not have a very clear idea of revolution, for he saw it as a question of personal salvation rather than of historical necessity. "His principal aim is to discover, in a revolution, the possibilities of expressing a supreme heroism . . ." But Nizan saw hope for Malraux: "It is already very important that he has joined the ranks of anti-Fascist fighters, the ranks of the defenders of the Soviet Union." In a subsequent interview in Literaturnaya Gazeta, Malraux was quoted as saying that he had begun writing a novel about oil fields, which would portray Soviet oil workers. Perhaps he really thought that he would do that.

As for Ehrenburg, he got himself ready for the writers' congress like a young girl preparing for her first ball, and available accounts suggest that it was indeed a festival. The walls of the meeting hall were decorated with portraits of Shakespeare, Tolstoi, Molière, Gogol, Cervantes, Heine, Pushkin, Balzac, and others. A flourish of trumpets announced the opening session; outside, a local crowd waited at the doors to try to see their favorite authors in flesh and blood, and at lunchtime the crowd was so dense that the delegates had to push their way in and out. Inside, the audience included delegations from the Red army, schoolchildren with trumpets, factory workers, and farmers from collectives (the women with enormous baskets of fruit and vegetables). The Western delegates were moved, although they could also see the naïveté and pathos. After the interminable sessions, they were literally covered with roses. Actually the workers and the farmers had come with a well-rehearsed message: to demand that the assembled authors write books about workers and farmers. To Ilya Ehrenburg, the packed hall seemed like a theater, for the audience applauded its favorites. Maxim Gorki was seen more than once wiping away a tear. Mikhail Koltzov and Isaak Babel drew laughs. And with Boris Pasternak, the brightest of the Soviet stars seemed to be present.

Later — much later — the congress was seen in another light. Louis Aragon, for example, had felt that the gathering represented a new consensus among Soviet writers. Internal dissension had disappeared; all embraced the Soviet system and Socialist Realism. But he discovered that the apparent harmony had been achieved by keeping dissenters like the poet Osip Mandelstam out of sight. And the Gorki who was presiding over the congress was also publishing a book praising forced labor camps for political prisoners. On the eve of the Malrauxs' departure, Isaak Babel took Clara for a walk. He told her how happy he ought to be: as a friend of Gorki he spent at least one evening a week in Stalin's company, he was living comfortably even without publishing a book. "I have the right not to write. But I am a writer. In my drawer I have two novels. If they are found, I'm a dead man." (Babel was later killed on Stalin's orders without seeing the two manuscripts to publication.) Ehrenburg confessed to Clara Malraux that the remarkable lyric poet Anna Akhmatova was among the absent, and that even Pasternak could publish only translations from Shakespeare, not his own work.

Gorki gave a banquet for participants in the congress at his country house. The guests included Nikolai Bukharin, soon to be purged and executed; Vyacheslav Molotov; even Klementiy Voroshilov, commander-in-chief of the Red army and later titular head of state. As Gustav Regler recalled, alcohol loosened tongues. Lenin's old companion Karl Radek made a Dostoyevskian speech revealing doubts about the Soviet system, and even managed to offend Malraux by calling him a "petty bourgeois." In his memoirs, Regler realized in retrospect that the Gorki banquet was the last of its kind. Never again would there be the same freedom of expression. Shortly after the congress Sergei Kirov was assassinated — the act that provided the pretext for the trials, deportations, executions of the Bukharins and the Radeks, the Babels and the Mandelstams, and of many of their policemen as well. Regler wondered if Radek imagined that the foreign guests could foresee what was coming, and possibly rescue him and the others from the fate in store for them.

The Moscow congress had been blessed in advance by the Association of Revolutionary Writers and Artists, whose slogans indicated how the event would be exploited in France:

> For a vast united front of struggle of the writers and artists of France side by side with the revolutionary proletariat! . . .
> For the popularization of Soviet literature and international revolutionary literature in France! . . . For the creation of international socialist culture under the banner of dialectical materialism, under the banner of Marx, Lenin, and Stalin!

From Paris — for he was not quite ready to make the journey himself — Gide sent a message calling for "a Communist individualism," which he admitted might seem a contradiction in terms. But he did not see how Communism could survive without taking account of the particularities of each individual. "Communism needs strong personalities," he concluded, apparently thinking more of his Left Bank community than of policed Moscow.

It was up to the foreigners — to the French, notably — to bring some of the Left Bank atmosphere to Moscow, and for the last time in that generation. Malraux became their spokesman. "If we were not bound to the Soviet Union, we should not be here," he assured the audience at the Moscow congress, describing himself as a revolutionary writer. But, out of design or naïveté,' he chose this platform to challenge the principles of Socialist Realism even as they were being polished up for global dissemination. "You are creating the kind of civilization from which Shakespeares rise," he began. "Don't let them suffocate under photographs, no matter how pretty the photographs are. The world doesn't ask you for the image of what you are, but of what transcends you, and soon you alone will be able to give it."

For one of his biographers, Malraux invented a conversation with Stalin at Gorki's country house (just as during his mission to Berlin he invented a meeting with Joseph Goebbels that never happened, either). The only direct encounter with Stalin took place during a parade on Red Square, where the Malrauxs stood close enough to the Soviet ruler to be able to speak to him, although they did not. Later at their hotel, when André asked Clara what she had thought of their neighbor, she irritated him with her reply: "I wouldn't mind spending a little time with him in bed."

★   ★   ★

Back in Paris, when everyone had returned at last from the Moscow summer, a rally was scheduled for the Palais de la Mutualité to hear reports. A nervous Gide was once more shanghaied into presiding. He told the enthusiastic audience that he looked forward to the day when Soviet art would be in a position to abandon its combative phase, to become "joyous." Gide had prepared his speech with care, but Malraux improvised. Yet Gide's *petite dame* found him as "dazzling, prodigious" as ever, although his ideas were a bit too subtle for this audience. Malraux conceded the right of the Soviets to Socialist Realism, in a context of civil war, five-year plans, the necessary construction of the country.

Soon, in the right-wing weekly *Candide*, Pierre Gaxotte would make the point that one found the names of Malraux, Gide, and their friends on petitions for victims everywhere in the world, but not for the victims of the Moscow purges.

9 Right and Center

SIDE BY SIDE, on a Left Bank that seemed colonized exclusively by intellectuals of the political left, was that other colony — the intellectual right. Often the active elements of the rival groups and grouplets were to be seen in the same public places — the Coupole on the Boulevard du Montparnasse, the Flore at Saint-Germain-des-Prés — just as they were published under the same imprints, such as Grasset and Gallimard. Social behavior being what it was then, one could share the scholastic life of the Latin Quarter, the drafty halls of the Ecole Normale Supérieure, the corridors and cubbyholes of *La Nouvelle Revue Française*, without really sharing any basic ideas.

Just as many on the left became victims of Nazism in the next decade, so many on the right collaborated with the German occupying forces. And it may be that our foreknowledge of the fate of the antagonists prevents us from a serene approach to the young right of the 1930s, even to some of those delicately labeled "nonconformist." It is also true that many young rightists, even those addicted to Action Française and professing antidemocratic, anti-Semitic sentiments in those years, moved into the mainstream under the shock of the declaration of war in 1939 and after France's defeat a year later at the hands of their supposed friends from across the Rhine.

They shared the same places: Robert Brasillach's world was circumscribed by the Left Bank university quarter, the Ecole Normale near the Pantheon where he lived (in an apartment on the Rue Lecourbe southwest of Montparnasse), but also by the Action Française student headquarters on a venerable, winding Left Bank street, the Rue Saint-André-des-Arts. Later Brasillach was published by Librairie Plon on the Rue Garancière, and for amusement he would go to the Union pour la Vérité on the Rue Visconti to bait the anti-Fascist speakers.

Rive gauche: the very name Left Bank was co-opted by a right-wing lecture group that in the mid-1930s provided a platform for young men like Brasillach, or for elder philosophers of Action Française such as Jacques Bainville (who spoke at Rive Gauche under the chairmanship of the movement's crochety chieftain, Charles Maurras). The meetings were held in the Vieux-Colombier Theater, on the street of the same name, until Maurras's provocative political behavior got them banned from it. From there they migrated to the Salle des Sociétés Savantes on Rue Danton, and to the Cinéma Bonaparte on Place Saint-Sulpice. Brasillach had the staff of the extreme-rightest paper *Je Suis Partout* organize some of these meetings, and some genuine Nazis had an opportunity to speak to receptive young artists under the auspices of Rive Gauche. Once Otto Abetz, then a Nazi propagandist specializing in German-French cultural exchange, lectured on the Hitler Youth Movement; he was introduced to the audience by Henry de Montherlant. As the collaborationist weekly *Au Pilori* recalled those years: "A number of true collaborationists came out of the Rive Gauche team, and at a time when this required a certain amount of courage and self-sacrifice."

It was in 1925 that Robert Brasillach, the young provincial, arrived in Paris to prepare for entrance to the Ecole Normale Supérieure.* Affiliation with the young royalists and racists of Action Française seemed a spiritual and intellectual awakening, and apparently nothing in the preparatory classes at the Lycée Louis-le-Grand, nothing in or around the Ecole Normale, discouraged a flirtation with Fascism (Brasillach later called this period his "pre-Fascism"). Bright young men of the right could be aided in their careers by veteran ideologues of Action Française, such as Henri Massis: Massis found Brasillach his publisher, Plon. Brasillach even received praise from Colette for his articles in *L'Action Française;* his first significant contribution to that daily organ of the movement was a review of Pierre Drieu La Rochelle's novel *Le Feu Follet.* Brasillach became a familiar of stage and movie directors, received recognition as an authority on theater and motion pictures, and dined with figures such as Georges Bernanos — another writer with a tender feeling toward Action Française — or *chez* the Countess Joachim Murat, and in the company of elders such as Léon Daudet, Abel Bonnard, René Benjamin, or Léon Bérard, all members of the ultraconservative elite. By 1937 Brasillach was working for Pierre Gaxotte, himself a graduate of Normale — the two had met in the library

* See Part I, Chapter 2, "Making Friends."

there — at *Je Suis Partout*, which gradually attracted all of the young pre-Fascists. They took it over when its publisher, Arthème Fayard, decided to close it down after the Popular Front won the elections in 1936. In a sense, the camaraderie of *Je Suis Partout* reflected, or perpetuated, the fraternity-house spirit of the Ecole Normale Supérieure.

And when André Malraux and his friends were in Spain with the loyalist forces, Brasillach was visiting the Franco side. If Malraux wrote *L'Espoir* about that war, Brasillach (with Henri Massis) wrote *Le Siège de l'Alcazar*, describing a heroic battle from the side of the insurrection against the Republic. Whereas Malraux visited the Soviet Union, Brasillach went to prewar Germany to meet Otto Abetz, Goebbels, and Adolf Hitler himself. The Nazi occupation of Paris would make it possible for *Je Suis Partout* to pursue virtually the same line it had taken before the war, and in the same violent key, until the liberation of France put an end to the movement, the paper, and its star. Brasillach was tried and shot in 1945.

★   ★   ★

Returning to the 1930s, we are constantly reminded of how it all ended: the activities of the Maurras movement, of the *Je Suis Partout* band, are superimposed on the years of the German occupation. Then, *L'Action Française* in Lyon, *Je Suis Partout* in occupied Paris, carried on their prewar ideological campaigns, but their rhetoric became the equivalent of death sentences for their enemies. What had been insolence, outspoken dissent before, became denunciation, treason thereafter. Case after case has been documented of arrests, deportations, executions following attacks in the columns of collaborationist periodicals.

But this is to anticipate. In the prewar years, Charles Maurras was sentenced to prison for advocating the assassination of members of parliament — and of Léon Blum himself — if they dared to take action against the Mussolini regime because of its invasion of Ethiopia. Imprisoned at the Santé (another Left Bank landmark not far from the vital center of Montparnasse), Maurras managed to write for *Action Française* every day of his eight-month term. And then, between his release from prison and the declaration of war, Maurras had the good fortune to be elected to the Académie Française. "The Academy has always hated democracy," was Julien Benda's comment.

The Action Française blend of Maurrasian royalist and traditional

Catholic doctrine was widely approved in the prewar years. It inspired
not only the student and youth groups that dutifully sold its literature in
front of churches on Sundays, but brigades of young toughs who brought
terror to the streets; they were the closest French replica to the Nazi
youth movements. Eventually, however, the Vatican itself placed both
Maurras's newspaper and his books on the Index of forbidden
works.

It was the era of the weekly large-format opinion newspaper, and the
most successful weeklies were conservative. No left-oriented
publication could compare in impact to *Gringoire*, subtitled "The Great
Parisian Political and Literary Weekly," whose circulation went as high as
640,000 copies during the Popular Front years. Arthème Fayard's
Candide, "The Great Parisian Literary Weekly," printed over 300,000
copies. Standing outside the political sphere, but always prepared to
comment on it, the satirical *Canard Enchaîné* printed an average of
175,000 copies weekly. Even *Marianne*, "Great Illustrated Literary
Weekly," published by Gallimard under the direction of Emmanuel Berl
and able to draw upon the literary establishment of the *N.R.F.* to fill its
pages, never printed more than 120,000 copies. And the weeklies
launched during the Popular Front era expressly to combat *Gringoire* and
Candide did no better. It was a time when *Action Française* sold more
copies each day than *Le Figaro*.

His apologists would maintain that Pierre Drieu La Rochelle is entitled
to greater consideration than the personalities already described in this
chapter, and that he moved with apparent ease not only among the
fanatics of the extreme right, but in and out of the best drawing rooms of
literary Paris. It is also pleaded that Drieu's writing vindicates his action
or excuses his behavior (although this particular argument is never
pursued). Drieu was saved by committing suicide before he could be
arrested and tried for Nazi collaboration, and the pose of helplessness
that succeeded so well with the ladies all his life also caused eminent
contemporaries to want to help him, or at the very least excuse his
behavior. In the recollection of Alfred Fabre-Luce, who wrote for
Drieu's *Nouvelle Revue Française* during the German occupation:

> Drieu was tall, naturally elegant, stamped with a nonchalance that at times
> gave way to an air of defiance. He often had a cigarette sticking out of the
> corner of his mouth as if to spare the effort of raising and lowering it . . . He

smoked his life as a cigarette, burning up one woman after the other — or rather, an idea after a woman, a woman after an idea. This balancing act was at once his weakness and his charm. He sought to win in politics the rooster feathers he needed to seduce, then returned to public life with the techniques borrowed from his flirting days.

Drieu's biography reads like fiction, which is why it can be preferred to his own books. Born in 1893, he was influenced by nationalism *à la* Maurice Barrès, by the romantic royalism of Charles Maurras. Often enough he was saved from the consequences of a foolish act by his first wife, who was of Jewish origin, and by the Jew Emmanuel Berl, but to be consistent in his Fascism he became an anti-Semite. He had been a camp follower of the Surrealists, even a companion of Louis Aragon, later of Malraux; he almost became a Communist before choosing the National Socialists. A friend of Gaston Gallimard, he was on speaking terms with all of the *N.R.F.* group; when Gallimard published his *Socialisme fasciste* in 1934, Julien Benda expressed admiration for the work in *La Nouvelle Revue Française,* and even the Communist Paul Nizan praised its style in Henri Barbusse's *Monde.* Berl asked Drieu to write a series of articles on the Fascist nations for *Marianne.* In those years Drieu could sit at the dinner table with his comrade André Malraux discussing literature, and then go off to write a pro-Fascist article, or even visit a Nazi Party congress in Germany.

Drieu even found a way to distinguish between the old friends who were his present political enemies — and the others. Thus in *L'Emancipation Nationale,* the organ of the Fascist Parti Populaire Française, Drieu (in 1936) identified Malraux and Aragon as Stalinist intellectuals who knew what they were about. Something in their natures, he said, lent itself to violence and ruse. "I understand how Malraux, who is a Nietzschean, an advocate of violence, an apologist for terror, can defend Stalin," he wrote. He was more concerned with liberals such as André Gide and Jean Guéhenno. They were the "real guilty ones, for they pretend not to feel this tyranny which offends them in all their fibers . . ."

Contradictions such as these have made Drieu interesting to read about, but he is hardly a representative figure of the 1930s. "He will die alone," Paul Nizan predicted. The German occupation of Paris made him an important person, as we shall see.

★   ★   ★

In retrospect, prewar extremism seems to have been readily assimilated by the literary establishment. Thus Marcel Jouhandeau, author of a brochure whose title translates as "The Jewish Peril" and of scurrilous contributions to *Je Suis Partout* and *L'Action Française*, could at the same time be a pillar of *La Nouvelle Revue Française* and a lifelong personal friend of that group's *éminence grise*, Jean Paulhan. Indeed, Paulhan later broke with his comrades of the anti-German resistance because of the blacklisting of Jouhandeau after World War II. Another who stood apart from movements was Henry de Montherlant, whose cult of virility made him appear ready to embrace Fascism at any moment, when in fact he held himself in check until the occupation of France by the Germans. The critic Paul Léautaud confined his politics to the pages of his journal, while the congenital anti-Semite Georges Bernanos, disciple of Edouard Drumont (whose *La France Juive* was an anti-Semitic classic) and a follower of Action Française, was saved in the eyes of posterity by his reaction against the behavior of Franco in Spain. However far they roamed from the mainstream of French thought, most of these internal exiles seemed to find a place at the café tables and dinner tables, and around the teapot at the Daniel Halévys'. Gallimard and Grasset, even the *Nouvelle Revue Française* and *Marianne*, offered a no-man's-land where they and their counterparts on the left could rest their swords.

Perhaps the common denominator was a feeling that *some* kind of change was necessary, that the corrupt old world incapable of dealing with France's economic straits cried out for a new deal. For some of the decade's young, the first goal seemed to be a private transformation. Rejecting the total politics of Communism, or of incipient Fascism, they might choose among a number of currents of thought that accorded priority to personal spiritual development, and to the building of communities of similarly disposed souls. It is difficult to put a label on these tendencies, although one historian has grouped them as "the nonconformists of the 1930s," and perhaps that should satisfy. Movements with names like Spirit, New Order, Plans, Combat, The Young Right, Reaction, in their idealism and slight remove from the ideological battlefield appealed to a layer of French youth whose influence is not to be underestimated. Some of these youth were to constitute the leadership of progressive Catholic movements, reforming if not the Church hierarchy then at least its avant-garde, making it possible for a good Catholic to be a good anti-Fascist, perhaps even a

Socialist; and in the 1930s, such dual options were not as frequent as they were to become.

But the priorities of the young Christians seemed to be a direct challenge to the political activists of the left. In *Commune*, in November 1933, the Communist Party's intellectual spokesman, Paul Nizan, called attention to an editorial by Emmanuel Mounier in *Esprit* that indicated that his movement was seeking to rescue the free enterprise system by purifying it. For Nizan, such movements as Spirit and New Order were primarily interested in preserving property values, and their doctrine of "personalism" was in fact paving the way for Fascism.

In the end, as Raymond Aron later observed, the practical failure of the Spirit movement was that it did not help its followers decide what to do, so that they were unprepared to react to real events, such as the Munich compromise with Hitler in 1938, or the advent of Marshal Pétain's Vichy regime.

★ ★ ★

There is no category in which to place Louis-Ferdinand Céline, who doesn't even belong to the Left Bank. If he is a character in this story at all, it is because of the part he played in Left Bank literary and political circles, or allowed to be played around him. Céline was never a member of anyone's movement; and he made it clear that, doctor though he might be, he cared little for mankind. There is considerable confusion about the Céline case, for in seeking to exonerate him from charges of serving the Nazis, his admirers did not content themselves with evoking his contribution to literary history: they liked to think of him as apolitical, even a-racist. A common misconception, for example, is that Céline wrote the extraordinary novels for which he is known during an earlier phase of innocence — and then turned bad. This happens not to be true, for his first anti-Semitic work, a minor play called *L'Eglise*, was published three years before *Mort à crédit* ("Death on the Installment Plan"). What saved Céline's reputation in those early years was public indifference to his minor works. Certainly the Communists didn't bother to read them, for Louis Aragon continued to seek his enlistment in the Party as late as July 1936, when Céline visited the Soviet Union to spend the rubles made available to him after the publication in the USSR of *Voyage au bout de la nuit* ("Journey to the End of the Night").

In December 1937 Céline published *Bagatelles pour un massacre*, the most violent tract to appear under the signature of a serious writer, and under the imprint of a serious publisher, in the prewar decade. It was a superb encouragement to the young Fascist generation. Lucien Rebatet and his comrades of *Je Suis Partout* were delighted with this "prodigious reinforcement": the rallying to their side of "a writer who remained on the extreme left, despite his announced disappointment with Communism; a man of the people, a naturalist par excellence, an atheist who could not be suspected of reactionary views." Anti-Semitism could even be profitable in those years. Céline's next book, *L'Ecole des cadavres*, was advertised in a leaflet containing some of the juicier quotes found in the book, such as: "The Jews are here for our misfortune . . . They are a thousand times more harmful than all the Germans in the world."

The intellectual history of prewar France was also made by this young and not so young right-wing crowd.

10 Unity of Action

On February 6, 1934, an angry mob charged police lines protecting the Concorde bridge and the Boulevard Saint-Germain leading to the French parliament building, a mob enflamed by the battle cries of right-wing extremist movements such as Action Française, kept in ranks by militants of the uniformed Croix de Feu, reinforced by rank-and-file members of World War I veterans groups, and by young toughs from that congeries of movements known as the *ligues*. The burden of their complaint was that their government was composed of thieves and their accomplices, who prevented the just punishment of the likes of Alexandre Stavisky, a stock manipulator of Russian Jewish origin found conveniently dead during the investigation of his activities.

At the same time and place, veterans belonging to a Communist-controlled movement assembled to protest against the evils of capitalist government. When the rioting ended, there were 2329 injured and 17 dead; 1764 of the injured were members of the police forces. The mob never got into the Palais Bourbon where the *chambre* was in session, yet what became known as "February 6" was not without its successes. The government headed by Radical Socialist Edouard Daladier saw the handwriting on the wall and resigned. When the leaders of left-wing political parties realized how close the government had come to being overthrown, they put a temporary end to interparty rivalry, initiating a process that two years later brought in a Popular Front government supported by the Communists. This is the shortest possible summary of the events that were to change not only French politics but French hearts, the way Communists and Socialists perceived each other, the way they faced up to Fascists, from then until the German occupation of France, and perhaps beyond.

In the heat of the action it was possible to misread it. Thus Pierre Drieu La Rochelle could telephone Malraux to express delight at having heard the Communists' "Internationale" and the right-wing favorite, "La Marseillaise," sung at the same time on the embattled bridge. (It might mean a rapprochement between Malraux's Communism and Drieu's Fascism.) The director of Les Nouvelles Littéraires, Maurice Martin du Gard, heard the news of February 6 firsthand from Drieu. "He raced around under bullet shots . . . with no other enemies than his countrymen," Martin du Gard recorded in his journal. "He threw himself down in the mud under the trees of the Champs-Elysées to watch the buses burn up and see the razor-blade attacks against the horses of the mounted police..." Drieu, who had visited Nazi Germany only a few weeks earlier, was disappointed that there had been no coup d'état.

★   ★   ★

Had the Fascists conquered the streets of the Left Bank? Was France about to slide into the madness that had taken possession of neighboring Germany only a year earlier, after Italy? The parties, unions, movements of the anti-Fascist left mobilized. This was the hour of the frantic contacts by telephone, the meetings in private homes, in cafés, on street corners, evoked in Clara Malraux's phrase, "Revolution is seeing each other a lot." "Each newspaper, depending on its political position, has its lies, its victories, and its heroes," Eugène Dabit commented in his diary. Friendships were broken — that between the André Chamsons and their mentor Daniel Halévy, for example. Chamson, who was then employed by Daladier as a cabinet aide, was warned by his chief to be prepared for anything, and that included possible attacks on the homes of government officials. So Chamson found his reserve officer's revolver in the back of a closet and made certain that it was in working order. Until then Chamson had seen himself as a pacifist, sympathizing with the Quakers. If Drieu became a Fascist then, Chamson could date his anti-Fascist engagement from February 6 and the following feverish days.

On February 12 a general strike was called by the non-Communist trade unions. The newly committed intellectuals joined the procession that crossed the working-class districts of eastern Paris from the Porte de Vincennes to the Place de la Nation; they were the embodiment of a manifesto inspired by André Breton of the Surrealists, and signed by René Crevel and Paul Eluard, as well as by André Malraux and Jean

Guéhenno among non-Surrealists, the Radical Socialist Alain, and the pro-Communist Jean-Richard Bloch; together they called for unity of action against the danger of Fascism. Malraux marched in the parade; so did the physicist Paul Langevin. As they approached the Place de la Nation, a separate Communist Party demonstration was arriving from another street. The two columns converged. "After a silence, a brief moment of anguish, to the astonishment of the party and union leaders, this encounter triggered a delirious enthusiasm, an explosion of shouts of joy," remembered André Chamson's wife, Lucie Mazauric. "Applause, chants, cries of 'Unity, unity' . . . In fact the Popular Front had just been born under our eyes."

★   ★   ★

Thus too was born an organization called the Committee of Vigilance of Anti-Fascist Intellectuals (CVIA), the first coalition of Communists and non-Communists in common cause that was to succeed, the first not founded by Communists but with Communists in its ranks. Until then, the ideological opposition between the parties had been too brutal, and Communist manipulation of movements such as Amsterdam-Pleyel had discouraged the nonaffiliated. If Paul Langevin, who had marched on February 12, was close to the Communists, the cosigners of the CVIA initiating manifesto were Paul Rivet, professor at the Museum of Natural History, a Socialist and a member of the non-Communist trade union federation CGT; and Alain, whose real name was Emile-Auguste Chartier, a Radical Socialist professor of philosophy.

Officially, the Communist Party was not quite ready for unity of action. As late as April 6, an editorial in L'Humanité signed by Maurice Thorez called for a front unique, but subordinate to the Communists, in movements such as Amsterdam-Pleyel; the Communists continued to refuse to be associated with what they called "Social Democratic puke." It took the intervention of the Comintern, through the discreet "Clément" (Eugen Fried), to put the Party on the new track. Official Communist Party history agrees that the first step was the unity-of-action policy decided by the Comintern on June 11, 1934, during a meeting of the executive group's political committee. The new line was ratified by the French Communist Party at a national congress which opened on June 23. On July 27, the Communist and Socialist parties solemnly approved a pact for unity of action: organizations, publications, meetings to be included. Henceforth everyone's commitment was going to be easier; no longer would one have enemies on the left.

The Committee of Vigilance of Anti-Fascist Intellectuals was a vehicle for a whole generation of writers, journalists, teachers, poets, and painters to take part, or feel as if they were taking part, in a movement directed against immediate danger. The Committee could dispatch André Malraux to Algiers, where he dropped down from the sky dramatically via seaplane, to join a CVIA rally against right-wing extremists whose local activities were causing alarm. It could bring André Gide and André Chamson — two authors who were not naturally suited to perform in public — in front of large audiences. Indeed, when CVIA found itself in crisis, the split was not so much between Communists and anti-Communists as it was a difference of opinion on the means to resist Fascism. For CVIA's pacifist majority would not entertain the notion of a *war* against Fascism.

★   ★   ★

At few times in the history of government has the role of intellect been so decisive. In recalling the events that fused into the spirit known as "Popular Front," Jean Guéhenno was reminded of Albert Thibaudet's "republic of professors." There was an apotheosis of sorts on that historic July 14, 1935, when Communists, Socialists, and Radical Socialists commemorated France's national holiday together, after weeks of maneuvering for position that seemed to be forgotten in the enthusiasm of the fête. What has come down to us from that day is the oath taken in the morning by participants in a rally held in a stadium for bicycle races; the very composition of the oath symbolized the marriage of intellect and politics, for the writers were André Chamson, Jean Guéhenno, and Jacques Kayser, a representative of the Radical Socialist Party. "We take the solemn oath," it concluded, "to remain united to put down disruptive movements, to defend and develop democratic freedoms, and to guarantee peace for humanity."

After the rally there was a parade from the Place de la Bastille to the Place de la Nation. If each political group came with its own banners and slogans, the divergences were lost on the crowd of onlookers. The impression was that the French working class and its spiritual guides were now united against domestic as well as foreign Fascism. In Robert Brasillach's dissenting view, the partisans of unity were "Radical Socialist escapees from the Stavisky affair, Muscovites, Socialist Jews."

A striking description of that day comes to us from a nearly forgotten participant at the stadium, who remembered when "the sun broke through the mist of this holiday morning, this July fog weighted with the heat of the crowd and clouds of tobacco smoke." And then, "at the instant that the 'Internationale' followed 'La Marseillaise,' we were closer to tears than to irony." The witness, the playwright Henri-René Lenormand, was in the afternoon parade, too, where he recognized a number of famous Frenchmen who had joined the procession in taxicabs: Léon Blum for the Socialists, Edouard Daladier for the Radicals, the Communist Marcel Cachin. The House of Culture was represented by André Malraux, Jean Cassou, Jean-Richard Bloch, Charles Vildrac, Jules Romains. Lenormand recorded these cries from the crowd watching the parade: "Long live intellectuals! Long live science! Long live Malraux!" They were all shaken by one particular cry: "Long live the professors! They must never die!"

Clara Malraux was marching alongside her husband in bare feet and sandals that stuck to the hot tar of the roadway. So André picked up his tiny wife to show her the sea of red flags floating behind them. Speaking of this demonstration, the Comintern's secretary general Georgi Dimitrov reported to his organization: "It is not only a working-class united front movement; it is the beginning of a vast Popular Front against Fascism in France."

A mutual assistance pact between France and the Soviet Union had been signed in May 1935, so that cooperation between Communists and the parties of the ruling classes was now quite possible without defying the Party line. Facilitated by the change in Moscow's policy, left and center-left political groups began working out their strategy together. The rival Communist and non-Communist trade union federations merged after a scission which had lasted fifteen years. One could even imagine a cabinet that would reflect the new party alignments, the new sentiments of rank-and-file voters.

On February 13, 1936, as he was being driven from the Palais Bourbon after a session of the Chamber of Deputies, the Socialist Party leader Léon Blum found himself in the middle of the funeral procession for Jacques Bainville, the popular historian and ideologist for Action Française (whom we have mentioned as a lecturer for the Rive Gauche lecture society). The young militants of Action Française recognized Blum, whom their organization had been denouncing with regularity as a *détritus humain*. They stopped his car and smashed the windows. Bleeding, Blum was able to find refuge in a building under repair; the workers slammed the gate behind him and laid him out on a rug in front of a fireplace. Later the same day, in an extraordinary session at the

Elysée Palace, the government approved a decree that outlawed the right-wing extremist movements: the Ligue d'Action Française, the Camelots du Roi, the Fédération Nationale des Etudiants d'Action Française.

★   ★   ★

But now the true apotheosis. For 1936 was a year of victories for the left, culminating in the spring elections, which gave the parties of the so-called Popular Rally a clear majority: 146 Socialist deputies, 116 Radicals, 72 Communists, bringing Léon Blum to power — the man who was not only the Socialists' political chief, but a Jew and an intellectual, a graduate of the Ecole Normale Supérieure who had been a literary and drama critic before entering politics, author of *Nouvelles Conversations de Goethe avec Eckermann* (as early as 1901) containing a theory of aesthetics, of a book on Stendhal, of a book on women and marriage. The writers and artists of the Left Bank could identify with this political leader who had been their schoolmate, who shared their concerns, although he had put aside the life of creation for public affairs. At midnight on May 3, the day of the second ballot, Ilya Ehrenburg recorded the street scene, as Parisians marched along singing the "Internationale," embracing passersby, crying, "Death to Fascists!" Soon Paris was unrecognizable. Red flags floated on the old gray-blue buildings. The sounds of the "Internationale," of "La Carmagnole" — a song of the Revolution Of 1789 — were heard everywhere. The stock market was down, the wealthy smuggled their money out of the country. Some in fright, others with hope, shouted, "It's the revolution!"

From André Gide's observation post on the Rue Vaneau, his confidante Maria Van Rysselberghe recorded the excitement: "Lord! how the atmosphere is heated and tense... The strikes are spreading; no newspapers this morning; it's hard to know what's happening. Will these events help Blum, or slow him down? . . . Moods change without motivation; yesterday everyone was anxious, today optimism reigns..."

Budding Fascists recorded the same events with undisguised bitterness. "The movies practically closed their doors to Aryans," remembered Brasillach, in memoirs published during the German occupation of Paris. "The radio had a Yiddish accent. The mildest-mannered citizens began to be fed up with the kinky hair, the hooked noses, which you saw everywhere." "Arriving from the depths of his oriental ghettos at the proclamation of racial victory," Lucien Rebatet noted in his own memoirs, also published during the occupation, "the Jew swarmed over us, in his original state of filth and presumptuousness certain to nauseate a full-blooded Frenchman... The alien nature of the disaster that struck us was crystal-clear."

To Jean Guéhenno, writing in the autumn of that year of victory, it seemed clear that "the experiment that our country is now going through has the greatest significance for the world." In the United States and elsewhere in that world, eyes were indeed turning toward France. "On the success or failure of the French Popular Front may depend, they assure us, the political orientation of the world for the next fifty years." Out of the experiment would come a new approach to social welfare, to the role of government as a monitor of industry, as protector of farmers as well as of industrial workers, and there would be nationalizations, educational reform, and wide acceptance of the notion that a government could have a cultural policy, too.

11   In Defense of Culture

No ENCOUNTER HAD more symbolic importance to the engaged writers of the 1930s than the International Writers Congress for the Defense of Culture in June 1935. It was a congress of stars; it would command newspaper space by the very fact of its being held. Putting the meeting together mobilized the best of the Left Bank intellectual community. The minor crises that marked the preparatory period were indicative of the major problems of the time; in a sense, the congress was a microcosm of the political wars raging outside the Palais de la Mutualité, as far away as Berlin and Moscow.

By unwritten rule, outspoken opponents of unity of action with the Communists were excluded or made to feel unwelcome. That included the Surrealists led by André Breton, as we have already seen, together with Trotskyists. Obviously conservative writers (or worse) were unwelcome, but not everyone considered conservative (or worse) accepted the label or felt that it justified exclusion. One of the excluded was Henry de Montherlant, and this drew expressions of disapproval from his political friends. "A congress of writers which deprives itself of the great majority of writers is only a clan of partisans," was the comment of a Radical Socialist newspaper, which mentioned François Mauriac, Paul Morand, Henri Béraud, Jacques de Lacretelle, and Charles Maurras among the absent. In fact this group, with Montherlant, could have formed an international congress on the other side of the barricades.

Another form of absenteeism was more troubling to the French participants. Maria Van Rysselberghe remembered a frantic telephone call from André Malraux after dinner on June 16 — just five days before the congress was to begin. Malraux told Gide that he had to see him at once, and he would be there in an instant (if he was walking from the

Rue du Bac a few hundred yards away, he would be there soon enough).
He explained that the Soviet Embassy had only then informed the
organizers of the congress that Maxim Gorki could not attend. In
Malraux's opinion, this would have a serious effect on its success, for
there were no other members of the Soviet delegation whose
international reputation matched that of the French, the British, and the
exiled Germans who were scheduled to participate. Malraux felt that
the Soviets were making fools of them. Malraux could not have known
that in the last years of his life Gorki was virtually a prisoner of Stalin,
who would not allow him to leave the Soviet Union. Gorki may even
have become ill by then, and in a year's time he would be dead. Soon
after that, his death would serve as a pretext for another treason trial in
Moscow, and several alleged plotters, including Gorki's doctor and the
head of the secret police, would be executed after being tried for the
murder of the sixty-eight-year-old writer. (It is possible that Gorki was
indeed murdered, but on Stalin's orders.)

What to do? The Mutualité had been rented, foreign delegates were
already en route to Paris — the Americans were on the high seas, for
instance. Malraux asked Gide to endorse his request that two Soviet
writers of international reputation be brought to Paris. One was Boris
Pasternak, a distinguished poet decades before he became known as the
author of the novel *Dr. Zhivago*. The other was the storyteller Isaak
Babel, who was to disappear during the Moscow purges. Gide agreed
that Malraux could use his name.

Shortly after Malraux made his request of the Soviet Embassy, as he
tells it, Pasternak's telephone rang and his companion picked up the
receiver. "Who? The Kremlin?" Pasternak took the phone from her, to
hear that Joseph Stalin himself was ordering him to purchase Western-
style clothing and to board a train that very night for France. At the
International Writers Congress the Russian poet read a poem and then
made a speech whose essence Malraux remembered as: "Talk politics?
Futile, futile... Politics? Go country, friends, go country pick flowers."
Pasternak confided to Ilya Ehrenburg that he suffered from insomnia and
had been in a rest home when he got the Kremlin's order to leave for
Paris. He had first drafted a speech in which the subject was his own
illness, and had to be persuaded to say a few words about poetry.
Pasternak himself later remembered having told the audience: "I
understand that this is a meeting of writers to organize resistance to
Fascism. I have only one thing to say to you: do not organize. Organi-

zation is the death of art. Only personal independence matters. In 1789, 1848, 1917, writers were not organized for or against anything. Do not, I implore you, do not organize."

As for Isaak Babel, he had not written a speech at all, but when his turn came he talked with humor and ease and in excellent French, his subject the love of Soviet man for literature. "He walked onto the stage, drew a lamp toward him, and sat down like a storyteller in an Eastern town," Gustav Regler described the scene. "He told Jewish stories; he was most comfortably relaxed, as though the huge auditorium . . . contained no more than a handful of students, instead of five thousand ardent and curious fellow-travelers."

★   ★   ★

Thanks to that extraordinary document, the diary kept by Maria Van Rysselberghe, it is possible to follow the eventful days preceding the congress from the Rue Vaneau. There we find Gide, weeks before the congress was to open its doors, distressed at the role he had been asked to assume. Yet he felt that it would be an act of cowardice to refuse. He worried that the one-sided nature of the sponsorship would frighten away potential participants, and said as much to Malraux. Malraux had to remind him how the project had come into being: the Soviet Union wished to have a suitably imposing platform for its leading writers to set forth their views. It was a service one could not refuse, whatever the cost. If Gide wanted a more representative attendance, why didn't he invite apolitical friends like Paul Valéry in his own name? As for Gide's unhappiness at the role he was expected to play, Malraux assured him that his responsibilities as chairman would be purely symbolic. "Malraux is prodigious in his clarity, his simplicity, his breadth," Gide's confidante told her diary. "He arranges everything as one would move the pieces in a game of chess. He dominates all situations with a gusto, a glibness, a frightening lack of hesitation and vagueness . . .

But as the day approached, Gide continued to feel unsure of himself. "When I think of this Congress at which I am expected to make a speech, it makes my head spin . . ."

★   ★   ★

Yet, in the view of *la petite dame*, the International Writers Congress was a triumph. "To hold a crowd of 2500 to 3000 persons for five evenings in a row, without counting the afternoons, to listen to speeches being read — almost all were read, and sometimes read twice, in French and in a foreign language — and most of which were tedious and inappropriate to the occasion, is rather extraordinary." There was never enough time to complete a subject; each day's program was carried over to the following day. "The public was as nice as could be; one felt that people were there because they were really interested: youth, students, writers, the brightest of the working class; it was a sensitive, enthusiastic, demonstrative public." "We didn't stop talking for five days and nearly five nights," recalled Jean Guéhenno, much disabused, twenty years after the event. "The smoke and the dust didn't have time to dissipate."

> For almost a week [reported the Toulouse daily *La Dépêche*], standing up to heat and exhaustion, delegates of fourteen nations devoted themselves, twice each day, to a brilliant debate of ideas... The heat was overpowering and many delegates took off their jackets. Yet the members of the presidium on the speakers' platform stood fast and even kept their detachable stiff collars on. Only M. Vaillant-Couturier spoke in a summer suit decorated with a white bow tie.

Despite the mugginess, Eugène Dabit did not regret postponing his vacation to attend the congress, "even though the atmosphere is sometimes feverish, confused, and disappointing," he told his private diary. He remembered with particular pleasure the discussions, which continued into the night at the outdoor tables of the Deux Magots and other Left Bank cafés.

★ ★ ★

On the morning following the opening of the congress, *L'Humanité* published its report on the front page:

FOR THE DEFENSE OF CULTURE

The most important writers of fourteen nations
met yesterday at the Mutualité

Gide and Malraux presided at the first session of the congress

The story that followed described the packed auditorium; "an eager crowd, dominated by youth, represented the working classes." The opening session should have begun at nine in the evening on June 21, but it got a late start, the seating of delegations taking up "a deplorable amount of time" (so complained Maria Van Rysselberghe, who arrived unescorted, so as not to place an extra burden on her friend). As honorary chairman, Gide greeted the delegates. "How troubled he seemed," Guéhenno remarked of Gide's first appearance before that large gathering, when, from the little room where we were all waiting, he had to be the first to climb up to the stage, to walk to the front while the crowd cheered him. On his face I could read his shyness and his joy. Not certain whether he should speak seated or standing, he got up, sat down again, mumbled some words as if to excuse himself for being there, and found himself only when he picked up his papers to read his speech in a ringing and serious tone." "In my opinion we must begin with the idea," Gide said that night, "that this culture which we seek to defend is the sum of the particular cultures of each country, that this culture is our joint possession, that it belongs to us all, that it is international." Guéhenno noted: "We took off our jackets and spoke in shirt sleeves. André Gide finally did the same, out of kindness. But how surprised he was at this new-found happiness."

Malraux was the effective chairman of the opening session. "We organized this congress in the worst possible conditions," he said. "With a few volunteers. Almost without funds." The other speakers that evening included E.M. Forster, Julien Benda, Robert Musil, Bertolt Brecht, and Jean Cassou. Messages were read from Romain Rolland, Comintern secretary general Georgi Dimitrov, and Maxim Gorki (from his sickbed). Gide evoked the tragic death of René Crevel.

E.M. Forster, whose name could not have meant much to the delegates of the working classes present in the hall, confessed that he was not himself a Communist, but perhaps would have been one, had he been younger and braver. In his talk Forster did what most of the other non-Communist participants were to do that week: he criticized the limitations on freedom found in his *own* country, particularly censorship on moral grounds, which to his mind represented a threat to sexual freedom and its literary expression. But then the Soviet and other Communist delegates would praise the Soviet Union, even as they criticized the situation nearly everywhere else. When it was his turn to speak, John Strachey pointed out that if his country's writing was essentially literary, there was a time when literature had to deal more closely with human concerns. Far from being destructive of culture, he insisted, Marxism preserved it, and itself represented the development of the European literary heritage.

The press reported that Julien Benda's talk provided the only discordant note that evening. "Showing himself, probably for the first time, to a 'proletarian' audience, he thought that he should come without the ribbon of the Legion of Honor," observed Henri-René Lenormand. Benda distinguished between Western and Communist conceptions of literature, noting that in the West reading belonged to those with leisure time. Such literature "is not popular, and that which is popular — is not literary." Guéhenno took the floor to reply. For him there seemed to be more than one road to heaven; it was indeed possible to be in communion with one's fellows. (This was an echo of a phrase recently employed by Malraux that was very much in the air that month, as will be seen subsequently.)

One speaker that evening went all but unnoticed, and one must turn to his collected works in German to find a trace of his speech. Bertolt Brecht was already the author of *The Threepenny Opera*, but he had not yet written the politico-didactic plays of his maturity. One other opening-night speaker, Robert Musil, could hardly have been known to the majority of listeners, for his important books had not yet been translated. There was also a speech by Edouard Dujardin, a somewhat forgotten Symbolist who was perhaps known better outside of France than within, for James Joyce was said to have been inspired by the interior monologue of his *Les Lauriers sont coupés*.

Meanwhile the Gide apartment at the Rue Vaneau was turning into a command post. Four typists worked continuously in the adjoining studio. The two poles of attraction, Maria Van Rysselberghe noted, were the telephone and the ice box, between goings and comings to sessions at the Mutualité, the planning sessions, the endless private discussions.

Gide as a chairman? His confidante warned him that he dropped his voice too abruptly at the end of sentences, "and that he must avoid applauding every speaker in that lifeless, automatic, distracted manner." In his own journal Gide tells a joke on himself. While chairing a session, he found it impossible to honor all the requests for floor time. Yet he was urged to call on a Greek delegate who had made the long journey in fourth class, her ticket paid for by a group of workers. He thought that he spied her on the speakers' platform, and went up to her to say: "It is a fine thing, comrade, that Greece is represented here."

In a soft voice she replied: "I happen to be India."

The congress gets no more attention than that in Gide's journal.

★ ★ ★

But it was now launched and away. "Under a white-hot sky," reported *Le Petit Journal*, "the Palais de la Mutualité boiled like a furnace. For four days the speakers' platform, the auditorium, the balconies, vibrated with an intense emotion." On Saturday, June 22, sessions were scheduled for three in the afternoon, and then again at nine, the subjects being "The Role of the Writer in Society" and "The Individual." Aldous Huxley, who had already written most of the novels that would assure his reputation, seemed to soar above the general preoccupation with quotidien politics as he addressed himself to the question of writers and propaganda. As examples of a literature of propaganda, he offered Erich Maria Remarque's *All Quiet on the Western Front* and H.G. Wells's *Outline of History*, whose influence had not, he thought, survived post-World War I prosperity. It was the literature of imagination that had a more lasting effect.

That evening it was Aragon's turn. The former Surrealist was virtually the Communist poet laureate; he offered homage to René Crevel. Crevel's speech written for the congress was not found in time to be read, but it was published in the July issue of *Commune*. His speech would have been a plea for an accord between poetic revolt and political revolution, the synthesis he failed to attain in real life by serving as intermediary between André Breton and the Communists. "Not to seek an accord between one's interior rhythm and the dialectical movement of the universe," he said, "is, for the individual, to risk the loss of all one's worth and all one's energetic power."

Mikhail Koltzov was another of the evening's speakers. In his memoirs, Arthur Koestler describes Koltzov as nothing less than the most brilliant and influential journalist of the Soviet Union, a confidant of Stalin, yet "a short, thin, insignificant-looking man, with a quiet manner and pale eyes, the exact opposite of the conventional idea of a famous reporter." (We see him again in Spain during the Civil War, before his disappearance into the Soviet night. When Artur London was interrogated in preparation for the Slansky purge trial in Prague following World War II, the Communists attempted to obtain evidence against Koltzov and two other participants in the International Writers Congress, Anna Seghers and Egon Erwin Kisch, who were accused of associating with Trotskyist intellectuals in Paris. But Koltzov had been killed on Stalin's orders long before the interrogation of Artur London, apparently soon after his return from the Spanish Civil War.)

Koltzov's speech received little attention, but when he had finished, the reporter for *L'Humanité* observed, there was an instant that summed up the very nature of this congress. Heinrich Mann, then in the chair, turned the microphone over to Gide. "After the voice of the country of Socialism [Koltzov], it was anti-Fascist France taking the hand of anti-Fascist Germany." Maria Van Rysselberghe remembered Gide as "simply perfect, having for the occasion rediscovered his fine voice. He spoke from his seat, calmly . . . without awkwardness as without mannerisms, with strength and simplicity." What Gide said was, "I believe that I can be deeply internationalist while remaining deeply French." It was an echo of his remarks on the opening night of the congress. "Just as I believe I can remain deeply individualistic in my Communism, and with the help of Communism. Because my thesis has always been this: it is in being the most particular that each of us best perceives the community . . ." Even Thierry Maulnier of Action Française could approve such language. He told readers of *Le Figaro:* "In the great hall of the Palais de la Mutualité, this grave, clear, admirably balanced voice, moving without superfluous flourishes, offered unexpected details to this over-enthusiastic and overly orthodox meeting."

On Sunday the American writer Waldo Frank went before the audience. Then forty-six, an authority on Hispanic civilization, his name was not quite unknown in France, for he had written both for *Europe* and *La Nouvelle Revue Française.* As a militant of the left, he had corresponded with Romain Rolland about his experiences in the violent Harlan County mine strikes in Kentucky, and Jean Guéhenno had published his report. He represented those American writers who were politically committed, and specifically the new League of American Writers, which was actually the counterpart of the Communist-front writers' groups of Europe. "Smallish, with a round child's face, he had something about him that seemed familiar to me," Clara Malraux remembered. After she had been seen in conversation with Frank, her husband snapped at her: "Why did you speak like a Trotskyist with Waldo Frank, which represents an insult to me?" (She had not realized that her remarks were Trotskyist, or that Frank was likely to be receptive to Trotskyist language.) In his speech Frank expressed a commitment to the working class — even to the Communist Party, according to *L'Humanité.* He distinguished between two Americas, the one for which he spoke and the other that disavowed him. "I learned a long time ago that my love for life and the humble part I wish to play in mankind's destiny implied declaring war on the capitalist system."

No one was likely to forget the contribution of Henri Barbusse, for his seemingly interminable speech gradually drove much of the audience from the hall. One participant recalled the efforts of the organizers to persuade them to return to their seats while Barbusse droned on. Somewhere in that speech Barbusse said: "Writers must take a stand, and participate consciously in the social drama in which they are involved."

Gide told his *petite dame* that Barbusse had been "of an inadmissible length and intolerably bad." Barbusse's performance made the speaker who was to follow him, André Chamson, "pale with anger," but Chamson's appearance was all the better for it. Chamson's literary contribution was in the portrayal of his austere southern French Cévennes region; he had come to public notice at the age of twenty-five with the story of *Roux le bandit*. His rural Protestants were naturally resistant to authority, natural conscientious objectors. By training Chamson himself was an archivist, by affiliation Radical Socialist. He and Lucie Mazauric had careers in museum administration. When Edouard Daladier read *Roux le bandit*, he had called in his fellow Provençal for a talk and offered him a job; thereafter, Chamson worked for Daladier whenever Daladier was a cabinet officer, and then when he became head of government. One of the organs of the future Popular Front, the weekly newspaper *Vendredi* was sponsored by the Radicals and published by Chamson and his fellow writers on the left.

What Chamson remembered later of the International Writers Congress was its clockwork organization. Each participant was given enough time to make a set speech, and that was all. But what a speech Chamson made! It was his first political performance, and he approached it as a writer. Although his theme was an attack on nationalism, in a rousing conclusion he warned "our adversaries that I am their enemy because I have been French ever since France existed . . . Because I am linked to this soil by its cemeteries and its furrows. Because I have tried to sing them, the first of a long line of peasants who could speak only in low voices, following the rhythms and the splendor of my people."

Monday was Pasternak's day. ("An immense ovation greeted the great Soviet poet," reported *L'Humanité*.) The American Communist Michael Gold, author of *Jews Without Money*, began his speech by paying his respects to Paris as the "marvel of the world," the capital of European culture. He told the audience that his own country was not represented only by the millionaire J.P. Morgan and the gangster Al Capone, any more than Hitler was the real Germany. America belonged to its workers and its creators. To resist Fascist demagoguery, he concluded, intellectuals had to learn to love their own countries and to get closer to the masses. Heinrich Mann, a writer of satirical novels, including the book that became the Marlene Dietrich movie *The Blue Angel*, was perhaps the best-known spokesman of the German resistance to Hitler, and an ardent fellow traveler of the Communists. He and not his brother Thomas (who was not present) held the center of the stage that evening.

It was also the evening of dissent. First, in the person of the Italian anti-Fascist professor Gaetano Salvemini. Then sixty-one, author of studies of the Florentine Republic, of the French Revolution, and of modern Italy, Salvemini had been a member of his country's parliament and editor of a newspaper of the pre-Fascist era Liberal Party. He had been arrested by the Mussolini regime for subversive activity, and had been able to leave the country. During his exile he was a lecturer on Italian civilization at Harvard University. As *Monde* saw it, in his address to the International Writers Congress Salvemini demonstrated that he was "far from having understood the true nature of Fascism," for he presumed to speak of "terror in Russia." He dared to equate Fascist dictatorship with dictatorship of the proletariat, added *L'Humanité*, and he was applauded by a few Trotskyists who took advantage of the opportunity to shout their disapproval of the Soviet system. Salvemini was *really* applauded, the Communist daily assured its readers, when he finally recognized the essential difference between classless society and Fascist repression.

Not *L'Humanité* but *Le Populaire*, the Socialist daily, informed its readers that Salvemini had raised the question of the way Victor Serge was being treated in the Soviet Union. This was apparently the first public reference to Serge at the congress.

Born in Brussels of Russian anti-Czarist parents, Serge had been raised in Western Europe. A revolutionary anarchist, he was an early convert to the Russian Revolution, but once settled in the USSR he found himself caught up in the campaign against nonconformism waged by an increasingly repressive regime; seen up close, the new Russia was not what it had appeared to be from abroad. Serge was arrested by the Soviet Police in 1933 and exiled to the Urals. By that time, he was forty-three years old and the author of a history of the October Revolution, a study entitled *Littérature et révolution*, and novels written in French. From the

Soviet Union he had managed to smuggle out a message asking his friends in France, including Magdeleine and Maurice Paz, to publish it in the event of his disappearance. In this message he defined the USSR as a totalitarian state, and later in his memoirs he remarked that he may have been the first to do so.

Unknown to rank-and-file congress participants, the Serge case had been an underlying issue from the first. The organizers were aware that it would be brought up, but thought that they could deal with it discreetly. The left-wing Socialist Magdeleine Paz was present, and she fully intended to speak for her friend. Henri Poulaille also demanded the floor to support Serge's case. A self-taught writer of genuine working-class origin, and spokesman for a group of self-styled "populist" authors who did not accept Communist Party discipline, Poulaille was not likely to find majority support in a congress guided by ideological enemies such as Louis Aragon; rebuffed, he left the hall. One newspaper reported that as he walked out, he managed to remove his photograph from a wall, where it hung beside those of Gide, Aragon, Malraux, and other congress celebrities. Aragon was quoted as commenting that even permitting Gaetano Salvemini to mention Serge had been "too much consideration for a counterrevolutionary." "Immediately, the audience was divided between Trotskyists and Stalinists," recalled Henri-René Lenormand. "Adversaries insulted each other in the jargon and with the arguments of the two political positions that had also divided Russian opinion . . . There were angry cries, a hubbub, almost fisticuffs, and Malraux, in a feverish and dramatic intervention, declared that anyone who mentioned Victor Serge would be expelled from the hall, thus showing the submission of the organizers to the orthodox Stalinist line." But the Serge case was not disposed of, only postponed.

Finally, at the very end of this evening session, by prearrangement and in a sense paid for by the life of René Crevel, Paul Eluard was given the microphone, to read the speech of Surrealist chieftain André Breton, who had been declared persona non grata after his assault on Ehrenburg. It was after midnight, the audience was thinning, and lights were being put out. "In addition to which, the chairman found it necessary to interrupt him . . . to warn the public, at that point quite divided, dominated by dissenters, that the electricity might be cut off . . ." So charged the manifesto entitled "When the Surrealists Were Right," signed by Breton with artists and writers such as Salvador Dali, Paul Eluard, Max Ernst, René Magritte, Man Ray, and Yves Tanguy, which was published after the close of the International Writers Congress to publicize its discrimination against the Surrealists and their doctrine of absolute freedom of speech. Breton's text was read too late to be reported in the next day's newspapers, and it was never referred to in *L'Humanité* at all. The confusion was such — "a tumultuous audience, which constantly drowned the speaker's voice" — that at least one member of that audience believed that Breton himself was at the microphone, and so recorded it in his memoirs. "Eluard spoke against the Franco-Soviet pact and against cultural collaboration between France and the USSR," reported Barbusse's *Monde,* and this is virtually all that the Communist press would say. But the complete text has been preserved. It suggests that what the Surrealists were complaining about was not France's alliance with the Soviet Union, but the latter's concessions to bourgeois France. For under the terms of the pact negotiated between Stalin and Pierre Laval, the French foreign minister, the previous month, the Soviet side recognized the need for a strong France. To the Surrealists, such a declaration clearly disarmed the ideological war of the French left against its own ruling class: "As if French imperialism, by the fact of the Moscow pact alone, could cease to be what it was!" Speaking through Paul Eluard, André Breton placed cultural preoccupations ahead of political ones.

Tuesday, June 25, was the final day of the congress. Once more Gide hesitated. Asked to speak again, he felt that if he did so he would have to bring up the Victor Serge affair, if only to show that those in charge of the congress were not seeking to avoid the subject. But he also feared that raising this matter could cause prejudice to his political allies: thus he explained it to Maria Van Rysselberghe. She was at home that afternoon when Gide phoned to suggest that she jump into a taxi to come see the fireworks at the Mutualité. She discovered that the meeting was taking place in a smaller room than was used for the plenary sessions. Indeed, Clara Malraux later said that her husband had agreed to Ehrenburg's tactics: to smother the Serge affair by moving the discussion to a time when there would be fewer witnesses.

The afternoon's speakers included Emmanuel Mounier of *Esprit* and Gide's Dutch writer friend Jef Last, who accompanied him to the Soviet Union the following summer. But when *la petite dame* entered the room, Magdeleine Paz was speaking, although from the back of the room her voice could hardly be heard. "Several times there was whistling, attempts to cover her voice, to prevent her from speaking." Malraux, in the chair, managed to impose order. Two Russians replied to Paz. Then, when another delegate intervened on Serge's behalf, "with the vehemence of a demagogue," in Van Rysselberghe's description, "there were cries, and whistling, and someone was forced to leave the room..." Gide closed the meeting with "words of appeasement and of confidence in Russia, which were moving." There is no more succinct account of that day. Barbusse's *Monde* reported that Magdeleine Paz and Charles Plisnier (a Belgian novelist who was to win the Goncourt Prize two years later) had both spoken on Serge's behalf, but the paper did not think it necessary to report the contents of their remarks. In fact Paz had evoked the congress's preoccupation with "dignity of thought . . . freedom of expression," censorship, and exile, all of which were pertinent to the Serge case. Plisnier, with a mandate from the Belgian delegation, supported her position. But if *Monde*'s reporters failed to catch these things, they did record the reply of the Soviet delegate Nikolai Tikhonov, who pointed out that as a Soviet citizen Victor Serge was subject to that country's law; having participated in the Trotskyist counter-revolutionary agitation that led to the murder of Sergei Kirov, Serge had been sent into exile, where he received a stipend from the state. (In reality, Serge had been arrested by the Soviet secret police and sent under armed guard in a convoy of deportees to a detention area on the frontier of Europe and Asia.)

Ehrenburg also had his word. The revolution had caused suffering, but was there childbirth without suffering? The Soviet Union had the right to defend itself against enemies of the revolution. Then Anna Seghers spoke for the German émigré delegation, "alarmed to note the pursuit of the discussion of a case that certainly merits careful examination, but not here." *Monde* also caught Gide's concluding words of appeasement: "The security of the Soviet Union must be the most important thing of all for us. Our confidence in the Soviet Union is the greatest proof of love that we can give it." ("Did he say 'love?'" the young writer Claude Roy asked a neighbor, for he could not hear everything that was being said; Gide had no microphone. "Yes, 'love.'") In his memoirs Serge pays tribute to his defenders, and notes that two Soviet delegates who had been his friends, Pasternak and Tikhonov, remained silent, while two others who attacked him, Koltzov and Vladimir Kirchon, were fated to disappear at the hands of Stalin's police. (Serge was apparently unaware of Tikhonov's attack on him at the congress.)

To anticipate: Serge was soon to be released from detention. At the close of the International Writers Congress, Gide drafted a letter on the case to the Soviet ambassador in Paris, and after discussing it with friends he walked the few yards separating his apartment from the Soviet Embassy on Rue de Grenelle to deliver it.

> For many French revolutionaries [Gide wrote], and revolutionaries of all countries, the USSR has become, as you know, an ideal fatherland; *we belong to it*; and we are ready to fight for it . . . It is important that its most ardent and devoted defenders not feel themselves morally disarmed and distressed when they have to defend it . . .

Then it was the turn of Romain Rolland. On a journey to the Soviet Union, he was received by Stalin, who promised him that Serge would be authorized to leave the Soviet Union with his family. But first he had to find another country that would accept him; refused visas by France, Great Britain, Denmark, and the Netherlands, Serge was finally taken in by Belgium. He eventually got to France, where he lived until 1940, and then moved to Mexico, where he died in 1947.

For the final session of the congress on Tuesday evening, the *grande salle* of the Mutualité was once again packed to the roof. Léon Blum, director of the Socialist Party's *Le Populaire* and soon to head the first Popular Front government, was in the press section, just under the speakers' platform. Henri-René Lenormand, one of that evening's speakers, later captured the moment in his journal: "Groups of workers, little girls and boys carrying banners, paraded with raised fists, swearing to defend culture." Lenormand's subject was the decline of the French theater, which led him to observe that the taste of workers was middle-class, a handicap for the development of a true proletarian theater. Since his emphasis seemed to be the attack on middle-class theater and not on the taste of workers, the speech passed. Indeed, since Lenormand complained of the decadence of the theater in his own country, while Vladimir Kirchon praised the blossoming of Soviet theater, *Monde* described the duet as a debate.

Aragon followed the debaters with a forceful argument for Socialist Realism, combined with an attack on his former love, Surrealism. "We must come back to reality," he argued, explaining that "only the proletariat and its allies can hope to achieve realism, which in their hands becomes Socialist Realism, the method of the writers of the USSR."

Gustav Regler, who only a few months earlier had campaigned for the Communists in the Saar plebiscite by which that territory was returned to Nazi Germany, brought a touch of drama, when he warned that the meeting hall was infiltrated by Nazi spies. "I address myself now to this phantom of the German Gestapo of Paris which has the habit of following us as shadow follows the sun, and who is certainly in this room, among you. And I say to him: You can close the frontier, our literature will cross it all the same." When he had finished, the audience rose to shout, *"Rot Front!"* (Red Front) and to sing the "Internationale."

Last but not least, André Malraux spoke. "His long body erect behind the speakers' table, his head leaning slightly toward the microphone, he spoke in a low, hurried voice," wrote Lenormand. "A nervous tic at times wrenched his face to one side . . . The crowd heard his message in deep silence — and then broke into heated applause . . ." Malraux seemed more concerned with eternal art than with the immediate struggle. "For each work becomes symbol and sign . . . A work of art is a possibility of reincarnation . . . To be a man is to strip to the minimum, for each person, his actor's mask."

★   ★   ★

The congress concluded by setting up an International Writers Association for the Defense of Culture. It was to be based in Paris, under the control of an international board that would meet each year in a different country, mandated "to struggle on its own terrain, which is culture, against war, Fascism, and in a general manner, against all threats to civilization." The executive council of the new association consisted of Gide, Barbusse, Rolland, the Mann brothers, Gorki, Forster, Ramón del Valle Inclán (the Spanish poet and novelist who was already a classic, and only a year from his death), Aldous Huxley, George Bernard Shaw, Sinclair Lewis, and Selma Lagerlöf of Sweden (Rolland, Thomas Mann, Shaw, Lewis, and Lagerlöf were Nobel prizewinners). Benda, Cassou, Chamson, Jean Giono, Guéhenno, Lenormand, and Malraux were members of the French bureau; their counterparts in the United States were Kenneth Burke, Malcolm Cowley, John Dos Passos, Theodore Dreiser, Michael Gold, and Langston Hughes, with Waldo Frank as secretary. Ehrenburg and Koltzov were the two Soviet secretaries.

Obviously, the incidents that broke out during the congress were the joy of the right-wing press. As *Commune* pointed out, the evocation of the Victor Serge case served *Candide, Gringoire, Je Suis Partout,* and the Socialist *Le Populaire* too. The libertarian Denis de Rougemont expressed himself in the quieter pages of *La Nouvelle Revue Française,* objecting to the corruption of language represented by the congress's use of the word *liberté.*' "Never did one lie as badly, never with more enthusiasm." Even more quietly, in a letter to his friend Marcel Jouhandeau, another *N.R.F.* man, Jean Paulhan, summed up the behavior of two of the congress participants he knew, and who, as it happened, represented the two poles between which most of the other delegates stood: "Aragon, sarcastic, hard, aristocratic, gave the impression at the Congress that he would last a long time, that one hadn't seen the last of him. But Malraux seemed to be crying (jerking his head nervously, agitated, at once handsome and dissipated) his last words. He was both moving and heart-breaking. If there is a revolution, which one will have the other shot? I suddenly feared for Malraux."

12   Malraux and the Intellectuals' War

In the 1930s the man to follow was André Malraux, the most engaged when he was engaged, the most detached when he was detached. (André and Lucie Chamson watched him fly off in February 1934, when all his friends were mobilizing their strengths and skills to keep Fascism out of France, to seek the legendary capital of the Queen of Sheba in the deserts of Arabia, an irrelevant adventure sponsored by a popular daily newspaper.) At rallies in Moscow or in Paris, Malraux could devote a long-awaited speech to his personal preoccupation with comparative art, to the confusion of a crowd hungry for a message. Actually, Malraux had begun to write about the anti-Fascist struggle before the time came to live it. Because his original subjects and concerns were far from French soil, he was considered to be an expert on foreign affairs, and later he seemed more comfortable fighting Fascists outside France than inside. Malraux's memoirs can be described as imaginative. But that may also be because he preferred to live his life as a novel, with himself as hero. *L'Espoir* ("Man's Hope") has been taken as a document on the Spanish Civil War, and an authority on revolution as seasoned as Trotski accepted Malraux's novels about China as eyewitness accounts, Malraux encouraging his reader to think that they were. A fellow writer and fighter of those years later confided that Malraux was, quite simply, devoid of political concerns. He was verbal, without any real interest in ideas. After a conversation he had dominated, if asked what he meant by a particular remark, he could disarm the listener by confessing that he had forgotten what he had just said. This is the reverse of the coin of Malraux's characteristic rapid-fire speech.

And yet: his first wife, Clara, companion of those years and not spar-
ing in criticism, insisted that his engagement in the anti-Fascist struggle
was total. It helped that he showed himself to be an excellent public
speaker in the best French tradition, "stirring by his very aggressiveness,
pathetic in his evocations of suffering and of hope, his speech now
broken, now modulated, the images fascinating in their unexpected-
ness." The same qualities as found in his books, intensified by his
physical presence, at times rendered excessive by that presence.

By extension, he became the man to hate, a target of the scorn of
Fascists such as Lucien Rebatet, who remembered his presence in anti-
Fascist demonstrations, "with his face of a sexual maniac devoured by
tics . . . a kind of Bolshevist under-Barrès, rigorously unreadable, and
who nevertheless had won the admiration of Saint-Germain-des-Prés,
even among the young right-wing idiots, thanks to a certain excitation of
vocabulary and a hermetic way of presenting Chinese news events
crumbled into a soup of adjectives."

Herself an active anti-Fascist, Clara Malraux was certain that her
husband was not a Marxist: "The efficacy of Marxism attracted him, it
seemed to me, more than its intellectual or moral justification." Which
meant also that Malraux could accept the Soviet dictator as an ally in the
struggle against Fascism without being troubled by Stalin's very personal
adaptation of Marxist doctrine. Malraux was able to dismiss the Moscow
purge trials as a private quarrel of Trotski's; he gave priority to the
defense of Republican Spain, and Stalin's Soviet Union was then also
assisting Spain. Trotski replied: "Mr. Malraux boasts of having always
'defended' anti-Fascists. No, not always, but only when that coincided
with the interests of the Soviet bureaucracy."

Le Temps du mépris was Malraux's contribution to the literature of
anti-Fascism. Written and published in 1935, a month before the
International Writers Congress, it was also serialized in La Nouvelle
Revue Française. His earlier fiction had dealt with the Far East; his
revolutionaries had been Chinese, and he struggled at their sides in
imagination. But by the time he sat down to write Le Temps du mépris,
he himself was a dedicated militant in the anti-Fascist struggle. The
evidence is that he began to write his book soon after his return from the
Soviet Union during the summer of 1934, when he attended that
congress at which writers were ordered down from their ivory towers.
But as usual, good sentiments made bad art. He himself dismissed the
slight work as a navet, a failed work. His hero, Kassner, is a

Czechoslovak Communist arrested and beaten by the Nazis; they will certainly use still more brutal methods to force him to talk about his activities when they discover his true identity. But another man turns himself in, identifying himself as Kassner and offering a confession. The real Kassner is freed, to be flown by the underground Communist Party apparatus to Czechoslovakia, where he arrives to join his wife at a rally on behalf of imprisoned anti-Fascists. An unsatisfactory plot, wooden characters; and Malraux possessed insufficient knowledge to be able to communicate the true horror of Nazi concentration camps.

What remains of the book is its preface. It was designed, the author said, as a reply to criticism of the story heard when it appeared in installments in *La Nouvelle Revue Française* shortly before publication. He confessed that his work was not in the Flaubertian tradition of detachment from the concerns of his hero, but rather in that of Aeschylus, Corneille, Hugo, Chateaubriand, even Dostoievski. "It is not passion which destroys the work of art," he wrote, "it is the will to prove something." French artistic sensibility had become too individualistic in the last half-century. In the eyes of his hero, Kassner, and of many Communist intellectuals — he did not specifically identify himself as one of them — Communism restores the fertility of the individual. He concluded with words that would inspire much debate that year: "It is difficult to be a man. But not more so in deepening one's communion than in cultivating one's differences — and the first nourishes with at least as much force as the second that by which man is man, that by which he surpasses himself, creates, invents, perceives himself."

The novel was the subject of an evening of debate at the Union pour la Vérité on the Rue Visconti. Here Jean Guéhenno referred to those who in Malraux's expression continued to cultivate their differences. In the audience, Gide thought that he recognized an allusion to himself. "To cultivate one's differences . . . By what misunderstanding was Guéhenno able to reproach me with that?" Gide asked himself in his *Journal* a short time after. "There is no need to cultivate the rest, which can always be found. But the rare, the exceptional, the unique, what a loss for all of us if that disappeared!" There was no chance of enrichment along that road, Gide pursued his thought. By limiting one's range to commonplace feelings about humanity, one impoverished humanity. "Every effort at depersonalization to the profit of the masses is in the end harmful to the masses themselves."

★ ★ ★

Soon commitment was to involve more than words. And there is no doubt that André Malraux, even the André Malraux tempted by the Queen of Sheba, was one of the chief heroes of the new engagement, the kind that could take a writer out of his study, out of his job in a publishing house, to do battle on a real battlefield.

In February 1936, less than three months before Frenchmen — not Frenchwomen, for they were not to get the vote until after the Second World War — elected a Popular Front majority, a similar coalition came to power across France's southern border. Malraux was a member of a delegation of writers, with Jean Cassou and Henri-René Lenormand, who traveled to Spain that spring to offer the support of the French left to its Spanish counterpart. The delegates were received by the new Spanish president, Manuel Azaña, himself a writer. But on July 17, Francisco Franco and fellow generals launched an insurrection against their government from army bases in Spanish North Africa. The Spanish Republic requested military assistance from France — by then, Popular Front governments were in power in both countries. But resistance from French conservatives, and above all from France's ally Britain, obliged the Léon Blum government to adhere to a policy of nonintervention in Spain. The militant French left decided that if it could not change its government's policy, it could intervene all the same, according to its means. This engagement was unprecedented, and quickly became an international affair, a model for intellectuals going to war in a just cause. But just as Spain was split, now violently, between left and right, so were the French who became involved in Spain. Soon there was a right-wing commitment as well as a left-wing one.

André Malraux was probably the first French writer to participate in Spain's war. Paradoxically, it was France's Popular Front, the same government that soon adopted a policy of nonintervention, that sent him there in the first place. As Clara Malraux recalled it, she and her husband were at the theater with their friends the Lagranges. Leo Lagrange was undersecretary of state for sports and leisure, a governmental position introduced by the Popular Front. During the intermission, Lagrange was called out of the box by Pierre Cot, the aviation minister, who informed him of the insurrection of the Spanish generals. It was agreed that Malraux would fly to Spain to investigate the means by which the French could assist the legal government of that country. So André and Clara Malraux flew to Spain, where they were met by Alvarez del Vayo, who had been a delegate to the International Writers Congress the previous year. Within weeks Malraux was engaged in secret and unofficial purchases of French aircraft (negotiated by a relative of Clara). In her memoirs Clara Malraux described the frantic scene at Le Bourget airport as the last planes were readied to fly out before the embargo on aid to Spain was to begin. Malraux, who wondered if he should now join the Communist Party (Clara tried to convince him that he should not), was soon back in Spain, in command of a squadron of fighter pilots who addressed him as "colonel." Soon he belonged to a rapidly growing community of foreign writers — some who were in Spain to fight, others to propagandize, or to help the Spanish Republican cause more subtly as foreign correspondents.

Was Malraux useful as a fighter for Spain? The evidence is contradictory. His enemies on the Fascist side charged that, among other things, he once shot down a French postal plane, killing a newspaper reporter. But his role as a mover of men, as a mobilizer of opinion, will never be contested. He commuted easily during that period between a Paris drawing room and the Spanish battlefield. Gide's *Journal* records meeting Malraux at the Rue de Bac in September 1936, during a brief interlude from Spain. "His face is less seamed by tics than it usually is and his hands aren't too restless. He speaks with that extraordinary glibness that often makes him hard for me to follow." Gide ended his diary entry with the information that Malraux's "intention, as soon as he gets back to Spain, is to plan the attack on Oviedo." In those days one could divulge a war plan in a Left Bank living room.

The next time Gide saw Malraux on a visit to Paris, the younger man was pessimistic about Spain, and more than ever prone to tics. This time Gide, in sympathy, indulged in tics of his own: "snorting, wrinkling of the nose," as he described it later to Maria Van Rysselberghe. "We must have looked rather funny."

On his return from the Spanish war, Malraux toured the United States to raise funds for Republican Spain, speaking at universities, at banquets (one in New York was sponsored by *The Nation*), to the Hollywood motion picture industry at the Mecca Temple Auditorium. It was in New York, not in Spain, that he met Ernest Hemingway for the first time, in the office of his (Malraux's) publisher, Random House.

Malraux returned to Paris and began the writing of *L'Espoir.* He finished that long novel in six months, and it was published while the war was still raging. A labor of devotion, a work of propaganda, it impressed even his enemies by its dramatization of battles that were at once so close and so remote to Frenchmen. It is a literary tour de force, a book one finds difficult to reread, as most of the books and poems that came out of that war are difficult to reread. One remembers W.H. Auden's comment on the engagement of English writers:

> Who managed in the Spanish War
> Not only to write well but be
> Of some use to the military?

But Malraux was soon back in Spain, to make the motion picture version of *L'Espoir*. It was filmed in Barcelona until Franco's army surrounded the city, and completed in Paris.

Manès Sperber, who was seeing Malraux regularly, later asked himself whether the reader of our era is capable of understanding what Spain signified to the non-Spanish of the 1930s. The *¡No pasaran!* of the Republic seemed of direct relevance to the anti-Fascists of the rest of Europe. In Spain they had an opportunity to take the offensive at last.

★   ★   ★

If the mass-circulation press avoided taking sides in Spain so as not to alienate readers, the leading figures of the intellectual right were not so reticent. A Manifesto to Spanish Intellectuals, released in December 1936, in the sixth month of civil war, carried the signatures of Paul Claudel and Ramon Fernandez, alongside those of Pierre Drieu La Rochelle, Abel Bonnard, Henri Béraud, Léon Daudet, and Henri Massis. Massis had written a propaganda tract on the heroism of Franco's forces with Robert Brasillach, who with his companions of *Je Suis Partout* observed the war from the Fascist side. Brasillach found himself under fire at the Madrid university campus, held by Franco's troops within thirty yards of Republican lines manned by the International Brigade. In *Bagatelles pour un massacre*, published in 1937 at the height of the war, Céline offered the thought that a war that allowed visiting writers to walk in and out of it like a railroad station waiting room was "a funny kind of war all the same." He called such visitors (he was speaking of the leftwing French, who of course were visiting the Republican side) "pleasure seekers, news-loving sadists." He was sure that they would not stand up to confront a regular army, whether it be Franco's or Hitler's.

Does all this suggest that the contributions of intellectuals to the Spanish war were a series of individual acts, largely the work of a few prima donnas of right and left? There was that. But there was also an effort to organize these contributions, whether spontaneous or directed. André Gide, for example, wished to send a group of representative French personalities to bear witness in Spain, in the hope of obtaining an end to the killing. Gide's plan was a personal one, but it followed on the heels of a similar proposal by Louis Aragon, which was not. Gide tried hard, but he could not get representatives of the extreme positions and the center to make common cause even momentarily. In December of that first year of war, left-wing intellectuals joined in an appeal to French opinion and "to the universal conscience," declaring flatly that France's failure to intervene on the Republican side was in effect intervention on Franco's. The signers included Gide, Aragon, Rolland, Benda, and Chamson. The Popular Front weekly *Vendredi*, published by Chamson with Jean Guéhenno and Andrée Viollis, opened its columns to the Republican cause, appealing for funds to purchase supplies for Spain. But *Vendredi* was also committed to the Léon Blum government, so it could not criticize the Popular Front policy of non-intervention, despite the editors' realization that Spain was in agony. On June 5, 1937, an editorial signed *"Vendredi"* meekly proposed "that we must leave ourselves entirely in the hands of the Government that our people freely chose." Later Chamson would admit that "the Spanish war dealt a death blow to the Popular Front, condemned our *Vendredi* as well, consecrated our doom." He realized that most of his paper's writers wished to help Spain, while there were also ardent pacifists, such as his co-director Guéhenno, who simply refused to accept war as a means. So Chamson could speak at a rally in favor of French intervention in Spain, while his newspaper had to avoid upsetting the fragile construction of the Popular Front, which had been put together with so much travail.

In Spain itself, the organization of the Republic's war effort, its supply lines, were increasingly in the hands of the Communists, often in the charge of envoys of the Soviet Union. Indeed, all available Soviet citizens with appropriate international contacts and fluency in Western languages were dispatched to the scene. And so Ilya Ehrenburg transferred his base from Montparnasse to Madrid, becoming a member of an international community that at one time or another included Italian anti-Fascists such as Palmiro Togliatti, Communist Party secretary general in exile and a Comintern official; Pietro Nenni, political commissar of the Garibaldi Brigade; and the writer Nicola Chiaromonte, a member of the Paris exile group; there were also Lazlo Rajk, Alexei Tolstoi, Egon Erwin Kisch, Anna Seghers, Jean-Richard Bloch, Antoine de Saint-Exupéry, Ernest Hemingway, John Dos Passos, George Orwell, and Stephen Spender. Officially Ehrenburg was in Spain as the correspondent of *Izvestia*, but he served also as the informal liaison between foreign writers and the Soviet ambassador. Mikhail Koltzov was also on assignment from a Moscow daily newspaper, *Pravda*, while acting as political adviser to the Spanish Republican government. For Koltzov, as for many other Communists who participated in the Republican war effort, Spain was the antechamber to camp exile or summary execution on return to Moscow. The Spanish years were also the Stalinist purge years.

Arthur Koestler was in Spain at Willy Münzenberg's request, seeking proof that Hitler and Mussolini were supplying help to Franco. On a tour of southern Spain, he was arrested and placed in solitary confinement by Franco forces, until he was released in an exchange of hostages. Gustav Regler arrived in Spain as the representative of the International Association of Writers, joining the International Brigade under French Communist André Marty; Regler was assigned as political commissar to the international battalions defending Madrid. One of his jobs was to take war correspondent Ernest Hemingway on a tour of the front. Hemingway was to speak on the responsibility of the writer in the anti-Fascist struggle at the Second American Writers Congress in New York in June 1937. His *L'Espoir* would be *For Whom the Bell Tolls*, but by the time Hemingway's Spanish war novel was published, Europe was enmeshed in World War II.

Most of the writers engaged in Spain were under Communist discipline, or they willingly accepted it for the good of the Republican cause. It also meant accepting a merciless purge of anarchist and Trotskyist volunteers on the Republican side, which often went as far as their execution as alleged traitors. Sooner or later, no matter what one's motives had been for enlisting on the Republican side, one came face to face with evidence of the Communist drive against the Trotskyists, and usually, for the good of the cause, one remained silent about it.

★ ★ ★

The International Association of Writers for the Defense of Culture, which had taken form at the star-studded Paris congress in June 1935, held its first regular meeting later the same year. In June 1936 it sponsored a session in London that featured a speech by Malraux and a resolution calling for a second international congress to be held in Madrid in 1937. By the time planning began for this congress, the Franco insurrection made it ever more timely — and dangerous. Madrid was under siege, so the Republican government had been transferred to Valencia, and it was decided to open the congress in that war capital. On July 4, 1937, the opening session took place there under the chairmanship of the Spanish Republic's prime minister, Juan Negrín. For the first time in the history of literature, *Commune* would say, writers from all over the world (two hundred of them, representing twenty-eight nations) met on the territory of a nation at war, to affirm their solidarity — "the solidarity of the intelligence of all nations" — and under a barrage of cannons. Once more Julien Benda took the floor to affirm that "the intellectual is perfectly in character in descending from his ivory tower to defend the rights of justice against barbarians." Mikhail Koltzov spoke, as did Regler. Alvarez del Vayo declared: "We are cultural fighters. The presence of uniforms among us reveals this, as do certain absences from our ranks." Tristan Tzara told how a Committee for the Defense of Spanish Culture, created by the International Association of Writers, was sending truckloads of propaganda to Spain and operating a courier service between volunteers of the international brigades and their families, bringing newspapers, books, and magazines to the front by plane. Malcolm Cowley explained how Americans were becoming pro-Republican, thanks to the firsthand reports of those on the scene, such as Louis Fischer and Hemingway, as well as the efforts of Malraux.

To get even closer to the front, the International Writers Congress shifted to Madrid for its meetings on July 6, 7, and 8. Delegates were assigned to a hotel near the university campus, close to the battle lines (which we have seen Brasillach observing from the other side). Each evening at the dinner hour, the Franco forces began firing their cannons; inside the dining hall congress delegates stood up and sang: "Madrid que bien résistes," based on a song by Federico García Lorca, who had been killed by the Fascists the previous year. As Ilya Ehrenburg remembered it, the barrage by Franco forces against the Madrid sessions of the Writers Congress was deliberate.

During the congress, specifically at five in the afternoon on July 6, a telegram arrived reporting a Republican victory on the Madrid front, and there was a proposal to make General José Miaja, who was in charge of the defense of Madrid, honorary chairman of the congress. When André Malraux spoke, it was to describe his fund-raising campaign for the Spanish cause in the United States and Canada, and even in a Hollywood film studio where, he recalled, Ernst Lubitsch was directing Marlene Dietrich in a movie.

On July 10, the delegates returned to Valencia, where one of the speakers was André Chamson. "For my part I should like to have the strength to take home so striking a message," he said, "that tomorrow in all the cities of the world that are still in security, in Paris, in London, in New York, at the dawn of each new day, at the hour when the air raids begin in Madrid, there is no man and no woman who fails to feel anguish."

The International Writers Congress held a final session in Paris on July 16 and 17, with Heinrich Mann and Louis Aragon as chairmen on successive evenings. This time André Gide was not on the platform. In Spain he had been denounced from the floor by José Bergamin and by Mikhail Koltzov. Now, in Paris, Aragon attacked him again (although this time there were protests from the audience). For Gide had committed the sin of writing frankly about what he observed in the Soviet Union; the controversy about his little book was raging as the congress opened.

13 Gide's Return

FROM THE MOMENT André Gide declared himself a Communist at heart, an admirer and a voluntary defender of the workers' homeland, he made himself available to the Soviet cause, refusing no petition, meeting, movement. Born in 1869, Gide was the senior member of most speakers' platforms, most sponsoring boards. His books, his influence, were more of a drawing card among the discerning than the works of those fading glories, Romain Rolland and Henri Barbusse. Gide was not robust, and his well-known aversion to drafts generated anecdotes. But the Communists were pleased with Gide's performance, and maintained a constant liaison with him via Paul Vaillant-Couturier and Ilya Ehrenburg, or indirectly through a network of fellow travelers.

It was the decade of pilgrimages to the Soviet Union. Gide had been planning such a journey for years. In 1933, for example, he had tried to tempt his friend Roger Martin du Gard into accompanying him, but Martin was evasive, finally immovable. Gide himself found reasons to postpone, to cancel: his colds, and Moscow's drafts, as well as the fear expressed to Maria Van Rysselberghe that he would be obliged to make speeches, would find himself saying more than he wished, while the translation into Russian and back into French for home consumption would make it worse, "and all the effort that I am making to keep my personal point of view in Communism will be lost." That was in October 1935. Ilya Ehrenburg pointed out to André Malraux that health wasn't everything, that Gide had a duty to the Party but also to the political situation: at the time it was considered vital to consolidate the Franco-Soviet alliance that had been made formal in the pact between the two nations in May 1935. Gide wondered to what extent it was in Ehrenburg's personal interest to see that he went to Moscow. Then

Gide's friend Pierre Herbart, who was to become the husband of Elisabeth (daughter of Maria Van Rysselberghe and mother of Gide's child), left for Moscow to work as an editor of the French edition of *International Literature*. Elisabeth joined him there early in 1936.

Gide's decision was taken in May. First he had another talk with Malraux, and with Ehrenburg, concerning what he would be able to say in the USSR and how his words would be treated. He wanted to talk about the plight of Soviet homosexuals, for instance; would he be listened to? He could choose his own traveling companions, at any rate. The first was his editor, Jacques Schiffrin, publisher of the Gallimard Pléiade library. Schiffrin was a keenly intelligent man of the left who was not a Communist and who possessed an irreplaceable asset: he was a native Russian speaker. Born in 1894 in Baku on the Caspian Sea, Schiffrin had been a student in Switzerland during the Russian Revolution. He settled in France, where he created the Pléiade library series, and remained as its director when it merged with Gallimard. Gide also invited Eugène Dabit, Louis Guilloux, and Jef Last, then thirty-eight, described by Gide's confidant as "a Dutch sailor, writer, winning, delicious, ironic, speaking an impossible French"; Last was to take part in the Spanish war and in the Dutch resistance during the German occupation of his country in the Second World War.

So Aragon told Moscow that Gide was finally on his way, and with Schiffrin as his interpreter. A telegram came back: Pierre Herbart was flying to Paris that very night to speak to Gide privately. For the Soviet hosts were upset that Schiffrin was going to interpret for Gide; that seemed like a lack of confidence on Gide's part, although Herbart had tried to pacify the Soviets by pointing out that Schiffrin was just a friend. Gide phoned Aragon and told him the whole thing was stupid: to reject Schiffrin, now that everyone knew he was going, would have a deplorable effect. In any case, Schiffrin and his other traveling companions were scheduled to arrive a week after Gide himself, and none of them would accompany Gide to official receptions. Aragon said that he would try to settle the problem. Maria Van Rysselberghe observed that Herbart was evasive, reticent about speaking of his experiences in Moscow. He was heard to comment on the lack of freedom of artists and writers there: "We must utilize Moscow as an experiment, not as an example."

Herbart also revealed that the Soviet Union had printed 300,000 postcards with Gide's picture on them. "Then everyone is going to recognize me," remarked Gide, worried. *International Literature* published an issue largely devoted to Gide; the University of Moscow opened an exhibition devoted to his life and works.

As Gide packed, the news of Gorki's illness became more alarming; clearly the old writer was dying. But if it was only to go to a funeral, thought Gide, better not to go at all. Ehrenburg reported that Gorki was getting better. So off went Gide and Herbart on June 16, 1936, flying from Le Bourget airport in a German airplane; there would be a stopover in Berlin. Schiffrin, Dabit, Guilloux, and Last sailed to Leningrad.

Gide arrived in Moscow with the best of intentions. His own diary expresses his state of mind: if he had once believed that man had to change himself first of all, now he was convinced that social conditions had to change before man could. Dishonest attacks on the Soviet Union had led him to wish to defend that country; he felt that the critics would begin to support the Soviet Union when he ceased to do so. He hoped that he would be able to keep his own attention focused on final goals, so that he would not be led to turn away from the USSR.

Certainly he had been shaken by the growing body of motivated criticism of the Soviet system. Before he left, Victor Serge, the man whose liberation from Soviet exile Gide had endorsed following the International Writers Congress just a year earlier, published an open letter to Gide in *Esprit*. How fight Fascism, Serge asked, if we have our own concentration camps? "Let me tell you that we can serve the working class and the USSR only with total lucidity." Herbart privately confirmed the truth of everything Serge said, but found it inadmissible for a Communist to declare such things publicly. Gide agreed. "Ah! But I should like to be able to tell Stalin everything I think about that."

Gide arrived too late to see Gorki alive. He paid his respects to him at his deathbed, and that evening attended a performance of Gorki's *Mother* before the rest of the audience was even aware that its author had died; an actor stepped to the front of the stage to announce it. The following day, Gide stood alongside the coffin with Herbart and Aragon (who was spending the summer in the Soviet Union). Gide delivered a speech in Gorki's memory on Red Square, then joined Soviet writers in the funeral procession. "The fate of culture is linked in our minds to the destiny of the USSR," he declared. "We shall defend it." But he could not resist returning to the theme that mattered so much to him: the individuality to which a creative person had a right, as well as a need. "I have often written that it is in being the most particular that a writer achieves the most general interest, because it is in showing the most personal side of himself that he reveals himself, by that very fact, the most humane." He observed that "no Russian writer was more Russian than Maxim Gorki." But he also said that while writers have always written against their regimes, for the first time, in the Soviet Union, the writer need not be in opposition.

Everywhere he went he was treated with deference. When he visited the Gide exhibition at the university, he talked to students assembled there. In Leningrad, where he had gone to meet Schiffrin and the other members of his party who had traveled by ship, he was also asked to speak, but there he experienced the heavy hand of the censor: he was asked to insert the word *glorious* before the phrase "the future of the USSR." And to remove *great* before *monarch.* While the group visited the Crimean port of Sevastopol, Eugène Dabit fell ill, apparently stricken by typhus. The others returned to Moscow, and Dabit died alone in Sevastopol on August 21, a month before his thirty-eighth birthday. The final entry in his private diary was a cry of pessimism, for he saw the coming of another world war. "We are hunted, we are lost. Life, in this world, becomes unthinkable." On his return to Paris, Gide accompanied Clara Malraux to the funeral at Père Lachaise cemetery, where Vaillant-Couturier and Aragon made speeches stressing Dabit's sympathy with Communism, Aragon referring to the dead man's expressions of moral satisfaction with the Soviet Union. "Alas!" was Gide's comment to his diary.

Although he was giving out hints, Gide had not yet delivered himself of his sentiments concerning the workers' paradise. Yet it was his practice to write about everything he did, saw, or thought about, and to publish what he wrote. There was also a tradition of writing about one's travels in the Soviet Union; by 1936 one could have filled a shelf with such accounts. Gide began writing his *Retour de l'U.R.S.S.* almost immediately after Dabit's funeral. In private conversations he made it clear that the Soviet government's severity with respect to homosexuality was only one of his objections to the regime. He was pleased, he told Maria Van Rysselberghe, that he had not seen Stalin, and had not even corresponded with him about the repressive legislation against homosexuals; there was now so much more to be said about the Soviet system than that. Certainly his Soviet hosts had done everything conceivable to satisfy his needs. Gide later confided to Roger Stéphane that they had filled a swimming pool with handsome young men, whom he discovered were Red army soldiers. (After the bombshell of Gide's book, the Soviets called attention to a homosexual act he had committed during his trip; apparently Gide had not realized that this encounter had also been prearranged.)

Maria Van Rysselberghe describes the evening — September 23, 1936 — when Gide read the first draft of *Retour de l'U.R.S.S.* to Jacques Schiffrin and Louis Guilloux. Presumably he had already read it to Jef Last, for Last stayed at the Rue Vaneau apartment before going off to Spain. The friends found Gide's report clear but harsh. "This little book will have the effect of an exploding bomb," Maria Van Rysselberghe observed with her habitual perspicuity. "You have to have a lot of courage to publish such a book," Guilloux commented. In his own journal, he shows himself to be less sympathetic to Gide: "I'm beginning to believe that he went to the USSR only to obtain the authority he needed to say what he is saying today." Gide went to southern France to show his draft to Herbart, obtaining useful suggestions for the final manuscript. By October 21 it was at the printer's.

Gide wanted to save the surprise of his conclusions for publication day. But he also thought that he had better warn his friends. He began with Communists such as Paul Nizan. By October 24, *Le Figaro* reported the "rumor" in a gossip column that Gide had returned from the Soviet Union troubled and disappointed. He was said to be preparing a small book for publication before the middle of November, and it might surprise. Meanwhile Gide had gone out to Versailles to talk to André Chamson, by then curator of the palace, asking whether *Vendredi* would publish his findings. How could Chamson refuse?

One of the anecdotes Gide told his friends — Chamson and Guéhenno both remembered and recorded it — was how, during his travels across the Soviet territories, he and his companions were greeted at train stops by banners of welcome, only later realizing that the banners were traveling on the train with them.

Now the pressures began to be felt. On October 26, Ilya Ehrenburg dropped by the Rue Vaneau. To Gide's surprise, he seemed fully aware of the contents of the unpublished book. Ehrenburg let Gide know that he even approved Gide's point of view, and in fact he himself could have said much more! But was this the right time, with the Spanish war raging, and the Soviet Union doing so much to help the Spanish Republican cause? Shouldn't Gide himself go to Spain? Gide liked that idea, for it suggested a means to prove that he was not breaking with the Communists. Meanwhile, Gide was getting telegrams from the Spanish war front warning that the book would represent "a mortal blow" for their cause.

Jef Last cabled from Spain, for example, begging that he at least postpone publication of *Retour* until they could talk in Madrid (Ehrenburg certainly put him up to that). Aragon phoned to say that he was back from Spain with a message from Last. The Dutchman had given Gide a letter of endorsement which was to have been printed at the end of the book; now that letter would have to be omitted. (Clearly Last had been identified as Gide's weakness.) Malraux also returned from Spain and asked to dine with Gide, who feared that this was to be another element in the campaign. But Malraux remained his independent self. "They are bothering you a lot, aren't they? Don't let yourself be had." But when Gide met Victor Serge, Serge wondered what Malraux's attitude would be if he were asked to choose for or against Gide. Gide said that Ehrenburg had obviously seen the text of his book, even though the printer had been asked to keep it confidential, to which Serge replied that Ehrenburg was a Soviet secret agent, or an aide of secret agents. For his part Gide had asked Magdeleine Paz to be sure that his meeting with Serge remain confidential so that no one could accuse him of having been influenced by Serge. "Try not to be followed," she had warned Serge.

All the while, Gide continued to make minor changes in his book, and before Schiffrin arrived to take the final proofs to the printer, he added a phrase at the very end, offering hope that Soviet aid to Republican Spain would represent a change in the Soviet system. When Gide's preface was published in *Vendredi*, Aragon phoned to say: "I am saddened not so much because of the probable reaction of our enemies but of that of our friends."

Even the faithful Herbart, who agreed with Gide's findings but not with his conclusions (Herbart was a member of the French Communist Party), now intervened. Gide was getting ready to accompany a delegation of French personalities representing left and right, Catholics and Communists, to Spain, in an attempt to end the fighting. Herbart suggested that Gide would have more influence in Spain if his book did not appear before the trip. Gide finally agreed to a week's postponement. But the planned delegation never left Paris.

★   ★   ★

Retour de l'U.R.S.S. was published on November 5, 1936, dedicated to Eugène Dabit (as "reflections of what I lived and thought alongside him, with him"). In the preface, which Chamson published in *Vendredi*, Gide explained that he had declared his admiration for the Soviet Union three years earlier, that as recently as this past March *La Nouvelle Revue Française* had published his further expressions of sympathy. But now he had to recognize his error. Was it he who had changed, or the USSR? In either case humanity seemed more important to him than even the Soviet Union; it was for that nation's sake that he was criticizing it now. He regretted that their common enemies would make use of his remarks, but he would not have written them if he had not felt that the USSR would eventually overcome its errors.

The body of the book — only seventy-three pages long if preface and appendices are subtracted — opened with a glimpse of the idyllic side of his journey: the friendly people, the natural beauty, the rest homes. But then there is the shock of coming upon long lines of consumers waiting their turn to purchase merchandise of inferior quality. Even the Persian saying (he quotes it in English): "Women for duty, boys for pleasure, melons for delight," did not apply there, for the melon was bad. He observed the indolence of workers, doubted official statistics concerning collective farm life. Everywhere he saw conformity, accompanied by boasts about how much better things were in that country. But he could perceive the slums and the poorly fed population behind the models; he discovered a genuine lower class. In the Soviet Union he felt that it was the revolutionary spirit that was considered counterrevolutionary. He doubted that in any other country, including Nazi Germany, thought was less free, more afraid. He described how his own public statements were censored, told of the extra praise of Stalin that his translator insisted on inserting into his telegram of greetings to the Soviet dictator. Stalin's personal rule, he went on, was contrary to Communist principles. He had seen how art was subordinated to the state; in passing, and in a footnote, he attacked the legislation against abortion and homosexuality.

Gide's little book was reprinted eight times between publication day and September 1937, a total of 146,300 copies. Overnight it was a sensation in the press, evoking reactions of happy surprise from the right (although in *L'Action Française* Thierry Maulnier regretted that the criticism of Soviet life was carried out "in the name of an inane egalitarianism . . . an anarchistic individualism . . . In time Gide was to disavow the applause he received from conservatives. Trotski praised Gide for his intellectual honesty, comparing him to Malraux, who, said Trotski, was "organically incapable of moral independence." Malraux was insisting that everything else be forgotten because of Spain. "His interest in the Spanish revolution," argued Trotski, "still doesn't prevent Stalin from exterminating veteran revolutionaries."

Of course *Pravda* and *L'Humanité* denounced Gide. Romain Rolland wrote a letter to foreign workers employed at the Stalin Steel Factory in Magnitogorsk that was published in *L'Humanité:* "This bad book is also a mediocre book," and more words to that effect.

Gide became a nonperson. His name disappeared from Communist-controlled publications, from the boards of their organizations. Polemicists were enlisted to denounce him on the floor at meetings of the Houses of Culture, in the columns of Party organs and like-minded periodicals. Aragon requested that Louis Guilloux, literary editor of *Ce Soir*, write a response to Gide's book. Guilloux replied that he could do no such thing, since he had gone to the USSR on Gide's invitation and in any case had seen little to write about. As we have seen, privately Guilloux had his own misgivings about Gide's exposé, believing that his friend should have departed from the Soviet Union as soon as he realized that he disapproved of it. "Why did he accept gifts until the very end?" And that eulogistic telegram to Stalin . . .

But Guilloux held firm. Jean-Richard Bloch, co-director with Aragon of *Ce Soir*, also pressed him to disavow Gide. Guilloux confided to his diary that if Bloch insisted, he would reply that he would not do it, and precisely because Bloch and Aragon wished him to. A few days later he was dismissed and replaced by Paul Nizan.

The consequences for Gide were predictable. Guéhenno found him suddenly alone. "The human warmth with which he had felt surrounded for several years, this affection which was perhaps on order, but nevertheless this affection which had borne him for a time, he felt that — again on order — it was being withdrawn." What hurt Gide, Guéhenno wrote in his diary, "was the silence of his friends of yesterday, the watchword of silence which they were following." Guéhenno was told by one Communist, "We're going to let Gide marinate a while." Seeing Gide walking on the opposite sidewalk one day, Jean Cassou crossed over to greet him. Gide said, "You dare to shake my hand when

everybody else is attacking me?" Cassou, concerned above all about
Spain, and believing that the Soviet Union was the only country that was
helping Spain, replied, "If I have any reproach, it's that you put yourself
above everything else." By that he meant that Gide cared more about his
own conscience than about their cause. Gide smiled, they shook hands
and parted.

   On a journey to Spain in connection with the plan for a peace
delegation, Pierre Herbart had taken a set of proofs of *Retour de
l'U.R.S.S.* He showed it to Malraux and to Regler, but also to Mikhail
Koltzov. While Herbart was still in Spain, Gide's book appeared in
bookstore windows in Paris, and the uproar began.   In Spain,
deviationists who were saying or doing less than Gide were being
arrested and summarily executed by Soviet agents, or by Spaniards
commanded by Soviet officers, and Herbart felt himself in danger. He
slipped away to see Malraux, then made his way back to France. Later,
when Jef Last arrived from Spain, he had to see Gide secretly, for he felt
he was being followed by his Communist comrades, who considered it a
crime to associate with Gide.

Soon Gide began to put together the information and reflections he had
left out of *Retour*, along with the information and reflections others were
bringing to him, in a second small book, *Retouches à mon Retour de
l'U.R.S.S.* Gide offered the new work as his answer to those who had
criticized the first book in good faith. Nizan had reproached him for
seeing the USSR as a country that no longer changed; on the contrary,
Gide felt that it was changing from month to month, and for the worse.
He drew a parallel between the attacks on *Retour* and the reactions to his
earlier books on French colonial territories. Those who visited the
Soviet Union with a guide, he argued, were like the "accompanied"
travelers in French Equatorial Africa. He confessed that only after
completing *Retour de l'U.R.S.S.* had he read Trotski and Serge. He
confirmed that Eugène Dabit had shared his disappointment with the
Soviet Union, something which Soviet apologists had contested.
Indeed, he said, he had purposely softened the blows in the first
book.

   Gide even aggravated his crime. He joined Georges Duhamel, Roger
Martin du Gard, François Mauriac, and Paul Rivet in sending a telegram
to the Spanish Republican government, asking that political prisoners be

given a fair trial. As it happened, these political prisoners were left-revolutionary militants of anarchistic and Trotskyist ideology; they were being liquidated by Spanish Republicans on the orders of their Soviet advisers. In *Izvestia* Ilya Ehrenburg published a fierce attack on those who were defending "the Fascists and provocateurs of P.O.U.M." (the dissident Communist movement). His specific target was "the new ally of the [Spanish rebel army] and the Black Shirts," the "wicked old man," the "Moscow crybaby."

14 Plunging into Barbarity

IT WAS A TIME of defeats.

On June 21, 1937, Léon Blum's Popular Front cabinet resigned. The following January, Blum tried unsuccessfully to form another government, and in April 1938 another Blum cabinet fell, having lasted less than a month. The Daladier government that followed —without Socialist Party participation — broke a general strike called to protest both the elimination of Popular Front reforms and Daladier's general policies, foreign as well as domestic. "The defeat of Léon Blum was our own defeat," Jean Guéhenno wrote in his *Journal d'une "révolution."* "We had stupidly thought that the revolution would come easily. Not for an instant did we accept the fact that it imposed as many duties as rights on us." The note was written in August 1937; rereading it that autumn, Guéhenno felt he had been undully harsh with the French left wing. "I should accuse more justly the era . . . and especially the sectarianism of parties and of individuals . . ."

Henceforth the Spanish Republic's military forces were reduced to defending rapidly diminishing pockets of territory. The aid that filtered in from France, the semiclandestine assistance from the distant Soviet Union, could not match that of Franco's Fascist allies. The successes of pacifists in France and elsewhere in preventing further internationalization of the conflict favored the aggressor: Spain's democracy died slowly as friendly eyes turned away, and at the end of March 1939 Franco was in Madrid. In France, the anti-Fascist effort turned now to assisting Spanish refugees. For its part, the French chapter of the International Association of Writers for the Defense of Culture set up a Reception Committee for Spanish Intellectuals, sponsored by Pablo Picasso, José Bergamin, Jean Cassou, Jean-Richard Bloch, Louis Aragon, and Tristan

Tzara. In a month's time it reported that five hundred people had been given funds or transportation to homes in France; sleeping bags were sent to refugee camps. Among those helped were the writers Antonio Machado, Rafael Alberti, Arturo Serrano Plaja.

To the east, Nazi Germany was on the move. The horror that had become a way of life in France's neighbor state was being exported. In 1936 Hitler reoccupied the demilitarized left bank of the Rhine, with no useful reaction from the Western Allies, just as there would be none when Hitler defied the Versailles treaty by introducing military conscription. As Italy completed its occupation of Ethiopia, Mussolini entered into a secret alliance with Germany, which had already signed such a pact with Japan. Germany then began the inexorable annexation of its neighbors. Austria fell to the *Anschluss* in March 1938. French writers normally in opposing camps joined in a declaration of national unity:

> Before the menace which weighs on our country and on the future of French culture, the undersigned writers, regretting the lack of union among the French, have decided to put aside their quarrels and to offer the example of their fraternity to the French nation.

Aragon, Chamson, Guéhenno, and Malraux endorsed the statement, but so did Georges Bernanos, Colette, Jacques Maritain, François Mauriac, Henry de Montherlant, Jules Romains, and other eminent personalities of the center and right. But where was Gide? He had become a nonperson. Actually, Gide found that being blackballed gave him a new kind of freedom. "This 'fear of the Index' that I expressed in the past, the absurd fear of being found wanting by the 'pures,' " he wrote in his *Journal*, "bothered me for a long time and a great deal, to the point that I didn't dare write any more."

Henceforth Gide's efforts would be private ones: financial assistance to refugees, usually Jews, who had fled Germany — cases usually called to his attention by Clara Malraux — and now, assistance to Spanish Republican exiles as well. We know of some of this activity thanks to a singular source. Gide had engaged as his private secretary a young man of the extreme right wing, Lucien Combelle, and while working for Gide Combelle had a friendly confessor in Paul Léautaud. Léautaud conscientiously recorded everything he was told. Combelle reported to Léautaud that he found Gide — even after his break with the Soviet Union — "chummed up, indoctrinated, preached to every minute of the

day," by left-wingers (no matter that they were anti-Soviet left-wingers).
Such people told Gide only the evil things about General Franco, for
instance, fearful that he might read the other side of the story in *L'Action
Française* and papers of the sort. Combelle discovered nevertheless that
Gide had moments of indocility, even revolt, in the face of leftist
indoctrination. And in the hearing of Maria Van Rysselberghe Gide was
also slipping back into cultural anti-Semitism. Roger Martin du Gard
tried to convince him that Jewish thought was *not* anti-French, citing the
examples of the "half-Jews" Montaigne and Proust. Both Gide and
Martin du Gard were pessimistic about the future. Gide, wrote his
confidante, "seems to believe that we are going to plunge into a period of
barbarity."

Without Gide, the International Association of Writers called a
meeting at the Palais de la Mutualité in July 1938, its agenda dealing with
assistance to Spain, to China threatened by Japan, to Czechoslovakia
threatened by Germany. The American Theodore Dreiser was present,
and the Englishwoman Rosamond Lehmann. They shared the speakers'
table with José Bergamin and Louis Aragon. Dreiser offered a Marxist
version of American history, stressing the importance of protest literature. Aragon pointed out that a survey of the League of American
Writers found that 410 of the 418 polled were supporters of Spain.
Among the other speakers were Langston Hughes, Stephen Spender, C.
Day Lewis, Rex Warner, Ernst Toller, and Anna Seghers, with Dolores
Ibarruri, who was called La Pasionaria of the Spanish Republican
cause.

A message was read to the meeting from Mikhail Koltzov, in the name
of the Union of Soviet Writers. He apologized for the absence of Soviet
delegates. "To our great regret at the present time the majority of Soviet
writers are either on vacation or traveling . . ." In fact, many of these
writers were in concentration camps or in prison — or dead. Of those
who attended the International Writers Congress in 1935, Babel and
Kirchon had already disappeared. Koltzov himself, who had withstood
the wave of denunciations in the columns of *Pravda*, was arrested on his
return from Spain later in 1938, and executed. Ilya Ehrenburg escaped
the purge of all who had foreign connections, all who traveled abroad,
claiming later that he didn't know how it had happened: he had won a
lottery, he remarked. In truth, his winning ticket was the letter he had
written to Stalin saying that he could be an effective agent of the Soviet
Union in the West, considering his knowledge of the area.

If Gide was one of the few on the left to see through the Moscow purges, he was not equally perspicacious in his judgment on the Munich compromise with Hitler. His *Journal* betrays an uncertainty felt by many: on the one hand, "reason (if not justice and right) won a victory over force"; on the other, his Dutch friend Jef Last had written him that the Munich agreement was a shameful defeat, which could only result in further demands from Hitler, further retreats for the democracies, and dishonor. After consolidating his takeover of Austria, Hitler had turned to another weak neighbor, insisting that Czechoslovakia cede territory occupied by the German-speaking Sudeten minority. In Munich, at the end of September 1938, the British and French prime ministers Neville Chamberlain and Edouard Daladier accepted Hitler's demands, giving Germany a slice of Czechoslovakia against the will of that nation. On his return to Paris, Daladier thought that the crowd waiting at the airport was there to boo or to spit at him because of the concessions to Hitler. Instead, he was cheered. "Damn fools!" he muttered. André Chamson saw him shortly after that. "You don't look happy," Daladier said. "No, I'm not," replied Chamson, although he himself did not see what else Daladier could have done. "Those people out there don't want to fight," Daladier told him. "What I must do now is to prepare them to fight all the same."

The division of feeling could affect the closest of friends. Simone de Beauvoir recalled that during the Czechoslovak crisis she had felt that "anything, even the most cruel injustice, was better than war." Sartre replied, "One can't give in indefinitely to Hitler." But even he found it difficult to reconcile his political convictions and his deepest feelings. Beauvoir was overjoyed by the Munich agreement. Raymond Aron found Sartre, his old school friend, similarly taken with the compromise. Sartre told him, "We can't dispose of the lives of others." A considerable number of left-wing intellectuals communed in the slogan, "The democracies have just declared peace in the world." The ambiguity was summed up by Antoine de Saint-Exupéry in *Paris-Soir* on October 1, the day the Germans began to occupy Czechoslovak territory:

> We have chosen to save the Peace. But . . . we have mutilated friends. And without doubt, many among us were ready to risk their lives for the duties of friendship. Such persons feel a kind of shame. But if they had sacrificed peace, they would have felt the same shame. For then they

should have sacrificed man; they should have accepted the irreparable destruction of the libraries, the cathedrals, the laboratories of Europe . . . And this is why we wavered from one opinion to the other. When peace seemed threatened, we discovered the shame of war. When war was no longer a threat, we felt the shame of Peace.

In May 1939, writers met again in Paris for their last significant gathering before the declaration of war. Ilya Ehrenburg was present, and so were his old friends Malraux, Aragon, Bloch, Paul Langevin, Marcel Cachin. "Everyone was pessimistic and the speeches seemed a repetition of things heard before," he remembered. "There was no longer any enthusiasm."

★ ★ ★

One might sum up the political history of the 1930s this way. At the beginning, most intellectuals seemed ready to believe that resistance to war and resistance to Fascism went hand in hand. The horrors of World War I could still be remembered, while Fascism was a distant threat. With the coming to power of Hitler, more than one French group split down the middle. In the Committee of Vigilance of Anti-Fascist Intellectuals, for example, the dilemma was between giving priority to saving the peace, even if this required appeasing dictators, or stopping Hitler, even if that meant war. The difference of opinion was an honest one, and even the silences on the left were the fruit of deeply held convictions.

Then, in August 1939, the bombshell of the pact between Nazi Germany and the Soviet Union made it clear that the left wing of the Left Bank was not one force but two. For bombshell it was. After marching into Czechoslovakia despite his promise to limit his demands, Hitler had made a claim on Poland's Danzig corridor, which separated segments of German territory, and prepared to attack that country, too. The Western democracies were readying themselves for battle at last when, on August 23, 1939, Stalin agreed to a pact of nonaggression with Hitler.

With that agreement, the very basis of the alliance of Communists and non-Communists against Nazism and Fascism was eliminated. Manès Sperber remembered it as "the greatest political and moral defeat" ever experienced by the anti-Fascist movement. It was a time of outraged and public resignations from the Communist Party, but also of many silent ones. Perhaps the luckiest were those who were not members of the Party and so did not have to make public protest or confession of error. Those like André Malraux could simply choose not to speak out, in the name of anti-Fascist unity. Ilya Ehrenburg fell ill, for no discernible cause, and was unable to eat normally for the next eight months; in all he lost nearly forty-five pounds. But he said nothing, just as he had said nothing about the Moscow trials. Louis Aragon was publishing *Ce Soir* each day; if one wrote regularly in a newspaper, it was difficult to avoid writing about the nonaggression pact. What Aragon said about it was that it was favorable to peace. With war less than a fortnight away, the French government shut down *Ce Soir* and the rest of the Communist Party press.

In truth, the twenty-one months between the signing of the Soviet-German agreement and Hitler's surprise attack on the Soviet Union in 1941 were among the most trying in the history of French Communists. The official line would have them treat the Franco-British war against Germany as imperialistic. Loyalty to the Soviet line required that, instead of opposing the Axis powers, they sabotage what the Communists called the "so-called anti-Fascist war," and that they consider the French and the British as the true aggressors. When the Germans occupied Paris in June 1940, Hitler's attack on the Soviet Union was still a year away. So the official Communist organ, *L'Humanité*, now published underground, treated the war in the west as one between rival groups of bandits, and there is evidence that the Communists asked the German occupation authorities for permission to publish their antiwar *L'Humanité* above ground. The Germans liked the idea, but the Pétain government in Vichy vetoed it.

One Communist intellectual took a public position: Sartre's schoolmate Paul Nizan, who was foreign editor of *Ce Soir*. He had been shaken by the Moscow trials, but had stood fast. Now, expected to swallow his Party's endorsement of the Soviet pact with the Nazis, he could not do that. Nizan did not attack the agreement itself, feeling that Stalin was justified in seeking such protection as that pact afforded. What he objected to was his own Party's approval of the agreement, as if French and Soviet interests were identical. Nizan was killed in battle near Dunkirk, but his reputation would pay for his break with the Party, as we shall see.

★   ★   ★

On September 1, 1939, the Germans marched into Poland, carrying out their part of the Soviet-German pact. On September 3 France and the United Kingdom declared war on Germany. Among the immediate consequences was a rather mindless roundup of German refugees in France, which made victims of leading anti-Fascists; absurdly, their country of origin made them enemy aliens (a similar hysteria took possession of the British Isles, just as the United States would turn against its own Japanese population after Pearl Harbor). Another consequence was the aggravation of the division between Communists and the rest of the left, now that the Communists were clearly unprepared to go to war against Stalin's new ally, Hitler. The absurdity was heightened when anti-Fascist refugees like Arthur Koestler and Gustav Regler, who had moved away from the Party, found themselves interned by the French alongside native French members of the Party with whom they could no longer have been as intimate in the world outside. Regler counted 560 refugees from every nation of Europe in his detention camp at the foot of the Pyrenees. Many were foreign Communist leaders; nearly all were anti-Fascists. No German Nazis or Italian Fascists were in the group at all.

What was happening back on the Left Bank? Simone de Beauvoir is one of the best historians of that time, and her war diary is also a guide to the cafés of Montparnasse and of Saint-Germain-des-Prés. She learns of the German entry into Poland from a waiter in her beloved Dôme; she passes her last hours with Sartre before his departure on military duty at the Café de Flore under a bright moon, while old Saint-Germain-des-Prés resembles a country church. But, "at the bottom of everything, everywhere, an indefinable horror." Back at the Dôme, the day before the declaration of war, soldiers mix with prostitutes. She notices a sign on a Montparnasse bookshop whose owner has a German-sounding name, proclaiming the store one hundred percent French-owned. She hears about Ehrenburg's illness, and that he is contemplating suicide. On September 3, curtains go up over the Dôme's windows to allow business as usual during the evening blackout. One must show identity papers to use the telephone (September 4); gas masks are issued at the school where she teaches; next day she notices that prostitutes are also carrying them. She sees André Breton in uniform. On September 5, she discovers that the Flore is closed. Reading Gide's *Journal* for 1914, she find analogies with the present. On September 6, she observes that crossword puzzles have been dropped from *Marianne* because of fear that they might contain a secret code. Next day she confesses her tender attachment to the cafés of Montparnasse: "I feel as if I'm home with my family and that protects me against anguish."

The following day, the sky is filled with antiaircraft balloon defenses. One must pay when served at the Montparnasse cafés in order to be able to leave quickly in the event of an alert. The Flore reopens in mid-October; she finds it superb with its new heavy blue curtains and red seats. "Now the cafés have learned how to camouflage themselves; they light up all their lamps and one is struck by this blaze when one arrives from outside." It is curious to read Beauvoir's diary alongside that of Alain Laubreaux, a member of the young Fascist band that put together Je Suis Partout, for his Saint-Germain-des-Prés occupied the same space and time. At the Brasserie Lipp on September 2, Laubreaux hears Louis Darquier de Pellepoix, soon to be the Vichy government's Commissar for Jewish Questions, attacking Jews so loudly that he is slapped by a young woman. He strikes back, and other customers come to the young woman's rescue. Darquier begins to use his cane and the incident degenerates into a brawl. When the Café de Flore reopens, Laubreaux goes there too. "I am choked and blinded by the thick tobacco smoke that makes the half-lit café even darker," he writes, "where an incredible assembly of Jews and half-breeds crawls about, gossiping excitedly." In the middle of this underworld, he spies Léon-Paul Fargue, who confesses that he too is looking forward to the defeat of his country, for only then will France be rid of the popular playwright Henry Bernstein, a Jew, and of "the moral muck in which we are wading." Laubreaux himself had told his friend Lucien Rebatet, who had been called up for military duty: "I can only wish for one thing for France: a short and disastrous war."

Ilya Ehrenburg was a privileged witness to these events. His country was not at war; he could observe with relative tranquility the foibles of Parisians during the drôle de guerre (or Phoney War, as the British called it) — an apt name for the long pause between the declaration of war in September 1939 and the German drive into France in May 1940. In fact, Ehrenburg was still under the shock of Stalin's rapprochement with Hitler. He read the telegram Stalin sent to Nazi Foreign Minister Joachim von Ribbentrop ten times. In it Stalin spoke of friendship cemented by spilled blood, and to Ehrenburg that seemed a blasphemy. Only a few old friends remained in contact with him, the others feeling that he had betrayed France — or they feared the police. Among the faithful were André Malraux and Jean-Richard Bloch. The right-wing press wondered why he was still in Paris, but so did he himself. The truth was, he was waiting for his exit visa. There is evidence that in the final desperate weeks of French defense against the German blitzkrieg, Ehrenburg was called in by members of the French government who wished to obtain emergency (and undoubtedly secret) military assistance from the Soviet Union in the form of airplanes.

★   ★   ★

With the declaration of war, the true exodus from the Left Bank began. Gaston Gallimard moved his family, the files of his publishing house, and even the cash box, in a convoy of five automobiles from the Rue Sébastien-Bottin due west to a large country house in Mirande, near Sartilly in the Manche *département*, surrounded by grazing pasture, facing the bay of Mont-Saint-Michel and the great old abbey. Gallimard insisted that Jean Paulhan join him there, for he intended both the *Nouvelle Revue Française* magazine and book publishing to be carried on from this dairy country. Only one clerk remained behind to handle mail; the younger employees were off to war. A circular was sent to house authors to assure them that Gallimard was always ready to publish their work.

One of Gallimard's star authors and editors, André Malraux, had removed himself from the political arena. That summer he devoted his efforts to his *Psychologie de l'Art*, traveling through southern France with his companion, Josette Clotis, visiting churches and museums, but also enjoying a gastronomic tour of the provinces. Josette had been with him in Spain and in the swing across the United States; for her, Malraux had virtually abandoned his wife, Clara. Henceforth, until her accidental death in 1944, Josette and Malraux were inseparable.

15 Fleeing the Left Bank

FRANCE'S *drôle de guerre*, the war without movement, lasted until May 1940, when the Germans bypassed the tunnel defenses of the Maginot Line to attack through Belgium, crossing the Meuse near Sedan on May 13, breaking through the so-called Weygand Line on the Somme three weeks later. On June 11 Paris was declared an open city, and German soldiers began marching in on June 14.

Many of our protagonists had good reason to fear the Germans and left Paris as soon and as fast as they could. Descriptions of the atmosphere must come from those who were able to stay. From Ilya Ehrenburg, for one, who although Jewish and Russian and a supporter of Communism, was protected by the Soviet alliance with Germany. It must have seemed the supreme irony to this intelligent man that he who had encouraged a generation of French anti-Fascists to rally around the Soviet Union now walked freely in Montparnasse while his anti-Fascist friends were obliged to take cover. He observed the "long lines of cars with mattresses on their roofs" crossing the Left Bank toward the southern exits of the city. The railroad stations were mobbed; those who possessed bicycles made use of them. Those without any means of transportation simply walked out of Paris, sometimes pushing handcarts. On the Boulevard Raspail "an interminable torrent of refugees streamed by." Opposite the Rotonde café, the statue of Balzac also seemed about to leave its pedestal. "I remained at the intersection for a long time," Ehrenburg wrote in his memoirs; "it was where I spent my youth. Suddenly, it seemed to me that Balzac was also leaving, with the others." When the German army entered the city he moved into the Soviet Embassy, but he continued to move about freely. When he finally left Paris he had sufficient material to write a novel about *The Fall of Paris*.

Paul Léautaud never had to leave. "I am staying. I was always determined to stay," he confided to his journal. "I don't want to sacrifice my pets. I wouldn't know where to go. I've got a bad character; I don't intend to live just anywhere . . . I don't want to take a chance of not finding any of my possessions when I return home." Léautaud was safe enough, and neither defeat nor its consequences troubled him. During the frantic flight of those around him, he went about his daily business at the Mercure de France, commuting from his distant suburb, buying and storing food for his animals, filling up the pages of his Pepys of a diary. The director of his firm, who was ready to collaborate with the Germans even before being asked, planned a quick translation of Hitler's *Mein Kampf*. Léautaud took secret pleasure in the anti-Jewish measures, convinced that they represented just revenge. Until the day the Germans pillaged a fine old bookstore. That the authorities punish Jews, who he felt might even deserve such treatment, was one thing; that it dispossess and eject them was another. "I could never approve such things."

But in talking to Lucien Combelle, Gide's former secretary, soon to become a conscientious collaborationist, he found it difficult to decide which he preferred: a German victory that would lead to a political, social, and moral reorganization of France, or a British victory, which would be the victory of the Jews — who he believed would then be more domineering than ever. Should one prefer the return to a past when scoundrels governed, but when there had been a certain freedom to say that they were scoundrels? His perplexity was a simplistic version of the dilemma facing much of the extreme right during the occupation years.

WHERE ARE OUR WRITERS?
André Gide, who had been devoting himself to the distress of foreign refugees, is in Cabris, in the [southern French department of] Alpes-Maritimes, and so is Jean Schlumberger. In Nice one finds Henry de Montherlant, who is writing his memoirs of his World War I volunteer work with the American ambulance corps; and Francis Carco. In Aix-en-Provence there are Edouard Peisson and Blaise Cendrars; in Saint-Tropez, Colette and Paul Géraldy. (*Le Figaro*, September 8, 1940)

The entire Left Bank was on the Riviera, the men with their mistresses, for the occupation of France by the Germans facilitated adulterous relationships: so Josette Clotis, Malraux's mistress, reported the situation to a confidante. To a young man entering the world of letters at that time, Nice in the early months of German rule seemed "truly a literary salon." But this is to anticipate. What is certain is that the armistice agreement between the victorious Germans and the defeated French divided the country into so-called occupied and free zones. The Germans were in Paris and the north, and controlled the Atlantic coast as well, while the government of Marshal Pétain had nominal control of southern France. Much of the Paris press had joined the exodus, and would henceforth publish in the Vichy zone — *Le Figaro* in Lyon, for example. Depending on who one was or what one believed, one might stay on in Paris under German control, settle in Vichy or another southern city under the Pétainists (with luck on the Riviera), or go into hiding.

★ ★ ★

Gide's diary was never a very private one. Designed for eventual publication, it would often appear in brief extracts in literary magazines not long after having been written. A selection of such entries covering the early months of German occupation was published in Algiers in 1944 under the imprint of Edmond Charlot, Albert Camus's first publisher, and it provoked a scandal. For in his notes Gide seemed to blame the French themselves for their defeat: their very qualities had rendered them helpless in the face of Hitler's ruse. Gide even endorsed, in those first hours of defeat, the opinion of Philippe Pétain, who attributed the German victory to a failure of will on the part of the French, ever since the First World War. As Pétain had put it, "the spirit of pleasure-seeking had replaced the spirit of sacrifice." Gide found Pétain's remark "simply admirable." Yet soon enough he would be criticizing Pétain for delivering France to the Germans, and those who approved Pétain's policies would be attacking Gide. For the collaborationist press, Gide became "the spiritual father of the defeat."

In the early months of the war, as has already been noted, Gide had been concerned with the problems of refugees, calling the attention of the press to the injustice of placing fugitives from Hitler in French detention camps, when many of them could have been of use to France. In defeat he continued to try to help these refugees. The Emergency Rescue Committee, an American organization created to assist prominent anti-Fascists who were threatened by the arrival of the Nazis, and which had already put Heinrich Mann on a ship bound for New

York, offered to evacuate Gide himself to the United States. He replied that he did not wish to leave France, at least for the time being, but he did enlist the Committee's efforts in behalf of his friends. He and Maria Van Rysselberghe invited the Emergency Rescue Committee volunteers to tea in Cabris, where he had a temporary refuge in the manor of a benefactor. Gide suggested that a French publishing house be established in the United States, for French authors might need such an outlet. The conversation took place on December 22, 1940, six months after the beginning of the German occupation, and a fortnight after Gaston Gallimard had handed Gide the first issue of the collaborationist *Nouvelle Revue Française*. Gide's old friend and editor Jacques Schiffrin, distressed and obviously ill, also came to see him. Soon Schiffrin and his family had found a ship sailing to Martinique in the West Indies, but their ship was not permitted to discharge its refugee passengers; it was ordered back to Casablanca in Morocco. From there Schiffrin wired the Gallimards for help. They turned to Gide, who asked that funds be drawn from his own royalty account in the publishing house to help. Thanks to Gide, Schiffrin and his family were not interned in Morocco as they might have been, for he let them use an apartment of his in Casablanca until they were able to sail again for the New World in the summer of 1941.

It was a trying time for Gide, who was going on seventy-two years of age, and who continued to be fought over as if he were war booty. An interzone card, the only kind of correspondence then possible between northern and southern France, arrived from Jean Paulhan in Paris: "P. V. [Paul Valéry] informs Uncle G. that if he wishes to return to Paris the [French] Academy is ready to elect him to membership." Pierre Drieu La Rochelle addressed him publicly in *Je Suis Partout*: "Come to Paris. The man who traveled to Moscow can certainly travel to Paris. Having compared the two zones, and their respective defects, you will perhaps also understand our position, which is to create a national socialism exempt from the errors of the old nationalism and the old socialism." But Gide was not going to be tempted.

Autumn found him freezing in Nice. He began writing a series of "Interviews Imaginaires" for *Le Figaro Littéraire*. In the very first imaginary interview, he mocked the notion that literature was responsible for France's defeat. But he remained prudent in what he wrote for publication; Roger Martin du Gard was even more prudent, and served as his faithful sounding board and censor. Then on May 5,

1942, Gide sailed from Marseille to Tunisia; he was to stay in North Africa until the war and the occupation were over.

★   ★   ★

The history of the year of defeat is filled with escape and evacuation stories. Paul Léautaud opened his morning newspaper to read with approval an ironic attack on Jules Romains, who had gone to New York with the files of the French P.E.N. Club:

> Why have these pseudo- "spiritual guides," these "historians of the French soul," these "humanists" abandoned Paris and the soil of France in such a cowardly way? Let them stay where they have gone with their panic, and let them die there of shame. They are not France.

At the outbreak of war Louis Aragon, then forty-two years old, had been called up for military duty and sent to the front below the Belgian border. After the collapse of the French lines, he was evacuated at Dunkirk to the English coast, to be transported back across the Channel to Brittany with the French troops who were expected to continue the war. Captured with his men, he escaped to France's sparsely populated southwest Dordogne, a region of hills and forests that sheltered many anti-Fascists in the German years. The Surrealist and Communist Aragon was at the dawn of a new career, as poet of the resistance. But his friends could always find him. The young writer Claude Roy caught up with Aragon and Elsa Triolet in Nice, where they were living in an apartment with views of the sea and of the old flower market. For Roy, Aragon and Elsa had never been as happy or as free as in those years of "misfortune and shackles."

Jean-Richard Bloch. Aragon's associate on *Ce Soir*, stayed on in Paris for a while, behind closed shutters; as a Jew he had more to fear. When the satirical illustrator Jean Bruller — soon to be the resistance author who signed his work "Vercors" — came to call on him, he learned that one of Bloch's sons was already in prison. Bloch's eighty-four-year-old mother would later be shipped to a German concentration camp, his daughter would be sentenced to death and have her head chopped off with an ax, and her own husband would be shot after escaping from a camp for hostages. Bloch himself was more fortunate. At the request of Germany's treaty partner, the USSR, he was allowed to cross Germany in a sealed train, as Lenin had before the October Revolution, to exile in the Soviet Union. In Moscow he was met at the station by Ilya

Ehrenburg, who was having troubles of his own. His novel on the fall of Paris seemed too anti-Fascist to the Soviet censors. When Stalin finally intervened to allow him to publish this attack on Nazi Germany, Ehrenburg realized that his country would soon be at war with Hitler.

Jean Guéhenno, of *Europe*, of *Vendredi*, had been transferred to a lycée in Clermont-Ferrand, in south central France. He wondered what he would do until the end of the German occupation. But in any case he promised himself to think clearly, and to employ ruse in order to continue to write. A segment of his diary of the occupation years entitled *Dans la prison* ("In Prison") was published through the underground. But he also wrote a lengthy biography of Jean-Jacques Rousseau during those years. In the summer of 1940 he was in Carcassonne, where he found Jean Paulhan and Julien Benda — Benda, "that curious old man [he was then seventy-two] . . . insupportable and yet sympathetic." Benda was bustling with projects. He showed Guéhenno a copy of the latest issue of *Gringoire*, once right-wing extremist, now extremist and collaborationist. It contained a caricature of Benda bearing the caption: "The bloodthirsty intellectual who dreamed of sacrificing France to the Jews." In his self-serving memoirs of the occupation years, the actor-director Sacha Guitry told how he assisted another old Jew, Henri Bergson (then eighty), in his return from the southwestern Landes region to his Paris home, obtaining for Bergson not only a German safe-conduct pass and sufficient gasoline, but a salute from German soldiers for this eminent representative of French culture. Presumably, the Germans in question did not realize that the famous philosopher was of Jewish origin. But the French Nazis did, for they attacked him on the Paris radio, and when he died soon after, he was buried without honors. Bergson had embraced the Catholic faith but refused baptism in order to remain among the persecuted.

After release from a detention camp in the Pyrenees, Arthur Koestler, fallen Communist, fallen Jew, lived in Paris during the *drôle de guerre*, often in hiding, for the French persisted in treating him as an enemy alien. One of his hiding places was Adrienne Monnier's apartment connected to her bookshop on the Rue de l'Odéon. Another hiding place was the headquarters of the French P.E.N. Club. When France fell Koestler joined the Foreign Legion, was arrested, and escaped to London via Algeria, Morocco, and Portugal. Before sailing from Marseille for North Africa, he encountered the critic and sociologist

Walter Benjamin, a German Jew. After being interned in a "voluntary labor camp" as an enemy alien, Benjamin was preparing his own escape over the mountains to Spain. He carried a visa for the United States, where he intended to join the growing community of émigré intellectuals in New York, but he also had a supply of morphine tablets to swallow in the event his escape plan failed. He killed himself at the Spanish border.

Manès Sperber enlisted in the French army, and was assigned to an émigré company. After the armistice he made his way to the south of France, aware of the danger he faced as a foreign-born Jew and an active anti-Nazi, and aware of the danger he represented to any friend who would give him shelter. False papers and true friends got him to Switzerland.

Willy Münzenberg was not that lucky. Though not a Jew, he was obviously a prime target of the Nazis and their French helpers. He and other anti-Nazis were released from a French detention camp before the arrival of the Germans. The freed prisoners split into small groups, Münzenberg heading east with two young men he had met in the camp. A few days later his bruised body was found in a forest, hanging from a tree. According to Koestler's information, the position of the branch to which the rope was attached excluded the possibility of suicide. Koestler attributed the death to Stalin's secret police, who also killed Trotski and the defecting intelligence officers Walter Krivitski and Ignatz Reiss. He could have added Thorez's confidant and adviser, Comintern agent Eugen Fried.

Until that troubled year, Jean-Paul Sartre and Simone de Beauvoir had been content to witness the action of others without participating in it. In Simone de Beauvoir's memoirs she confesses their passivity, blaming it on individualism and a feeling of helplessness. Sartre went further. He told an interviewer much later, "I had no political opinions and, of course, I didn't vote." He had admired the Popular Front, but from afar; at the time of the Munich concessions he was torn between his pacifist convictions and the urge to fight in his own way against Nazism, for he was an anti-Nazi "at least in my head." The 1939-40 war was the decisive event. Sartre was thirty-two when it began. Drafted, he served in a grim outpost on the dormant eastern front. In early February 1940 he was in Paris on leave, for a week of walking and talking with Beauvoir. He thought a good deal about what the postwar world might be like; he was determined not to remain aloof from politics as he had been until then. One had to assume responsibility for one's situation, and the way to do that was to commit oneself to action. Sartre was taken prisoner at the close of hostilities; by the time he returned to Paris at the end of March 1941, he was ready to participate in resistance activities.

But of what kind? In Beauvoir's Montparnasse hotel room he met with friends such as Maurice Merleau-Ponty, Jean-Toussaint Desanti, and his former student Jacques-Laurent Bost to discuss their options. Acts of individual violence? None of them could have thrown a grenade. Collecting intelligence? Making propaganda? That was more like it. Sartre scoured the Left Bank in search of better-organized groups. Their encounters took place at the Closerie des Lilas or in the nearby park, in the monk's cell student rooms of the Ecole Normale Supérieure, in hotel rooms. They called their movement Socialisme et Liberté, and in the first issue of their bulletin Sartre proclaimed that if Germany had won the war, their job would be to make sure it lost the peace.

During the 1941 school holidays, Sartre and Beauvoir slipped across the line dividing the German- and Vichy-controlled zones for a vacation (Sartre began the writing of his *Les Mouches*, "The Flies," in Marseille), but above all to begin making contacts with Parisians who had taken refuge in the south. They found Gide in Grasse; he suggested that Pierre Herbart might be a more suitable recruit than himself. To Sartre Gide seemed vague. Sartre told him that he was a "traveling salesman of ideas" — subversive and even dangerous ideas. He also told Gide that he was on his way to see Malraux, and Gide wished him "a good Malraux."

★   ★   ★

At the time of the declaration of war, we have seen, Malraux was traveling in southern France with his companion Josette Clotis. His attempts to enlist led to the tank corps (he was then thirty-eight). After months of idleness east of Paris, he had momentary exposure to battle before being made prisoner; his brother and their friends got him released from a detention camp in Sens. He made his way to the Riviera, where Dorothy Bussy (the sister of Lytton Strachey and Gide's English translator and lifelong admirer) put her Roquebrune villa at his disposal, completely furnished and with a butler. Manès Sperber, for whom the Mediterranean coast was a temporary refuge on his way to Swiss exile, found Malraux through Gide. To him we are indebted for a description of the villa, known as La Souco, whose dining room opened to the sea, the cliffs, and the bay of Monte Carlo on one side, and to the Italian coast on the other. The butler wore white gloves when serving, although Sperber remembered nevertheless eating rutabagas, the ubiquitous turnip of wartime France. The villa was on a tongue of land called Cap Saint-Martin, on the edge of an old village dominated by a medieval castle. "I'm waiting for you in a pink house, with an orange grove, a magnolia tree, and a little dancer of a cat," Malraux wrote to Josette Clotis. Friends who saw him in those years reported him as preoccupied with his writing — the aborted novel *Les Noyers de l'Altenburg* ("The Walnut Trees of Altenburg") and an essay on T.E. Lawrence.

The history of Malraux in wartime France is incomplete without referring to his life with Josette, who had now given him his first son, and who expected him to divorce Clara so that she could become the second Mrs. Malraux. Josette Clotis — with her striking young woman's features, her penchant for good clothes and good food and other kinds of fun — was not only a persuasive argument for the conquering hero's deserved rest. There is convincing evidence that she was a positive force, too, offering Malraux an alternative to his political commitment. The evidence takes the form of her notes and correspondence, used by her friend Suzanne Chantal in her biography of Josette, which was published with Malraux's endorsement. From the mid-1930s Josette Clotis had been an increasingly active influence on Malraux. In an intensely political milieu, she was stubbornly apolitical, with even a disposition to racism, feeling closer to the self-proclaimed Fascist Pierre Drieu La Rochelle than to any of Malraux's anti-Fascist friends. About Malraux and his Jewish wife she simply said, "Their noses aren't in harmony." She suggested that for a Jewess to bear a child out of wedlock mattered less than for a Christian like herself to do so.

We learn a good deal about Josette Clotis's influence on her man from Suzanne Chantal's book; it is clear that Josette's pressure on Malraux to desert the anti-Fascist struggle for her sake was constant. While he fought in Spain, she beseeched him to abandon the war and even the pro-Spain political rallies, and hide away with her in the country, or abroad. "You ought at least to have the time for your book, between Spain and their war [the coming Second World War], the time, also, to be a little tranquil and happy." He: "I won't let myself be eaten by you, ogress." But doesn't he? At the outbreak of the war she thinks: "If I could always keep the world's drama away from him . . . to carry it alone." She feared that the war would draw him back to "intellectuals outside of life, pederasts, crackpots, people who need to get tight, to take drugs, to sleep around, to go through psychoanalysis."

And so the forced retreat from Paris brought about by the German occupation was her chance. "At last it was the life that Josette so long desired, waited for," Suzanne Chantal wrote of life at La Souco. "The Mediterranean, being together, a pleasant and comfortable daily existence in a ravishing decor, with their butler Luigi, a handsome, curly-haired, smiling Italian, who can do everything, the housework, the cooking, and serve meals in a white jacket." Although Josette had written novels and a gossip column for *Marianne*, she was quickly bored by Malraux's friends. As for Drieu La Rochelle: "He's so good-looking! If all André's friends were like him!" Thanks to Drieu's connections with the Germans, she had received a pass to leave Paris with her first son — in grand style, in a mink coat and via sleeping car — to join Malraux on the Riviera. And Drieu became the godfather of her second son. Later, when Malraux finally joined the active resistance and was on an incognito trip to Paris, Josette alarmed him by making a telephone call to Drieu, to arrange an appointment to see him.

Nothing less than the foregoing must be known if we are to understand the astonishment of Sartre, in that first summer of French defeat, when he arrived for lunch at La Souco, to be served broiled chicken à l'américaine — with bacon strips and tomatoes, in an elegant setting — no mention of humble rutabagas this time. Malraux listened politely to Sartre's plan for resistance to the enemy occupation, but commented that he did not believe action possible. Only Russian tanks or American planes — neither of which was then engaged — could vanquish the Germans. Suzanne Chantal describes the parade of visitors who attempted to enlist Malraux, with no greater success: Jean Cassou, Roger Stéphane, Claude Bourdet among them. She cites Clotis's contemptuous reaction to these beseechings: "The one who speaks of risking prison flees abroad a week later. The other who dreams of a patriotic and underground magazine hopes to cover himself with glory in the back of a printer's shop, protected by his father-in-law's connections."

Boris Vildé, a linguist employed at the anthropological museum, the Musée de l'Homme in Paris, may have been one of the visitors to whom

Clotis referred. A founder of one of the very first resistance groups, with other members of the museum staff and their friends, Vildé was in southern France in January 1941, lying low. A few members of the network had already been arrested in Paris. He called on his mentor, Gide, but made no overture to him. He called on Malraux, and invited him to join their resistance effort. Malraux replied, "Let's be serious. Do you have arms?" On the contrary, the Vildé group had resolved to use every means except armed action. Malraux smirked and replied, "All this is very nice, but not serious," or so Vildé reported it back to Jean Cassou and others of the network. Malraux promised to join the resistance against the Germans when the United States joined the war. He was right about the dangers, for Vildé was soon arrested and, with other members of the network, executed by the Germans.

To his credit, as Sperber pointed out, Malraux did refuse to write for any Paris periodical, or even to have a book published in occupied France. If he rejected the solicitations of his friends who had already moved into the underground, it was in order to be available when he could fight with something more than words.

PART III

The German Years

16 Capturing the N.R.F.

No SINGLE EVENT in the cultural life of German-occupied France reveals as much about the forces involved as the takeover of *La Nouvelle Revue Française*. It may be difficult for readers familiar only with the postwar reincarnation of that magazine to understand its role in France between the wars, when it was the place one expected to find the best in contemporary literature and thought. The German ambassador in occupied Paris, Otto Abetz, was quoted as saying, "There are three forces in France: Communism, high finance, and the *N.R.F.*"

When the Gallimards left Paris for Normandy at the outbreak of war, much of the Left Bank followed them, at least in heart. And followed them down to the ramparts of Carcassonne, not far from the Spanish border. But if the Gallimards were to save their publishing business, they would have to do it in Paris. Getting started again was a matter of paramount importance not only for the publisher but for his authors, for many of them depended on their income from the company. Gide, for example, worried about the state of his finances when the Gallimard treasury was unable to disburse royalties; Valéry, Malraux, and other literary celebrities were in the same predicament.

Saving the house of Gallimard required a pact with the devil, and in that eclectic publishing house a devil was not hard to find. Pierre Drieu La Rochelle was virtually the house Fascist. His biographers show the gradual evolution of Drieu's ideology in those years preceding World War II, when it seemed as if he were training himself to be a better National Socialist, a better anti-Semite. On May 1, 1940 — the eve of the decisive German attack in northern France — he informed Gaston Gallimard that he would no longer write for an *N.R.F.* that published Louis Aragon. In his journal he noted: "In any case, I have decided never to set foot in the office of the *N.R.F.* dominated by Jews, Communists, old Surrealists, and all kinds of people who believe in principle that truth is on the left." Nonsense, Paulhan told him. "If there are people who think that the *N.R.F.* becomes Communist when it publishes a poem by Aragon, Fascist with you, Radical Socialist with Alain, pacifist with [Jean] Giono, and belligerent with [Julien] Benda, well, they are simply foolish."

Paulhan, Drieu confided to his journal, was a "little bureaucrat, pusillanimous and sly, wavering between hysterical Surrealism and the nutty rationalism of the Republic of Professors."

Suddenly, in less time than anyone had imagined possible, the Germans were in Paris, and everything, everything changed for Drieu. Just a week after the fall of Paris, he entered this remarkable note in his diary: "As for the *N.R.F.*, it's going to crawl at my feet. That pack of Jews, pederasts, timorous Surrealists is going to be shaken up miserably. Paulhan deprived of his Benda is going to scurry along the walls, his tail between his legs." He had indeed summed up the future of the *Nouvelle Revue Française*.

Luckily for Drieu, he had the patronage of his prewar German comrade Otto Abetz, who arrived in Paris shortly after the first Nazi troops to represent the German government; soon he had the rank of ambassador. As the promoter of prewar Franco-German cultural movements, Abetz had brought Drieu to Germany as early as 1934; as head of the French section of the Hitler Youth Movement and consultant on France to Hitler's foreign affairs adviser, von Ribbentrop, he had played a key role in Nazi propaganda in France. Abetz had come not to destroy Paris, but to maintain it in the service of Nazi Germany, and he intended to encourage creative activity consistent with this goal. Drieu convinced many of his peers in literary Paris that Abetz was a man of great understanding with whom dialogue was possible.

In the early weeks of the occupation, Abetz and Drieu agreed that the latter should publish a literary magazine, drawing on former contributors to the *N.R.F.* Almost immediately it made sense to both men that the simplest arrangement would be to take over the *N.R.F.* itself. Only Gaston Gallimard needed to be convinced, and he quickly saw the positive side of the bargain. With the *Nouvelle Revue Française* coming out regularly under German patronage, Gallimard's book-publishing activity would also benefit from protection. Jean Paulhan, to whom he explained this, found Gallimard naïve, just as he felt Drieu naïve in thinking that his N.R.F. would represent true Franco-German intellectual collaboration.

★   ★   ★

The weeks to follow saw frantic activity on the part of Drieu La Rochelle and equally frantic activity and certainly anguish on the Gallimard side. For the role of Gallimard was to convince the eminent founders and writers of the N.R.F. to pursue their cooperation with a magazine of the same name published with German encouragement, and with Drieu as master. Gaston Gallimard called on Gide in his temporary refuge in the hills of Cabris, to tell him that if they didn't revive the N.R.F., the Germans would simply take it over; and so Paulhan had to go, to be replaced by Drieu. At this stage, there was even the hope that Antoine de Saint-Exupéry and André Malraux would join Drieu's editorial board. Maria Van Rysselberghe found Gide "happily" uncertain about what to do, and she was able to persuade him to refuse to lend his name. But to show good will all the same, Gide offered to contribute an unpublished selection of his journal for the first issue. It would end with the promise, "To be continued." Gide thought that he could always hold back the next installment if he didn't like the way the magazine looked, and that would be a way of warning his readers.

Jean Paulhan made a desperate attempt to keep the revived magazine from calling itself La Nouvelle Revue Française, and thus to keep the precious symbol out of German hands. He lost the battle, not because of Drieu, but because one of the N.R.F.'s apolitical editors insisted that the name be kept.

Then, on the eve of publication of the first issue, the Germans raised the ante by marching in to shut down the publishing house. The pretext, so the story went, was that German officers billeted at the Gallimard manor in Normandy had discovered anti-Nazi books there. In fact the event was less fortuitous than that. As Gallimard described it to Gide, he had been asked to turn over 51 percent of control of the publishing business to a German publisher, and when he refused the Germans replied: "Very well, then we are going to close down your plant; you've got two hours to clear out of it, and the magazine won't be published any more."

Drieu was obviously the one to do something about *that*. Now, in addition to his privileged relations with Ambassador Abetz, he had made a new German friend in Gerhard Heller, an unusual Propaganda

Department aide. Heller was imbued with French culture and less than enthusiastic about Nazi brutality, making him an ideal representative of Germany from the point of view of French publishers and authors. During the final weeks of preparation for the *N.R.F.*, Drieu called on Heller at Propagandastaffel headquarters at 52, Avenue des Champs-Elysées. There was little to worry about, or so it seemed, for Abetz himself had assured Drieu that the magazine would not be subject to censorship. Heller added a personal word. As a student he had attended some of Drieu's lectures and had read some of his books. He suggested that they meet outside his office, and Drieu replied: "Let's say this evening, at my apartment." Heller warned him that he would have to show up in the uniform of a German officer, boots and all. "It doesn't matter." So that evening he crossed over to the Left Bank — a particularly luxurious section of the Left Bank, the broad Avenue de Breteuil behind the Hôtel des Invalides, where Drieu had a large bachelor's flat with a sweeping view of the skyline. It was not only Heller's first visit to a Frenchman's home, but he would have the first Scotch whisky of his life there. He also decided before the evening was over — but kept this to himself — that his own political opinions were to the left of Drieu's.

Heller himself went to Feldpolizei headquarters, where he convinced a captain, a professor of French in prewar days, that the forced closing of the Gallimard building deprived the publisher of pre-Christmas sales. Then he accompanied the police official to Rue Sébastien-Bottin, where Heller helped remove the seals (strips of paper bearing the Feldpolizei stamp). From an upstairs office, which he later learned was Paulhan's, Heller phoned Drieu to tell him that he could inform Gaston Gallimard that the company was open for business.

Shortly after that, on December 7, 1940, Gaston Gallimard visited Gide in Cabris again, carrying the first issue of Drieu's *Nouvelle Revue Française* and the story of his own tribulations at the hands of the Germans. Gide and his *petite dame* were convinced that it was because Gallimard had resisted the Germans that the *N.R.F.* could now be published, not because he had made concessions to them. And Gide found that first issue not bad at all.

"Well, this time, whether they like it or not, the French have begun," wrote Drieu in the collaborationist weekly *Le Fait*. "The Germans were there and it was necessary to work things out with the Germans . . . We are collaborating, and that is a guarantee of survival . . . Those in the government, those in business, intellectuals, are all collaborating . . ."

★   ★   ★

Holding in one hand a copy of a prewar issue of *La Nouvelle Revue Française,* and in the other a copy of the Drieu version, how could one tell the difference? The same off-white covers, with the title of the magazine and subject headings in red ink, the *nrf* colophon at the bottom. There was even a continuity in the numbering of the issues, and the selling price remained the same. The first issue of Drieu's *N.R.F.* was dated December 1, 1940. Faithful subscribers might remember that in the last issue before the fall of Paris, a novel by Aragon called *Les Voyageurs de l'impériale* had begun to appear, with a promise of continuation. But Drieu La Rochelle was not going to let his old friend and enemy, the personification of the Communist aesthetics, into the pages of *his* magazine.

That first issue contained as strong a representation of the old *N.R.F.* group as could have been hoped for, bolstered by the arrival of some of Drieu's friends: Jacques Chardonne, Jacques Audiberti, Marcel Aymé, Marcel Jouhandeau, Jean Giono, Paul Morand, and Ramon Fernandez were conspicuous contributors. There was even a brief contribution from Alain, the venerable Radical Socialist teacher-philosopher; music criticism by the composer Georges Auric; and book reviews by Brice Parain as well as by Kléber Haedens and Claude Roy. More, there was a promise to publish Marcel Arland, André Gide, Henry de Montherlant, Antoine de Saint-Exupéry, Saint-Pol-Roux, and Paul Valéry in future issues (but nothing ever came from Saint-Exupéry). The back cover of the second issue even promised forthcoming works by Paul Eluard, André Malraux, and François Mauriac (but neither Malraux nor Mauriac ever snapped at the offered bait).

Of course, the real change was in the presence of pro-Fascist, anti-Semitic newcomers, writers who would have received short shrift from Paulhan. They set the tone. Yet when a new poem by Paul Eluard filled five pages of the February 1941 issue, it contained a dedication to Jean Paulhan. The new *N.R.F.* also allowed itself a respectful tribute to the philosopher Henri Bergson and a homage to modernist James Joyce. One thing is certain: no lasting literature came out of the *Nouvelle Revue Française* during the occupation, no new work that would mark contemporary literary history; there was no equivalent of the serializa-

tion of Malraux's *La Condition humaine*, for example.   Camus's
L'Etranger could have been such an equivalent, but Camus flatly refused
to allow the *N.R.F.* in German Paris to publish it. In the long run, this
failure to win over the best of the present and the future convinced
Drieu, if not his readers, that his experiment in collaboration could not
be pursued.

Yet pressure continued to be applied to those whose prestige could
save the venture, and first and foremost to Gide. Fortunately for him,
he was virtually out of reach in southern France. Using all the tact he
could muster, Drieu expressed his gratitude to Gide for having allowed
him to publish selections from his diary, which showed that Gide had
confidence in Drieu's efforts to preserve the *N.R.F.* as the bastion of
French and world literature. But in the same mail with Drieu's message
came a copy of Jacques Chardonne's new book, *Chronique privée de l'an
1940*. Gide had read sections of it in the *N.R.F.* that alarmed him; now
he realized that Chardonne was offering a philosophy of collaboration
with the occupying authorities and invoking Drieu as one of its guiding
lights. This time Gide was firm. He asked that his name be removed
from the covers of Drieu's magazine, and then made his decision public
in *Le Figaro*; it was published alongside his severe review of Chardonne's
book.

But still the struggle for Gide's soul wasn't over. Gaston Gallimard
feared the consequences of Gide's withdrawal to his own strategy, and
told him as much. The defection would make Gallimard look bad and
represent a mortal blow to the magazine. Thanks to Maria Van
Rysselberghe, we have an eyewitness to the subtle and occasionally
unsubtle battle for Gide, which lasted almost as long as the
collaborationist *Nouvelle Revue Française* itself. Van Rysselberghe was
present when Malraux visited Gide in Nice in February 1942, informing
him that Drieu intended to call on him to solicit his help in making the
N.R.F. more literary, this time with Paulhan's participation. As for
himself, Malraux told Gide, "I have a daughter whose mother is Jewish,
and I am determined not to collaborate with anti-Semites like Drieu,
which doesn't diminish the consideration I have for him."

After two years of publishing a magazine that today seems sad and
drab, Drieu offered his own summing up in the January 1943 issue. The
"elders" had abstained from participating in his experiment? "Peace to
their silence." It had allowed him to put forward a new generation who
otherwise would have had to wait; and he thanked Paulhan for *his*

support. Drieu observed that he had been criticized for involving the magazine in politics, but that it always had been involved. The difference, he insisted, was his commitment to Hitlerism. "I am a Fascist because I have measured the progress of European decadence." His political position allowed him to criticize what he felt were the lukewarm tendencies of Vichy, with its "half concealed Catholics, badly washed democrats" who refused the opportunity to establish a true Fascism in France.

If there appears to us something morbid in the behavior of Drieu La Rochelle, there is something positively joyous in Paulhan's. Is it because Paulhan was playful even when being serious? That Drieu thanked him for his help on the magazine was proper, for there is evidence that Paulhan not only passed manuscripts on to Drieu, but that he openly solicited contributions, while himself refusing to write for the magazine because it barred Jews and other writers whom he had published before the war. Not surprisingly, Paulhan's office in the Gallimard building during Drieu's reign resembled a resistance cell. Dominique Desanti remembered being led up the stairs with her husband by Bernard Groethuysen, and tiptoeing past Paulhan's former office (then occupied by Drieu) to join a group that visited Paulhan once a week as a token of solidarity; they stood side by side in the little office as if in a subway train. And we know something that Drieu and presumably the Gallimards did not: that Paulhan was at the center of a whole world of underground resistance activities: secretly printed books, mimeographed news bulletins and tracts, and that he carried out most of this work in that small office not far from Drieu's.

On the surface Paulhan's relations with Drieu remained cordial, whatever either has been quoted as saying sotto voce. When Paulhan was arrested for his role in the Musée de l'Homme resistance network, for which, as we have seen, Boris Vildé and other leaders of the group were to be executed, Drieu acted quickly to get Paulhan out of the hands of the police, even though the charge was serious: Paulhan had hidden the underground movement's duplicating machine. On his release from detention on May 20, 1941, Paulhan expressed gratitude to Drieu, but he also explained that he could not have refused to conceal the machine when he knew that Anatole Lewitsky, the Musée de l'Homme anthropologist, was being followed; he added that he would hide Lewitsky himself if necessary. Lewitsky was executed with Vildé in February 1942.

★ ★ ★

The bargain was kept on the German side: Gallimard's book publishing blossomed. Just to cite names that are still remembered, in a typical month in 1941 the firm brought out books by Paul Morand, Armand Salacrou, Paul Eluard (a selection of poems), Henri Michaux, Jean Rostand — and Drieu La Rochelle, in addition to works of Ivan Turgenev and Sören Kierkegaard. In another month, in 1942, there were Camus (*L'Etranger*, "The Stranger"), Raymond Queneau, Paul Claudel, and a French translation of James Joyce's *Ulysses*. Perhaps there was a little more German literature than before, and a great deal more of the work of Drieu's N.R.F. companions? But most of the Gallimard stable was also being published. Jean-Paul Sartre's ambitious philosophical treatise, *L'Etre et le néant* ("Being and Nothingness"), appeared in Paris in 1943, as did Simone de Beauvoir's first novel, *L'Invitée* ("She Came to Stay"). No Jewish authors, living or dead, were published: that was also part of the bargain. For the house of Gallimard had to follow ground rules laid down by the Propagandastaffel and agreed to by the French Publishers Association. Thus Gaston Gallimard was able to keep his house out of German hands, and could stand up for Paulhan, Groethuysen, or Queneau when the Germans wished them removed as editors. It is also true that Gallimard published writers who could hardly have been appreciated by the Germans.

For if Aragon's *Les Voyageurs de l'impériale* could not be serialized in Drieu's N.R.F., it could appear as a book elsewhere in the same building, over the colophon of "Editions de la NRF." Later Aragon said that he had permitted Gaston Gallimard to change his unsympathetic German characters into Dutchmen. But after the war Aragon claimed to have discovered that his references to the Dreyfus affair had *also* been changed, in a manner that suggested that the author believed that Captain Dreyfus was guilty after all. The result, according to Aragon, was an anti-Semitic work. He set it right after the liberation of Paris.

If the Gallimard book company flourished, or seemed to, the magazine faced a losing battle with the cultural elite. Some alternative outlets for poems, essays, and stories were becoming available in southern France and elsewhere in the French-speaking world — or underground. By the spring of 1942, Drieu was ready to rid himself of the burden of *La Nouvelle Revue Française*, hoping to place it in the hands of a board of eminent literary personalities whose moral authority and reputation were uncontested. But how to persuade such persons to accept this unwanted gift? The negotiations, ultimately unsuccessful, were pursued for over a year, the chief negotiators being Gaston Gallimard, Paulhan, and Gerhard Heller, the Propagandastaffel representative.

We know from Drieu's private diary just how discouraged he was. In December 1942 he writes:

> I have put myself in a situation that is frightfully boring: the magazine, collaboration, all of that has irritated me from the beginning, almost constantly. And now that everything is working out badly, I am fed up with the part I'm supposed to play until the end. I often feel like killing myself without further ado.

The notion of suicide occurs again in his diary and in his conversation. Toward the end of the German occupation, it became a leitmotif.

In the underground *Les Lettres Françaises*, which was being produced with the active support of Drieu's office neighbor, Jean Paulhan, Drieu and his magazine had become a favorite target. Thus, in the January-February 1943 issue of *Les Lettres Françaises* — there was no January issue because the office where it had been duplicated was discovered by the Germans — an anonymous article, actually written by Claude Morgan, was entitled "Drieu's Anguish." It commented on Drieu's confession in La Nouvelle Revue Française that he was alone in his combat. "After a thousand pirouettes," the article said, "Drieu La Rochelle is suddenly discovering the depth of the abyss beneath his feet and he hangs back, like an animal who is afraid." In his private diary Drieu now scribbled:

> Certainly I'm afraid . . . To labor for two years for Europe when one isn't certain what the Germans want to make of it, with a few collaborationists who are divided among themselves by the Germans themselves, and in the middle of a population that wants Europe to be English, American, or Russian, this is wearying in the end. And weariness breeds fear, especially when the news is bad . . .

Another unsigned report, this one written by Paul Eluard, Edith Thomas, and Claude Morgan, was entitled "The Last Gasp of the *Nouvelle Revue Française*." Clearly based on inside information, it referred to a decline in subscriptions and to Drieu's plan to kill himself.

"The latest news," it concluded, "is that Drieu still hasn't committed suicide."

But the most forceful analysis of the situation was the work of Jean-Paul Sartre, in the form of another anonymous contribution to *Les Lettres Françaises* in the mimeographed issue of April 1943. "Like Montherlant, [Drieu La Rochelle] fought World War I for fun... Then he went back to women and was even more bored..." Sartre painted the portrait of a vengeful Drieu denouncing his enemies to the Vichy regime, threatening those in the zone occupied by the Germans with prison. "He amuses himself as he can, sadly . . . He didn't arrive at Nazism by elective choice; at the bottom of his heart, as at the bottom of Nazism, there was self-hatred, and the hatred of mankind that it engenders."

In the final months of the collaborationist N.R.F., Drieu allowed himself an escape from the depressing atmosphere of his magazine through writing, but he also ventured into the political arena to support the Jacques Doriot brand of Fascism through the Parti Populaire Français. His magazine was managed in all but name by Paulhan, who was also soliciting manuscripts for a successor magazine, which was expected to be published on Drieu's departure. But a magazine without Drieu was not to be.

"It is false to write that the Nouvelle Revue Française is dead," read a note in *Poésie 43*, the scarcely veiled pro-resistance monthly published in southern France. "The N.R.F ... has just reimbursed its subscribers... the N.R.F. of M. Drieu La Rochelle is no longer published. But hadn't it ceased to exist a long time ago?"

17 Paris vs. Vichy

As THE YEARS roll on, putting another generation between us and the Second World War, it becomes increasingly difficult to remember or even accept the notion that there were two Frances in the years of German occupation. One of them centered on Paris, under direct control of German military and civilian authorities, with only the token presence of a French government. The other was a fully structured "French State" whose capital was Vichy, whose leader was a World War I hero, Marshal Philippe Pétain, with nominal authority over a so-called unoccupied or "free" zone. In Paris the Germans were concerned with maintaining order while carrying on their war: this could mean tolerating a certain degree of cultural and even political pluralism. In Vichy, where Pétain had been voted full powers on July 10, 1940, by what survived of the prewar Third Republic, a coalition of ideologues relished the opportunity provided by defeat to promote a certain philosophy of the state and of the citizen's duty.

A paradox was quickly apparent. If one were a creative writer or artist — say, a Mauriac or a Picasso — one could be freer, or at least *feel* freer, in German Paris than in Pétainist Vichy. At least one was more likely to know where one stood. "I even go so far as to find preferable, for a while, German servitude with its painful humiliations, less prejudicial to us, less degrading, than the stupid discipline that Vichy offers us today." That from André Gide, writing in his diary on May 6, 1941, when he was living in the southern zone controlled by Vichy. He published these pages in wartime Algiers, warning in a preface that they represented immediate impressions left as they were written. (In his definitive version he removed only the word "stupid.") Comfortably installed in Vichy as a journalist, Maurice Martin du Gard, founder of *Les Nouvelles*

Littéraires, came up to Paris in August 1941 to observe this paradox at first hand. "Although this may seem strange," he told his diary, "to one who comes back to it after a long absence Paris gives the impression of ease and even of freedom . . . I overhear relaxed language on the back platforms of buses; at the sidewalk café tables no one worries about being overheard, as in Vichy."

Maurice Martin du Gard — who must be distinguished from his cousin Roger, Gide's comrade — lived in a Vichy of transplanted Parisians, yet envied those who could not resign themselves to abandon Paris, who returned to their beloved city soon after the June 1940 exodus to face "an unheated room, the anguish of the dawn with no employment certain, the poor food" — and the presence of the Germans. "But perfection and beauty are always dear."

A related paradox was that extremists — rabid Fascists, uncompromising racists — *also* preferred Paris, where they felt that their positions were better defined and defended. Thus Lucien Rebatet, in the autobiographical *Les Décombres,* condemned the softness of the Vichy government and of life in the shadow of Pétain. After a taste of it in the immediate months of defeat, Rebatet reported that "everyone who possessed the slightest 'Fascist' and anti-Jewish feeling came back to Paris." Fascist movements, fanatically anti-Jewish newspapers such as *Je Suis Partout, Au Pilori,* and *La Gerbe* flourished.

In Paris the Germans had found highly structured, preexisting institutions, such as the publishing trade, newspaper plants, radio studios; these often remained in the hands of the people who had run them before the Nazi victory. Vichy contained an elegant spa whose fame as a resort had endowed it with a considerable number of comfortable hotel rooms, but everything else had to be created. Yet with the attrition of the war and the trauma of defeat, some two-thirds of the newspapers and magazines of Paris and northern France disappeared. Prestigious publications such as *Le Figaro* and *Le Temps,* popular papers such as *Paris-Soir, L'Action Française,* and the Catholic *La Croix* migrated to the south, to be published in the Vichy area with lower printings and less influence. In this "free" zone, it was often enough to set up one's publishing enterprise a hundred miles away from Vichy — in Lyon, say — to feel free to defy Pétainist conformity.

★ ★ ★

It may have been Otto Abetz, the German occupation ambassador, writing his memoirs in a French prison in 1950, who first circulated the notion that occupied France produced more books in 1943 than any other country, including the United States and the United Kingdom. His figures were: 9348 books for France, against 8320 for the United States and 6705 for the U.K. The best available statistics show average annual title output for the years 1940-1944 for France, the U.S., and the U.K. as 6379, 9452, and 7874 respectively. France's own book trade organization provides further significant statistics for the war and occupation years:

YEAR	TITLES PUBLISHED	TRANSLATIONS (TOTAL)	FROM ENGLISH	FROM GERMAN
1940	5400	676	281	80
1941	3888	119	72	17
1942	7008	322	79	113
1943	7918	130	24	62
1944	8680	81	10	46

The official figures fail to confirm those offered by Abetz, but they do show vigorous book production, although of course they do not indicate what kind of books were available or in what quantities, and what books were *not* published. Abetz was also proud to be able to say that under German occupation France's scientific and intellectual activity was comparable to that of prewar years. No journalist or author was made to suffer for prewar anti-German opinions; even works by Jean Giraudoux, the French government's war propaganda chief, could be published, along with works of the notoriously anti-German Paul Claudel, or of an ideological adversary such as Jean-Paul Sartre. All true. Indeed, we have the testimony of André Thérive, a frequent contributor to the press of occupied Paris, that on the opening night of the Comédie-Française production of Claudel's *Le Soulier de satin*, when the author climbed to the stage amidst ovations to embrace the leading lady, the German generals in the front boxes shouted bravos. One would have to know something of the personal commitments of particular French men and women — whether he or she was Jewish, for example — to be able to observe differences in the Left Bank scene before and after June 1940.

Not everyone bothered or cared to make the distinction. In June 1942, Jews were required to wear yellow stars on their clothing. But Simone de Beauvoir noted that many ignored the order, and she herself never saw anyone wear a yellow star at Montparnasse or at Saint-Germain-des-Prés. Presumably not many Jews frequented cafés in such exposed neighborhoods in those times, and indeed, a month after she made her observation, Jews were barred from all public places, including restaurants, movie theaters, and libraries (although Beauvoir's bolder Jewish friends continued to turn up at the Café de Flore). Most Jews of prominence had abandoned Paris for isolated corners of southern France, or for safer asylum abroad. Certainly there were none in the theater, the concert hall, on the radio: the French Commissariat General for Jewish Questions saw to that. Jews were not allowed to work in publishing or printing, but in theory they could write books, at least at the beginning of the occupation. Later on, at the request of the Germans, French publishers agreed not to publish them.

Otherwise, German censorship seemed more flexible than Vichy's. If there was no apparent challenge to Nazi thought and goals, the work passed, while Vichy's censorship was founded on rigid doctrine: nationalism, religious conservatism, the repudiation of Socialism. Another reason a writer took a greater risk in Vichy was that the Pétain regime was staffed with native Frenchmen, who knew more about the mentality of the various authors whose works were submitted than the Germans. Thus the Germans allowed Gallimard to publish poetry by Louis Aragon, while Vichy denied circulation in its zone of the notorious Communist's book. Even after November 1942, when the Germans took over the southern half of the country, the Pétainist regime's censorship continued, and a work could still be distributed in Paris but barred from southern France.

Fortunately for the German occupation army, whose small group of French-language specialists at Propagandastaffel headquarters could hardly have read the thousands of books submitted for publication each year, help soon came from the French publishers themselves. In September 1940, the French Publishers Association signed a convention with the Propagandastaffel making each house responsible for its own production. The French promised to produce nothing that was anti-German, no books that were banned in Germany. And when a publisher could not decide whether a book might be acceptable, the Association was to carry out prepublication censorship. The convention also provided for the elimination of undesirable books that had been put on the market before the agreement was signed.

The Publishers Association lost no time in circulating a list of "Works Withdrawn from Sale by Publishers or Forbidden by the German Authorities." Dated September 1940, it was officially known as the "Liste Otto," a curious tribute to German Ambassador Otto Abetz. In a preface, French publishers justified the list by their desire "to contribute to the creation of a healthier atmosphere and the concern to establish conditions necessary to a more accurate and objective understanding of European problems." Their preface continued on an ideological note:

> These are books that, by their lying and biased nature, have systematically poisoned French public opinion; especially undesirable are books by political refugees or Jewish writers who, betraying the hospitality granted them by France, promoted war unscrupulously in the hope of furthering their selfish goals.

This first "Liste Otto" contained all the obvious books — all of Benda and Léon Blum, Malraux's anti-Fascist novels *L'Espoir* and *Le Temps du mépris* (but not earlier works such as *La Condition humaine*), Thomas and Heinrich Mann, Sigmund Freud, Arthur Koestler, Louis Aragon, Paul Nizan, Erich Maria Remarque *(All Quiet on the Western Front)*, eight works of Vicki Baum including *Grand Hotel*, the books of Stefan Zweig (when Zweig killed himself in exile in Brazil in 1942, *Le Figaro* was not even permitted to mention the death of this German Jew, let alone his life and work). Heinrich Heine was also on the list, and this Jewish-born German soon disappeared from literary history in France as he had in Germany.

Even authors who became sympathetic to the occupation, or whose ideas were not inconsistent with Vichy doctrine, were on the list with their anti-German books. Ironically, in this period when Nazi Germany and Stalin's Soviet Union were collaborating, the "Liste Otto" banned anti-Soviet works, such as a book by Trotski translated by Victor Serge. And Gaston Gallimard notified Gide that among the 153 proscribed titles were his *Retour de l'U.R.S.S.* and the follow-up *Retouches*, as well as Gide's *Journal*. (In fact, *Retour* and *Retouches* were not on the first list at all, but on the second, and the *Journal* appeared on neither.)

In July 1942, over the signature of the president of the French Publishers Association, a second "Liste Otto" replaced the original one. It included books missed the first time and still older titles found in second-hand bookstores; now the police were scanning the bookstalls along the Seine for dusty copies of such books. An explanatory note pointed out that the ban now included translations from English, with the exception of the classics, as well as from Polish, a culture that would be annihilated, according to Nazi doctrine. The ban on books by Jews excluded scientific works, but biographies of Jews, even if written by non-Jews, were also forbidden. "These measures," the president of the Publishers Association explained, "which do not seem to cause a serious material prejudice to French publishing, allow French thought the means to continue its development, as well as the civilizing mission of bringing peoples together."

Any exceptions to the ban on translations from English (save for classics) would have to be approved case by case by the German occupying authorities. Exceptions might include George Bernard Shaw, specifically identified as Irish, and Rabindranath Tagore, a "Hindu." As examples of biographies of Jews to be banned, the Association cited works on the composers Jacques Offenbach, Giacomo Meyerbeer, and Darius Milhaud. The third "Liste Otto," released in May 1943, again with the endorsement of French publishers, contained an appendix listing several hundred Jewish authors writing in French. But some who felt that they had no place on the list complained to the Association, which transmitted their protests to the Germans. The reply came that the list of Jews was only a first effort, based on information supplied by the publishers themselves and other sources; that because of "the indifference manifested in France until now to making known the names of writers of Jewish origin, it is natural that this first list contains errors." The Publishers Association itself insisted that it had nothing to do with a list that "by its nature necessitates an investigation for which it is not qualified."

Soon the system became routine. When a work was banned, its publisher would announce its withdrawal from sale by advertising in the book trade magazine *Bibliographie de la France*. In the February 5, 1943, issue, for example, Gallimard served notice that it was no longer selling Antoine de Saint-Exupéry's *Pilote de guerre* ("Flight to Arras"), by order of the occupation authorities. Gerhard Heller, the Propagandastaffel officer sympathetic to French writing and writers, once found himself inside a vast garage on the Avenue de la Grande Armée where seized books were piled up, awaiting destruction. A "frightful spectacle," he told his diary. Heller was reminded of the Nazi book burnings he had seen at the University of Berlin in 1933. He was ashamed for his country; later he would read Sartre, quoting Marx, to the effect that shame is a "revolutionary sentiment."

★　★　★

No attempt will be made to assess the effect on French literature past and contemporary of the combined censorships of the Germans, Vichy, and the French themselves. Certainly some very important works, or lesser works by important authors, were published during the years of censorship. It is also true that the climate of oppression did not encourage creation. If Camus could publish *L'Etranger* and other works conceived far from Paris, the manuscripts Malraux produced in this period were inferior specimens of Malraux. Gide, after hesitation, agreed to be published under the Germans, as did Sartre and Simone de Beauvoir; Paulhan, Mauriac, Eluard, Aragon also published some of their books under German censorship (and others in the underground). "Alas! how much kneeling and renunciation there is in French letters in 1941!" Jean Zay, Léon Blum's Minister of Education, wrote from a Vichy prison cell (before his murder by French Fascists). "If a few great writers save honor by the dignity of their silence, how many others, and not the least among them, rush to serve the new gods, curiously forgetting their past and their own works!"

18 The Structures of Collaboration

THERE WERE COLLABORATIONISTS through conviction, sincere French Fascists bewitched by the myth of a super race, by the sheer virility of the Nazi revolution. There were embittered antidemocrats, antisocialists, anti-Semites, and those seeking revenge for the victory of the partisans of Captain Dreyfus, who discovered a kinship in Hitlerian ideology. At the other extreme were businessmen concerned with carrying on profitable enterprises by manufacturing and building for the German war effort — or publishing and selling books or magazines or newspapers. Perhaps the middle range of collaborationists were more pathetic. They simply intended to continue to do what they had been doing before the German army occupied France. Certainly most movie and stage directors, writers for the theater or the screen, actors and actresses, and performers of all kinds, willingly pursued their careers, generally without malicious intent. Journalists, essayists, even novelists, and their publishers had a harder time, for it was more difficult for them to avoid serious content, to avoid committing themselves for or against.

Collaborationism was not defined after the fact — say, at the moment of the liberation of France. It was a conscious policy elaborated by the Germans and their sympathizers, and accepted by the nominal government of France. On October 24, 1940, Philippe Pétain, Chef de l'Etat Français, crossed into the German-occupied zone to meet Chancellor Adolf Hitler in Montoire-sur-le-Loir, a small town in the château country south of Paris. Whatever the actual dialogue between the two leaders and their aides may have been — whatever the negotiations, reticences, and second thoughts — what came out of

Montoire as far as the French were concerned was Pétain's public declaration on October 30:

> It is with honor and to maintain French unity — a unity of ten centuries in the framework of constructing the new European order — that I am today entering the path of collaboration... This collaboration must be sincere. It should include a patient and trusting effort . . .

All sources agree: this declaration by a still-respected hero of France had a deep influence. In 1940, most of the French were "Pétainists."

On his arrival in France at the beginning of the occupation, Otto Abetz served as the chief representative of the German civil government. Soon he had the rank of ambassador, and by November 1940 he had taken over the German Embassy on the Rue de Lille. But unlike other ambassadors in Paris or elsewhere, he exercised power. In the organizational structure of the German occupation authorities, responsibility for control of French cultural production — books and periodicals, theater and music and the other arts — belonged to the Propaganda Abteilung (Propaganda Department), which reported to the German military command. Operational responsibility was vested in the Propagandastaffel on the Champs-Elysées, which employed separate staffs to deal with literature, music, general culture, active propaganda. Here is where French publishing was watched, encouraged, censored; everything produced in Paris in the four years of German occupation owed something, for good or for evil, to this office. If it has a place in this story, it is largely thanks to the unorthodox behavior of Sonderführer (or lieutenant) Gerhard Heller. As the occupation became a settled fact of life, the components of the German command cooperated ever more closely; by 1942 there were regular meetings concerning cultural production between appropriate officials of the German Embassy, the Propagandastaffel, the Sicherheitsdienst (SD) — this was the SS Security Service, often confused with the Gestapo, which had only a small staff and little responsibility in occupied France — and the Deutsche Institut (German Institute), a cultural propaganda organization that took over the Polish Embassy on Rue Saint-Dominique, a fine eighteenth-century mansion built for a princess of Monaco.

The lavish German receptions in the grim occupation years were popular affairs. Alfred Fabre-Luce recorded his impressions of one held at the embassy — Ambassador Abetz standing virtually alone in one drawing room, while the adjacent room containing the buffet was besieged. "I never saw people eat with such enthusiasm . . . The blocks of butter that disappeared rapidly, the chicken wings that flew into eager mouths were investments for which the Propagandastaffel hoped to earn interest later on . . . " In his journal, the German officer-author Ernst Jünger offered a similar perception of an evening at the German Institute; the guests of director Karl Epting included sculptor Arno Breker, Abel Bonnard, Vichy Minister of Education and a member of the Académie Française, and Pierre Drieu La Rochelle. "And then," records Jünger, "a bunch of hack writers, of the sort one can live without. All these people stew in a mixture of self-interest, hatred, fear, and some already wear on their forehead the stigmata of horrible deaths." But few of the eminent Parisians cited in the memoirs of Karl Epting's widow as having joined these soirées at the German Institute — famous authors and playwrights and at least one of Paris's prestigious literary publishers, famous actors and actresses and stage directors, artists and scientists and men of the Church —were seriously chastised after the departure of the Germans.

In practice, the behavior of the occupying authorities varied. Those imbued with doctrine saw no reason to avoid brutality when dealing with the French. Others, who served the Nazi cause in another way, acted more tactfully; this allowed them to make maximum use of France and the French in the German war effort. Fortunately for the Germans, there were legions of French men and women ready to make the job easy, and publishing houses with glorious names were prepared to include pro-Nazi books, violently anti-Semitic pamphlets, in their catalogues. Bernard Grasset was one of the Germans' luckiest catches. An employee observed how the Germans quickly identified Grasset as a special friend, flattering him as "the greatest French publisher." In his circulars to booksellers, Grasset boasted that he had the endorsement of the occupation authorities.

Nearly every major contemporary author had been published — and many were discovered — by Grasset. That included Marcel Proust, who had been too unorthodox for the N.R.F. clique at the beginning; André Malraux, who later went over to Gallimard; and François Mauriac, who did not. Bernard Grasset also stood apart from his peers in the energy he employed on behalf of his German friends. In a series called In Search of France, he published the most ardent of the collaborationists, such as Jacques Doriot, Drieu La Rochelle, and Georges Suarez (who was executed at the liberation of France). Grasset set forth his own views in a book also called "In Search of France" (A la recherche de la France), published in 1940. "The French," he wrote, "find themselves entirely in the hands of a nation that has risen to the summit of unity and strength, and by the virtue of one man."

No less pathetic was the case of Robert Denoël, whose publishing house actually received German capital during the occupation of Paris. After the liberation it was remarked that he had published "only" eleven pro-Nazi books during the occupation, among them anti-Semitic manuals (such as one whose title translates as "How to Recognize the Jew"), a collection of Hitler's speeches, and the two most famous anti-Semitic literary works of the time: a new edition of Céline's Bagatelles pour un massacre, and Lucien Rebatet's Les Décombres. But during the occupation years Denoël also advertised two prewar books by well-known authors of the left — Louis Aragon's Les Beaux Quartiers and Eugène Dabit's Hôtel du Nord — and published the stories of Aragon's companion, Elsa Triolet, announcing the work of this Russian-born Jew in such unlikely media as the intensely anti-Semitic, pro-German La Gerbe. "The author... is on the road to celebrity," read one of Denoël's advertisements for Triolet. (Aragon's biographer believes Triolet intended in these stories to write "Resistance prose.") Even as Denoël announced Triolet's march toward celebrity, she was hiding out with Aragon in Villeneuve-lès-Avignon, where a roundup of Jews was under way.

The venerable house of Calmann-Lévy, founded in 1836 by Michel Lévy — the original publisher of Gustave Flaubert, of Alexandre Dumas father and son, of Sainte-Beuve and George Sand — was owned by Jews. After the inevitable confiscation, its name had to be changed, and eventually it became "Editions Balzac." Paul Léautaud reports Gaston Gallimard as telling him in September 1941 that a consortium of publishers had been formed to acquire Calmann-Lévy to prevent a German take-over. Apparently this joint effort failed, for a letter dated January 20, 1942, has been found in the files of the Commissariat General for Jewish Questions from one of the publishers of this group (and not the least among them), offering to purchase the Jewish-owned house and to create for it an editorial board that would include Pierre Drieu La Rochelle and Paul Morand (another familiar signature in the press of the period). This publisher assured the authorities that his company "Is an Aryan house, with Aryan capital."

During their tenure, the French carpetbaggers who managed Calmann-Lévy sold off everything of value, including letters from the eminent literary men and women of the nineteenth century. The house also became a manufacturer of mediocre works not destined to survive the German years. As its manager of the time confided to Paul Léautaud, everything that is published sells.

Hardly any well-known publisher of prewar significance went without procollaborationist and even pro-Nazi books in its catalogue then. The most noble found it necessary or useful to put forward works in the spirit of the times, such as an *Anthologie de la Nouvelle Europe* offering a literary alibi for collaboration, or an anthology of German poetry omitting the work of Heinrich Heine.

A resolution voted by the underground Comité National des Ecrivains (National Committee of Writers) entitled "Warning to Publishers" declared that the enemy had its helpers inside Parisian publishing houses. Collaborationists were in a position to examine the manuscripts submitted by patriotic writers, so they could denounce or blackmail them, while publishers were inundating the bookstores with German literature and pro-Hitler propaganda. The resistance writers promised that any person who lost a job because of the occupation would get it back after the war. The Writers Committee also intended to oversee the purging of guilty publishers, without prejudice to whatever legal action the postliberation authorities might take.

Writers who chose not to remain silent during the German years could choose among a wide variety of periodicals, from the scrupulously non-political to the violently racist — and such periodicals had to be taken seriously when they exposed the hiding places of anti-German, anti-Fascist militants, or of Jews, so that the French police or the German Sicherheitsdienst could find them. Some of these publications were old and once-respected institutions that had been unable to resist the material temptations of the New Order. Others were newcomers, published expressly to take advantage of the prevailing climate; an example was *Au Pilori*, launched with the subtitle "weekly of combat against the Judeo-Masonry." The literary right was represented by *Je Suis Partout*, thanks above all to the *normalien* Robert Brasillach and his team of witty and cruel contributors, who specialized in polemics. Its claimed circulation during the occupation was in the neighborhood of 200,000 copies. On one occasion, *Je Suis Partout* denounced what it called the "Gaullists" of Nice, like Louis Aragon and Claude Roy, even naming the bar in which they congregated. Soon after, Roy received the visit of a police inspector. Aragon's friend Pierre Seghers remembered that *Je Suis Partout* was pleased to report the news of the death of Max Jacob in a detention camp: "Jew by race, Breton by birth, Roman Catholic by religion, sodomist by habit," was its epitaph.

★   ★   ★

Perhaps the most curious intellectual product of German Paris was *Comoedia*. It was a weekly — still another — in the prewar tradition, in the format of a large daily. From the start, *Comoedia* attracted the contributions of eminent figures in letters and the arts who seemed willing to believe that a strictly cultural enterprise could exist under enemy occupation; because it would not deal with politics, the paper need not compromise itself or its contributors. The list of writers may have reminded readers of the prewar *Nouvelle Revue Française*, for only the most committed anti-Fascists were missing, and of course Jews. Marcel Arland, a close associate of the *N.R.F.* group before the war and after, was responsible for *Comoedia's* literary department. His front-page review of Camus's *L'Etranger* in the July 11, 1942, issue was the first significant presentation of that new novel in occupied Paris.

Even Sartre, committed in principle to anti-Nazism, could believe that a free publication might appear under the German regime. When the publisher of *Comoedia* outlined his plan for a strictly cultural newspaper and asked Sartre to handle the book-review column, Sartre agreed. A translation of Melville's *Moby Dick* had just been published by Gallimard, and Sartre wished to write about it; he did, in *Comoedia*. But then he had second thoughts, feeling that the paper was less independent than it had been presented. Still, Simone de Beauvoir tells us in her journal, in their opinion *Comoedia* was different from the rest of the occupation press, because it protested against denunciations of the kind in which *Je Suis Partout* specialized, while defending works that contradicted Fascist and Vichyist morality. "Nevertheless, the first rule on which resistance intellectuals agreed was that they shouldn't write in the press of the occupied zone," concluded Beauvoir. (When a young admirer of Albert Camus showed him an article he had written about Camus for *Comoedia*, Camus advised him not to publish it in Paris. So the young man gave it to *Confluences*, a magazine published in Lyon.)

Throughout the occupation, *Comoedia* presented familiar names in literature and the arts, as if cultural life could be carried on as usual on streets patrolled by Hitler's army. It published a weekly page devoted to "Europe," which glorified German literature and emphasized the affinities of French and German culture. Jean Paulhan felt that the paper's literary columns had never contained a dishonorable phrase, but the underground resistance didn't see it quite that way. *Les Lettres Françaises*, in November 1943, declared: "Everyone knows that *Comoedia* devotes a 'European' page to Nazi propaganda each week. This is why the paper is published and seeks to bring together in its other pages eminent literary, artistic, and theatrical names."

19 Everybody Collaborated

IF ONE WERE ABLE to tabulate the memoirs of those years, one might conclude that nearly everyone in Paris resisted the Germans during the occupation. But it is also possible to make the case that "everybody collaborated." The persistence of the latter notion may in part result from the efforts of the collaborationists themselves, for whom it was comforting, even useful (often to save themselves from jail or worse), to prove that they were not alone in this possibly criminal activity. If everyone was compromised, how could anyone be punished?

The "everybody collaborated" line is disseminated notably in the recollections of those who associated with the German occupying forces, and who attempted to exonerate themselves by offering a record of all the others who were similarly associated. That so many of the most active collaborationists were never punished, or received only minimal sentences (which were soon suspended and later amnestied, making it unlawful under French law even to refer to the original convictions!), facilitated their return to good society, where they often attained positions of influence, as publishers of newspapers, television and radio stars, members of the Académie Française. Such persons are likely to perpetuate the complaisant notion that "everybody collaborated" (or the equally current notion that "everybody resisted") even down to our day.

Fighting for his life in his trial in January 1945 for collusion with the enemy, and questioned about his relations with the Germans in Paris, Robert Brasillach told the court: "I met a certain number of people at the German Institute, a certain number of writers, several of whom would perhaps be embarrassed if I didn't have the charity to remain silent about their names." Pursuing this defense, he offered some details:

Let me say that the only time in my life that I met M. Gallimard, an eminent publisher today, was at the German Institute. Another whom I saw at the German Institute was M. [Georges] Duhamel. (*laughter*) I lunched with Jean Giraudoux at the German Institute and I don't believe that Jean Giraudoux was a traitor.

Brasillach was sentenced to death and shot by a firing squad, but his brother-in-law, Maurice Bardèche, published an open letter to François Mauriac in 1947 repeating Brasillach's affirmations and adding that "everyone" autographed his books to Lieutenant (Gerhard) Heller (Mauriac was one who did), "that Aragon was sheltered by Denoël, that Paulhan was saved by Drieu . . ."

Jean Galtier-Boissière, editor and bookseller, was friendly with many of the collaborationists, although he himself rejected that option. But after the liberation, he took obvious joy in exposing what he called "The Hypocrisy of the Purge" (the title of a series of articles he wrote for a Paris daily newspaper). Attacked for these articles in the left-wing press, he also seemed to enjoy exposing the ambiguous behavior of his left-wing critics. Galtier-Boissière concluded: "During the occupation there were thousands of heroes and hundreds of traitors. Between the two groups, the immense majority of the population opposed to enemy propaganda a force of inertia that, by its weight, annihilated all the efforts and all the ruses of collaborationism."

Surely no one personified the ambiguities of the occupation years better than Paul Léautaud, or perhaps it is because we have a frank record of his doings and his thinking (four dense volumes of his *Journal littéraire* deal with the German years) that the contradictory reactions of Léautaud and his friends are so vivid even today. Coming into town each day from a bleak neighborhood on the outskirts of Paris to a routine job at the Mercure de France, picking up food for his dinner and for his pets along the way, Léautaud saw a good deal of the literary Left Bank, and if he did not understand everything he saw or heard, he had the ability to record it honestly so that we can try to understand. This very average person never knew for sure whether he should admire the Germans because their anti-Semitism was a logical development of his own, or hate them because he was a patriot. He was skeptical of the most extreme statements of the collaborationists — the descriptions of kindly German officers by a Jacques Chardonne or a Drieu La Rochelle, for example. Yet he wrote for Drieu's magazine and was happy to be recommended to the German director of Radio Paris for a broadcasting job. Léautaud felt that the French deserved what had happened to them for declaring war on Germany. "In what way can we complain about the physical presence of the Germans? Polite, straightforward, almost unobtrusive," he told a friend. He opposed acts of resistance. "The Germans are our masters. They are on our soil... I find the behavior of these [resistance] people stupid . . . Do they think they are going to change anything?"

Perhaps the right word for it is not ambiguity, but color-blindness. A number of leading authors pursued their careers during the German years with no apparent misgivings. A writer concerned with nothing more political than the relations between the sexes could publish books in a Paris dominated by swastikas, just as an actor could mouth someone else's words, a musician perform concert music without intelligible content. If true collaboration with the Nazi authorities was an ugly fact, the transgressors generally an unsavory lot, the innocent, color-blind behavior of so many well-known authors is almost always interesting, and it may be worth the effort to turn the pages of Drieu's *Nouvelle Revue Française* to separate the consciously corrupt from the color-blind. Criticizing Colette for publishing in a collaborationist newspaper, the underground *Lettres Françaises* suggested that she had not realized in what company she was going to be published. "And this maneuver," the resistance organ explained, "proves that in giving the press controlled by the occupying forces the least bit of article, even one without political significance, a writer plays his part in the concert of enemy propaganda orchestrated by Goebbels . . ."

★   ★   ★

Consider the careers of that singular couple, Jean-Paul Sartre and Simone de Beauvoir. In point of fact, the German occupation coincided with their celebrity. Sartre's plays *Les Mouches* ("The Flies") and *Huis clos* ("No Exit") were first performed in German-occupied Paris. Beauvoir's first novel was published then. In her memoirs, usually as frank as Léautaud's and often as ingenuous, Beauvoir records her delight with an article by Marcel Arland praising her *L'Invitée* ("She Came to Stay"). The article was published in *Comoedia* — "a real newspaper," she exclaims — and never mind that it was published, as her book was, in Nazi Paris. She was also touched when Ramon Fernandez, although solidly in the enemy camp, walked into the Café de Flore — where he usually never set foot — to congratulate her on *L'Invitée*. She even thought that she had a chance to win the celebrated prize of the Goncourt Academy, at a time when that Academy was dominated by collaborationist writers. Sartre gave her a message from the National Committee of Writers to the effect that she would be allowed to accept the prize if it came, provided she not give interviews or articles to the press. A strange message, since in *Les Lettres Françaises*, the National Committee had already warned that the Goncourt Academy "would have much to answer for."

In Paris, Beauvoir worked for the Pétain government's Radio Nationale, producing a cultural program of her own invention. The Sartre-Beauvoir personal code of behavior allowed her to work for this propaganda organization: "it all depended on what one did there." She later described her productions as "insipid," but of course they provided some of the filling that made the Vichy station worth listening to, and thus more dangerous to unsophisticated listeners.

Meanwhile Sartre was coming to public notice with *Les Mouches* — and no matter that the Sarah Bernhardt Theater where it was produced had been purified by having the Jewish actress's name removed from over the doors. The ambiguity of the situation was underlined when both the *Pariser Zeitung*, the newspaper of the German occupation forces, and the underground *Lettres Françaises* praised the play. In truth, Sartre's play was far more ambiguous than his admirers then and since have wished to believe. When *Huis clos* was staged at the Left Bank Théâtre du Vieux-Colombier, the opening night was remembered as "the event that opened the golden age of Saint-Germain-des-Prés in making the neighborhood known, not yet to the crowds . . . but to the drawing rooms of Paris and of France."

Pariser Zeitung praised Sartre's play as "a theatrical event of the first order." The same critic also liked Albert Camus's *Le Malentendu* ("The Misunderstanding"), when it was produced in the final weeks of the occupation. If the Germans enjoyed the philosophical adventure of tolerating Sartre and Camus on the Paris stage, the collaborationists were often more severe, for they sensed the danger of ideological contamination. Still, Camus's *L'Etranger* and *Le Mythe de Sisyphe*, and Sartre's *L'Etre et le néant* — all published by Gallimard during the occupation — became literary events without stirring political passions, for they contained no obvious political references.

From that point on, Sartre and Camus were central figures of the intellectual Left Bank. Authors of little or no political significance, whose works were even less concerned with the here and how, enjoyed free sailing in German Paris, and a better chance of rapid success in the absence of their potential rivals — those who were banned, in the underground, or who refused to be published in their occupied country. If an author or director or actor refused to be represented by a work at that time, his place was quickly taken. Did those who came to prominence between 1940 and 1944 realize that their careers had been facilitated by the vacuum created by the Nazis, and that their competition had often become prisoners and inmates of concentration camps, unable to speak, to write, to publish?

Among those conspicuously present was Paul Claudel, already a classic author. His *Le Soulier de satin*, directed by Jean-Louis Barrault at the Comédie-Française, was the theatrical event of occupied Paris. The production of Jean Giraudoux's *Sodome et Gomorrhe* brought the debut of a young actor, Gérard Philipe, while Philipe's future director, the innovative Jean Vilar, was making his own debut at the head of a small company. Jean Anouilh and Sacha Guitry were familiar names on the stage by then, and the list of motion picture directors and stars who appeared with new films under German censorship may surprise the unsuspecting.

If Jean Cocteau and Jean Marais were troubled in their careers of dramatist and actor-director, it was not for anti-Nazi behavior, but because their aesthetics and life-style were broad targets for the young Fascists who ruled the streets of German Paris. This did not prevent Cocteau from being represented on the Paris stage, or from associating with eminent Nazis such as Arno Breker, the sculptor and Hitler's chosen guide through conquered Paris. When Cocteau complained to his German friends about the attacks on him in *Je Suis Partout*, they replied: "It's the French who are attacking you; you're not liked by your colleagues." Marais physically assaulted the distasteful collaborationist critic Alain Laubreaux and was saved from arrest, it is said, by a phone call from Cocteau to Breker — the German had given his private number to Cocteau for just such an emergency. Perhaps it was Cocteau's charm, his many-faceted talent, that saved him from the postliberation purge that claimed so many less imaginative peers, nor did it hurt that he had drafted a petition to Ambassador Abetz asking that the Germans liberate Max Jacob from detention — a petition signed by leading collaborationists as well as by Pablo Picasso.

If collaboration was encouraged by the weak wills of so many men and women of letters and cultural celebrities, the behavior of French Communists facilitated it from the beginning. We have seen that Stalin was Hitler's active partner in the war against Poland, in the breaking up of that country, from the outbreak of World War II in September 1939 until June 1941, when Hitler turned against his ally. To this day the controversy has not ceased in France over the role of the Communist leadership in the early months of the occupation. What is certain, as we have seen, is that representatives of the French Communist Party formally asked the Germans for permission to resume publication of L'Humanité in occupied Paris. "We have been the only ones to protest against the war, to demand peace at a time when it was dangerous to do so," the delegates argued. "L'Humanité will have as its task the pursuit of a policy of peace in Europe and the drawing up of a German-Soviet friendship pact, thus to create the conditions for an enduring peace." Even without German endorsement, the underground L'Humanité attacked Britain's "Imperialist" continuation of the war against Germany and called for peace and reconciliation between the working classes of France and Germany. (Apparently the Party later forged issues of L'Humanité in an attempt to show that it had favored resistance.) After the Soviet Union entered the war against Germany, of course, French Communists were among the most militant resistance fighters; certainly, rank-and-file Party members threw themselves into secret warfare without hesitation, as if their leaders' early collaboration with the Germans had been only a bad dream.

Then there was the persistent German effort to win the minds and hearts of French intellectuals, sometimes by inviting them to visit Germany. The first large-scale delegation was organized to attend an international congress of writers in Weimar in October 1941. Robert Brasillach, a member of the French contingent, found himself in the company of eminent colleagues such as Marcel Jouhandeau, Jacques Chardonne, Pierre Drieu La Rochelle, and Ramon Fernandez, and Abel Bonnard, the Vichy minister of education. In Germany they encountered a collection of literary personalities from other parts of Europe, occupied and not. One of them was John Knittel, a bestselling Swiss novelist, who after a speech by Chardonne expressing hope for permanent Franco-German friendship, offered a toast to France. "Then," reported Brasillach, "the whole audience rose to its feet, held up its glasses, applauded; everyone shook the hands of the nearest

French delegate." There was even talk of establishing an International Society of Writers. The following day the foreign visitors were invited with Goebbels, the propaganda minister, to a ceremony at the tombs of Goethe and Schiller; later they were the guests of Arno Breker at his Berlin studio.

A second Congress of European Writers met again at Weimar the following year. One member of the French delegation, Georges Blond, wrote a front-page account of it for *Je Suis Partout*. He had traveled to Germany, he said, with Chardonne, Drieu, André Thérive, André Fraigneau — "all five of us guided, encouraged, kept informed, kept together by our dear Gerhard Heller." In Weimar Goebbels made a speech, asking the writers to engage not only their lives but their works in the common struggle. The correspondent of *Je Suis Partout* discovered that his German literary counterparts were noble, free, humane.

The Germans had even greater success among artists, if famous names mean anything. At least once, they lured to Germany a delegation that included some of the most popular painters of the period: Maurice de Vlaminck, André Derain, Othon Friesz, and Kees van Dongen among them. In their contacts with artists, the Germans possessed a master of ceremonies in the gregarious sculptor Breker, whose memoirs record his many good deeds on behalf of France's artists, and in saving French-owned works of art coveted by the Nazi leadership. He even claims to have won the agreement of the Germans not to prosecute Jews who failed to wear the obligatory yellow star. Not only was Breker's Berlin studio a port of call for French collaborationists, but the exhibition of his sculpture at the Orangerie in Paris in May 1942 — heroic statuary sufficiently attuned to Hitler's theme of racial superiority to make Breker the artistic ambassador of his country — was a major event. The Vichy ministers Abel Bonnard and Jacques Benoist-Méchin delivered inaugural speeches, the latter offering a moral, lest the significance of the event be lost on anyone. "One of the thoughts formulated on many occasions by Chancellor Hitler," Benoist-Méchin explained, "and to which I subscribe without the shadow of a reservation, is that no political act has meaning unless it serves as a framework and a support for a spiritual act."

The Breker exhibition even tempted the French sculptor Aristide Maillol, then eighty, from his Mediterranean retreat to bestow a still more weighty blessing. The frail Maillol, with his prophet's white beard, was photographed with Breker among the statues, as Jean Cocteau had been, and was received with honors at the German Embassy reception afterward. In his memoirs Breker denies Simone de Beauvoir's own recollection, that Parisians had boycotted the opening of his show, citing an eyewitness report by Jacques Chardonne and readily available photographs as proof. Among the eminent visitors to the Orangerie, in the following days, were Hermann Göring and Pierre Laval.

★   ★   ★

Such is *la petite histoire* — in the apt French expression — of the German years, significant only in demonstrating that the occupying power could draw support for its presence from a reservoir of French talents and celebrities. Still, most collaborationists are not worth footnotes in literary history, and their very names require further identification today. Only one author whose work has survived behaved ambiguously during those troubled years: Louis Destouches, who signed his books Louis-Ferdinand Céline. His *Voyage au bout de la nuit* and Mort à *crédit*, novels that stirred the prewar decade, are among the few books of that time that continue to move readers. Céline attempted to repeat himself, or his characteristic prose, in a series of ephemeral political and racist pamphlets, and then, after the liberation, returned to autobiographical fiction. Some of these pathetic echoes are still more interesting to us than the productions of his more reasonable contemporaries.

Out of respect for his work, and probably also for commercial reasons, an attempt was later made to gloss over Céline's prewar role in the popularization of racism, his irresponsible behavior under the Germans. One even wonders whether concern for his reputation explains why his most outrageous books have not been reprinted. That he was an evil genius and a deranged personality is clear from any serious examination of his life and works. If Céline has a place here, it is because others treated his symptoms of paranoia as political statements and prophecies.

The myth was that Céline was not a collaborationist, and indeed — if the term signifies an active role in publishing or editing, public appearances or speechmaking, or holding an official position of leadership in a political movement — he was not. What he did do was equally extraordinary: he published books and articles during the occupation that advocated still more collaborationism than existed: "working together, without fraud . . . under discipline." In *Les Beaux*

Draps, a book in the form of a tract published in Paris nearly a year after Hitler's troops marched in, Céline warned that Jews were still to be seen everywhere. He called for their extermination, and that of their supporters as well. Céline's definition of a Jew was more rigid than that of Hitler's Germany or Pétain's Vichy: "I mean by Jew," he explained in a footnote, "any person who has a single Jew among his grandparents." The book may have been too much even for Vichy, for copies were seized in the south.

Céline's other favorite activity at the time was writing for the occupation press, often through letters to the editor, and chiefly to take the French to task for not being violent enough in their anti-Semitism. He wanted to see more denunciations. The writer Ernst Jünger, then a German officer stationed in Paris, had an opportunity to see this man up close at the German Institute in December 1941. Céline told Jünger "how surprised and stupefied he is that we soldiers don't shoot, hang, exterminate Jews — he is stupefied that someone possessing a bayonet doesn't make unlimited use of it." Céline added: "If I carried a bayonet, I'd know what I had to do." Jünger decided that he had learned something, after two hours of such talk, about "the monstrous power of nihilism." Céline and his kind were using science uniquely as a means to kill. (Still, one wonders if Jünger really had to cross the Rhine to meet such people.)

On June 22, 1944, less than a fortnight after the Allied landing in Normandy, Jünger learned that Céline had already rushed to the German Embassy to obtain the necessary travel documents, and immediately took refuge in Germany, two months before the German withdrawal from Paris. "Curious to see," noted Jünger, "how people capable of demanding the heads of millions of men in cold blood worry about their dirty little lives. The two facts must be connected."*

---

* Jünger avoids identifying Céline in his diary entry for June 1944: he is called "X" in the first edition (Of 1953) and "Merline" in the revision of 1980. In the original translation of the first volume of the journal (1951), Jünger's entry for December 1941 identifies Céline by name; however, by 1980 this reference too has become "Merline." Jünger does not wish to confirm that "Merline" is Céline; the reader must judge from the content whether he is.

20 The Resistance, Through the Looking Glass

IT IS POSSIBLE to say that "everybody resisted," but proving it would require some mind-reading. For if in principle "everybody" opposed the German occupation of France — French political leaders, members of the Establishment, writers and artists included — their opposition seldom produced consequences. Sometimes a single minor act in a four-year period would be magnified to heroic proportions. Some very important literary figures are credited with one or two specific deeds, such as writing a pseudonymous book or anonymous article, while all the rest of the time they were passive, resisting only in spirit. Sometimes a single act of clandestine opposition was negated by daily acts of tacit or active collaboration, and then where are we?

One of the most striking presences in the Left Bank of the occupation years was a German, the man we have already met whose particular responsibility was the world of literary publishing. Gerhard Heller represents both the ambiguities and the possibilities of his time. By the nature of his work, he was closer to many of the leading pro-Nazi collaborationists than to the passive or active resistance, and it is he who had "guided, encouraged, kept informed, kept together" the band of French collaborationists during their visit to Germany in 1942. But if so many literary stars of the prewar anti-Fascist left wing survived the German years unharmed, Heller and the mentality he represented deserve some of the credit.

Heller was born in Potsdam, in a French-oriented environment he attributed to the Huguenot origins of the community, and perhaps of his own family. He learned French at school, then studied the Romance languages and civilizations at the ancient University of Heidelberg. In the first year of Hitler's rule he was sent on a scholarship to the University of Pisa and in the following school year, thanks to Karl Epting, then director of the German University Bureau in France, to the University of Toulouse in southwest France. Back in Germany, he worked in the cultural section of the German radio network, one of his duties being to report on French and Italian propaganda broadcasts. With the defeat of France, his skills were put to other uses. Despite his lack of military training, Heller was given a uniform and a grade, *Sonderführer*, corresponding to lieutenant. He boarded the train for Paris on his thirty-first birthday, November 8, 1940.

Although he had been a candidate for Nazi Party membership in his student days, Heller never became a full-fledged member. As a Protestant he resisted oath-taking, even to the Führer. He and his student comrades found the Nazis distasteful. But he had a feeling of kinship with Ambassador Abetz, whom he had met in prewar France. This was a connection he felt he could draw upon in difficult moments.

In Paris Heller was assigned to the literary section (Gruppe Schrifttum) of the Propagandastaffel on the Champs-Elysées. His wife to be, Marie-Louise, was also assigned there. During her years of work for him, he never confided his political feelings to her or told her of his occasionally unorthodox acts. His superiors knew little French, let alone French literature, so he was set loose in a room with a heap of manuscripts. He decided that he had better remind the French Publishers Association that individual companies, and the Association, were supposed to carry out their own censorship, submitting only doubtful cases to the Germans. Heller told French publishers: "Don't do anything unwise, such as trying to publish Jewish authors or anti-German tracts." By March 1941, the system was functioning satisfactorily, and Heller's work gave him frequent contact with famous publishers and editors. In a sense he had joined the Left Bank literary scene, if in a new and strange manner. By the summer of 1942 he was living in it, too, for his office and living quarters were transferred to the German Institute's elegant town house on the Rue Saint-Dominique (although he and his activity were controlled not by the Institute but by Abetz's embassy).

If the Germans working in propaganda generally lacked interest in French culture — often dismissing French as a subculture for half-breeds — Heller's private goal was to preserve a French cultural presence, and when he could perform a small and secret act of resistance, he did it. When the students of Paris demonstrated on November 11, 1940, Heller (who had just arrived in France) was ordered into the street with other soldiers on duty at Propagandastaffel headquarters to help arrest them. While escorting a group of students upstairs, he stopped the elevator before it reached his floor, and allowed his captives to slip away. It was the first time he had said no. Later he was able to help innocent victims; for instance, he argued successfully for the release of Jacques Chardonne's son from German detention. But when a resistance activist was arrested and earmarked for a concentration camp, Heller knew that nothing could be done to save him. Suspecting that a number of French acquaintances such as Jean Paulhan were involved in acts of resistance, Heller worried about them and when possible tried to protect them, but could he have done much in a serious case? Apparently it took a collaborationist with something the Germans needed — a Pierre Drieu La Rochelle — to save a Jean Paulhan. Yet when a denunciation of Paulhan — among others — was sent to the Germans over the signature of an *N.R.F.* author's wife, Heller was able to act. He discovered that the denunciation had been sent not to the ferocious SD but to the Feldgendarmerie, the police force of the Wehrmacht, and there he was able to vouch for Paulhan and Bernard Groethuysen, at least.

The argument Heller used in his interventions with the SD (the Sicherheitsdienst, or SS Security Service), which was responsible for dealing with subversive activities in occupied territories, went this way: "We must not create martyrs; we don't want the French against us." Ambassador Abetz said more or less the same thing: "Leave culture alone; that gives us less to worry about." At times Heller could approach Abetz in the late evening, after the ambassador's secretary had gone home, to explain a particular case, or to obtain authorization to act. Heller felt that the SD and related services were not concerned with intellectual resistance, for they did not feel such activity could really harm Germany. And in truth, few French writers suffered for what they wrote during the occupation. Most of those arrested, deported, or otherwise punished were involved in more violent forms of resistance: intelligence collection, sabotage, paramilitary operations.

So Heller pursued his day-to-day role as self-appointed trouble-shooter. Gaston Gallimard had him read the manuscript of Albert Camus's *L'Etranger*. Heller did not put it down until four o'clock the next morning, and then telephoned Gallimard's secretary as soon as he reached his office to offer his approval and his help in the event of difficulties.   He also approved *Pilote de guerre* ("Flight to Arras") by Antoine de Saint-Exupéry.   Saint-Exupéry was then in the United States, which had joined the war with Germany, and his book concerned the final weeks of France's war; Heller was blamed for letting it pass. He was subsequently obliged to tell Gallimard that the book was banned, and Gallimard dutifully called back the copies already sent to bookstores, while Heller was sentenced to some days of house arrest. For a French reader could not have failed to see the subversive message in *Pilote de guerre*.   In the privacy of his wartime diary, Jean Guéhenno noted its "admirable pages," for Saint-Exupéry had rejected the notion that the French victims of German occupation were "guilty" of anything, and he hinted at an "awakening of resistance."

Heller also approved the allocations of paper for the printing of work by Louis Aragon and Elsa Triolet (the Germans around him did not even know that she was Jewish, Russian, and a Communist), as well as by Eluard.   He gave the green light to Grasset for the publication of Mauriac's *La Pharisienne* ("A Woman of the Pharisees"); he respected Mauriac's art.   Although there was nothing subversive in this novel, Mauriac himself was suspected of harboring unorthodox thoughts if not acts, so Heller's decision brought criticism from both the Germans and the French collaborationists. Heller was invited to the publisher's office when Mauriac came in to autograph press copies, and his was dedicated "To Lt. Heller, who expressed concern for the fate of the Woman of the Pharisees, with my gratitude." Later this copy, which Heller had given to friends in Paris at the time of the German retreat in August 1944, turned up to cause postliberation embarrassment for Mauriac, or so Mauriac's enemies hoped.   Heller ran into Mauriac several times, notably at Ramon Fernandez's funeral, but he made no effort to seek a closer association, with him or with others he admired, such as Camus or Sartre, for fear of compromising them.

Some Frenchmen on the Left Bank were aware of Heller's true sentiments: Marcel Arland, for one, as well as Marcel Jouhandeau and Pierre Drieu La Rochelle. The Fascists of *Je Suis Partout* found him sympathetic, although they were more outspoken in their admiration of Hitlerism. Heller admired Lucien Rebatet for his culture, his knowledge of music and of motion picture art, but he detested Rebatet's book *Les Décombres*, in which the author said of a Jewish comrade in arms: "If it were useful, I should have his head cut off without blinking an eye." He was also appalled when Brasillach advocated sending Jewish children to the camps together with their parents; that day Heller cried. At a dinner for Karl Epting's assistant, Karl-Heinz Bremer, who was to leave the German Institute for the Russian front, Robert Brasillach offered a toast: "We are sorry that Bremer is leaving, but we still have Gerhard Heller, even though he is a liberal." The remark could have caused trouble for Heller, but nothing came of it. Jacques Chardonne later said that he never met a real Nazi during the occupation, even during the Weimar journeys. Indeed, Heller arranged the travels of his French friends so that they would meet only relatively liberal Germans. Chardonne also said: "Don't talk to Heller, he's more French than the French."

One of Heller's admirers was Paul Léautaud, that singularly apolitical diarist, who remembered hearing him say: "We are disgusted by the number of Frenchmen who come to us to denounce other Frenchmen." In the weeks before the German retreat from Paris, Léautaud wrote: "I intend, if things get definitively worse for the Germans . . . to go to [Propagandastaffel headquarters] to express to Heller my feelings of cordiality and to ask him to express the same to Captain Jünger." Léautaud added for himself (and what he wrote would not surprise careful readers of his diary): "I may add . . . my regret for the defeat of the Germans, continuing to feel as I do that the political interest of France was in a victory of Germany and an understanding with that country."

Only on returning to Germany after the liberation did Heller face real danger. Assigned to propaganda work against the provisional government of Charles de Gaulle, he was alerted by a friend in Berlin that someone in the Propaganda Ministry had decided that he was a defeatist. In fact Heller had opposed, and perhaps even blocked, a plan for taking French hostages to Germany in August 1944. He had seen a list of French writers known to be hostile to Germany,— names such as Mauriac and Eluard were on it — both at the German Institute and at SD headquarters on the Avenue Foch, and he had managed to remove and destroy it in both places. Now a report was circulating on Heller himself, severe in tone and recommending extreme measures. But it was routed to the office of another friend, and so got no farther. Still, to keep out of danger he obtained an assignment to Sigmaringen, where the Germans had regrouped the Vichy government and assorted collaborationists under Pétain. There he became aware of the first symptoms of a nervous disorder, diagnosed by Céline in his true-life role as Dr. Destouches, that would mark him for the rest of his life.

By the time he left the hospital, in Konstanz, the French army had occupied that region of southwest Germany. He turned himself in to them, offering Jean Paulhan and François Mauriac as references, and had no problems after that. In postwar West Germany, Heller published a French cultural bulletin, then the German cultural magazine *Merkur*, and participated in founding a publishing house.

★   ★   ★

Years after, Heller made an attempt to reconstruct his occupation diary. He had buried the original on the Esplanade des Invalides, shortly before the German withdrawal from Paris. But although he counted the rows of trees to find the exact spot, he could not locate his cache. So he rewrote the diary, retelling the story of his meetings with many of the leading literary personalities of those years, with the Gallimards, with the elusive Jean Paulhan — whose own ambiguities must have struck a familiar note, although Heller confessed that from 1941 to 1944 "we never spoke openly of things that had to be left unspoken at the time." He expressed a particular indebtedness to Paulhan: "It is through him that I became another man." He remembered how, fearing for Paulhan's safety, he served as an unofficial sentinel below Paulhan's windows on the Rue des Arênes, to be on hand should something happen, casting an occasional glance at a neighboring building on the connecting Rue de Navarre, where Paulhan's friend Jean Blanzat lived, and where for a time he hid François Mauriac.

From Heller's lost and remade diary, we can learn something of the Thursday luncheons given by Florence (Mrs. Frank Jay) Gould, where one might meet Marcel Jouhandeau, Paul Léautaud, and others; and about a less orthodox salon, that of two German soldiers, the Valentiner brothers, who had a tiny flat under the roof on Quai Voltaire, with a view over Saint-Germain-des-Prés. Once Céline arrived in Heller's office at the German Institute and scrawled "N.R.F." on the door, explaining, "Everybody knows that you're an agent of Gallimard and the private secretary of Jean Paulhan." Céline removed two pairs of goggles from his pocket, gave one to Heller and one to Marie-Louise (the future Mrs. Heller), and explained: "They'll be pretty useful when German cities go up in flame and smoke." Indeed, after an air raid on Berlin in February 1945, when the air was filled with smoke and dust, Heller found Céline's goggles and put them on.

21 Midnight Presses

ON A FINE SUMMER day in German-occupied Paris, Jean Bruller, the illustrator who had achieved a certain prewar reputation with his satirical drawings in the left-wing press, was walking on the Rue du Vieux-Colombier when he was hailed by a onetime friend, André Thérive, the writer and literary critic. Although Bruller had liked Thérive in the past, he was less than enthusiastic about him now, for the man was contributing articles to periodicals published under German control. Bruller, who was becoming active in an underground publishing venture, hardly felt like discussing current events with him. By the time they reached the subway station at the intersection of the Boulevard Raspail and the Rue de Sèvres, Thérive was showing Bruller a book he carried under his arm: Ernst Jünger's *Jardins et Routes*, a day-by-day account of the officer-writer's participation in the battle of France. With Germans like Jünger, Thérive remarked, "we can have an understanding." He praised Jünger's sensitivity and comprehension, his love for France. So Bruller got hold of the book, and became absorbed in the officer's description of his campaign, his relations with local populations, and with young women as well, his respectful visits to cemeteries along the way. But Jünger's very sincerity alarmed Bruller. Would not the average French reader imagine that the kindly Jünger represented the behavior and intentions of all Germans?

Bruller was soon at work writing *Le Silence de la mer* ("The Silence of the Sea"). In this little story he evoked the "good German officer." Bruller's German is billeted in a country house inhabited by an elderly Frenchman and his young niece. The officer reveals himself to be of considerable learning and good will. He explains to his involuntary hosts that he actually descends from a French Huguenot family that had immigrated to Germany after the revocation of the Edict of Nantes. He is well read in French literature, he cites Shakespeare, and he plays the piano in the house. But all the while the old Frenchman and the girl remain silent. They are determined not to reply to anything the German says.

The officer takes leave to spend a fortnight in Paris to participate in a cultural event that, he promises, will seal the bond of partnership between his country and theirs. But on his return his mood has changed. He announces that he has serious things to tell his hosts. He asks that they forget everything he has said during his six-month monologue. For in Paris he spoke with other German officers, who revealed to him the true intentions of the Nazis: to destroy France. "Not only its power: its soul as well. Its soul especially." Disgusted by what he has learned, the good German has requested to be returned to active duty on the Russian front. As he takes leave of them, the young woman is visibly moved. But she keeps her silence. Only after the officer's final adieu does she form the same word on her own lips. The officer smiles as he walks out.

Bruller originally wrote *Le Silence de la mer* for an underground periodical at the request of his friend Pierre de Lescure, a former bookseller and publisher of a literary magazine, who during the occupation was an agent of British Intelligence. Lescure had already recruited Bruller for the same job, which then consisted of planning escape routes for British war prisoners. There had been a plan to transform an underground magazine, *La Pensée Libre,* from an exclusively Communist publication into a magazine representing a broader range of opinion. But the Germans had found the printing plant, arrested the printer, and confiscated the machinery. The project had been too ambitious, requiring too much material support. Henceforth all such efforts were devoted to smaller publications, bulletins of only a few pages that could be typed on a stencil for duplication.

So what to do with the relatively bulky manuscript of Bruller's story? Its author decided: publish it as a book. Thus began the most unusual publishing house of the Left Bank, then or ever. Bruller approached a printer who had reproduced some of his Goya-like sketches in prewar years, and through him found a smaller, less conspicuous plant (on the Boulevard de l'Hôpital), which specialized in death announcements. What Bruller wanted was a very small-format book of about one hundred pages, with elegant composition and layout, and stiff covers; he was convinced that a good printing job would strike the reader's imagination, making the message all the more effective. The printer could turn out only eight pages at a time, after which he would redistribute the type to do another eight pages; it would take weeks to finish the job. Each week Bruller brought eight more pages of manuscript, which were destroyed as soon as the type was set, and took away the printed pages, dropping them off at a friend's office on Boulevard Raspail, where they would be picked up by another friend who was to do the binding.

While serving in an Alpine regiment at the beginning of the war, Bruller had broken a leg during maneuvers, and was sent to convalesce in a home at the foot of a low but forbidding mountain chain called the Vercors. So he took Vercors as his pseudonym. Later it happened that the same mountains became a center of partisan activity against the Germans. Only 350 copies of Le Silence de la mer were printed. They were ready in February 1942, but soon after that a British Intelligence secret radio operator was arrested, and Pierre de Lescure had to go into hiding. To protect Lescure, the book could not be released for a while.

But Bruller was a publisher now. He called his company Editions de Minuit (Midnight Press) and had a distribution list for his productions: writers, teachers, scientists. Through a contact of Lescure, Jacques Debû-Bridel, he was able to reach Jean Paulhan, the person with the widest access to potential authors. Paulhan was already becoming the pivot of much literary production, chiefly clandestine.

Paulhan gave his own copy of Silence to a friend, Professor Robert Debré of the Academy of Medicine, who like Paulhan himself was in touch with the Musée de l'Homme resistance network that had ended tragically. Debré had Bruller's story duplicated, so that it was circulating in that form even before the printed copies were distributed, and he contributed funds through Paulhan for the further operations of Editions de Minuit. Soon a guessing game began: who was "Vercors?" Bruller was able to keep his secret, because even his closest associates didn't realize that he was the author. He was following rules of security learned from Pierre de Lescure; for example, don't even tell your wife what you are doing. He never met Paulhan, Debû-Bridel remaining their intermediary; he even avoided encounters with old friends whom he knew to be involved with the enemy, for he didn't wish them even to *think* about his existence.

By the fall of 1942, Bruller was able to begin distributing *Le Silence de la mer*. The next book to be set in type was *A travers le désastre*, by the Catholic philosopher Jacques Maritain, first published in New York as *France, My Country, Through the Disaster*. But Bruller and his friends hoped to find more books actually written on occupied French soil. Meanwhile Bruller, his friend Yvonne Paraf (who was in charge of binding), Debû-Bridel, Paulhan, and Julien Benda each wrote brief texts to be published as an anthology (in April 1943) under the title *Chroniques interdites*. Paulhan's contribution was a tribute to Jacques Decour, prewar editor-in-chief of *Commune* and cofounder of underground *Les Lettres Françaises*, who had been arrested in February 1942 and executed as a hostage in May.

Each volume published by Editions de Minuit reproduced a manifesto drafted by Pierre de Lescure before his disappearance into the underground. "In France there are still writers who . . . refuse to take orders," it said. "They feel deeply that thought must have expression. To act on other thoughts, without doubt, but especially because, if it is not allowed to express itself, the spirit dies." Soon the little books, each scarcely four and a half by six and a half inches in dimension, began to form a library in which some of the country's best writers were represented, although each employed a pseudonym borrowed from a region of France. François Mauriac became Forez, for *Le Cahier noir* ("The Black Notebook"), published in August 1943; Jean Guéhenno was Cévennes, for *Dans la prison* ("In Prison"), which appeared a year later. Other pseudonymous volumes were written by Jean Cassou, André Chamson, Louis Aragon, and Elsa Triolet (the last two rejected geography, but signed as "François La Colère" and "Laurent Daniel" respectively). There were also to be Edith Thomas, Yves Farge, Claude Morgan, Gabriel Audisio, Jacques Debû-Bridel. Vercors returned with *La Marche à l'étoile*, a story in which Bruller imagined the fate of his own father, a Hungarian Jew, had he lived during the German years. The old man in the story is arrested as a hostage and shot by Vichy police with other naturalized Jews in reprisal for an act of resistance. Uncertain as to the worth of his second manuscript, Bruller submitted it first to Paul Eluard, who by then was the chief literary adviser of Editions de Minuit, assisted by Lucien Scheler, a kindly and committed antiquarian bookseller in whose home Eluard had taken refuge. Eluard was enthusiastic about the new contribution by the mysterious Vercors, and it was prepared for printing.

The little books were now the talk of reading France, and they were circulating outside France as well. *Le Silence de la mer* appeared in London in a translation by the critic Cyril Connolly, and in New York in *Life*. It was even attacked from the besieged Soviet Union by Ilya Ehrenburg, who rejected the portrayal of a kindly German officer, for no such specimen had been seen on the Eastern front. Ehrenburg's attack was repeated by a Free French émigré periodical, which denounced Vercors as a provocateur. But on the occupied mainland *Les Lettres Françaises*, itself controlled by Communists, called Vercors's book "the most moving, the most deeply human that we have had the opportunity to read since the beginning of the German occupation."

Each new book published by Minuit was henceforth distributed in at least one thousand copies, and sometimes two thousand, notably for François La Colère's *Le Musée Grevin*, which was rapidly recognized as "Aragon's poem," just as *Le Cahier noir* was often recognized as by Mauriac; this was one of the reasons why Mauriac eventually decided to move out of his apartment. Paulhan enjoyed telling his friends who wrote what, and that was one of the reasons why Bruller made sure that Paulhan didn't know the true identity of "Vercors." *Le Silence de la mer* was reprinted in 1943 in fifteen hundred copies. But such a figure does not tell the whole story of the book's circulation, for it and other Minuit productions were reprinted here or there without authorization, and after the liberation Bruller even saw handwritten copies of his *Silence*. Another book was brought in from abroad for translation by Editions de Minuit: John Steinbeck's play about the resistance, *The Moon Is Down*.

One of the most memorable projects was a two-volume anthology of poetry entitled *L'Honneur des poètes*. In Paul Eluard's view, honor belonged to those who refused to limit their writing during those dangerous years to poetry for poetry's sake. The second volume of the anthology bore the title *Europe*, and part of its contents consisted of poems from other occupied nations. To fill it out, some of the ostensibly foreign contributions were actually written by French poets. The word-of-mouth success of the first volume of *L'Honneur des poètes* was immediate, in part because of curiosity aroused by the use of false names. When the publishers ran out of copies, they reprinted it on cheap paper as an eight-page tract that could be mailed. Meanwhile Jean Lescure (no relation of Pierre de Lescure) and his wife distributed it around town by bicycle. "It is an act by which French poets speak out loudly for their place in the struggle for the liberation of their homeland

and the freedom of the world," proclaimed Les Lettres Françaises. "How infuriating not to be able, because of police terror, to support our ideas with our names . . ."

Perhaps Editions de Minuit was largely a solace to morale. It gave its authors an opportunity to express themselves and to feel engaged; it gave readers the feeling that at least a pilot light of free expression existed in the German years. If writers were so dangerous that they had to be censored, if books had to be burned, then it was significant that one could express oneself. "We are greatly honored," Cévennes (Jean Guéhenno) wrote in Dans la prison. "A tyrannical power, in attributing so much importance to our thoughts, obliges us ourselves to recognize the singularity and the scandal of what we believe."

Les Lettres Françaises was a more sober enterprise, with less concern for appearance and more message. Actually, the monthly newspaper had two starts, two histories. Jacques Decour, a specialist in German civilization whose real name was Daniel Decourdemanche, had organized an underground group attached to the Communists' Front National, first called the Front National des Ecrivains (National Writers Front). Jean Paulhan, who had known Decour as a young man and had published his novels at Gallimard, was an early recruit, with Paulhan's friend Jean Blanzat, Guéhenno, and Charles Vildrac. Decour collected material for what should have been the first issue of Les Lettres Françaises, but on his arrest his sister burned the manuscripts. With Decour, not only the manuscripts but the liaison techniques and the connection with a plant for reproducing the newspaper disappeared.

Enter Claude Morgan, the pseudonym of the son of Georges Lecomte, of the Académie Française. A member of the Communist Party since the Spanish Civil War, Morgan had been assigned by the Party to work with Decour in setting up the writers' front, and Decour had shown him samples of periodicals duplicated by mimeograph as an indication of how they would operate. On the arrest of Decour and his associates Georges Politzer and Jacques Solomon, Morgan did not go into hiding, confident that they would not talk. A Party emissary contacted him to ask that he put together an issue of Les Lettres Françaises, but this time without assistance — without the contacts, or the articles that Decour had already collected. Morgan composed an "Adieu à Jacques Decour," a report on the war, and added the manifesto of the National Writers Front. At the last moment his printer was discovered, so the first issue, dated September 1942, and many more to follow, were duplicated by mimeograph.

Henceforth Morgan lived the life of a secret agent, taking all possible precautions for his meetings, outwardly living as the government functionary he was. Late in September 1942, the writer Edith Thomas returned to Paris from the southern zone and put Morgan in touch with Jean Paulhan and Jacques Debû-Bridel. She also contributed an article to the second issue of *Les Lettres Françaises,* so Morgan was no longer its only writer. Soon the informal staff included Paulhan, Debû-Bridel, Guéhenno, and Vildrac. Early issues were published in editions of four thousand copies (to the best of anyone's later recollection); by 1944, printed issues were published in as many as twelve thousand. They were not generally sent through the mail, but dropped into letter boxes in Paris, while bundles were handed over to couriers for distribution among partisan fighters in southern France.

Claude Morgan tried to make his paper more literary, both to justify its existence and to distinguish it from other underground periodicals. But without being able to offer contributors the possibility of seeing their names in print, he could not always find writers. He did receive a text from Paulhan on the collaborationists who had gone to the Weimar writers' congress and an article by Debû-Bridel on British philosophy. They went to the printer to make up the third issue; but once more the printer was caught, the manuscripts lost, and Morgan had to write the whole issue again.

Then he met Paul Eluard, who after Paulhan was certainly the most dynamic personality of Left Bank resistance. Eluard wrote a poem, "Courage," while Morgan waited, and henceforth the two met daily. Morgan was soon recruiting other first-class writers such as Mauriac and Jean-Paul Sartre. He found the time to help Editions de Minuit by distributing their little books or forwarding manuscripts to them. And at last he found a printer for *Les Lettres Françaises.* (Its headlines were composed in the plant used by German occupation forces to print the *Pariser Zeitung.*) The paper was put together first at Morgan's office in the Louvre, where he worked in a division responsible for the security of works of art in provincial museums, then at the apartment of a writer off the Rue de Vaugirard near Montparnasse, and later on in the office of Les Cahiers d'Art on Rue du Dragon, one of Eluard's command posts. By that time Morgan was living on the same street, steps away from Saint-Germain-des-Prés. Until the liberation of Paris, *Les Lettres Françaises* published anonymous contributions by authors such as Albert

Camus, Jean Cassou, Paul Eluard, François Mauriac, Jean Paulhan, Raymond Queneau, and Jean-Paul Sartre.

The National Writers Front, to become the National Committee of Writers, proclaimed itself representative of "all tendencies and all confessions: Gaullists, Communists, democrats, Catholics, Protestants..." That first manifesto, composed before his arrest by Jacques Decour, had promised: "By our writings we shall save the honor of French letters." But the group also set itself a combative goal: "We shall thrash the traitors who have sold out to the enemy. We'll make French air unbreathable to these German hacks." And the hacks would hear of it. Even the ingenuous Paul Léautaud recorded receiving a copy of the paper from an unknown correspondent and reading an attack on Pierre Drieu La Rochelle and the *N.R.F.* milieu he frequented. He spoke to Paulhan about it, and mentioned finding a good poem in the same issue; Paulhan told him that it was Eluard's. (In fact it was a poem by Aragon that Claude Morgan had brought back from the southern zone; presumably Paulhan knew as much.) Léautaud was pleased, for he had just met Eluard downstairs in the Gallimard lobby. During the same conversation, Paulhan told Léautaud about the arrest and probable torture of Benjamin Crémieux, a prewar *N.R.F.* author and Jew who had been hiding in southern France. That made Léautaud reflect seriously about resistance, which he decided was quite possibly noble, even if stupid. Crémieux, formerly secretary general of the French P.E.N. Club, was sent to Buchenwald concentration camp, where he died.

On the value of even a little resistance, Paulhan made his own position clear in a contribution to the underground journal *Cahiers de Libération*:

> And I know that there are those who say: they died for precious little. A simple piece of intelligence (not always precise) wasn't worth it, nor was a tract, nor even an underground newspaper (often badly printed). To such persons one must reply: "It's that they were on the side of life. It's that they liked things as insignificant as a song, a snapping of fingers, a smile. You can squeeze a bee in your hand until it suffocates. It won't suffocate without stinging you. That's precious little, you will say. But if it didn't sting you, bees would have become extinct a long time ago.

22 CNE and Company

LOUIS ARAGON'S BIOGRAPHER credits him with convincing the underground Communist Party that the way to resist the Germans and their helpers in Vichy would be to encourage unity of action between Communists and non-Communists, rather than through wholly Communist endeavors such as the stillborn *La Pensée Libre*. Both *Les Lettres Françaises* and the Comité National des Ecrivains (CNE) — the National Committee of Writers — were products of the new line. Aragon himself set up the southern-zone headquarters of this Committee.

Since his return from active duty in northern France, the war and its unhappy consequences had been the main motifs of Aragon's poetry. He seldom rested his pen in the German years. When he wasn't organizing, he was writing poems that appeared anonymously, pseudonymously in numerous resistance publications. Pierre Seghers, a poet who began to publish his own work because Paris did not seem to want it, created a poetry magazine from his home in the village of Villeneuve-lès-Avignon, across the river from the ramparts of Avignon. Meeting Aragon in Carcassonne, he made a friend and obtained an eminent contributor to the first issue of *Poésie 40* (whose title was to change from year to year). "Slender, dark-haired, young and lively, tall on his feet, fast-moving, he greeted me as if we were old friends, took me by the arm, and dragged me along." Thus Seghers's first impression of Aragon, who with Elsa Triolet was soon a long-term house guest. Later Aragon went on to Nice, where young Claude Roy came under his spell, "taken little by little with the sinuous movement of his gradually accelerating comings and goings, his sudden turns, the figure eight which his body formed in the small flat."

From the old flower market in Italianate Nice, Aragon and Triolet transferred their base into the Drôme region at the foot of the Vercors chain, then to another hideaway in the home of another literary magazine publisher, René Tavernier, in the outskirts of Lyon. It was an itinerary not without hazards, for Aragon's enemies had not quite forgotten him, and Pierre Drieu La Rochelle, his old friend, was not above using the austere pages of *La Nouvelle Revue Française* to attack him, along with the small reviews of southern France and French North Africa that dared to publish Aragon and other authors Drieu considered unpatriotic. Aragon's visits to Paris were as clandestine as he could make them. Lucien Scheler tells of the arrival of Aragon and Triolet at the Gare de Lyon in eastern Paris early in 1943. They had traveled with false papers, but another couple who were hardly inconspicuous in occupied Paris, Paul Eluard and his beautiful wife, Nusch, greeted them on the platform. That year Gallimard published Aragon's novel, *Les Voyageurs de l'impériale.* (His volume of poems called *Le Crève-Coeur* was published by the same house in 1941, although a small softcover edition appeared in London with a preface by Cyril Connolly that erroneously claimed it had been banned in Paris by the Germans.)

In Lyon, during his year with René Tavernier, Aragon worked on another long novel, *Aurélien,* in part a fictional attempt to come to terms with Drieu La Rochelle. Tavernier lived in a large house on a hillside in a suburb called Monchat, with paths leading from the house at top and bottom that facilitated unobtrusive arrivals and departures. It was here that Aragon established the headquarters for the southern zone of the National Committee of Writers, which attracted other visitors at least as conspicuous as Aragon himself, such as his comrade Georges Sadoul, another Surrealist-turned-Communist; Francis Ponge, the poet and secret Communist agent; the boisterous Father Raymond-Léopold Bruckberger. There was also a pale young man unknown to most of the Left Bank veterans, for he had spent little time in Paris until then. He was up from his native Algeria to convalesce after an attack of tuberculosis, but the Allied landings in North Africa in November 1942, followed by the German takeover of the southern zone, had cut him off from home and family. So Albert Camus spent the occupation years in Le-Chambon-sur-Lignon, seventy-five difficult miles from Lyon, where his friend and benefactor Pascal Pia worked for the Vichy-zone *Paris-Soir* before going underground in the Combat resistance movement. Taking time off from writing *La Peste* ("The Plague"), Camus would pay Pia friendly visits in Lyon; on one such visit, he was taken to the Tavernier house for a meeting of underground writers.

★   ★   ★

In Paris, the counterpart to Aragon was Paul Eluard, quite another sort of person. "A large man, stout without being heavy, full-blooded without being meaty," remembered Claude Roy, whose modest flat on the Rue du Dragon Eluard and Claude Morgan used to produce *Les Lettres Françaises*. To Roy, Eluard was good will personified. This poet of lyrical love was chosen — chose himself — to be at the center of things, turntable of the CNE in the occupied half of France, adviser to Jean Bruller and the Editions de Minuit group, all the while composing ardent resistance verse under various names including his own, but also insisting on retying all the parcels of underground publications to show how they should be done. "His hands, trembling perpetually, but skillful thanks to concentration, wrested the wrapping paper, the string, from us, but gently . . ." Anecdotes abound, lovingly told, of how he pursued his particular role in the intellectual resistance. He would hang compromising papers near the toilet each night, as if they were scrap paper, to reduce the likelihood that they would be noticed in a raid. He tried unsuccessfully to remember codes. If he was supposed to say on the telephone, "I'm waiting for the La Fontaine," or "Send me the Pascal book," he would say instead, "I didn't receive the Balzac, no, I mean the Molière — oh, you know what I mean, Jean Lescure's article." From time to time, Claude Roy tells us, the Party dispatched an envoy with a list of grievances. They would oblige him to go into hiding — say, to a psychiatric hospital deep in the sparsely populated Lozère hills region of southern France. Then he would rush back to Paris to get some books from his apartment — whose address was widely known — after which he might call on Picasso, then turn up at the Deux Magots and other familiar meeting places.

In principle, only a few trusted persons knew where Eluard lived. In principle, he avoided Place Saint-Germain-des-Prés. But other cafés were closer to his temporary lodgings, in the apartment of bookseller Lucien Scheler on the Rue de Tournon. And when Max-Pol Fouchet, the young poet from Algiers, who published a poetry review called *Fontaine*, came to France early in 1942 to contact writers in occupied Paris, he met Eluard by appointment in a restaurant on the Rue de Grenelle, just south of Saint-Germain-des-Prés. Fouchet was alarmed to hear German spoken at another table, and later he learned that the restaurant was a favorite of the German police. "Paul entered . . . sat down, and in a loud voice spoke to me about the ineluctable victory of the Allies, the certain defeat of the Germans." On the street again, Eluard remembered that he had left his briefcase behind. He returned to get it, and opened it to remove a packet of resistance leaflets. Eluard also gave Fouchet a copy of the poem that became known as "Liberté." Back in Algiers, when the censor of *Fontaine* glanced at it and discovered it was a love poem, he did not read on to the conclusion of the twenty-first stanza, missed the punch line, and so let Fouchet publish it:

> In my pupil's notebook
> On my desk and the trees
> On the sand on the snow
> I write your name
>
> • • •
>
> And by the power of a word
> I start my life again
> I was born to know you
> To name you
> Liberty.

"Liberté" was soon reprinted in New York and in London, was heard on the Voice of America and BBC radio, and was published as a leaflet dropped over France by the Royal Air Force. Eluard himself published it openly, in a small volume he entitled *Poésie et Vérité 1942*. The Gallimard bookstore on the Boulevard Raspail displayed it in a window with other volumes by Eluard. But a German officer, attracted to the title by its evocation of Goethe's *Dichtung und Wahrheit*, leafed through the book and told a clerk, "This is Communist, Monsieur"; the book was quickly removed from the window.

The occupation brought Eluard, who had been expelled from the Communist Party with André Breton and René Crevel in 1933, back in. He also had to be reconciled with Aragon, the Party's ideological executioner of the 1930s. This happened, Pierre Seghers remembered, when Aragon received a volume of Eluard's poems and reviewed it anonymously in *Poésie 41*. Eluard recognized Aragon's style in the unsigned note, the story goes, and contact began through the interzone postcards then in use. Their meeting took place in February 1943 on the upper floor of a nondescript restaurant on the Rue des Ecoles, with their wives and Seghers as witnesses. (Presumably this banquet followed the encounter in the railroad station.) Soon Aragon, as "François La Colère," joined Eluard, as "Jean du Haut," among the contributors to Editions de Minuit.

★   ★   ★

The Left Bank headquarters of militant writers, corresponding to René Tavernier's house perched on Lyon's slopes, was Edith Thomas's apartment at 15, Rue Pierre-Nicole, in the quietest possible corner of the Latin Quarter — near the Luxembourg gardens, closer still to Val de Grâce church.   There was another advantage: the concierge, that omniscient Paris institution, was lodged in a neighboring building. After a career in the left-wing press that included an assignment in civil-war Spain, Edith Thomas had left Paris at the beginning of the Second World War for reasons of health. When she returned in the autumn of 1941, she was thirty years old.   Because she refused to write for the collaborationist press, she found work at the National Archives (she had been trained as a historian).   One of the first resistance contacts she made was Claude Morgan, then frantically engaged in his one-man *Lettres Françaises*.   It was Thomas who put Morgan in touch with Paulhan, as already noted; and Paulhan gave her names of other likely recruits for underground activity. Starting in February 1943, meetings of resistance writers took place in her large apartment one floor above the narrow street. The participants were supposed to arrive singly or in very small groups, and there were not to be more than five at any meeting. But it did not work that way: sometimes ten or more came, and once, when they needed a decision of the full assembly, there were twenty-two, among them familiar faces: François Mauriac, Paul Eluard, Raymond Queneau, Jean Paulhan, Jean Guéhenno (and some who soon became familiar, such as Sartre and Camus).   That day, Edith Thomas counted fifteen bicycles parked in her lobby, and asked Claude Morgan to be more careful about the size of future assemblies.

At meetings of the northern-zone CNE, news of the war was exchanged, and the latest productions of collaborationist writers analyzed. Rules were drawn up; for instance, it was agreed that writers in the southern zone should not send review copies of their new books to Paris newspapers. There were no formal agendas for these meetings; Paulhan, Eluard, or anyone who wished simply took the floor. There were times, particularly early on, when members of CNE actually convened in Paulhan's office at Gallimard, quickly passing through the lobby, where they might run into Drieu La Rochelle, or worse, and climbing the winding stairway to Paulhan's room.

★ ★ ★

One of the most prestigious recruits to CNE was François Mauriac, the only member of the Académie Française to engage himself body and soul in the underground. His biographer credits Father A.-J. Maydieu, a Dominican and the prewar editor of liberal Catholic periodicals, together with Paulhan and Jean Blanzat, with saving Mauriac from collaborationism. And Mauriac seemed to move as easily into conspiracy with left-wingers as he had among his conservative Catholic and royalist right-wing friends before the war. So he became a target of the collaborationist press. Guéhenno's diary records an anti-Mauriac lecture in June 1941 entitled "François Mauriac, agent of French disintegration," where Father Maydieu led the booing, assisted by Guéhenno and other Mauriac partisans. The Fascists of Je Suis Partout warned Mauriac that if he appeared in a Saint-Germain-des-Prés café he'd be chased out. Accompanied by Jean Blanzat, "strong as an ox," Mauriac visited the cafés one after the other, but nothing happened. Another time, as he walked out of Brasserie Lipp, he ran into a group of toughs who shouted, "Mauriac, friend of Jews, you have no place in Paris! Get out!" Protecting his face with an arm, the frail novelist in his broken voice retorted, "You don't scare me! Who laughs last laughs best ... Lice!" He got back in Le Cahier noir, published by Editions de Minuit. "Whatever we observe that is shameful around us and in our own hearts, let's not be discouraged from giving credit to man: it's what will keep us alive."

★ ★ ★

And Sartre, who in the first postwar decade would be hailed as the symbol, as well as the product, of the intellectual resistance? What did he actually do? Certainly he tried to participate; the aborted Socialisme et Liberté was a try. But with the disappointing reception he and Simone de Beauvoir encountered on their field trip to recruit members for their intellectual resistance group, he abandoned active resistance. After discussion with her, in October 1941 he decided to return to work on Les Mouches. It represented, Beauvoir later wrote, "the only form of resistance that was accessible to him."

But then a form of resistance offered itself that was possible even for Sartre. He joined the National Committee of Writers. A pamphlet published in the southern zone had attacked him as a disciple of the German philosopher Martin Heidegger, considered an admirer of Nazism; Claude Morgan promised to warn his southern-zone counterparts of their error. Sartre wrote a devastating analysis of Drieu La Rochelle for *Les Lettres Françaises* and henceforth participated regularly in CNE and a parallel organization for theater people. Simone de Beauvoir decided not to join him. She felt it would serve no useful purpose to have both of them involved, since they shared opinions; moreover, Sartre told her, the meetings were dull.

★ ★ ★

Still, in good faith one could doubt the efficacy of intellectual resistance. How could words help when a brutal enemy occupied one's soil? Here is how Jean Galtier-Boissière, an influential and unorthodox journalist as well as an unconventional bookseller, posed the problem in retrospect:

> Some blew up trains.
> Others touched up quatrains.

Much of the poetry of resistance, or poetry by resisters, was published openly and over the signatures of the authors; one could read and even enjoy this poetry without necessarily seeing the subversive message it concealed. Clearly, if Aragon's *Le Crève-Coeur* could pass German censorship despite Aragon's reputation, if the Germans could admire Pierre Seghers's *Poésie* magazine (as Karl Epting of the German Institute later claimed), an argument was being proposed that poetry bore no effective message at all.

But there were intellectuals in the militant resistance too. The poet Robert Desnos, for one, contributed a pseudonymous poem to *L'Honneur des poètes* that began: "This heart which hated war now beats for war and battle!" Desnos was a member of a clandestine resistance network. On his capture he was deported to Buchenwald, then to Terezin, where he died of typhus. He continued to write poems, some of which got through to friends outside, until the end.

23 Topography of German Paris

LIFE WENT ON. Elegant ladies received among flowers and paintings. A legion of writers filled the pages of the daily and weekly press, publishing houses hummed with activity. Theaters were packed with audiences hoping to be stirred, and sometimes they were. Such movement, even intense movement, may give a misleading impression of what Paris was like during the Nazi occupation. Leaving aside the private feelings of its inhabitants — the inevitable sadness, even bitterness (hardly measurable sentiments) — there is adequate testimony that the Left Bank was not merry. In September 1941, a year and a summer after the Germans marched in, Paul Léautaud observed: "Paris, at least the 5th, 6th, and 7th arrondissements, continues to be quite deserted: few passersby, few cars, many closed shops." Claude Roy, up from the provinces, was impressed by the direction posts in German, the dramatic flags with their swastikas flying over hotels and public buildings, the green uniforms of sentinels. On the first Christmas Eve of the occupation, Jean Bruller discovered posters on the corner of the Boulevards Saint-Germain and Raspail announcing the execution of a young engineer who had struck a German soldier.

Maurice Martin du Gard, a Parisian stationed in Vichy, visited the capital in August 1941 to experience "this incredible silence" — for bicycles had replaced noisy automobiles, there was an occasional rider on horseback, and taxis were horseless carriages pedaled by their drivers. "One takes refuge in work, in reading — never have so many books been read — in friendship as well." He describes the necessary simplicity of receptions: "Some deprive themselves of bread for a fortnight, saving their ration tickets so they can offer their guests little sandwiches." If one earned money but could not purchase a new car or travel, one might go to the auction house to bid on a painting. In working-class neighborhoods, Martin du Gard noticed small coffins, a reminder that children resist privation badly. Rumors abounded. There was faith in Marshal Pétain: the feeling was that he had been sponsoring coercive laws and restrictions so that the French would become angry and revolt against the Germans. But one also heard a refrain: "Pétain to bed. Off with Darlan's head.* De Gaulle, go ahead!" Martin du Gard noted the briskness of cultural life: theater, concerts, art exhibitions. "The desire to think of other things is combined with the desire to encourage directors and artists who overcome considerable difficulties to prove to Paris that it is still Paris." Only movies are unpopular, for they are patently "German."

Adrienne Monnier, the owner of the Rue de l'Odéon bookshop, described her life and that of her literary friends for readers of Le Figaro Littéraire in the Vichy zone. She stressed the scarcity of food, the need to eat vegetables one doesn't like: "Valéry scrapes a little nutmeg on the dishes he is served . . ." But the worst was the cold (in February 1942). Monnier set up a sawdust stove in her shop, but in her apartment she was too cold to read or write. So each evening she turned on the kitchen oven and sat beside it to compose her articles. As for the bookselling business, new books were rare, and often one had to line up at the publisher's office for them, the good books being handed out one by one. The bargains that had taken up so much space before were almost all sold now, while certain works, especially by English or American authors, would disappear for a time. In the first days of the occupation, buyers rushed for the classics, for poetry, because, wrote Monnier, "a homeland is a language first of all." That meant Charles Péguy, Mallarmé, Apollinaire, Rimbaud, but also Paul Claudel, Paul Valéry, Henri Michaux.

What of Adrienne's American friend Sylvia Beach, now that the United States was engaged in the war? She was still in Paris, reported Monnier. Beach had recently closed her bookshop and was working on her memoirs. "Dear Sylvia! it's thanks to her, to the friends she has in the Touraine region, that we receive a rabbit almost every week. She

---

* Admiral François Darlan was second in command of the Vichy state in 1941 and until April 1942.

was even able, after a year of working on the project, to get us a Christmas turkey." Beach had carried on with Shakespeare & Company until she had a run-in with a German officer to whom she refused to sell a copy of *Finnegans Wake*. After closing the shop, she disappeared from circulation, although she returned to the Rue de l'Odéon discreetly each day for news of Adrienne and their friends in the underground.

In an open letter to Gide, also published in *Le Figaro Littéraire* in Lyon, Monnier described the young people who came into her store. Their clothing was less formal than ever; they wore their hair long; they admired Sartre, Michaux, Jacques Prévert, and the newly translated *Moby Dick* (which, as a classic, escaped the German ban on American literature).

By the autumn of 1942, things seemed to be looking brighter. Monnier tells her readers of lunching on the Rue de Babylone with Colette and being served an omelette with fresh eggs, a magnificent steak with "lots, really lots of sautéed potatoes, beautifully crisp." The talk was of food and pastry, and of where one could get good chocolate.

★   ★   ★

In the ingenuous, often tediously commonplace observations of Simone de Beauvoir, we have a still closer view of Left Bank life through the German years (much of it seen from the cafés of Montparnasse and of Saint-Germain-des-Prés) — of the street scenes and shortages, for if it was possible to eat decently in a small restaurant, food stores and street markets were bare. Meeting friends, writing books in favorite cafés, were Beauvoir's joys; she froze in her hotel room, but cafés were heated. She worked on her novel and read Hegel at the Dôme. Evenings she spent at the Flore, where the Germans never set foot. She went to the theater, but not to nightclubs, because the Germans had taken them over.

At the Café de Flore the clientèle had not changed significantly, but if the overflow crowd of provocative young women in search of adventure was familiar, the coffee and the beer were ersatz. When Beauvoir moved to a dingy hotel on the Rue Dauphine, she had to rent a pushcart and drag all her possessions across town with the help of a friend. By the harsh winter of 1942, when coal and electricity were in short supply, some subway stations closed, and movie theaters shut down in the afternoon. But Beauvoir soon found that she could work best at the Flore, where gas lamps functioned when the lights went out. One could actually feel at home, feel sheltered, there. She tried to arrive at opening

time to secure a table near the stove; that could be as early as eight in the
morning.   Others worked at neighboring tables: Thierry Maulnier,
Dominique Aury, Jacques Audiberti; collaborationists, too. But most of
the customers were anti-Fascist, when they weren't actual participants in
the underground resistance.

While they were observing, they were being observed. Alfred Fabre-
Luce, whose best-known contribution to the occupation years was the
Anthologie de la Nouvelle Europe, recorded his impression of Sartre and
Beauvoir "in this zoo [the Flore] where they were, as was said, on
permanent exhibition." Beauvoir "had the crisp face of a pretty
schoolteacher"; Sartre "was heavy-set as a bull under his reddish shock
of hair and crossed eyes . . . On their little marble tables one saw, instead
of drinks, inkwells. They worked there between the telephone and the
toilets, among drafts and questionable odors." Fabre-Luce concluded
that the filthiness of the Flore's regular customers had nothing to do with
shortages. "These young people were just as slovenly before the war. At
the Ecole Normale Supérieure the dirty ones [as the left-wing party was
called] won over the cleans [the insulting name for right-wingers]." But
he admitted that the occupation drove people who might otherwise be
guests at one or another literary salon into the cafés, wartime scarcity
making entertainment difficult and the lack of transportation requiring
that one concentrate one's life in one place. "And the café is the only
place where one can eat, drink, receive, and work all at once."

Those who frequented the Flore and those who preferred the Deux
Magots, just a couple of doors away, were quite different sorts. Legend
had it that if a customer of the Flore wished to cheat on his mate, he or
she could meet the new conquest at the Deux Magots and not be found
out.

Toward the end of the German years, Beauvoir and Sartre had to flee
Paris, when a member of a resistance group with which they had become
associated was arrested. When they returned, "out of prudence" they
moved to a different hotel, ten yards from their usual hotel on the Rue
de Seine. Soon they were back at the Flore, seated at an outdoor table
with their new comrade, Albert Camus.

"Never did sunny Paris seem sweeter than at the Allied landing [in
June 1944]," remembered Claude Morgan, who, the very day of the
Normandy invasion, moved *Les Lettres Françaises* into Claude Roy's tiny
flat on the Rue du Dragon. "The outdoor cafés were crowded and along
the Boulevard Saint-Germain young women on bicycles rode by, their

skirts floating behind like banners. The sweetness seemed too much like indifference."

But much of the movement on those Left Bank boulevards was represented by men and women on missions. Members of the Musée de l'Homme resistance group passed plans of the naval base at Saint-Nazaire in the ladies' room of the Café des Deux Magots. Resistance journalists met around the corner, on the Rue des Saints-Pères, at the corner of the narrow Rue Perronet, in the back room of a small, unglamorous café-tobacco shop with a gabled roof.

Some neighborhood publishing houses also served as ad hoc meeting places. One cannot forget the top-floor office of Jean Paulhan *chez* Gallimard. "There was always a crowd and we were packed together like herrings," Dominique Aury recalled. Claude Morgan frequented a more discreet publishing hideaway, Les Cahiers d'Art on the Rue du Dragon, which in fact was closed for business during the occupation. "This is where the cyclists delivered, by the trailer load, the tracts, newspapers, pamphlets that we were producing. A giant reproduction of a Matisse painting presided over our movements. The folding sessions took place on the mezzanine and Paul Eluard took part with that attention to detail that he brought to bear on everything."

Another Saint-Germain-des-Prés apartment played a singular role: the home of Marguerite Duras and her husband and their companions at the bottom of the Rue Saint-Benoît. In that old house, opposite a favorite cheap restaurant of Left Bank intellectuals (the Petit Saint-Benoît), Sainte-Beuve had lived after the Revolution of 1848, virtually in hiding. Closer to our own time, Léo Larguier, the author of *Saint-Germain-des-Prés, mon village,* had lived and died there. On his return to occupied France after meetings with the Free French in London and with Charles de Gaulle in Algiers, François Mitterrand turned up at the Duras flat, and he and others sat around smoking English cigarettes as Mitterrand recruited them into his resistance organization. The Duras apartment had a bed in every room, often all occupied.

Life here was complicated by the proximity of Ramon Fernandez, a regular contributor to the collaborationist press and cultural adviser to Jacques Doriot's pro-Fascist Parti Populaire Français. Fernandez lived two floors above the Duras apartment. Indeed, the Fernandezes had found the apartment for Marguerite Duras in the first place, and she and they were close until the goings and comings of the Duras group made it prudent to avoid encounters.

On Sundays the Fernandezes had their own informal salon, an open house that attracted a different crowd. Gerhard Heller was an occasional guest, and here he met many French writers for the first time. A frequent visitor was Drieu La Rochelle, Fernandez's editor at *La Nouvelle Revue Française*. Collaborationists also met at the Rive Gauche bookstore, strategically located on Boulevard Saint-Michel at the Place de la Sorbonne; Jean Guéhenno heard students refer to it as the "Left Bank of the Rhine." Although its name came from the prewar lecture group that introduced Fascist ideology to Paris and served as a breeding ground for collaborationists, the Rive Gauche bookstore was owned and operated by the Germans themselves and sold German literature as well as the works of their French friends. It was no small contribution to Left Bank morale when someone threw a bomb at the shop, and that happened more than once. Thus in November 1941 the windows of the store were blown out; students filed past "with closed mouths but laughing and speaking with their eyes," Guéhenno noted. One window had contained photographs of Henry de Montherlant from childhood on, with early letters and manuscripts. "All of that was blown to bits by the grenade explosion. What an irreparable loss!" The damage was repaired the same day, after which the remains of the books were displayed in a window with a sign reading, "Bombs against an idea!"

★ ★ ★

To sample the hospitality of literary salons in the German years, one had to be a collaborationist, or to wear a German uniform. One could also try it if one had the nonchalance of a Jean Paulhan. Thus we can follow the crowd in and out of Florence Gould's (although in the earlier postwar editions of Ernst Jünger's diary — one of the best sources — he gallantly disguised the French-born wife of American financier Frank Jay Gould as "Lady Orpington"). Jünger, carefully concealing his misgivings about Hitlerism, became a welcome guest at the homes of the most prominent literary and artistic personalities of occupied Paris — *chez* Marcel Jouhandeau, for example, or *chez* Paul Morand. He also met French friends at the German Embassy or the German Institute, or even at the Valentiner brothers' on Quai Voltaire.

On their side, the noncollaborationists had little public exposure. A more private form of celebration were the all-night parties described by Simone de Beauvoir, the "fiestas" held at the homes of friends possessing sufficiently large apartments. If a guest decided to stay beyond the curfew, he or she had to spend the night. Beauvoir recounts some memorable nights in the final months of the occupation, one of them at Michel Leiris's apartment on a Left Bank quay. It followed a reading of Picasso's play *Le Desir attrapé par la queue*, with Sartre among the actors, Camus directing, and Picasso, Georges Braque, Jean-Louis Barrault, Jacques Lacan, and Georges Bataille among the spectators. When the curfew (and the party) began, Sartre, Camus, and their comrades declaimed poetry, sang songs. Some days later Picasso invited his actors around the corner to his Rue des Grands-Augustins studio for a drink.

Like Florence Gould, who despite being an American could entertain both during and after the occupation, Pablo Picasso was a protected institution. He has been called an interior exile. If the ideologists of Vichy branded him and other modern artists as decadents who had contributed to France's decline, the Germans made a point of showing respect, and even tried to win him over. His studio became an obligatory port of call for cultured German officers, as well as French admirers, and it got so crowded at times that he could not work. He was often seen with a large group at the black-market Catalan restaurant on his street (once it was shut down for serving beef on a day when restaurants were not allowed to serve it under the rationing rules, and Picasso himself was fined). Although he engaged in no political activity, made no political statements, his very existence was a symbol. In *Comoedia* Vlaminck denounced him: "Pablo Picasso is guilty of having directed French painting into the most deadly impasse . . . to negation, impotence, death." Such an attack reinforced the respect in which Picasso was held by those who refused to collaborate. In the first issue of *Les Lettres Françaises* published in the open after the German departure from Paris, Louis Parrot wrote in homage: "By his very presence among us, he gave us hope . . . While it would have been so easy for him to leave Europe, Picasso refused to abandon the city where he had known misery and glory."

When Picasso joined the Communist Party some weeks after that, a five-column headline in *L'Humanité* proclaimed:

THE GREATEST LIVING PAINTER OF TODAY,
PICASSO HAS JOINED THE PARTY OF FRENCH RESISTANCE

The bookseller and writer Jean Galtier-Boissière in his journal mocked Picasso's resistance record, for he remembered only his expensive lunches at the Catalan restaurant.

24 Parisians Far from Paris

IF ONE WAS YOUNG, ambitious, and not too scrupulous about the people and groups with which one mingled, or if one was a member of the Establishment concerned with the protection and possibly the augmentation of one's privileges, Vichy was the place to be in 1940. Just as Paris had always attracted talented French-speaking people away from their own countries — from Belgium, from Switzerland — so Vichy drained brains from Paris in the year of the armistice. Even before the end of hostilities, the French government had begun to evacuate public and private services to that elegant south-central watering place. Then Philippe Pétain and Pierre Laval brought their parliament there, to meet in the baroque, turn-of-the-century Petit Casino, where only shortly before the pampered ill had gambled, drunk, been entertained. The luxury-class Hotel du Parc, with its three hundred rooms, became a seat of government. With France officially divided, it made sense to migrate to Vichy. "Overpopulated by vanquished soldiers, bureaucrats anxious to betray, socialites looking for society, Vichy . . . seemed to be an operetta," the young Roger Stéphane remembered. Arriving in Vichy early in the Pétain reign, Claude Roy, the young rightist who soon became a Communist and even a resistance activist, found much of the Parisian world he knew transplanted here. At the Youth Secretariat he discovered a kind of House of Culture called Jeune France (Young France), a rallying point for young theater people, musicians, poets, even left-wing journalists.

Yet in France under the Germans, to be able to think or create, even under official Vichy auspices, was already a luxury. For many Frenchmen and Frenchwomen, survival meant to flee. This was true for Jews and for known Communists or active left-wingers, especially if they lacked influential friends. Certainly Jews were in the avant-garde of "this legion of deserters," to cite the uncharitable phrase of one of the eager collaborationists. In that hour of exodus Alfred Fabre-Luce discovered that "the Jewish world" was larger than he had imagined: "It takes in not only the Jews, but all those they corrupted or seduced." Those who could not "desert" to Spain or England took refuge on the Riviera, which for a time was even controlled by the more benign Italians. The humorist Tristan Bernard, a Jew who found his way there, was credited with the line: "What do you call inhabitants of Cahors? Cadurciens. — Inhabitants of Juan-les-Pins [a Riviera resort]? Jews." Gide's Journal tells how Bernard, lecturing in Cannes, warned his listeners, "I myself belong to this people that has often been called 'the elected.' That is, 'waiting for the second ballot.' " Later Bernard, at the age of seventy-six, was arrested in a roundup. Influential friends obtained his release from a transit camp, which would have been the first step toward confinement and perhaps death in a concentration camp.

Manès Sperber, under the double handicap of being a Jew and a former Communist, served in the French army with an émigré company. When he managed to reach southern France, he found a refuge in Cagnes; on the recommendation of Malraux, Roger Martin du Gard hid his manuscripts. Eventually Sperber slipped across the border into Switzerland, where he spent the Vichy years. Julien Benda, banned from Drieu La Rochelle's Nouvelle Revue Française and, as a Jew, in certain danger, lived out the occupation in southwest France. All of his papers back in Paris, including those in the office of his publisher, were seized and never found. Emmanuel Berl, a Jew not known for his radicalism, was actually summoned to Bordeaux the week of the armistice to work on Marshal Pétain's speeches, apparently including the statement of June 25, in which Pétain told the French people: "A new order begins . . . I summon you to an intellectual and moral recovery first of all." Berl went on to Vichy, where he found Drieu La Rochelle, who in his "generosity" did not fight with his former friend, now so vulnerable. Berl and his wife, Mireille, a singer, spent a year in Cannes, where she was able to pursue her career, although from Paris Je Suis Partout denounced her as Jewish and expressed indignation that she was still allowed to perform. From Cannes the Berls moved to the remote Corrèze region, where Berl met up with his friend Malraux.

Jean Cassou had warned his superior at the Luxembourg Museum, then the repository of modern art, that it would not be wise to make him curator of the Museum of Modern Art, then in the planning stage. But his superior was certain that it would be all right, and he convinced Vichy that Cassou's record as a Communist sympathizer, and even his wife's being Jewish, should not prevent the appointment. So Cassou was informed that it had gone through. Returning home, he switched on the radio to hear a news report that "the Spanish Jew and Freemason" Cassou had been appointed curator of the Museum of Modern Art. He was fired at once, but stayed on in Paris and had an opportunity to help his friends in the Musée de l'Homme resistance cell. When the leaders of that group were arrested, he knew that he would soon have to go into hiding. Lacking a steady income, he began selling his personal library. When Cassou visited Robert Emile-Paul, one of the few publishers in Paris to side with the resistance, Emile-Paul opened a copy of the Fascist weekly *Au Pilori* and pointed to a headline denouncing the presence in Paris of the "Spanish Jew." "Old man," Emile-Paul said, "you've got to get out of town right away."

Cassou took refuge in Toulouse, a center of asylum for Spanish Republicans and Jews both. Max Ernst, the Surrealist, and Jacques Lipchitz, the Cubist sculptor, lived there before migrating to the United States. The refugees met in cafés that stayed open until midnight, or at a bookstore owned by an Italian anti-Fascist; it was a bit of the Left Bank transplanted. Cassou joined a military resistance group, the first to receive arms parachuted from the British, but he was arrested in December 1941. On his release, in the spring of 1943, he joined what was then a better-organized resistance. He became Charles de Gaulle's Commissioner of the Republic for the region. During the liberation of Toulouse, Cassou was wounded and spent weeks in a coma. While in prison, he had spent solitary days and nights composing poetry in his head; on a mission to Paris for his resistance organization, he met Jean Bruller and handed him the poems that at last he had been able to write down. Cassou's 33 *Sonnets* were published under the name "Jean Noir," with a preface by "François La Colère" — Aragon. (After the war Cassou returned to museum administration, as creator and first curator of Paris's Museum of Modern Art.)

Clara Malraux was both Jewish and an outspoken anti-Fascist. Paradoxically, her survival depended on her relationship to André Malraux, that singularly immune anti-Fascist. His chief priority was to obtain freedom to marry Josette Clotis, the mother of his sons. But Clara needed the protection of the Malraux name, for herself as well as for their daughter, and André Gide undertook the delicate task of convincing Malraux of this. Malraux brought up the matter of divorce again, even visiting Clara in Toulouse. "I don't want an illegitimate son," he explained. To which Clara replied, "How I wish that my daughter were illegitimate and without a Jewish mother!" So Malraux refused his permission — and permission was necessary — for Clara and their daughter to leave France. The same day — January 19, 1942 — Malraux told Clara that he would not participate in the resistance until the Americans landed. "I'm sick and tired of defending lost causes," she quotes him as saying.

Malraux's life in southern France could fill a book of its own. When he was ready to leave his Riviera villa, with its gloved valet serving seaside lunches under the orange trees, he created a myth of "interallied" resistance and, with his characteristic brashness, succeeded in making it real. Captured by the Germans, apparently through his own imprudence, he was saved by the German retreat.

But during the first two years of the occupation Malraux's chief preoccupation was a philosophical novel. He completed the first half, which he called Les Noyers de l'Altenburg ("The Walnut Trees of Altenburg"), and published it in Switzerland. Since he was working in self-imposed retreat, this might have been his best book, summing up a life of action and contemplation. But once again this dramatic era produced a failed work. The author had been trying to say too much, perhaps, or trying to write the book expected of the public figure he had now become. It was a meditation on war, art, mankind, hardly readable as fiction. Malraux himself realized this, and rather than allow it to be reprinted after the war, he broke it up and used parts of it in his Anti-mémoires. During the occupation he also worked on an essay on another man of action who was also a thinker, T.E. Lawrence.

Maria Van Rysselberghe provides the best description of Malraux during his "resistance year." On a visit to Paris from the southern zone, he asked the Bernard Groethuysens to arrange for him to stay at Gide's Rue Vaneau apartment. "He goes directly to the balcony, walks back and forth on it, inspects the cornice, the gutter, the roof, the breaks in the façade, with the eye of an expert — one never knows, does one? He takes note of all the exits... All this rapidly, without a superfluous word. If he were making a movie called 'Malraux' he wouldn't play it better." He also offered to have the British drop meat, tea, and cigarettes for the Van Rysselberghe family by parachute. When he relaxed and abandoned his personnage, Gide's confidante found Malraux even more interesting. During his exile on the Riviera, he had pursued not only his relations with all his Left Bank friends, but his literary affairs as well.

Receiving a manuscript from his onetime comrade Pascal Pia, he read it and recommended it at once to the Gallimards. It was *L'Etranger*.

★   ★   ★

No more curious Left Bank affinity survived the German years than the quasi-fraternal relations of Malraux and Pierre Drieu La Rochelle. It seems established that Drieu provided a protective umbrella for his occasionally insouciant friend throughout the German and Vichy rule. At the outset, we know, he told his contact at the Propagandastaffel that nothing must happen to Malraux (and some others), and the man from the Propagandastaffel — aware of Malraux's forays into occupied Paris and even of Drieu's journey to see him in southern France — was quite prepared to intervene if necessary. During the years of Drieu's active collaboration with the Germans Malraux continued to see him, apparently willingly. Thus in the summer of 1941, Drieu spent some days at the Riviera villa. In May 1943, still director of *La Nouvelle Revue Française*, Drieu noted in his diary: "Saw Malraux in Paris. He no longer believes in anything, denies Russian strength, thinks that the world has no meaning and goes to the dogs: the American solution. But it's that he himself has renounced being something to be only a literary man. Will he be great enough in this area to justify his existence? . . . He advises me to do as he does . . ."

In a will drafted in October 1943, after the collapse of his *Nouvelle Revue Française*, Drieu named Malraux as one of his literary executors. Later, in a final will before his suicide, he requested that Malraux attend his funeral.

★   ★   ★

In Tunisia, where he arrived from the Riviera in early May 1942, Gide settled down to a routine of writing and meditating — a routine that had not been possible during his unsettling months on the Riviera, with the constant pressures from Paris to collaborate with *La Nouvelle Revue Française*. Still, he did not settle down without doubts, for he wondered what he had left to say. "In what way can I serve henceforth?" he asked his diary. "In what way will I be needed?"

He was translating *Hamlet*, indulging his senses, reading classics. He finished *The Red and the Black* during an Allied air raid (Tunisia was in the hands of the Axis). In November 1942 he was cut off from mainland France by the Allied landings in North Africa, a situation that did not change when the Allies liberated Tunis in May 1943. A rumor spread in Paris that Gide was seeking writers to sign a petition requesting his repatriation. Gide's friend Roger Martin du Gard devoted himself to circulating a denial.

As soon as he could, Gide flew to Algiers, now safely in Allied hands. "The Americans, in our old world, are liked by everyone and everywhere," he wrote with elation. "So quick with their generosity, so friendly and smiling, so natural, that one joyfully accepts being in debt to them."

Arriving in Algiers, Gide had the pleasure of finding Antoine de Saint-Exupéry already on the scene. The pioneer pilot, his old friend, had served in reconnaissance during the brief months of the 1939-40 war, had gone on to the United States after the German victory, and in New York wrote an account of his experiences and impressions. This was *Pilote de guerre* ("Flight to Arras"), the book the Germans banned in Paris (although Jean Galtier-Boissière, the nonconformist bookseller, testified that it continued to be sold in occupied Paris under the counter).

In New York Saint-Exupéry also published *Lettre à un otage*, a small book written as an open letter to a Jewish friend in occupied France. In fact, the author pointed out, there were forty million hostages in France, and the duty of those outside the country was to serve those left behind. "Perhaps you won't read our books. You won't hear our speeches... We are not creating France. We can only serve her..." Saint-Exupéry himself returned to serve, and then disappeared on an aerial mission to southern France at the end of July 1944.

New York — with Jules Romains, André Maurois, Jacques Maritain, Julien Green — was a magnet for voluntarily exiled writers and thinkers. By now Jacques Schiffrin, Gide's friend and editor, was there, publishing books in French and in the familiar softcover French format; among them were Gide's *Interviews imaginaires* and Vercors's *Le Silence de la mer*. Soon Schiffrin joined forces with another émigré publisher, Kurt Wolff, and created Pantheon Books. Another French-language publisher in New York, Editions de la Maison Française, intentionally evoked the familiar Gallimard covers in its book design. Among its authors were Raymond Aron, Julien Benda, Julien Green, Jacques Maritain, André Maurois, Jules Romains, and Philippe Soupault, the veteran Surrealist, who had written an account of his captivity in Vichy-controlled Tunisia called *Le Temps des assassins* ("Age of Assassins").

Thanks to the Emergency Rescue Committee, the private American program of aid to refugees, a number of intellectuals who were in danger in France — outspoken anti-Fascists, Jews — were assisted during their stay on or near the Riviera and sometimes could be evacuated to safe haven in the Western Hemisphere. The Committee set up a base in Marseille, in the Vichy zone, for the United States maintained relations with Pétain even after it entered the war in December 1941. André Malraux used this channel to obtain funds from his American publisher, who paid advances on his royalties to the Committee in New York. Malraux received French currency from the Committee in Marseille (the Committee got the francs from departing refugees, who in turn would be reimbursed in dollars when they reached the United States). Thus, in the first winter of German occupation, André Breton and Victor Serge, among others, inhabited a spacious villa on the outskirts of Marseille, as guests of the Emergency Rescue Committee. They discovered it to be a rendezvous of Surrealists, among them Hans Bellmer, Victor Brauner, René Char, Max Ernst, André Masson, and Benjamin Peret. When Marshal Pétain visited Marseille, the police arrested Breton and his American hosts and subjected them to interrogation. But eventually Breton reached New York, where he stayed throughout the war, broadcasting to France through the Voice of America. He also mounted an international exhibition with Marcel Duchamp to benefit prisoners, and published a magazine with Duchamp and Max Ernst.

★ ★ ★

The writers who stayed behind — in Paris or in the more forbidding and therefore more hospitable provinces of southern France, especially the hills of the southwesterly Lot and Dordogne regions, which seemed almost designed for hiding — could publish without shame in a number of journals in Vichy France. Some of these were founded with the express purpose of saying what could not be said on the Left Bank. Pierre Seghers's *Poésie* was one such magazine, certainly the closest mainland counterpart to *Fontaine* in Algiers, but taking the risk of greater proximity to Vichy and to the Germans, not to speak of the danger of sheltering that marked couple Louis Aragon and Elsa Triolet. In Villeneuve-lès-Avignon, just opposite the walls of Avignon across the Rhône, Seghers was more than an editor. He often served as a liaison between members of the intellectual resistance who might not otherwise have been able to keep in touch. When necessary, a writer for *Poésie* used a pseudonym, just as he would when contributing to the underground press.

Confluences began innocently enough, as the venture of several young men of good family who wished to publish and be published. But in that time and place — July 1941, and Lyon — such an enterprise was certain to attract writers denied access to the Paris reviews, or who refused to write for them. As director of *Confluences*, René Tavernier published Aragon, Eluard, Louis Martin-Chauffier (the prewar editor of *Vendredi*), Pierre Emmanuel, and Pierre Seghers. Although its program called for a cultural diversity that would include "acceptable" authors — Maurice Barrès, Paul Claudel, Henry de Montherlant, and Jean Giraudoux, as well as Henri Bergson, Marcel Proust, and Gide — *Confluences* was fated to publish the damned. Clara Malraux's name appeared on its cover, as did the names of Sartre and Mauriac.

Because it printed a poem by Aragon called "Nymphée," Vichy suspended *Confluences* for two months. The same issue (July 1942) contained contributions by Gertrude Stein, who was of Jewish origin and American, and by Max Jacob, a convert to Catholicism but still a Jew according to German and Vichy yardsticks. Gertrude Stein and her companion, Alice Toklas, lived in a village near the Lake of Bourget in central France, where they received packages simply addressed "to the American women," although a German security office was nearby. Another contribution by Gertrude Stein appeared in a symposium issue of *Confluences* on "Problems of the Novel," together with work by key figures in the intellectual resistance: Jacques Debû-Bridel, Robert Desnos, Martin-Chauffier, Claude Morgan. There was also an essay by that young man just becoming known in mainland France, Albert Camus. On the death of Max Jacob during detention, *Confluences* offered him a poetic homage, and in the same issue there was a review of Robert Brasillach's poetry, citing passages likely to provoke laughter at his expense. None of this was lost on Vichy, which informed Tavernier that his magazine would receive "reinforced control." In Paris, a collaborationist daily reported:

> The literary magazines of the southern zone have always manifested, more or less slyly, the greatest tenderness for the defunct Third Republic, its Jews, pederasts, and Freemasons.
>
> Among these magazines, *Confluences*, which is published in Lyon... has always distinguished itself by its zeal in opposing new ideas. To write for this magazine it is sufficient to be an American Jewess, without talent, like Gertrude Stein.
>
> A writer is interned? At once his name appears in the table of contents of the next issue of *Confluences* . . .

25 Liberation

THE MORE LUCID of the collaborationists did not have to wait for the Anglo-American landings on the Normandy beaches in June 1944 to realize that the time was approaching when, in Simone de Beauvoir's phrase, "they were to be expelled from the press, from France, from the future." Among themselves they manifested significant differences of opinion, the most reckless pushing on with their pro-German militancy and attacking the others — those who realized that their side was losing the war — as "quitters." In a vain attempt to boost the morale of the hard-liners, the fanatics of *Je Suis Partout* sponsored a public meeting in January 1944, while Allied troops were moving slowly but inexorably northward in Italy. By then Robert Brasillach was sounding like one of the quitters, for he had lost faith in Fascist might, if not right.

Already — and he was among the first — Céline had rushed to the German Embassy and demanded authorization to flee to Germany. Others among the most violent collaborationists began to leave, or to take cover in anonymous hotel rooms, in the homes of sympathizers. Those who could get out went to Germany or to Italy. Sigmaringen, in the southwest corner of besieged Germany, provided shelter for the hard core of Vichy's rulers, including Philippe Pétain, virtually a captive in his castle. Even Céline was there for a while. His eerie description of Sigmaringen in *D'un château l'autre* are his best postwar pages.

Lucien Combelle describes a sentimental *soirée d' adieu* in Paris in the company of Pierre Drieu La Rochelle, while Karl Epting, their friend from the German Institute, packed to return to Germany. Over cognac they discussed the errors of the collaborationists and what they felt to be the double or even the triple game Vichy was playing. Drieu, Combelle remembered, was "lucid, pessimistic, still rather nervous, slightly disdainful." Silent about his own plans, he wished Combelle a future career in the Communist Party, since "the Communists will be the heirs of Fascism in Europe." On August 10, a friend encountered Drieu in the early morning, walking near his Avenue de Breteuil apartment.

"What are you up to, my friend?"

"I've made my decision," Drieu replied. "I'm leaving." His departure was to have taken the form of suicide, although in that August attempt he failed. Gerhard Heller, preparing his own evacuation from Paris, had a passport made out that would have taken Drieu to Spain or to Switzerland. He phoned Drieu on August 13 to discover that he was in a hospital. Leaping onto his bicycle, he went straight to his bedside, and was there when he opened his eyes for the first time. He slipped the passport under his friend's pillow.

The liberation of Paris came about when advancing Allied troops obliged the Germans to withdraw all along their front, making the evacuation of cities such as Paris essential if the Germans were not to be trapped. This is military history, but history is also composed of myth, and myth wants the liberation of Paris to be the work of its citizens. True, its citizens willed liberation, and many died in its streets in one heroic week in August 1944. At the request of Charles de Gaulle, the insurrection was timed to the approach of Allied forces, which included elements of the Free French, and a French column was in the avant-garde when the Allies entered Paris. The combined result — of volunteer fighters in the streets, of Allied tanks — allowed Frenchmen to hold their heads high in the difficult months that would follow.

> At six o'clock in the morning, I ran along the Boulevard Raspail: the Leclerc division paraded on the Avenue d'Orléans, and along the sidewalks, an immense crowd applauded it [recorded Simone de Beauvoir] . . . From time to time a shot was fired: a sniper on the roofs; someone fell, was carried off, but no one seemed upset: enthusiasm stamped out fear.

All day long she and Sartre walked through flag-decked Paris, watching women in their Sunday clothes offer kisses to the liberating armies. "What emotions in my heart!" Soon Sartre would be publishing his own observations in Camus's *Combat*, in a series of articles entitled "Un promeneur dans Paris insurgé" ("A stroller in the Paris insurrection"). While the firing continued, and the passing tanks shook his old house, Pablo Picasso was absorbed in painting a *Bacchanale* inspired by a seventeenth-century painting by Nicolas Poussin. What could a Sartre or a Picasso do? The glory belonged to young men with rifles that week.

Up from Villeneuve-lès-Avignon, Pierre Seghers found it impossible to remain indoors while the insurrection raged and barricades were thrown up at vital crossroads. He and Paul Eluard collected a bundle of tracts, copies of *Les Lettres Françaises*, of *L'Eternelle Revue*, the vest-pocket-sized magazine Eluard had begun to publish, and a collection of resistance songs, and off they went to hand them out along the Rue du Dragon. "Suddenly German soldiers appeared, hugging the walls along the Boulevard Saint-Germain, machine gun or grenades at the ready."

Sylvia Beach tells of fighting along the Rue de l'Odéon. When at last the jeeps arrive, one stops in front of her building, number 12. She hears a deep voice shouting her name. Adrienne Monnier cries, "It's Hemingway!" Beach rushes downstairs. In battle dress, grimy and bloody (or so she remembered it later), Hemingway picks her up and swings her around, kissing her as onlookers cheer. At the request of the two booksellers, Hemingway orders his company out of the jeeps and up to the roofs to clear out the snipers, and that puts an end to the firing on the street. Hemingway and his men come down again and take their leave, "to liberate the cellar at the Ritz," as he tells her. Myths are made of such stuff.

★   ★   ★

During the German occupation, one of the best organized resistance movements was Combat, founded to carry out sabotage and paramilitary action, to collect intelligence, and to supply false papers and other logistical support to its underground warriors. It was also one of the best-known movements, thanks to a monthly newspaper, also called *Combat*, that distributed tens of thousands of copies of each issue. From the beginning *Combat* attracted writers and journalists. Its Paris activities were in the charge of Claude Bourdet, son of the playwright Edouard. Albert Camus, arriving in Paris in the fall of 1943 to work for Gallimard — who by then had published *L'Etranger* and *Le Mythe de Sisyphe* ("The Myth of Sisyphus") and became his regular publisher — was immediately recruited into the Combat movement by an old mentor, Pascal Pia. Pia, a prewar companion of André Malraux, had been Camus's superior at the Popular Front daily *Alger Républicain*; as we have noted, he sent the manuscript of *L'Etranger* to Malraux. An underground resistance activist, Pia had become editor of *Combat*, but when he was called to other secret duties, he nominated Camus to replace him. So Camus was an editor at Gallimard by day, an editor for underground *Combat* by night. At the time, *Combat* was printed on a small page that facilitated printing and distribution. The crowded pages were carefully laid out so that printers working far from headquarters could set them into type without further recourse to the editors.

Camus and his colleagues were also planning the first issues of a daily version of *Combat*, which they intended to publish openly in Paris as soon as the Germans had departed. The Combat movement, like many other resistance groups led by young idealists and veteran patriots, hoped to carry the spirit and ideology of the liberation struggle into the politics of postwar France. Nearly all of these groups had drawn up political programs. *Combat's* was summed up in a motto printed each day in postliberation Paris just under the masthead: "From Resistance to Revolution." It had the chance to present the right image at the right time — of a young left-wing generation impatient with its elders, whose compromises and corruptions had weakened France on the eve of the Second World War.

So it happened that *Combat*, born of resistance to the occupation, introduced a new generation of intellectuals: Camus first of all, a new arrival who would henceforth never stray very far from Saint-Germain-des-Prés, his new friends Jean-Paul Sartre and Simone de Beauvoir, who would rapidly become the most famous personalities of the Left Bank, and a versatile, sometimes brilliant collection of young men and women who were the editors, reporters, and critics of the daily *Combat*. To improve their chances, they also engaged experienced journalists of the prewar press; later they were joined by Raymond Aron.

By prearrangement, each underground paper took over the building and presses of one of the established dailies that had collaborated during the German years. The *Combat* staff was one of three assigned to the large plant that had been used by the German army's *Pariser Zeitung*. They began to move in while German tanks still patrolled the streets, and found German uniforms and grenades in the offices they were to occupy. Although the *Combat* staff was in place by August 18, they delayed publication at the request of Gaullist resistance leaders, to avoid provoking the withdrawing Germans during the fragile truce that had been arranged. But on August 21 their first issue came out. Distributed on the streets of Paris to the accompaniment of shooting, it contained news of the uprising of Parisians and of the progress of Allied troops outside the capital.

An editorial by Camus, but not signed, appeared on the first page each day. "Paris fires all of its bullets in the August night," began the editorial of August 24, presenting the ideals of those leading the liberation movement against the background of continued fighting in the streets. "One cannot ask those who fought in silence for four years . . . to allow the return of the forces of resignation and injustice . . ." Day after day *Combat* and the other new dailies and weeklies, whether Communist-controlled, independent left-wing, or liberal, served as a check on the provisional government of the authoritarian Charles de Gaulle and on its consultative assembly, which had moved to Paris from Algiers; *Combat* commented on the first laws, the first court decisions, the behavior of citizens as well as leaders. The paper also supported punishing those who had sold out to the enemy during the German years. And all this in the context of a postwar France that had to throw off years of German pillage, Vichy law, and humility to raise itself from the ruins.

★　　★　　★

On October 29, 1944, the column at the top right of the front page of *Combat* was headlined:

ON THE VOSGES FRONT

THE ALSACE-LORRAINE BRIGADE: COLONEL MALRAUX

The story, by Jacques-Laurent Bost, a former student of Sartre, reported an encounter with "two writers in the struggle": André Malraux, "slender and nervous, wearing a beret with officer's braid" (he soon turned up at the *Combat* office in this attire, to be photographed for posterity alongside his admirer, an equally slender Albert Camus), and *commandant* André Chamson.

In the southwest Dordogne, Malraux had organized an armed resistance movement, had been arrested and imprisoned by the Germans, until the advance of Allied troops from a beachhead on the southern French coast forced their withdrawal; Malraux was one of the prisoners they abandoned. Soon after that, he attached himself to a group of Alsatian resistance fighters, and they to him, believing that he could lead them in the liberation of their province.

At the outset of the occupation, André Chamson, as a museum curator, had been assigned to protect monuments and works of art, until the attacks on his fellow curator Jean Cassou made it advisable that he too remove himself from public scrutiny. In Montauban in southwest France, where art treasures such as the Mona Lisa were under the care of a Louvre museum team that included Chamson's wife, Lucie Mazauric, Chamson took up writing again, although he was determined not to publish anything under the combined servitudes of the Nazis and Vichy. When the Chamsons and their treasures were evacuated to a still more secure corner of France, Chamson joined the local *maquis*, and when General Jean de Lattre de Tassigny landed in Provence, he offered his own troops to the advancing French army. Soon Chamson had joined his battalion to the two battalions of "Colonel Berger" — as André Malraux styled himself and a character he invented for his autobiographical *Les Noyers de l'Altenburg*. Thus was formed the Brigade Alsace-Lorraine, most of whose soldiers, natives of those provinces, had refused to accept their annexation by Germany.

One day, as he and Chamson inspected the front lines together, Malraux began reciting what sounded like a chant: "I have been French ever since France existed . . . Because I am linked to this soil by its cemeteries and its furrows . . ."

"What are you quoting?" Chamson asked. "You don't recognize your own words?" It was the peroration of Chamson's rousing speech to the International Writers Congress at the Palais de la Mutualité in 1935.

PART IV

1944
and After

26 Picking Up the Pieces

COULD ANYONE HAVE doubted, in the weeks following the liberation, that Paris would never again be the same? Certainly not any of those who had taken part in the fight to free it, any more than those who had accepted or even facilitated the German occupation and were now in jail awaiting trial, in hiding, or in flight. No thinking person could have expected prewar conditions to return. The new government was a provisional government; the legislature was a consultative assembly; there could be no regression to the Third Republic of the 1930s, any more than a continuation of the Vichy state. Charles de Gaulle had arrived from Algiers with the best representatives of France in exile, to join forces with mainland Frenchmen who had lived still more dangerously.

It was a heady time for writers and other intellectuals. The streets of Paris seemed to be theirs for the asking. "To be twenty or twenty-five in September 1944 seemed an enormous bit of luck: all roads opened before one," exclaimed Simone de Beauvoir afterward. In 1944 she was thirty-six; Sartre was thirty-nine. "Journalists, writers, budding filmmakers discussed, planned, decided with passion, as if their future depended on themselves alone."

Not only the people, but what the people read and listened to, were different. All of a sudden underground publications came to the surface; the Communists and their fronts alone sponsored enough new periodicals to fill a newsstand. Those who published far from Paris were attracted to the liberated capital like moths to a lamp. As soon as he could obtain an allocation of paper, Max-Pol Fouchet moved *Fontaine* from Algiers; *L'Arche*, the Gide-sponsored rival, also transferred to Paris; the Algiers publisher Edmond Charlot brought his company, and soon rivaled the veteran Gallimard with the quality of his authors, the

significance of the books he published.   René Tavernier brought
Confluences from Lyon, Pierre Seghers his *Poésie* from Villeneuve-lès-
Avignon.   Summoned back to edit *Ce Soir* by the Communist Party,
Louis Aragon invited Jean Cassou to return and direct the Party's
monthly, *Europe*; only Romain Rolland, the founder of that magazine,
was missing, for he died on December 30, 1944.   The board was
expanded to include resistance veterans sympathetic to the Party, such as
Vercors.

There was an empty space on the racks, however. It should have been
filled with the familiar shape and colors of *La Nouvelle Revue Française*,
but that magazine was under a ban.   Appointed "liquidator" of the old
N.R.F., Jean Paulhan began to plan an elegant literary review to be called
Cahiers de la Pléiade, in memory of the N.R.F., for he would be soliciting
contributions from the surviving eminences, such as Gide, who
contributed *Thésée*, a short play he had been saving for a revival of the
N.R.F.   "*Cahiers de la Pléiade* doesn't feel obliged to take a stand on
major economic or national conflicts," announced the presentation
accompanying the first issue, in an apparent disengagement on Paulhan's
part.   "It simply hopes to bring together a number of curious, modest,
and seemingly useless texts that other periodicals, busy with great and
noble projects, might neglect."

Paulhan was reacting, mildly in this instance, to the vigorous purging
of Paris's intellectual life, the fruit of an understandable and long-
repressed desire for revenge, the fruit of an atmosphere in which
"everybody collaborated" was becoming "we all resisted." "I notice that
there were never more than fifteen of us at meetings [of the National
Committee of Writers] held at Edith Thomas's," Jean Guéhenno noted
in his diary, "but with Paris finally liberated, at our first gathering in
September 1944 we curiously found ourselves in a crowd of over a
hundred, at least eighty of whom we had never seen before and who,
with all reasons for living lost, had nevertheless lived very well."

It was enough to discourage Guéhenno from attending further
meetings of the CNE.   But that organization was now enjoying the
privileges of victory, and who could have wished to deny its membership
— those who had risked arrest, prison, or death every moment of those
dark years — their time of exultation? Jean Bruller was among those who
attended the first CNE meeting after the liberation, held in the former
plant of *Paris-Soir*, where *Les Lettres Françaises*, now a weekly
newspaper, was being produced in broad daylight.   Claude Roy
interviewed him for *Front National*, a Communist-front daily also

published in that building. How did Bruller feel, having become a "great French writer" overnight? Jacques Debû-Bridel, director of *Front National*, told him: "This time, Vercors, you mustn't laugh; you're going to join the Académie Française!"

The first issue of *Les Lettres Françaises* after the liberation was dated September 9. It proclaimed itself the organ of the CNE, and its front page reproduced a Manifesto of French Writers signed by three members of the Académie Française — Georges Duhamel, François Mauriac, and Paul Valéry — along with fifty others, including Camus, Eluard, Guéhenno, Michel Leiris, Jean Lescure, Paulhan, Queneau, and Sartre, and a dozen more from the south, such as Aragon, Benda, Cassou, Malraux, and Roger Martin du Gard. The manifesto concluded:

> Let us remain united in victory and freedom as we were in sorrow and oppression.
>
> Let us remain united for the resurrection of France and the fair punishment of the imposters and traitors . . .

The call for "fair punishment" divided the Left Bank into two unequal parts. On one side, the overwhelming majority was determined to wipe out the last traces of pro-Nazi and collaborationist ideologies, and the supporters of those ideologies. On the other, a smaller group motivated by humanitarian instincts, and at times by personal ties to one or more transgressors, demanded that bygones be bygones. The leading activists of the CNE, the Communists, and also the idealists of *Combat* led by Camus, were among the most ardent advocates of the purge. Two writers, Mauriac and Paulhan, became spokesmen for "forgive and forget." The irony was that both had been among the early architects of a black list of collaborationists.

> Those who have forgotten evil in the name of good
> Those who have no heart preach pardon

So began a poem by Paul Eluard, a leader of the avengers, printed on the front page of *Les Lettres Françaises* in March 1945.

> No jewel is more precious
> Than the desire to avenge the innocent
> . . .

★   ★   ★

In its first public issue, *Les Lettres Françaises* reported a unanimous decision of the National Committee of Writers. CNE members would refuse to write for any periodical or book series that also published the work of collaborationists. Already, in a plenary meeting of that organization, a preliminary blacklist of collaborationists had been drafted, featuring the most obvious and prominent, such as Brasillach, Céline, Drieu La Rochelle, Marcel Jouhandeau, Charles Maurras, Henry de Montherlant, and Paul Morand. It was not a blacklist in the usual sense, for it did not call for a ban on the writers it condemned. Instead, CNE members would simply refuse to be published wherever the condemned writers were published. The second weekly issue of *Les Lettres Françaises* offered a longer list, containing over a hundred names, including writers who were later found guilty in the courts and sentenced to death or to long stays in prison — minor writers with major transgressions, but also some major writers guilty of minor transgressions.

The CNE list did not include publishers as such. Resistance writers were not going to refuse to be published by Gallimard, say, if Gallimard continued to publish Jouhandeau, or by Plon if it published Brasillach. A separate Purge Committee of Publishing and Bookselling had been formed, composed of representatives of the government and of publishers, together with such writers as Sartre, Vercors, and Pierre Seghers. The Committee suggested, for example, that Jean Paulhan be appointed extraordinary adviser with the mandate to liquidate *La Nouvelle Revue Française*, which was not to be allowed to appear under any title, and to see that the publishing house itself no longer called itself "Editions de la N.R.F.," i.e., Nouvelle Revue Française Publishing House. (Just before one of the Committee's sessions in the Cercle de la Librairie headquarters on Boulevard Saint-Germain, a group of members met with Sartre in his small hotel on the nearby Rue de Seine to coordinate their positions. Vercors wished to be harsh with the Gallimards, but Sartre pleaded their case.)

In the end, as Vercors and his friends protested in the pages of *Les Lettres Françaises*, the worst of the collaborationist publishers not only continued to function, but even received paper allocations in a period of acute scarcity, so that authors were obliged to take their manuscripts to them if they wished to be published. These established houses had been able to build up stocks of paper precisely because they served the Germans, alleged Vercors, while his Editions de Minuit, the underground publisher that became an above-ground publisher in liberated Paris, could not obtain enough paper to produce new books or even to reprint its underground series.

Sanctions, in any case, did not represent eternal punishment. Many of those blacklisted — and even writers who received more serious punishment, such as a ban on publication of their works for a given period (ordered by the official National Purge Committee of Men of Letters, Playwrights, and Composers, which was authorized to sit as a court) — returned soon enough to active creation, and often to fame. To membership in the Académie Française, for example, or to celebrity on the government-owned radio and television networks.

The purges destroyed many wartime alliances between Left Bank intellectuals. At first Jean Paulhan served as a court of appeal, accepting the blacklist as a necessary evil while seeking to attenuate its effect on writers who he felt had been misguided. Both Arthur Rimbaud and Romain Rolland would have been on the blacklist, Paulhan argued, the former for applauding the Prussian occupation of France in 1870, the latter for his opposition to World War I. Paulhan's first public dissent appeared in *Les Lettres Françaises* itself. With blacklists and governmental purge committees, he argued, genuine resistance veterans will get all the assignments, and so will have no time for serious work. "During this time, collaborationist writers, left to themselves, will work on their own. After five or ten years they will return in force with seasoned works . . ." He thought a great deal about his friend Marcel Jouhandeau, and sought testimonials on his behalf. Jouhandeau, Paulhan insisted, had joined a writers' delegation to Nazi Germany only to help French war prisoners, and he had actually refused to contribute to the violent collaborationist press. Paulhan told Vercors that he placed Jouhandeau above Goethe, and he asked Vercors to promise that Jouhandeau would not be denounced in *Les Lettres Françaises* (which would lead to his prosecution), if he, Paulhan, published Jouhandeau's work in *Cahiers de la Pléiade*. (Meanwhile, Paulhan explained to Jouhandeau that if he had not used his work in the first issue of his magazine, it was to avoid creating difficulties for him.) Paulhan promised that he would resign from CNE if it did not remove Jouhandeau from its blacklist. And he published Jouhandeau in the second issue of his *Cahiers*.

In the same issue — dated April 1947 — Paulhan's own essay, whose title can be translated as "Of Chaff and Wheat," pointed out that it was up to the police to deal with authors who committed crimes. The effect of the blacklist, he said, had been to close publishing houses and magazines to some writers, so that a novel by Montherlant had to be

published in far-off Ecuador, an essay by Jouhandeau in Switzerland, a
novel by Drieu La Rochelle in Argentina; and just to find out what
Gabriel Marcel thinks of the purges — "he thinks badly of them" — one
must go to Canada. What had begun as a democratic ideal — not to
write for a medium where collaborationists were published — had
become fascistic.

Like Paulhan, François Mauriac also regretted his early and ardent
position in favor of purging collaborationists. In that first public issue of
Les Lettres Françaises, he had contributed a stirring appeal for drawing
lessons from the acts of the collaborationists: they should never again be
allowed to harm France. "From those who shared in this error the least
that the Republic can demand is withdrawal and silence." He warned his
colleagues of the Académie Française that if they did not expel Charles
Maurras after his conviction for collaborationist crimes, he himself
would resign. But the trials of collaborationists, which often enough
concluded with a death sentence, caused the good Christian in him to
react against the purge courts. The inconsistency of the sentences
reminded him of a lottery. Soon he was engaged in a battle of the front
pages with Albert Camus — Mauriac in the conservative Figaro calling
for charity, Camus in Combat placing reliance on "human justice with its
terrible imperfections," corrected "by a desperately maintained
honesty." The duel reached a climax with an editorial by Mauriac
mocking "our young master" who emitted his judgments "from the
height, I suppose, of his future work." Although Camus later revised his
own position concerning justice and charity, and removed himself from
the National Committee of Writers as its Communist orientation
became more evident, the bitterness of that feud forever separated these
believers, respectively, in a Christian and a lay morality.

The debate raged in Les Lettres Françaises. Julien Benda protested
that "international socialites" circulated expressions of pity for
collaborationists in the drawing rooms of high society. In the Catholic
Esprit, challenging Mauriac, a writer mocked those who saw in the
purges "a literary theme on charity," and quoted Charles Péguy on the
need to punish enemies of one's country. Sartre and Beauvoir approved
the CNE blacklist. Vengeance was vain, they felt, but certain people had
no place in the new world they were trying to build.

27 Consequences

THE MOST ASTOUNDING THING — a testimonial to the strange attraction Pierre Drieu La Rochelle exercised on his friends — was the energy committed anti-Fascists employed to help him. For Drieu was a fugitive, ripe for a firing squad, from the day Paris was free of German occupation troops until his suicide in March 1945. He spent nearly seven months in hiding, never leaving Paris, and during that time Robert Brasillach and many other notorious collaborationists were tried and executed. Reporting the twenty-year prison sentence given to an associate of Drieu in January 1945, *Les Lettres Françaises* reminded readers that Drieu himself was still at large.

One person who might have helped him was André Malraux, now engaged at the front with his Alsace-Lorraine Brigade. Malraux was indeed asked, although history does not tell us by whom, whether he would accept Drieu in his brigade. "Of course," he replied, but made it clear that Drieu would find himself in an uncomfortable environment. Another source suggests that Malraux posed conditions that Drieu found unacceptable, Malraux being more interested in his own role than in the fate of his friend.

Emmanuel Berl, whom Drieu had cast off because of his Jewish origin, continued to think of Drieu, and even mapped out some hiding places for his onetime comrade in the remote Corrèze region. But when Drieu escaped capture and punishment by killing himself, Berl was angry. "He accepted the idea of living in hiding when I was the victim, but he himself couldn't take it." A no less surprising offer to help came from Emmanuel d'Astier de la Vigerie, a prewar right-wing extremist who had since converted to anti-Fascism and amassed a distinguished record in the underground resistance (later he became a famous friend of the

Soviet Union and of Joseph Stalin in person). As Charles de Gaulle's first Minister of the Interior, installed in liberated Paris in September 1944, d'Astier expressed concern for his prewar comrade. He even suggested that Drieu slip across the border to Switzerland to escape the justice for which he himself, as Minister, was the guardian. Finally d'Astier told a mutual friend: "Hurry up and use my help, for I'll only be Minister for another three days."

Malraux could not be reached for Drieu's funeral, after the third and this time successful suicide attempt, by gas and drugs. Jean Paulhan was there, and Gaston Gallimard, Paul Léautaud, Jacques Audiberti, Brice Parain. Paulhan wrote to Drieu's half-Jewish first wife that perhaps the dead man had sacrificed himself so that others would not be troubled. "It is certain that the Drieu trial would also have been the trial of Chardonne, Jouhandeau, Fabre-Luce . . ."

★ ★ ★

Not all of the manhunts and prosecutions of postliberation Paris had to do with melancholic romantic heroes like Drieu La Rochelle. But Robert Brasillach was a well-liked man. A friend wrote of him that he "was all of youth. He was the revolutionary of kindness, of a love of life, of intelligence." Never mind that he had been the archetypical collaborationist, admitting to having "more or less slept with Germany." One of the accusations at Brasillach's trial was that after the fall of France the Germans had released him from a prisoner-of-war camp because of his potential usefulness, and he had given full value, denouncing the resistance and exposing his enemies to the German and collaborationist police. His only regret, after the roundup of Jews in Paris in 1942, was that the Germans might spare Jewish children (this was the statement that made Gerhard Heller of the Propagandastaffel break down and cry).

But Brasillach was a graduate of the Ecole Normale Supérieure, he was an author, almost an intellectual, a member of the Left Bank club who had strayed. After he received the death sentence for collusion with the enemy in January 1945, François Mauriac, his son Claude, Marcel Aymé, and Thierry Maulnier campaigned for a pardon, drafting a petition to Charles de Gaulle, head of the provisional government. Mauriac took on the job of persuading fellow members of the Académie Française to sign the petition; Valéry and Claudel accepted, and among resistance activists, Paulhan and Camus. Camus after much hesitation, for he believed that Brasillach had encouraged the arrest and torture of his comrades, and had never asked for clemency for the resistance writers in enemy hands.

In a private meeting with de Gaulle, Mauriac pleaded the case for clemency. The evidence is contradictory, but the most reasonable version of their talk is that de Gaulle was particularly angered by Brasillach's journey to Germany to encourage French volunteers who fought alongside German troops against the Soviet Union; when Brasillach went on trial, the war against Germany was still raging on both the eastern and western fronts. Brasillach stood before the firing squad on February 6, 1945.

Although leading figures of the daily press and radio were executed, no other creative writer received capital punishment. Clearly it helped that the guilty ones had delayed their arrests and trials by hiding until the fever of liberation justice dropped. Thus the prosecution of Lucien Rebatet and Brasillach's other *Je Suis Partout* colleagues took place only in November 1946, over a year and a half after Brasillach's execution. (Rebatet had left Paris with the Germans for Sigmaringen, while Brasillach stayed behind and was arrested.) This time the nonconformist Galtier-Boissière set about rallying support for Rebatet, although Galtier-Boissière had been a frequent target of the accused's polemics. The letter he obtained from Pierre Bourdan of the Free French radio of wartime London summed up a state of mind. "Without seeing any excuse for Rebatet's criminal behavior," Bourdan wrote, "I nevertheless consider, as many Frenchmen do, that our courts show flagrant partiality in prosecuting acts of collaboration. Writers and journalists who with their signatures accepted responsibility for their acts are sanctioned with the full force of law. On the other hand, remarkable leniency is shown to lawyers who denounced other Frenchmen... to generals and admirals ... manufacturers who reinforced the German war machine... finally and especially the publishers of newspapers who inspired collaborationism ... and financed it ...."

Rebatet was not executed. Charles Maurras, who at seventy-seven was tried in Lyon in a hostile atmosphere (while tracts were distributed threatening reprisals in the event of his conviction), faced the death penalty but received life imprisonment, together with "national degradation." "It's the revenge of Dreyfus!" he shouted when the sentence was pronounced. Céline had the benefit of a five-year propaganda campaign by friends and apologists and of a skillful letter-writing campaign of his own. "The Jews should put up a statue of me for all the harm I didn't do them, but which I could have done," he wrote to his judges. He was able to return to France a free man. The writers' purge commission found a notable target in Henry de Montherlant, who was forbidden to publish for one year; then his sentence was made retroactive.

That unique but essentially honorific institution, the Académie Française, had been a veritable gentlemen's club for the extreme right in the prewar years. With academicians such as Philippe Pétain and Charles Maurras, Abel Hermant and Abel Bonnard becoming defendants in purge trials, the case for cleaning out the Academy itself seemed clear. "Seeing such Abels," Paulhan had written in a poem circulated from hand to hand during the occupation, "one wonders . . . what the Cains are doing." Four members of the Academy, including the two Abels, had been on the sponsoring committee of an organization created by the Germans and Vichy to send volunteers to fight on the German side. During the early postliberation months there was talk of dissolving the Academy and starting afresh. Georges Duhamel, its secretary, brought the crisis to the office of Charles de Gaulle, suggesting that everything would be easier if de Gaulle himself accepted membership. "The chief of state is the protector of the Academy," he replied. "How can he be a member of it?" But de Gaulle did suggest that the surviving Academicians take advantage of existing vacancies to elect writers who had shown themselves patriots during the occupation, even if these writers did not apply for membership.

Nothing came of any of the brave plans for renewal. Instead, de Gaulle was to note with regret, the Académie Française simply returned to its old ways, its leaders having observed with relief that the worst of the crisis was over.

★   ★   ★

And so, whatever the fate of the Left Bank's personae, its infrastructure was not dismantled. Publishing houses survived, even if some of their writers went into limbo. No prestigious imprint disappeared.

Yet it was not for lack of trying. In their statements issued from the underground, resistance writers had promised that publishers would be held responsible for what they printed, or failed to print, during the German years. The Purge Committee of Publishing drew up a list of companies that it believed deserved to be punished, but it had no power to carry out the punishment. Few were given the clean bill of health that Robert Emile-Paul received, as a publisher who had refused to sign the convention between the publishers' association and the occupying forces, who refused to respect the "Liste Otto" or to publish works the Germans wished to see published.

★   ★   ★

André Gide and Maria Van Rysselberghe flew back from Algiers in May 1945, to a Paris not yet organized for comfort: they had to carry their baggage to a checkroom and then descend into the subway for the journey to the Rue Vaneau, loaded "like mules" with heavy bags, coats, umbrellas, shawls, a cane, looking for all the world like lost tourists. Before his return, Gide had submitted some pages from his unpublished *Journal* — his eyewitness account of the Allied entry into Tunis — to *Les Lettres Françaises*, which ran them at the top of page one on November 18, 1944, with an introductory note informing readers that Gide had joined the National Committee of Writers.

The very next week Louis Aragon took the same space in that newspaper with an open letter to Claude Morgan protesting the publication of Gide in a paper reserved for writers who "showed calm French courage before the enemy." Aragon did not object to Gide's membership in CNE, but that was as far as he would go. He realized that Gide had not written for *Je Suis Partout,* nor had he "carried on the work of his *Retour de l'U.R.S.S.*" by sponsoring the recruitment of volunteers to fight the Soviet Union. Yet, said Aragon, Gide had been the predecessor of the wartime collaborationists in his anti-Bolshevism, "a major asset of enemy propaganda." Presumably Aragon did not know, or did not care to remind readers, that Gide's *Retour de l'U.R.S.S.*, far from being used in German propaganda, had been banned by the Germans in occupied Paris. Aragon went on to denounce Gide's behavior in North Africa, citing entries in Gide's own diary dating from the beginning of the occupation, and seeming to accept it.

The gravity of this attack, in the climate of purging, caused Claude Mauriac to write Gide early in January 1945: "Despite the violent desire I have to see you again, I don't advise you to come back immediately: passions are at their height..." And young Mauriac was private secretary to de Gaulle when he wrote that. The Gide affair split literary Paris in two. Camus placed his moral authority on Gide's side (he had been living at Gide's Rue Vaneau apartment, but had not yet met the elder writer). Even Paul Valéry told his young friend Eugène Guillevic, "You'll have to choose between me and Aragon." Guillevic, deeply committed to the Communist cultural line represented by Aragon, felt that he had no choice; he never saw Valéry again. Then passions began to diminish. Gide returned to preside over the surviving N.R.F. circle and lived to see the coming to power of the next literary generation of the Left Bank: Camus, of course, and the "unreadable" Sartre.

In his *Journal*, some weeks after receiving the Nobel Prize for Literature at the end of 1947, Gide replied to the criticism that he had never really committed himself. "This is precisely where the leaders of the new generation differ from us, judging as they do a work according to its immediate efficacy. They also seek immediate success, while we found it quite natural to remain unknown, unappreciated, and ignored until the age of forty-five. We aimed for duration . . ."

28 New Faces and Old

AT NO OTHER TIME in French history had a transformation seemed as radical. A new generation literally emerged from the shadows: young men, young women, whose only credentials for admission into the society of letters were their records of courage and commitment. An older generation largely compromised by enemy occupation slipped into purgatory. There could be no repetition of the split between Dreyfusards and anti-Dreyfusards at the beginning of the century, for this time the consequences of being on the wrong side were more disabling. In the months following the peace, the pronouncements of the National Committee of Writers virtually had the force of law; its blessings as well as its exclusions could play a decisive role in a career.

Few writers wished or dared to stay away from the receptions organized by the Committee in the elegant salons of the Maison de la Pensée Française, opposite the palace of the chief of state, where Louis Aragon was the host of this most coveted of literary teas. *Les Lettres Françaises*, the weekly organ of CNE, was useful if not essential to a literary launching. If an admired author did not actually contribute an article, story, or poem, or an artist a drawing, the newspaper would interview him instead and feature his portrait on the front page. *Europe*, the Committee's unofficial monthly organ, shared the top rank among left-literary reviews with *Esprit*, and later with *Les Temps Modernes*, in the vacuum created by the ban on *La Nouvelle Revue Française*. The CNE came tumbling down only when the cold war forced it to disclose its undeviating loyalty to the Communist Party. When François Mauriac finally reproached the Committee for being under Communist domination, the year was 1949. A Soviet-inspired coup had already taken place in Prague, the Atlantic Pact was being signed by the Western Allies.

Editions de Minuit entered the postwar scene less spectacularly. Jean Bruller had not wished to keep his underground press alive after the liberation. He was persuaded to do so by writer friends who deplored the paucity of publishing houses that had not compromised with the occupation authorities. Indeed, the resistance publishers who joined in a Groupement de la Fidelité Française in the months after the German withdrawal could be counted on one's fingers; Emile-Paul and the infant Editions du Seuil were the best known among them. Editions de Minuit published facsimile editions of its pseudonymous little resistance books, as well as new works by Vercors, Jean Cassou, and other CNE writers, as well as concentration camp veterans. But the sponsors of Minuit were amateurs. They soon came up against the hard facts of business, made even harder by postwar scarcity. Paul Eluard told Pierre Seghers that it had not been difficult to publish L'Eternelle Revue underground. But when he wished to produce a magazine openly in liberated Paris, it took four months to obtain administrative approval. "The underground had its good side," Seghers concluded. Editions de Minuit survived as a collective enterprise of veterans of the intellectual resistance until 1948, when an augmentation of capita cost them control of the company. The name was carried on by new owners who combined political and literary engagement, and Minuit became the publishing house of Samuel Beckett and Alain Robbe-Grillet, and the birthplace of the nouveau roman with Michel Butor, Nathalie Sarraute, Marguerite Duras.

The new Left Bank had new heroes. The most improbable was a partly blind professor of philosophy who could not even claim a particularly distinguished record of resistance activity: Jean-Paul Sartre. He and his friends, and those who wished to be his friends, their groups organized or informal, their books and magazines, their slightest movements suddenly seemed to occupy everybody's attention — as well as a considerable number of café tables on and around the Place Saint-Germain-des-Prés. Something about this atmosphere made Ernest Hemingway, meeting Sartre for the first time in Paris in 1946, squeeze the little man in his muscled arms and exclaim: "I'm only a captain; you're a general!" (Hemingway had been drinking, Simone de Beauvoir points out in describing the scene.)

Beauvoir speaks of the offensive existentialiste in the first autumn of peace, the autumn following the defeat of Japan. In a brief lapse of time a number of things happened. The first issue of Les Temps Modernes, the Sartre group's magazine, appeared, with two novels by Sartre, L'Age de *raison* ("The Age of Reason") and *Le Sursis* ("The Reprieve"). Simone de Beauvoir brought out a novel of her own and put a play on the Paris stage. Her play and their magazine were launched in a single week, and Sartre gave an often-cited lecture, "Is Existentialism a Humanism?" The literary couple was as surprised as everyone else by the tumult. Overnight Sartre and Beauvoir were celebrities whose every move was reported in the press. *Combat*, the product of a team whose best-known member was Albert Camus, "commented favorably on everything that came from our pens or our mouths . . ." They were the targets of photographers as they walked the streets; they were accosted by passersby; they were the object of stares at the Flore; people whispered about them as they passed. At Sartre's lecture the crowd was too big to fit into the auditorium; there was a crush, and women fainted.

Soon the "existentialist offensive" had conquered all. To the delight of diarist Jean Galtier-Boissière, a wit was heard to say that Saint-Germain-des-Prés was now "the Cathedral of Sartre" (Simone de Beauvoir was *la grande Sartreuse*). Sensational weeklies had a field day. *Samedi-Soir*, with nearly half a million lowbrow readers, published an account of café and nightclub life on the literary Left Bank, making it clear that all the drifters and dancers were "existentialists." Later Sartre commented: "But those who read in *Samedi-Soir* the interesting testimony of a girl that I was supposed to have lured into my bedroom to show her a Camembert cheese were not readers of *Les Temps Modernes*." Printing over a million copies weekly, *France-Dimanche* devoted a copiously illustrated page to "Sartre, this unappreciated man," describing him entering the Café de Flore "with his short steps, his head buried in the dirty wool of an unkempt jacket, its pockets bursting with books and papers, a Balzac novel from the public library under the arm..." He sat at a table, "gazing about him with emotion, while removing the scarves from his neck and . . . warmed by a few cognacs, the small pipe stuck in his sensual lips burning cheap tobacco . . . taking a two-bit pen from his briefcase . . . to scribble forty pages of manuscript." Then, *France-Dimanche* told its readers, with a small band of disciples "gathered around him like a school of sardines," Sartre went off to an evening of nightclubbing.

What was it that made, and perpetuated, the existentialist myth? Beauvoir offered her own explanation: "Having become a second-class power, France defended itself by glorifying, for purposes of exportation, its home-grown products: fashion and literature." And Sartre offered an ideology even for the *petits-bourgeois*, for existentialism, in its claim to reconcile history and morality, helped them "confront horror and absurdity while maintaining human dignity."

There was another consideration. To a Left Bank intellectual frustrated by the years of German occupation and the omnipresence of Vichyist ideology, with the only outlet a dangerous but occasional act of defiance, an opportunity was being offered to descend from one's ivory tower, and this for the price of a copy of *Combat* or *Les Temps Modernes.* For Sartre and Beauvoir, who had rejected the temptation to take part in prewar anti-Fascist movements and had been relatively passive during the German years, had learned some lessons. Now they had friends in the seats of power. "Politics had become a family affair," Beauvoir explained, "and we intended to be involved." They read with approval Camus's position statement in an early issue of *Combat*: "Politics is no longer dissociated from individuals. It is a direct call of men to other men." No longer could public affairs be a career or even a leisure-time activity: "The complicity of politicians was swamped by the camaraderie of a struggle into which each of us had thrown his entire self." Although they later claimed to find him superficial, avoiding difficult questions, thumbing through books instead of reading them, emitting snap judgments, during the years of Saint-Germain-des-Prés and its glory Sartre and Beauvoir enjoyed the company of their country cousin, Camus. Their lives, if not their works, were so closely intertwined that Camus was forever being identified, against his protests, as another "existentialist."

★ ★ ★

It is difficult for us now to re-create the surprise and delight that greeted the inaugural issue of *Les Temps Modernes* ("Modern Times") in October 1945. Its editorial board, its table of contents, seemed to bring together everyone and everything that was vital in postwar Paris. Camus was absent from the board, for he was said to be too busy with *Combat,* but there was Albert Ollivier, who with Camus and Pascal Pia composed the notorious "Ocapia" which edited that daily newspaper. *La Nouvelle Revue Française* may have disappeared, but Jean Paulhan, its moral heir, was on Sartre's board. Another member was Sartre's schoolmate Raymond Aron, returned from Free French headquarters in London and an intellectual aide to André Malraux, de Gaulle's intellectual Minister of Information.

The first issue of Sartre's magazine carried a twenty-page "presentation" by Sartre himself, in which he made a case for the writer's commitment. As for art for art's sake, he called it irresponsibility. "Since the writer has no way to escape, we want him to take hold of his era firmly; it is his only chance; it was made for him and he for it." Again: "Our intention is to work together to produce certain changes in the Society that surrounds us." Not to change souls — that was for specialists (and here Sartre alluded, perhaps, to the Catholics of *Esprit*) — but to deal with "the social condition of man and the conception he has of himself." He promised that the magazine would take a position on every new political or economic event. And in conclusion he warned that "in *littérature engagée* [committed literature], commitment must in no case allow literature to be forgotten."

Later, in her memoirs, Sartre's companion enumerated the underlying motives of the group that founded *Les Temps Modernes*. Sartre hoped to influence his contemporaries. It would be useful to have a means to express impatience, surprise; present choices. Books took too long to write and to publish. In the magazine, almost as quickly as in a letter, they could address their friends, reply to their adversaries. "Our intellectual polemics had the intimacy, the urgency, and the warmth of family quarrels." All of Sartre's important political statements, including *What Is Literature?* — the seminal study of the writer's commitment — appeared first in the magazine, which also became a record of relations between the Sartrians and the French Communist Party, and which later presented (in the form of articles not reported) the break with Camus within its pages. *Les Temps Modernes* was published monthly in a small office in the Gallimard building until it criticized Gallimard's most precious asset, André Malraux; then, it was immediately chased across the narrow Rue de l'Université to a rival publisher's attic.

Sartre and his group and their magazine had another function in the immediate postliberation period: to serve as guinea pigs. The experimental question was: could independent intellectuals work in harmony with the French Communist Party without being subordinated to it? One might have thought so, taking the National Committee of Writers as an example. But from the beginning CNE was an instrument of Communist Party cultural policies, a jealously guarded preserve of Louis Aragon and other Party intellectuals. Sartre and his friends thought they could share goals with the Communists, even join them in campaigns, while remaining independent. But the Communists demanded more than that: after the first issue of *Les Temps Modernes*, Sartre was actually summoned to a meeting with Party ideologists, who blamed him for propagating a non-Marxist philosophy that was attracting the young, drawing them away from their Party.   Communist intellectuals began attacking Sartrian existentialism as anti-Communist, if not worse. (Once again, Sartre was attacked as a "disciple of the Nazi Heidegger.")

Poor Sartre: without knowing it, he had made his entry onto the public scene at the very moment when Communist Party policy, at Stalin's direction, was returning to a hard line. He became a target of *Pravda*, which characterized existentialism as "a nauseating and putrid concoction." *Les Lettres Françaises* published a front-page exposé on December 28, 1945, by Communist ideologist Roger Garaudy under the headline:

> ON A REACTIONARY PHILOSOPHY
> A FALSE PROPHET:
> JEAN-PAUL SARTRE

Garaudy not only denounced the contradictions between Sartrian philosophy and Marxism, but virtually expelled Sartre from the anti-Fascist movement, by alleging that he had seen in the resistance only an opportunity to exercise his penchant for negation. This attack was only the first of many. Sartre's onetime friend Jean Kanapa published, under Party auspices, a small book whose title translates as *Existentialism Is Not a Humanism* — an allusion to Sartre's famous lecture — and Kanapa employed wit and mockery to put Sartre and his friends in their places. "The question is: is the Sartrian simply a little animal already out of fashion, violent-tempered but inoffensive, noisy but vain, or does it merit that one demand of it political decency?" Kanapa saw Sartrian doctrine as "a little ideological delinquency that actively plays the game of reaction and . . . anti-Communism." He placed existentialism in the same camp as other ideological enemies of the Left Bank's Communist intellectuals: Surrealism, "literary-café Trotskyism, aestheticism à la Paulhan or à la Malraux . . ."

At the height of the Communist offensive against the Sartrians, the opportunity arose for effective rebuttal, and in the name of the best cause of all: defense of an old comrade.

The comrade was Paul Nizan, Sartre's classmate at the Ecole Normale

Supérieure. Ever since his withdrawal from the French Communist Party when it approved the Stalin-Hitler agreement of August 1939, Nizan had been the object of a Party campaign that sought to brand him a government spy. Maurice Thorez himself had fired the opening gun in a Communist periodical in March 1940, treating Nizan as "the police informer." Nizan's death during the German attack on France that May did not end the campaign. It was said, and repeated, that Nizan had been an agent of the French Interior Ministry (the cabinet department responsible for the police) even before August 1939. An attempt was even made to link Nizan's preoccupation in his fiction with the theme of treason to his alleged activity as a police informer.

In March 1947 Sartre and his friends, who then still included Raymond Aron, André Breton, Julien Benda, Albert Camus, Jean Guéhenno, and François Mauriac, released a statement entitled "The Nizan Case." The statement declared that Aragon had alleged in private that Nizan furnished information on the Communists to the Interior Ministry. Yet, the signatories declared, the real reason for Communist attacks on Nizan was his departure from the Party when it supported the pact with Hitler.

The Party replied in *L'Humanité*, accusing Nizan's defenders of being "moralizers." In *Les Lettres Françaises* the CNE followed up by protesting the anonymous allegation that Aragon was the source of the whispering campaign against Nizan. To this Sartre replied: "I was the one to whom M. Aragon made the statements cited... Does he consider them of such a nature that their pure and simple repetition throws discredit on their author?" The Communists offered no proof of the charges against Nizan; a chronology of the affair was published in *Les Temps Modernes*. The break between independent intellectuals and the Communist Party was now complete; it would end only through the determination of Sartre.

29 Changing Saint-Germain-des-Prés

THE CITYSCAPE of Paris seldom changed perceptibly in those days. Streets, the public and private meeting places of the Left Bank, looked much the same in the first years of postwar Paris as in the prewar decade. Façades were grimier, perhaps, and they had to wait more than a decade for a scrubbing, but the lights were on again, the curfew was off. The real differences were of another kind. The generation that occupied the conspicuous tables in the cafés of Montparnasse and of Saint-Germain-des-Prés, that staffed the new magazines and newspapers, and whose books appeared in display windows did not define itself by opposition to Fascism, as in the prewar decade, nor by a determined if often silent rejection of its surroundings, as during the German years. Instead, these were outspoken representatives of a new breed; they were going to use the infrastructure of the literary Left Bank in new ways. First of all, in an extended and exuberant celebration of their victory (no matter that it was not entirely theirs). The celebration seemed to last for years, and gave birth to a night life bearing little resemblance to any other: intellectual cabarets and cellar jazz clubs, that is, cabarets and clubs favored and sometimes even managed by intellectuals. The fête began in the first days of liberated Paris. "Day and night with our friends, chatting, drinking, wandering, laughing, we celebrated our deliverance," Simone de Beauvoir described that time. "What an orgy of fraternity! . . . Big khaki soldiers chewing gum proved that we could sail the seas again . . . For me, in the informality of the young American soldiers, there was the incarnation of freedom: ours and — we didn't doubt it — the freedom they were going to spread around the world."

Once again Beauvoir's diary is the most complete guide to the landmarks of the Left Bank. But the very moment the generation of Sartre and Camus took possession of the territory, it was contested by prying journalists, by a growing public, including rubbernecking tourists from the world over. Sartre moved to a Rue Bonaparte apartment with a plunging view over the Saint-Germain-des-Prés intersection, but he and Beauvoir could no longer work at the Café de Flore; they were too well known. They took refuge in the basement bar of the Pont-Royal hotel, down the street from Gallimard — as an earlier celebrity, André Malraux, had done in the 1930s. Beauvoir managed to work there, despite the inconvenience of the barrels that then served as tables, and although the new refuge had been identified in the press. There were new places to explore, some as much as five hundred yards from the Deux Magots. There was a certain degree of isolation, for example, in the austere trappings and businessmen's restaurant atmosphere of Brasserie Lipp.

The cellar clubs were the novelty. "We wanted to change the world during the daytime, and exchange ideas at night," Claude Roy said later. At Le Méphisto, on a corner of the Boulevard Saint-Germain a few short blocks from the famous cafés, one discovered "an agitated meeting place of agitators." On the Rue Dauphine there was the new Tabou, where Sartre liked to listen to Boris Vian's jazz trumpet. "The place was so noisy, so jammed, so filled with smoke that we could neither hear each other nor breathe." But talk they did, and presumably breathed.

Later the crowd moved still closer to its old haunts — to the Club Saint-Germain, nestled in a cellar within steps of the Café de Flore and the Deux Magots. "Saint-Germain-des-Prés already was no longer the village of the 1940s, a village clustered around a church steeple with courtyards echoing to the tools of craftsmen, its little people of little trades," Claude Roy recorded in his memoirs. "Nor was it yet Las Vegas plus Greenwich Village." The oral history of the period, and the occasional memoirs that have been written, suggest an uninterrupted drinking contest between the eminent men and women of letters on the Left Bank. "To think that in a few hours I'm going to talk about the writer's responsibility!" exclaimed Sartre during one of those nights fueled with alcohol, and Camus laughed. Beauvoir accompanied Sartre to the Sorbonne the next morning, where he presented himself ravaged with fatigue, bolstered by stimulants, to the assembled students. "If they had seen Sartre," she thought, "at six in the morning!"

Some things did not change: André Breton's permanent drawing room at a sidewalk café table, for example. Claude Mauriac's notebook captured one such moment in June 1946:

> . . . The old master André Breton, surrounded by some fifteen aging disciples, smoking an evening pipe with dignity at a sidewalk table of the Deux Magots. Someone who had been expelled from the ranks of the Surrealists [elsewhere Mauriac identifies this person as Antonin Artaud] passes by and bows deeply; Breton bows still more deeply; and there is an exchange of courteous, indeed friendly, phrases over the tables that separate them. Only this tender complicity remains of former anathemas, the violence of past battles . . .

Indeed, in a sense several literary and political generations without much in common shared these places now. Roy identified them: "the group of the first villagers of the 1930s, the Jacques Prévert band, the Sartrian 'family,' the young birds of the night whom the newspapers called 'existentialists' . . . and the Communist 'cell' . . ." Their common denominator was anti-Fascism, and Communism their reference: either they had been Communists, were presently Communists, or would become Communists.

★   ★   ★

There was also a time for work. The office of *Les Temps Modernes* in the Gallimard building became a port of call for the literary elite. Following the *N.R.F.* tradition, the director of the new magazine received contributors with their manuscripts, or readers simply wishing to talk, at given days and hours. But soon that good intention had to be abandoned, and Sartre received by appointment only. Simone de Beauvoir describes an afternoon at Gallimard in the spring of 1946 with Elio Vittorini and Raymond Queneau in the *Temps Modernes* office and, in the corridors and adjacent cubbyholes, André Malraux and Roger Martin du Gard. Once a week, the Gallimard editorial conference brought together an assembly more significant to literature than the Académie Française could have summoned to its own chamber only a few hundred yards away. Every other Sunday Sartre invited his staff and leading contributors for a discussion of current and future policies, to elicit suggestions, to assign articles. Jean Paulhan might be present, or the versatile Boris Vian, who was among other things an author Sartre admired, although he might show up with a trumpet if he was going on to perform in a club, for this was how he earned his living. Both Sartre and Beauvoir did their own writing at the Rue Bonaparte apartment now. From their work table they could rest their eyes by gazing out at the sidewalk café tables and the crossroads, now considered to be their domain.

Only a block away, a small house set back from the street — an eighteenth-century house with a tree in the garden that suggested some distant provincial retreat, rather than the geographical center of intellectual Paris — was the home of Editions du Seuil and, on the fourth floor, of the influential left-Catholic *Esprit*, whose director, Emmanuel Mounier, also received by appointment only, and also gathered around him future opinion-makers. Like the old Gallimard and *Nouvelle Revue Française* duo, Le Seuil and *Esprit* were as much a literary-political movement as a business. The weekly committee meetings were smaller and less formal here than those at Gallimard, but in the heady atmosphere of the time they were also more serious, for an association with *Esprit* or Le Seuil implied moral as well as political commitment.

★   ★   ★

On the Rue Saint-Benoît, around the corner from Sartre's apartment, the home of Marguerite Duras and Dionys Mascolo now served as another command post in the literary-political wars of the Left Bank. The Rue Saint-Benoît was best known for the Club Saint-Germain, a jazz cellar farther up the street, and for the Montana bar, so unobtrusive compared to the Café de Flore next door that Sartre's group continued to meet there for drinks throughout the postwar decade. There was also a nondescript bistro, the Petit Saint-Benoît, where most writers and artists in the neighborhood, even if they could afford something better, took meals with their peers before the war, during the German occupation, and since. It was hard to dine there tête-à-tête, for the tables were meant for communal dining.

Just across the street from this little bistro, the Duras apartment had become, in Claude Roy's phrase, "one of those houses out of the Russian novels of the period of the intelligentsia, where one sees coming in or going out, at every instant, three ideas, five friends, twenty papers, three indignations, two jokes, ten books, and a samovar of boiling water." It was a beehive dominated by Marguerite Duras as queen. "She had an abrupt mind, a baroque and often droll vehemence, an infinite capacity for fury, appetite, warmth, and astonishment. . . ." Actually, she contributed little to the discussions, for women did not participate much in those days. But she did the cooking, wrote her books, and had a baby. In retrospect, she decided that the silence that custom imposed on women had helped make a writer of her.

Duras was becoming known to discerning readers for small, intense books in which human relations and amorous ones take precedence over the world's business, but in her Russian-style apartment, ideology prevailed. "There was never a need to open the session," explained Roy, "because it had never been closed." Visitors who were not expected would bring their own food and an extra loaf of bread, the talk went on all through the apartment, and at night the house was a dormitory.

In the immediate postwar years, all of the inner circle there were Communists — more about that soon enough. Party cell meetings were held just around the corner, on the Rue de Rennes, in a building standing between Sartre's house and the Deux Magots. Afterward the comrades returned to the Duras apartment to continue the discussion. When they were still Communists, these post-cell meetings took on the character of fractional meetings, strictly forbidden by Communist Party rules.

★   ★   ★

Albert Camus was increasingly at the center of the scene. This French Algerian just turned thirty had no roots in the city, but the war and the occupation had shipwrecked him in mainland France and on the Left Bank, his only baggage a promising beginning in literature, and Mediterranean charm. He lacked the polish of his peers at Gallimard, just as he lacked their old-boy links, and many of them never let him forget it. But *Combat* and his early books had made him a celebrity all the same, an asset to his publisher and a young hero to the world beyond the Rue Sébastien-Bottin.

Soon after his arrival in Paris, Camus moved into André Gide's studio room, which Gide's *petite dame* had arranged for him to use, and in the first months of liberated Paris 1 bis, Rue Vaneau, again became a meeting place of the literary and political elite, but a younger elite, and without Gide. Later Camus was given an old Gallimard office imperfectly transformed into living quarters, on the ancient Rue Seguier between the Rue Saint-André-des-Arts and the Seine quay. From this modest, ill-heated building — Camus was hardly well-to-do, and fuel was hard to come by during France's long recovery — his walk to Gallimard took him past most of the landmarks of the literary Left Bank. If he turned onto the Rue de l'Ancienne-Comédie, leaving the Rue Dauphine with the Tabou club behind him, he would pass the old Procope café, then (on Boulevard Saint-Germain) Le Méphisto, with its cellar club. Continuing, he might find Sartre and Simone de Beauvoir at the Rhumerie Martiniquaise, just before arriving at the Saint-Germain-des-Prés crossroads with the famous literary cafés. And at any moment he could stop, at the Bonaparte, the Montana, even the brassy and popular Royal Saint-Germain. Farther along, near the Gallimard building, was the tranquility of the Pont-Royal.

In the immediate postwar years, when he was dividing his working hours between *Combat* and Gallimard, and finding time to write as well, and when he wasn't fighting off a new seizure of tuberculosis or writer's block, Camus was a familiar face at Saint-Germain-des-Prés. And one of the most attractive. "Humphrey Bogart young," journalist Jean Daniel described him. Daniel later evoked an incident in a nightclub, when a young movie critic, after breaking several glasses and a bottle of whiskey, climbed onto the bar to proclaim: "I'm going to speak to you about an injustice worse than those we denounce [in *Combat*]; this injustice is alive and it is standing here before us. It's Camus — he has everything you need to seduce, to be happy, to be famous, and in addition to that, he dares to have all the virtues!" One of the virtues, if we are to accept the recollections of contemporaries, was knowing how to pick out and then pick up the most beautiful women in the group, whatever the group might be. "They said I had charm, imagine that!" says the protagonist of Camus's novel *La Chute* ("The Fall"). "Do you know what charm is? A way of having people say yes to you when you didn't even ask a question." Reading that, Simone de Beauvoir decided that Camus had taken himself as the model for his hero.

When *La Peste* ("The Plague") was published in Paris in 1947, its author began to be mentioned as a candidate for the Nobel Prize. Had Camus received the prize then, he would have been the youngest winner in the history of the award. Already he had a secretary one of whose principal duties was to protect him from admirers.

As for Gide, he was showing his age. His remarkable confidante, Maria Van Rysselberghe, was ever loyal, but she was frank, too. Perhaps she was also betraying her age, for the tone of her diary becomes increasingly critical. She spent less time with Gide and more in her own apartment across the landing, for she was distressed by the chaos that surrounded him. In that city of scarcity, Gide received visitors in a Moroccan-style robe and an incongruous canvas hat. He lived and worked in a small room where he could sit strategically between two radiators, with an electric heater underfoot.

Still, Maria Van Rysselberghe was there to help him when necessary, to withstand the assault of the telephone, the doorbell, the photographers and interviewers, when the Swedish Academy announced that he had won the Nobel Prize in November 1947. Now she found him increasingly self-important, "obsessed by his personage," resentful of criticism even by close companions. In the end he seemed to her irresponsible in his politics, too, signing a petition he should not have signed, and then forgetting that he had done it. "This little story is typical of his behavior, which is vaguer and vaguer, unjustifiable, changing, illogical; he is already like that in minor matters, so when it's a matter of the fate of Europe . . ." That was in August 1950. Gide was living his last year; he died the following February, at eighty-one. Still a symbol worthy of polemical energies, for the Communists never forgave him his rejection of their USSR. "It's a cadaver that has just died," commented L'Humanité. Among the more personal remarks, another journalist quipped that Gide "lived dangerously under three layers of flannel sweaters." With this sort of attitude in mind, Sartre opened the next issue of Les Temps Modernes with a tribute to that old man who had not been his comrade. "The mental restrictions, the hypocrisy, to speak frankly, the abject stink of the obituaries written about him," explained Sartre, "irritate me too much for me to be able to speak here of what separated us from him." He continued: "They would have forgiven Gide for risking his thought and his reputation if he had risked his life and, particularly, pneumonia." Of course Gide had been prudent, of course he had weighed his words, had hesitated before signing petitions.

But the same man dared to publish the profession of faith of Corydon, the indictment of Voyage au Congo; he had the courage to take the side of the USSR when it was dangerous to do so and that, still greater, of changing his position publicly when he decided, rightly or wrongly, that he had made a mistake. It is perhaps this mixture of cunning and of audacity that makes him exemplary; generosity is praiseworthy only among those who know what things are worth . . .

★ ★ ★

Something else was happening in Paris: the Americans had returned. But these were different Americans: black writers, artists, musicians. The war had brought a growing awareness to American minorities that their condition could be bettered. For qualified individuals, it could be improved most rapidly if they took the initiative of sailing away to Europe; to leave the United States, in those days, was already a protest.

Certainly Paris seemed freer to Americans, black or white, than the puritanical society they left behind. And a black man abroad who possessed an American passport automatically acquired a touch of white, or so one of them, the young novelist William Gardner Smith, discovered in Paris. He felt he was treated with more courtesy by the French than, say, a Moslem from North Africa would be. "A black person could live in greater peace with his environment in Copenhagen or Paris than in New York, not to speak of Birmingham or Jackson," Smith later wrote in *Return to Black America*. "But at times he found it harder to live at peace with himself. The black man who established his home in Europe paid a heavy price. He paid it in a painful tearing of himself from his past . . ."

Richard Wright, with a number of well-received works behind him (the novel *Native Son*, the autobiographical *Black Boy*), felt that Paris was a place where a black American could preserve his dignity, breathing freer air. He had found a guardian angel in Gertrude Stein, with whom he had been corresponding from the United States. Early in 1946 he met Jean-Paul Sartre in New York, and found the man and his doctrines attractive. Sartre had already published a story of Wright's in the first issue of *Les Temps Modernes*, and later he serialized *Black Boy*. Wright became a frequent contributor to the magazine. Arriving in Paris in May 1946 under quasi-official sponsorship, he was the guest of honor at a Gallimard reception, where he met that house's celebrities. Soon he had been introduced to a considerable number of the cultural eminences of the Left Bank, including Gide. After eight months he returned to the United States, but racism there seemed more acute than ever, and in 1947 he returned to Paris with his family again, this time to stay.

Black Americans such as Wright, William Gardner Smith, James Baldwin, and the mystery writer Chester Himes seemed to move with ease in French society, or at least in the literary world of the Left Bank. It was easiest for Wright, an older man with a body of work behind him, and with potential political allies. He had been a Communist before the

Second World War, a founding member of the fellow-traveling League of American Writers; Moscow's *International Literature* had published a poem of his as early as 1936, dedicated to Louis Aragon and to Aragon's incendiary poem "Red Front." Although Wright reacted to the Sartrians with a feeling of personal unease, he was comfortable with their politics. Gradually he became integrated into the life of Parisian intellectuals, without losing his cousinhood with fellow black Americans, who could be found at their own café meeting places — the Café de Tournon, on the street of that name, or the Monaco, at the Carrefour de l'Odéon, just steps from Wright's apartment on Rue Monsieur-le-Prince. Wright died at a comparatively young age, fifty-two, in November 1960. William Gardner Smith was only forty-seven when he died, in 1974. Few black Americans have stayed in Paris as long as he did. While Smith was writing his novel *The Stone Face* in the early 1960s, the civil rights movement in the United States began to achieve its first victories. Smith made a last-minute change in the manuscript, and had his self-exiled hero decide to leave France to return to the country of his birth, and so to "help to turn the States into a place nobody will want to flee."

★ ★ ★

Nor should we forget the Latin Americans who chose Paris as a refuge from the right-wing dictatorships on their continent. The poet Pablo Neruda for one, whose Chilean Communist Party membership forced him to flee his country. Another was Jorge Amado, a novelist and fighter for the economically deprived of the Brazilian northeast. A Communist Party representative in Brazil's legislature, Amado was expelled from that body with other members of his party; since he was under indictment for subversive activities and had now lost his parliamentary immunity, he slipped out of the country early in 1948 to join the colony of Brazilian writers and other intellectuals in France. He had already been published in Paris by Gallimard before World War II, and by Sartre's publisher, Nagel, since; in fact, he first ran into Sartre on a visit to Nagel's office. He became a friend of both Sartre and Simone de Beauvoir and was later their host in Brazil. In Paris he saw Eluard, Aragon, Picasso when he could, Tristan Tzara, Jean Cassou, Anna Seghers, and French friends whom he had already met in Latin America, such as Roger Caillois. But he was not a café-goer, nor a man for literary teas. He never felt himself part of a group, Sartre's or any other; he was a Latin American writer and not a French one. Indeed, the Brazilian

Portuguese language, his culture, and his national experience (notably Brazil's minor involvement in the Second World War) kept him and fellow Brazilians out of any Parisian circle but their own. He met other Latin Americans, often at Pablo Neruda's apartment on the Ile Saint-Louis. He and his family lived in a small hotel on the Rue Cujas, around the corner from the Sorbonne.

But Jorge Amado soon became active in the Communist-controlled peace movement, and a delegate of his country's left-wing writers at the Congress of Intellectuals for Peace in Wroclaw, Poland (discussed in subsequent pages). On his return he participated regularly in peace movement activities and attended meetings of the National Committee of Writers. Aragon serialized one of his books in *Les Lettres Françaises*, and then published it under the imprint of a Communist Party house. In Wroclaw, Amado had become a friend of Ilya Ehrenburg, whom he saw again on visits to Moscow, and then in Prague.

For Amado packed again, and moved on to Czechoslovakia. He had been invited by the Union of Czechoslovak Writers to spend a vacation in a castle near Prague, and found it easier to live in that country than in France, thanks to royalties that were accumulating in Eastern Europe but that could not be transferred to the West. He spent two years in that castle and completed an epic novel on pre–World War II Brazilian Fascism. Then it became possible to return to Brazil and his beloved Bahia, where he was to write the comic novels for which he is best known.

30 The Parting of Ways

HOWEVER AMBIGUOUS the behavior of many French Communists was in the early months of World War II, however bitter the memory of their hesitations and compromises and occasional pro-German statements to those who were consistently anti-Nazi before, during, and after the war, the Communists performed more than honorably in the anti-German resistance, and by the final months of the occupation the coalition of Communists and non-Communists that had marked the 1930s seemed stronger than ever. Stalin's Soviet Union had been an ally of France, of the United Kingdom, and of the United States in the conclusive battles. Even before the war ended, Charles de Gaulle went to Moscow to negotiate a Franco-Soviet pact, and when Stalin brought up the case of the French Communist leader Maurice Thorez, a good Frenchman who he felt did not belong in prison — "at least," added Stalin with a smile, "not right away!" — de Gaulle replied, "The French government treats Frenchmen according to the services it expects of them." Thorez did not go to jail for having deserted in the first days of the war. Instead, he went into de Gaulle's cabinet.

Indeed, under de Gaulle's approving eye, the Communists seemed to have thrown their weight on the side of moderation, in the interests of national unity, at a time when they might have set off a revolution. Later some wondered why their Party had not made an attempt to seize power in 1944, when it might have succeeded under the cover of the resistance. But this was to treat France as a vacuum, to consider its Communists independent of external influences and free to act as they wished. In postwar France the Party continued to adhere to a line, first a soft one, then a hard one, when the Soviet Union challenged its Western allies for control of the center of Europe, and for once-independent nations all along its borders that would serve it better as satellites. With the USSR, the somewhat liberal policies that had been necessary during the war, such as toleration of Western culture and of the fresh air brought in by foreign Communists temporarily resident in Moscow, were quickly abandoned. The abandonment became doctrine.

In France, Communists held cabinet posts as late as May 1947, and in June of that year, at the Eleventh Congress of the Party, they still used moderate language; they were not yet ready to reject cooperation with the West. In September 1947 the Cominform (the Communist Information Bureau) was founded as an up-to-date version of the prewar Comintern. The star of the inaugural session was Andrei Zhdanov, a World War II general who had taken part in the siege of Leningrad and who was now a member of the political bureau of the Soviet party; in postwar Moscow, he was responsible for ideological conformity.

To Zhdanov, speaking with Stalin's voice, the world was already divided into two camps, one imperialist, the other anti-imperialist — the former led by the United States, the latter by the Soviet Union. The role of the Communists was to resist the United States through a policy of national independence," and that also meant waging ideological warfare against "right-wing Socialists." Unity was a thing of the past. At a meeting of the French Party's central committee in October, Thorez confessed his errors, and the new Stalin line was in force.

This much Party history must be understood if one is to make sense of the intellectual wars of the Left Bank in the postwar decade. Not that September 1947 was an absolute dividing line, for Zhdanov had been denouncing Western influence for over a year before the Cominform's inaugural session, and in France itself there had been a parallel hardening of lines. But now the schism was becoming visible everywhere in French life. Just as the central trade-union federation, the CGT (Confédération Générale du Travail) was to split into Communist and non-Communist movements (the latter to call itself CGT-Force Ouvrière), so writers and artists and other intellectuals chose sides in their respective organizations and institutions. In the Communist magazine *Démocratie Nouvelle*, an article entitled "Ideological Expansionism of the Yankees" described how the United States was colonizing France with its culture:

They know that they can count on such and such a publisher who sits on the books or newspapers written by progressive Americans, but who praises to the skies the name of Henry Miller, professor of eroticism, sower of despair . . . They keep the atomic bomb at home as a state secret, but they send us Faulkner. But if they need philosophers they find them on the scene . . . It's in Paris itself, at the Café de Flore, that the most reliable poisons are developed.

At the time that would have been understood as an attack on Sartre. The Party leadership anticipated dissidence and attacked potential dissidents before they became dangerous. A Commission of Intellectuals was created deep inside the Party, headed by Laurent Casanova, Thorez's chief deputy for ideology. One member was Pierre Daix, who as a student had taken part in public demonstrations against the German occupying forces, was arrested as a "terrorist," and was sent to the Mauthausen concentration camp. Daix now seemed a rising star in the postwar Party's ruling group. At Casanova's request he organized a Critics Circle directly attached to the Central Committee. The emphasis on critics instead of writers was not an accident: it allowed the Party to bring in whomever it wished. Among writers, the Circle included Aragon, Eluard, Guillevic, Claude Roy, and Marguerite Duras, all still Communists in good standing. This Circle would allow the Party to exercise control more forcefully. Intellectuals could debate with relative freedom during its meetings — but free discussion would end when the meetings ended.

The French Communist Party also took charge of the publication of Les Lettres Françaises, which by 1947, under amateur management, was in financial trouble. Pierre Daix was brought in as editor-in-chief, to purge the staff of unreliable elements, to return it to strict Communist orthodoxy. Daix met regularly, and secretly, with Casanova, to be kept up to date on the Party line; he also met with Aragon, who was moving gradually into control of the paper.

No longer could a Left Bank intellectual hold on to his Party membership card and hope to speak his mind. The Communist founded La Nouvelle Critique, assigning Jean Kanapa as editor-in-chief, to provide a guide to what its thinkers should think. When Dominique Desanti published an attack on Gide in this paper, she lost her friends — by now dissident Communists — of the Marguerite Duras circle on the Rue Saint-Benoît. In the Soviet Union, Andrei Zhdanov was condemning such prominent representatives of Soviet culture as Boris

Pasternak, Sergei Eisenstein, and the composers Sergei Prokofiev, Dimitri Shostakovich, and Aram Khachaturian. In Paris, Laurent Casanova and other Party functionaries undertook a similar purification of the ranks. Of course, the difference was that one could be purged on the Left Bank and still remain free and alive, and perhaps even make a living.

But if one stayed close to the Party line, as did André Stil, a protégé of Aragon, one might win a Stalin Prize for a novel and become the most translated French author in the world, hailed in banner headlines in *L'Humanité*, the object of daily meetings all over France, covered with gifts. The painter André Fougeron, another Aragon protégé, enjoyed a similar promotion; he was launched in a newspaper campaign unlike that given any other artist of his time.

For the Communist world was so complete, with its daily and weekly newspapers, its cultural and political magazines, social affairs and rallies, national and international congresses (not to speak of its cell meetings), that one could believe it was the whole world.

★   ★   ★

Zhdanovism created havoc in the little house on the Rue Saint-Benoît where Marguerite Duras and her companions lived. One of the first shocks came in the form of a high-pitched attack on leading non-Party writers, Sartre and Paulhan among them, by Jean Kanapa, the Communists' ideological scout and a member of the secret Commission of Intellectuals, in Pierre Seghers's *Poésie*, a magazine usually devoted to more poetic concerns. Kanapa accused French authors of creating a neutral literature to avoid signifying anything; he also noted that the same writers happened to be procapitalist and anti-Communist. He attacked Sartre and others who wished to create a Socialist Europe without the Soviet Union, accused Arthur Koestler of defending Fascists, even attacked François Mauriac for having published *La Pharisienne* with the authorization of the German occupying forces. (Of course Kanapa failed to speak of Aragon's *Les Voyageurs de l'impériale*, which had not only been published with German authorization, but which had compromised its author more profoundly because Aragon had accepted censorship.) Kanapa demanded that writers treat of "the laboring masses" rather than the closed world of the bourgeoisie. "Literature of propaganda? Yes, of propaganda for man."

The tumult caused by Kanapa's attack moved Casanova to ask Pierre

Daix to organize a debate on the issue. During this meeting, held in the
spring of 1948 at Communist Party headquarters, Robert Antelme of the
Duras group, in a paper prepared with Dionys Mascolo, argued that
literary creation had to remain independent of the shifting requirements
of the Party. Daix saw no basic conflict between Antelme and the Party
and said as much to Casanova, but at the next meeting of the
Commission of Intellectuals, Casanova insisted on a vote of
unconditional support for the ideological positions of the Party, and told
Daix privately, "The Party is not a party of discussions . . ."

There was also the Elio Vittorini affair. The Duras circle had met the
Italian writer when he was invited to Paris by the National Committee of
Writers in 1946 (though as a guest of CNE he was then a virtual prisoner
of what they considered the "high society" Communists around
Aragon). A respected novelist and translator of contemporary authors
such as Faulkner, Vittorini had worked in the underground Italian
Communist resistance press during the war, and became the postwar
editor-in-chief of the Party's daily, Unità. He also published a magazine
of his own, Il Politecnico, which experimented with cultural diversity;
refusing to reject non-Communist art and artists, it published
translations of Faulkner, T.S. Eliot, Hemingway, Kafka, Joyce. When
Vittorini met Sartre in Milan, in the summer of 1946, he found that they
had much in common, and indeed Il Politecnico was closer to Les Temps
Modernes than to Aragon's Europe. Then, in a famous exchange of
letters, Italy's Communist Party leader, Palmiro Togliatti, contested
Vittorini's open policy. Vittorini replied politely that Soviet aesthetic
doctrine could not be applied to Italy. Rejected as a deviationist, the
Italian author lost the support of his Party, and his magazine suspended
publication in December 1947, at the height of Western Zhdanovism.

During the controversy, Vittorini visited Paris again. This time he
escaped the pomp of the Aragon salon and lived at the Rue Saint-
Benoît, which from then on would be his Paris base. Duras and Mascolo
began to take vacations with Vittorini and his wife, in Italy, France, or
even in Spain. Using the pen name "Jean Gratien," Mascolo joined
Edgar Morin in interviewing Vittorini for Les Lettres Françaises. Coming
upon the interview without preparation, today's reader is likely to see it
as properly Communist, suitable for that time and place. Should a writer
be committed? Vittorini was asked. He replied, "The word doesn't
matter. For me, it means to be a Communist. It is as natural for me to
be a Communist as to write." He did not believe that "the end justifies

the means" was a Communist principle, but he felt that neutrality of the kind he attributed to Albert Camus was "collaborationist." For Vittorini, true Communism was "protestant," placing freedom ahead of order.

For a meeting of the Critics Circle at the Palais de la Mutualité — in one of the smaller rooms — Casanova assigned a report on the Vittorini affair to Edgar Morin, who promptly defended the independence of culture with respect to politics. Still, Morin stayed in the Party, swallowing the Prague coup of February 1948, the denunciation of Tito, and the Rajk purge trial in Hungary. He left only when he was thrown out. Duras, Mascolo, and Antelme were also expelled, apparently as much for their life-style, which the working-class membership of the Saint Germain-des-Prés cell could hardly be expected to understand, as for dissidence. At the time there were six hundred Party members in their district, and from one day to the next Marguerite Duras felt as if she had been excluded from the universe. Morin wrote about the loneliness that followed exclusion, when "everyone was in a warm place, in homes, at meetings. I was alone like a phantom while everywhere in the world workers were marching together . . . I had lost communion, fraternity, forever. Excluded from everything, by everybody, from life, warmth, from the Party. I began to sob."

Claude Roy, who stayed on much longer in the Saint-Germain-des-Prés cell, until his own expulsion, nevertheless continued to frequent the Duras group. But when he was in the presence of the ardent Communist Paul Eluard, he felt ashamed of those nights spent on the Rue Saint-Benoît "blaspheming the religion of Socialism, criticizing its priests, doubting its premises. It was if I were reading forbidden books in hiding."

In such a climate, most of the Left Bank Communists waited to be expelled; few had the courage to break. One who did was Edith Thomas, whose apartment had been the meeting place of the underground National Committee of Writers. For her, the excommunication of Tito was the final straw, and she traveled to Yugoslavia with Clara Malraux to bear witness to the sincerity of Yugoslav Communism. On her return, she was denounced in L'Humanité as one of those who had joined the Party in the days of "relative facility," when in truth she had joined in the dangerous days of the German occupation, when the affiliation could mean jail, torture, even death. Now her friend Dominique Desanti, who like Edith

Thomas had joined in the dark days, realized that as a loyal Communist she would henceforth have to pretend not to notice Thomas when they passed on the street. Desanti knew that she should now disavow her own Communist allegiance (she had written a book expressly to attack Tito). "The contrary happened," she later confessed. "The more the 'heretics' troubled us, the more the Party shocked us, the more we were determined to shake off all self-respect, to lose face in the eyes of the bourgeoisie, to commit ourselves."

Zhdanovism continued to spread outward; not only the Sartrians but the Surrealists came under its guns. Being of the left but not of the Party was sufficient to be tarred as an instrument of capitalism, imperialism, allies of Fascism. Roger Vailland, before the war a right-wing militant who had been expelled from Breton's circle, now wrote a small book for the Communists to denounce Surrealism as antirevolutionary. In *Les Lettres Françaises* in early 1949, Ilya Ehrenburg, still serving the Soviet Union as roving correspondent and publicist, denounced Sartre's play *Les Mains sales* ("Dirty Hands") as "an anti-Communist and anti-Soviet pamphlet." Noting that the play would be produced in the United States, for it was "a good export product, better than French wines and perfumes," Ehrenburg went on:

> An advertisement in English found in a recent issue of a Paris entertainment guide: tourists were invited to visit a Saint-Germain-des-Prés café where they would be able to see with their own eyes the chief attraction of Paris, France — Jean-Paul Sartre. Chicago shopkeepers and Oxford (Mississippi) farmers contemplate with fascination this "terrible rebel," not knowing that this "rebel" has been tame for a long time . . .

Those on the left who were active fellow travelers but not subject to Communist Party discipline had no less difficulty than their friends inside the Party, when it came time to separate the sheep from the goats. That gregarious man Jean Cassou, who had gone along with the Communists of *Europe* after the withdrawal of Jean Guéhenno, who had taken up with the Communists again during the euphoria of the liberation, was another who could not accept the Stalinist attack on Tito. When he returned from a visit to Yugoslavia and described (in an article in *Esprit*) what he had seen, he suddenly discovered that he was not as free as he had thought. Summoned to a leadership meeting of Combatants for Peace and Liberty, a Communist front, he listened as a formal indictment was read. He was on trial; he was being asked by a

Communist Party officer to retract his beliefs. He did not retract, and became an enemy of the people.

Cassou's article in *Esprit* was accompanied by a similar one by Vercors; the two articles appeared together under the title "One Must Not Fool the People." "I am not passing into the American camp," Cassou insisted. "Like many intellectuals of my generation, I fought for causes that the Communists also fought for, against Fascism and in favor of the Popular Front..." He was aware of the "frightful danger" of the American "empire," but must one submit to the Cominform because of that? Apparently one must. When the Communists began to attack them, Vercors requested an opportunity to reply in *Les Lettres Françaises*, but Daix refused. Vercors replied that if he could not use the pages of a paper for which he wrote regularly to answer a personal attack, he would write for that paper no longer. So Daix had him rewrite the article in more acceptable language, but then refused the preface, in which Vercors revealed the difficulty he had had in getting it published. Vercors said the preface had to appear or he would withdraw the article. Faced with another refusal, he ceased to write for *Les Lettres Françaises*. But he remained a supporter of the National Committee of Writers for many more years.

31 Communists and Anti-Communists

IN THE DECADE following World War II, Louis Aragon became one of the most powerful figures of intellectual Paris. Not only did he control daily, weekly, and monthly periodicals capable of making reputations or breaking them, but he knew how to use his power. In the spring of 1947 he became director of *Ce Soir*, the Communist Party afternoon daily, which looked more or less like any other mass-circulation newspaper, for it made more subtle use of the same ideological material that *L'Humanité*, the official Party organ, published with less subtlety. With the Party's blessing Aragon (through Pierre Daix) functioned as director of *Les Lettres Françaises*, which had become a general cultural weekly covering theater, movies, and the fine arts as well as books. He was also the power behind the politico-cultural monthly *Europe*, whose nominal postwar directors were Jean Cassou and later Pierre Abraham. Aragon also held a number of organizational posts. He was secretary-general of the Union Nationale des Intellectuals, founded in 1945 as a fusion of existing intellectual resistance veterans' groups. Moreover, he became a member of the Central Committee of the French Communist Party and a confidant of Party secretary Maurice Thorez. As the chief executor of the hard line on culture propounded in the Soviet Union by Andrei Zhdanov, Aragon was in many ways the French Zhdanov. He was as close to being a commissar of culture as one could find outside the Soviet Union and its bloc of East European allies, with more power over writers and artists than any official Minister of Culture could wield in a Western country.

It was not easy for a writer or an artist to create in such an atmosphere, in those early postliberation years when the high-strung, susceptible Aragon sometimes seemed to be mimicking the tantrums of his beloved Stalin. But if Stalin's excommunications could kill, Aragon's could only wound. He wore his responsibilities proudly, and the receptions in the salons of the National Committee of Writers were splendid affairs. To Dominique Desanti, Aragon and Elsa Triolet were *le couple royal,* and these monarchs had their courtiers. If the Party accepted Aragon's ways, it was because his life-style challenged minor taboos, but never any major ones.

If Aragon had a rival in Communist literary circles, it was Eluard, that other popular poet of Surrealism and resistance. For all his lyric enthusiasm for freedom, Eluard was stubbornly Stalinist, refusing to accept the possibility that the Soviet Union could be wrong. Pablo Picasso was a different sort. An artist whose work was impermeable to the doctrine of Socialist Realism, he was unmoved by Zhdanovism in Moscow or in Paris. Yet he remained loyal to the Party he had joined in October 1944. He certainly did not need the publicity he received henceforth in the Communist-dominated, Aragon-dominated press; readers of those papers did not buy his paintings. "You understand," he told Claude Roy, "I was a foreigner and without a family. I entered the Party the way one finds a family." Picasso realized that the relationship brought with it some of the inconveniences of family life: the family would like to make a druggist out of you when you really want to be an artist, or a Socialist Realist when you only want to be Picasso. But in the postwar decades, many a Party member who never read poetry or looked at paintings must have been proud that an Eluard and a Picasso shared their allegiance.

★ ★ ★

Like Aragon, André Malraux knew how to care for his image. The end of the war saw him as another intellectual hero — hero of intellectuals, and of newspaper readers, rally-goers, voters; he was destined to become even more of a *personnage* than Aragon. For he had picked himself up from his Riviera hideaway at the right time, and entered the resistance movement late but at the top, and in so doing had created a new character at least as compelling as any in his books. But even wars end. Soon, Malraux confessed to Marcel Arland that he was hesitating between "being a writer, making movies, or entering into action." But what action? Could being Minister of Information "satisfy a man of our class?" The two friends were talking in their regular bistro on the Rue du Dragon. Two days later, as Arland recalled it, Malraux entered into action, at a congress of resistance veterans: the all-important session of the Mouvement de Libération Nationale (MLN) that rejected unity with Communist resistance veterans.

Malraux did not make movies, but he did continue to write. Not fiction, but fiction of sorts, for the autobiographical works of his last years contain as much invention as fact; but above all, he wrote his ambitious and contested works on the psychology of art. He withdrew from the literary and even the political life of Paris as he had lived it before the war, and rejected the very idea of entering the Académie Française. Yet from the end of World War II until his death he held a court of his own, as an official or at least a public personage. (Once, he refused to relieve his wife of any of the armload of packages she was carrying, explaining: "If General de Gaulle carries packages, he is no longer General de Gaulle.")

In the months between the liberation and the German surrender, the harmony between Communists and non-Communists seemed total. But then the Communist plan to fuse all anti-Fascists into a single body amenable to control was challenged, and decisively. The Front National, ostensibly a broad anti-Fascist movement of resistance veterans but in fact tightly controlled by the Party, sought a merger with the Mouvement de Libération Nationale, a more heterogeneous coalition, some elements of which were left-wing and even pro-Communist, while others such as Combat were independent; in all, MLN represented some 500,000 members and several periodicals, including Parisian daily newspapers born of the resistance.

The first congress of the MLN was held at the Palais de la Mutualité in January 1945, and fusion with the Front National was on the agenda. Malraux took the floor, and his intervention has been accepted as crucial to the outcome; the MLN congress voted against a merger by 250 to 119. In his speech Malraux appealed for a mobilization of non-Communists: "If we want to maintain our mobilization of energy, we must employ a technique similar to that of the Communists..." In effect, Malraux was anticipating his own role in the Gaullist movement, and in the anti-Communist crusade of the cold-war years — and this before he had even met the General.

Charles de Gaulle had moved his provisional government from Algiers to Paris to fill a vacuum left by the departure of the Germans and the dismantling of the Vichy State. In November 1945 he was elected *chef du gouvernement provisoire*, pending the adoption of a constitution for the postwar republic. That same month he formed a new cabinet, bringing in Malraux as his Minister of Information — in effect, as his spokesman. This same cabinet included Maurice Thorez and four other Communist Party leaders. Malraux's chief of staff was Raymond Aron, whom he had first met at a prewar summer seminar at the Pontigny Abbey.

But soon after that de Gaulle resigned, to dramatize his disagreement with the traditional parliamentary regime, which seemed to have the favor of political leaders and voters. He returned only when France was prepared to throw over the constitution of the Fourth Republic in favor of a system of government with more authority for the chief of state than the parliamentary system allowed. Between de Gaulle's withdrawal in January 1946 and his return after what was virtually a coup d'état in May 1958, a faithful band of supporters, most of them veterans of the Free French of London and Algiers, labored to bring him back, and to impose his conception of strong government on France. The movement opposed both political parties and Communists, and André Malraux was its intellectual, taking de Gaulle for the incarnation of France, and the Communists for the Antichrist. The Gaullists founded the Rally of the French People (RPF), which was to be at once a party and antiparty, and which organized mass rallies, published newspapers, magazines, and other propaganda, and possessed its own security service, which engaged in pitched battles with equivalent Communist forces. In charge of Gaullist agitprop, Malraux set about his task with the same intensity he had shown before the war in Communist and anti-Fascist causes, working from elegant offices on the Place de l'Opéra. Stories circulated about his growing self-importance, his luxurious life-style, his automobiles, and his lackeys.

In Malraux's mind — this he makes clear in *Antimémoires* — his task in the Gaullist entourage was to mobilize intellectual energies behind anti-Communism, and de Gaulle's conception of the state, just as Willy Münzenberg had organized the left behind international Communism back in the 1930s. Malraux confided to Arthur Koestler in October 1947, when the Gaullist campaign had reached fever pitch, that he knew he was taking a risk in serving reactionaries to bring de Gaulle to power. That is, if de Gaulle did not act as Malraux expected once he attained power, Malraux would feel that he himself had betrayed the working class, and so would have to kill himself.

"Neither right nor left: the country," Malraux concluded one of his political messages. Just as the Stalinists were not really on the left of the political spectrum, the Gaullists (he argued) were not on the right.

★   ★   ★

If Malraux's appeal at times seemed unworldly, opposing as it did a mystique to the down-to-earth deeds of Communist subversion, Albert Camus's message was more concrete. But recurring illness, an anguished private life, and the desire to fulfill the promise of his first books kept him from the political arena in the early postwar years, despite solicitations from all sides. After his withdrawal from *Combat* (with the others of the original founding group), he lacked an organ in which to express himself, his better instincts keeping him away from the Gaullists, just as they kept him from *Les Temps Modernes*. Camus had had an experience that neither Malraux nor Sartre possessed, nor indeed most of the intellectuals he knew. He had actually been a card-carrying member of the Communist Party, in prewar Algiers, and at the age of twenty-three he had already been its victim. When he refused to follow the Party after it ceased to support Moslem nationalism, he had been tried privately and expelled. Still, he shared the suspicions of American might and American civilization current among left-wing intellectuals, for if the Communists had not injected this malady into the French bloodstream, the Gaullists were doing so now. (In a speech in March 1948, Malraux called for a French, a European culture distinct from both America's mercantile civilization and Stalinist totalitarianism.)

Camus was aware of the need for paying as much attention to the abuses of freedom in Stalinist-controlled areas as had been given to the abuses of Nazism and Fascism in the past. He wrote a series of articles for *Combat* under the general title "Neither Victims Nor Executioners," which came to represent his major political statement of that time. In an age of terror, he argued, those who rejected both the Soviet and the American ways, and who rejected a world where murder was considered a legitimate act, were men without a country. Socialists had to choose between the Communist doctrine that ends justify means — i.e., that murder can be a legitimate act — and the rejection of Marxism except as a critical tool. The end of ideology had ushered in a world dominated by the great powers; the alternative to bloodshed was universal order, not a utopia but a realistic system. Henceforth, in Camus's view, the world was divided between those who agreed to be murderers in the name of abstract principles and those who refused with all their strength.

The Communists and their fellow travelers did not fail to see that Camus's soft analysis was as dangerous to them as the hard approach of a Malraux or a Koestler. In refusing to choose between Communism and capitalism, in trying to "save bodies," Camus became (or so charged Emmanuel d'Astier de la Vigerie) an unwitting accomplice of capitalism. Then, as in later years, Camus's discreet, introspective commitment often seemed to the unsuspecting to be noncommitment, and so it made him vulnerable to attack by those more conspicuously engaged. Camus's enlistment in the ideological struggle of his time was expressed in his writings, most notably in *L'Homme révolté* ("The Rebel"), the synthesis of his antitotalitarian philosophy. "My role," he wrote in a reply to d'Astier, "is not to transform the world, or mankind . . . But it is, perhaps, to serve in my own way the values without which even a transformed world is not worth living in." He eschewed petitions and large-scale campaigns, although for a time he made an exception for Garry Davis, a Don Quixote much like himself, a young American war veteran who had renounced his nationality to become a citizen of the world.

★   ★   ★

Besides André Breton, who on his return from the United States broke a lifelong friendship with Picasso because of the painter's membership in the Communist Party, another conspicuous anti-Communist of Left Bank Paris now was Arthur Koestler. He had written the most influential anti-Communist book of the time, and in the form of a novel. *Darkness at Noon,* an account of the purge trials of the old Bolsheviks in Moscow, appeared first in London during the war (the original German manuscript having been lost), and was translated from the English into French only after the liberation. Koestler's essays on Stalinism, collected in *The Yogi and the Commissar,* brought a denunciation in *Les Temps Modernes* by Maurice Merleau-Ponty, then still a sympathizer with Soviet Communism. Because of the Sartrian group's opposition to Koestler, Camus concluded an argument with Merleau-Ponty and Sartre at a party at the Boris Vians by slamming the door.

But for a while Koestler had been admitted into Sartre's circle. Sartre and Simone de Beauvoir found him conceited, ever prepared to quote his own words. "We were made uncomfortable," Beauvoir later remembered, "by his pedantry of the self-taught man, by the doctrinal assurance and the scientism derived from his superficial Marxist training... But he also had much warmth, liveliness, and curiosity; he brought a tireless passion to our discussions; he was always ready, no matter what hour of day or night, to deal with any subject at all." Koestler was generous with his money as well as his time, and Sartre and Beauvoir enjoyed some memorable Parisian nights with him, Camus, and their women — nights liberally fueled with assorted alcohols, the descriptions of which are one of the high points of Simone de Beauvoir's postwar journal. She has Koestler throw a glass at Sartre in a fit of anger, of polemic, and perhaps of jealousy. "No friendship without political agreement," insisted Koestler. And then Sartre told him that they no longer had anything to say to each other.

Just as Koestler and his comrades in prewar Paris, then under Münzenberg's wing, had composed the basic documents for the anti-Fascist struggle, so Koestler's anti-Communist books now offered facts as well as theory for postwar anti-Communism. It was even said that the Communists had attempted to block the publication of the French translation of Darkness at Noon; the pressure was such that the translator removed his name from the title page. When it appeared in bookstores the Communists bought up as many copies as they could, but they certainly did not purchase all of the half million copies sold in the first year. Koestler was proud that a French newspaper called Darkness at Noon the most important factor in the defeat of the Communists in the May 1946 referendum on the draft constitution. On the front page of Les Lettres Françaises, Claude Morgan counterattacked with a defense of the prewar Moscow trials, which he said had purged the Soviet Union of dangerous traitors. "Without the Moscow trials," Morgan asked, "would France now be free?" Morgan went further, as a writer in Esprit did not fail to notice; he reminded the French Jewish publishers of Koestler's book that Jews owed much to Stalin's army for having vanquished Hitler. Vercors, for his part, criticized Darkness at Noon in the name of hope, for one had to believe in the Soviet Union.

The high priest of Communist ideological conformity, Laurent Casanova, was even moved to devote space to Koestler in the theoretical organ of the Party. Koestler was only recently naturalized as a British subject, observed Casanova (a reference to his Hungarian origin), but his work was anti-French, because Koestler opposed the Communist line of national independence. In a small book entitled *Le Traître et le Prolétaire ou l'entreprise Koestler and co. ltd.*, Jean Kanapa advanced a more personal thesis against the author. He recalled that after Koestler's arrest by Franco troops in Málaga in February 1937, he had been released by the Fascists; indeed, he had allowed himself to be arrested by the Fascists in the first place. So Koestler was a deserter, and a traitor in the bargain.

32   Cold Warfare

DEPENDING ON ONE'S ALLEGIANCE, one defines the cold war as the Western response to Eastern threats, or the contrary. The founding of the Cominform may be accepted as the first official manifestation of the cold war on the Communist side, although many less conspicuous signs preceded it, and as has already been said, the hardening of the ideological line by Zhdanov and his French counterparts began a year before the Cominform did. It simply took time for most of the French to recognize that the Soviet Union was in an expansionist phase, that it had kept its armies in the territories it held at the close of hostilities with Nazi Germany, and was installing puppet regimes in those places, first as coalition governments and later as tightly controlled Communist dictatorships. Perhaps it took the spectacular coup d'état in traditionally democratic Czechoslovakia in February 1948 to draw the attention of many in the West to what was taking place in the East.

But half a year earlier, in Rennes in July 1947, Charles de Gaulle (who was no longer head of state) denounced the threat represented by Soviet power, which already controlled a bloc of four hundred million persons held together by constraint. "Its frontier," he warned, "is separated from ours by no more than five hundred kilometers [300 miles], or not more than two laps of the Tour de France bicycle race."

The cold war has been dated as starting still earlier, from the day and the hour in March 1947 when Harry S. Truman asked Congress for military and economic aid for Greece and Turkey, this at a time when a Communist-inspired insurrection in Greece threatened to bring one or both countries into the Soviet orbit. Greece and Turkey received help, but the pressure continued elsewhere. The Prague coup in 1948 was followed by the Soviet blockade of Berlin, the reply to which was the historic airlift that kept that city alive, and then the Soviet-bloc excommunication of Tito and his Yugoslavia. On April 4, 1949, the Western democracies including France signed the North Atlantic Treaty, which provided for mutual protection in the event of armed attack, but it was only when hot war began in Korea in June 1950 that NATO became organized into a unified military command.

Today it is difficult to comprehend how real the likelihood of European war, of a Communist coup d'état in France, seemed to sensible men and women, including the writers and artists of the Left Bank, in the final years of the 1940s. The dramatic language of Charles de Gaulle was also the language of his aide, André Malraux, and Malraux was the leading agent in spreading the message to his peers. A number of eyewitness accounts document his role as messenger of despair, or at least alarm. While he was de Gaulle's Minister of Information — that is, between the end of November 1945 and January 20, 1946 — Malraux invited his friend Marcel Arland to the Opéra. During the intermission, he whispered, "In less than a week the Communists are going to take over Paris, or at least try to, by fire and blood." He reassured Arland: "An aircraft will be placed at your disposal to take you to Brussels." Was Malraux speaking of a domestic Communist insurrection, or a Soviet invasion? The naïve Arland would not have known the difference. But Malraux also confided to American journalists — on January 18, 1946, just before de Gaulle withdrew from office — that the Soviet Union and the United States would clash over the "prone body" of Europe, which would bring the Russians to Paris. Nearly a year later Malraux was still talking that way; he told Georges Bernanos that the Soviets were sure to attack France by the spring of 1947 at the latest. Once more Bernanos took leave of France, and a friend insists that it was because he was convinced that Soviet tanks would soon be in Paris. Jean Galtier-Boissière dined with Malraux in January 1948 and was told that the Communist coup would take place in March, beginning with political assassinations and sabotage of railway tracks by Yugoslav experts . . .

The Communists were also preparing for the worst. There were scare headlines in L'Humanité, talk of a police roundup of Communists and a siege of their headquarters. After the beginning of the Korean War, Camus and Sartre sat in the Brasserie Balzar alongside the Sorbonne, arguing their respective positions with some heat. "Have you thought about what will happen to you when the Russians arrive?" Camus is supposed to have asked Sartre, adding, "Don't stay!" For his part, Camus said that he would join the resistance; Sartre replied that he could never raise a hand against the proletariat. The intensity of Camus's plea, "If you stay, they'll take not only your life but your honor," affected Simone de Beauvoir, she confesses in her journal. In the days following that café meeting, she repeated Camus's argument in her discussions with Sartre. Merleau-Ponty's wife told Sartre, "What is expected of you is suicide." Another time, according to Beauvoir, Roger Stéphane pleaded, "In any case, Sartre, promise me that you'll never confess!"

In October 1948 a political weekly, Carrefour, launched a survey of leaders of public opinion under a headline in red and black inks:

IF THE RED ARMY OCCUPIED FRANCE
WHAT WOULD YOU DO?

"The Russian occupation isn't fatal, but it is possible," the editor explained. Malraux's was among the first responses. "You ask me: what will you do? The same as from 1940 to 1944." But most of those interviewed rejected the question itself, affirming that the French would know how to prevent war on their soil. Some, like Louis Martin-Chauffier, considered the question dangerous, because it contributed to an attitude of fatalism. "Why 'the Red army'?" asked Vercors. "Why not 'the American army'?" But he and others on the left affirmed that they would resist any invasion at all, any occupation. Sartre refused to reply in the columns of a newspaper that often attacked him; in any case, he commented in a roundtable political discussion, should either the United States or the USSR occupy France, he and his friends would go into the underground.

The cold war was a time of purge trials in Eastern Europe, when the leaders of one Soviet satellite after another, who had been heroes of Communist propaganda during the war, suddenly became traitors meriting the executioner's block. The last of the staged trials took place in Moscow itself during the final months of Stalin's life, when a group of well-known Kremlin doctors, most of them Jewish, were accused of assassinating Soviet leaders such as Zhdanov.

Then Paris became the scene of two landmark trials, each of which took the form of a criminal libel suit, while each in its way exemplified the East-West struggle.

Victor A. Kravchenko was an official in the Soviet Purchasing Commission in the United States when he defected in 1944. His first revelations about the crimes of Stalinism came when the war against Germany and Japan was in full swing, and U.S.-Soviet cooperation was an essential element in that war. Then, the exposé of the Soviet police state from the point of view of a member of the working class and a functionary of that state that appeared in his book *I Chose Freedom*, published in the United States in 1946, had international repercussions. In French translation the book was a popular success the following year, and an immediate target of French Communists. The burden of the attack on Kravchenko was left to *Les Lettres Françaises*, which on November 13, 1947, charged that the book was a fake. The story was attributed to a journalist who was given the name "Sim Thomas," purportedly a former agent of the wartime American intelligence agency OSS (Office of Strategic Services). "Thomas" claimed that Kravchenko's book had actually been written by anti-Soviet specialists for U.S. intelligence. ("Sim Thomas," it is now known, never existed; the article claiming that *I Chose Freedom* was fabricated by U.S. agents was in fact fabricated by Soviet agents.) On April 25, 1948, *Les Lettres Françaises* followed up with a second article, this one signed by André Wurmser, a Communist polemicist, who concluded: "It's one or the other: either Kravchenko lies or he is an abject creature."

Kravchenko had explained in the original version of his book that he had written the manuscript in Russian and that it had been adapted under his supervision for American readers. Now he filed a complaint for criminal libel against *Les Lettres Françaises* and Claude Morgan, its director, as well as against "Sim Thomas"; he filed another against Wurmser when his article appeared. The trial began on January 24, 1949, in a newly refurbished Paris courtroom, and immediately became a cause célèbre. Reporters jammed the section of the room made available to them, and it seemed as if everybody who counted in Paris had to watch at least part of the trial. It was clear that the Soviet system itself was being judged, for this was the first official forum at which evidence on the deportations and camps would be heard. Just before the hearings began, Kravchenko outlined his complaint at a press conference — more a rally than a conference — at the Salle de Géographie on the Boulevard Saint-Germain (near the Café de Flore). "January 24, 1949, wasn't the opening of a trial, it was a first night," the defendant André Wurmser later recalled. "Movie cameras, newsmen from Panama, New Zealand, Germany, America; they were everywhere, on the benches, the steps, so close to the judges that it was indecent."

As the plaintiff claiming damages, Victor Kravchenko spoke in Russian, with an interpreter translating into French. "What I did," declared Kravchenko, "I did for the whole world, for all free people who must know the truth about the life of the people under Soviet dictatorship, and who must see that this regime is not a regime of progress, but one of barbarity." He was the grandson and the son of workers, he had been a worker himself, and had even been a Communist against the will of his father. "I appeal to all workers, to peasants and intellectuals all over the world . . ." Pointing to the defendants, he said, "The goal of my enemies is to smear me and to compromise me by every possible means . . . a job that was assigned to them by the Kremlin."

The trial proceeded in the French courtroom tradition of free and easy debate, frequent interruptions. In his testimony Wurmser stressed the exploitation of Kravchenko's defection by Nazi propaganda. He added that whoever is anti-Soviet is also anti-French (which brought an indignant "Oh, oh, oh!" from Kravchenko's attorney, Georges Izard). The defense argued that Kravchenko could not have written the book; for example, he was demonstrably not familiar with Ibsen's play *The Doll's House*, which was cited in the book. Kravchenko conceded that the text had been adapted for Western readers. Hours passed that way.

A parade of Communists and Communist sympathizers testified as character witnesses for the defendants. But the importance of the case to the Soviet Union became apparent when the defense flew witnesses in from Moscow — all the more since that country did not readily open its borders. Kravchenko's ex-wife took the stand to denounce him; Kravchenko pointed out that she was forced to testify, because her father was in a camp. "It's the Soviet police state that obliges this woman to come to France to make a statement that is unworthy of her."

The Communist side then produced an engineer from Moscow to denounce Kravchenko, and the two men had to be separated by court attendants. When the engineer told Kravchenko not to dare mention the name of Stalin, Kravchenko retorted, "I can speak of the 'beloved' leader because I am in free France and I don't care what the 'beloved' leader might think about it . . . I've waited for this minute all my life!" A Soviet general who had been head of the Soviet Purchasing Commission in Washington threw doubt on Kravchenko's character; Kravchenko accused him of being a representative of the Communist Party and not a military officer at all.

Among the most effective witnesses for Kravchenko's book was Margarete Buber-Neumann, daughter-in-law of the Jewish philosopher Martin Buber and later the wife, or widow — for his fate was not known — of Heinz Neumann, a German Communist leader who had been arrested in the Soviet Union in 1937 by the secret police. She herself had been deported to a Siberian deportation camp and turned over to the Nazis after the Soviet-German pact in August 1939. The Nazis sent her to Ravensbruck concentration camp, where she spent four years.

The confusion instilled in Parisian intellectuals by the Communist campaign against Kravchenko before and during the trial, the difficulty of demonstrating the truth of Kravchenko's indictment of the Soviet system, come through in the diary of Simone de Beauvoir. She attended a session of the trial with Sartre. "Whatever his lies and his venality," she wrote of Kravchenko, "and although most of his witnesses were as suspect as he, a truth emerged from their testimony: the existence of work camps. Logical, intelligent, confirmed by many facts, the story of Mme Buber-Neumann carried conviction." "The testimony of Margarete [Buber-Neumann] was staggering and I came out tormented," Dominique Desanti, the self-confessed Stalinist, later recalled. "But if Margarete Buber-Neumann did shake me an instant, I didn't for a minute believe in the truth of what all the witnesses said . . ."

On April 4, 1949, the judge issued his verdict to a packed courtroom: Kravchenko, he declared, was indeed capable of having written I Chose Freedom, although Claude Morgan's record in the underground resistance while Kravchenko was abandoning his own country also had to be taken into consideration. Guilty of libel, Morgan was fined and ordered to pay damages to Kravchenko. A similar judgment was rendered against Wurmser, while Les Lettres Françaises was declared responsible for court costs. That paper continued to advance the Soviet cause, resembling L'Humanité and Pravda more and more each week, printing Stalin's name in ever larger type, until the day came that the camel's back broke. On that day Aragon and Daix refused to support a new Soviet move against Czechoslovakia, and the Communists removed their backing; the paper was forced to shut down.

The defendant Claude Morgan later confessed that vhen Victor Kravchenko died he was tempted to write an art le entitled, "Kravchenko, you were right."

★　★　★

The last years of Stalin, years of arbitrary accusations and arrests, placed increased strains on Communist credibility. French Party members and fellow travelers were required to accept not only the purges of veteran Communists once praised for their courage and loyalty, but to write and to make speeches justifying the purges, to visit the countries where they were taking place, just as French collaborationists had been brought to Germany during the war. In Hungary, the trial of Lazlo Rajk saw this Communist leader, Minister of the Interior of the Soviet puppet government, and a former member of the International Brigade in Spain, confess to his own crimes, in a repetition of the scenario of the Moscow trials of the 1930s. The Communists in Paris duly staged a rally to denounce Rajk, and the once fiercely independent Julien Benda spoke. When Vercors submitted an article to *Les Lettres Françaises* pointing to contradictions in the confessions of Eastern European Communist leaders, Pierre Daix told him that the paper had to show solidarity with the Hungarian Communist Party, and so could not publish his article.

Soon Daix's paper had a writer in Sofia to report on the trial of Traicho Kostov, Bulgaria's Communist deputy prime minister, but now a "traitor and spy." When the Czechoslovak Communist leadership was similarly purged, in the Rudolf Slansky trial, Vercors asked for space to denounce the anti-Jewish nature of this case. Daix and Morgan persuaded him to postpone his article, but a reading of the indictment shook Daix himself. He realized that the defendants had done nothing other than what he himself had done in the course of his political life. *Esprit* printed a detailed exposé of the Hungarian purges by François Fejtö, who until then was an official Hungarian cultural attaché in Paris. His article, entitled "The Rajk Affair Is an International Dreyfus Affair," was prefaced by Emmanuel Mounier, who denied that it was being published for anti-Communist, cold-war motives. Dominique Desanti later explained why most Communist intellectuals still did not believe that the trials were faked. It would have been necessary to admit not only judicial error but the "truly demoniac plan" behind the trials, and to stay in the Party after such an admission would have required a "political cynicism" she felt that they did not possess. "It was therefore, literarily, impossible for us, inconceivable, inadmissable, excluded." For many such persons it would take Nikita Khrushchev's authoritative, if secret, revelations of Stalin's crimes in 1956, and the entry of Khrushchev's tanks into Budapest to crush the insurrection later that year, to shake their faith.

★   ★   ★

Now the Communists were using their fellow-traveling intellectuals without any pretense of allowing them to exercise independent initiative. Events were international, Paris and its literary Left Bank only a cog in a vast machine. Communists were expected to offer their reputations in defense of the Soviet philosophy of science, for example. Louis Aragon devoted a whole issue of *Europe* to praise for the theories of Stalin's preferred biologist, T.D. Lysenko, who in defiance of accepted theory put forth the view that environment could affect genetics. French Party scientists had to concur or face expulsion and infamy. The Party dissolved the Commission of Intellectuals, which had provided a framework for discussion, even though the discussion was not public, making it clear that henceforth artists and writers would have to conform to a more narrowly construed doctrine of Socialist Realism. On the death of the Soviet dictator, Pablo Picasso drew a portrait of a young Stalin that his friend Pierre Daix published in *Les Lettres Françaises*. In sharp contrast to the fatherly image that the Party faithful had learned to accept, Picasso offered a virile, even somewhat revolutionary figure. There was a roar of protest, a moral lynching of Picasso; *Les Lettres Françaises* was required to apologize, and for some time to come the sacrilegious nature of this portrait, which Picasso had conceived as a homage, seemed the most important business with which the Party had to deal.

The French Communists, with guidance and material assistance from their big brothers in Moscow, were now beginning to transport intellectuals by the planeload to ambitious international conferences, such as the Congress of Intellectuals for Peace in Wroclaw, Poland, at which Picasso, Paul Eluard, Fernand Léger, Julien Benda, Jorge Amado, Pierre Seghers, and Vercors participated, with Laurent Casanova, Jean Kanapa, and Pierre Daix in the wings, and Aleksandr Fadeiev, president of the Soviet Writers Union, providing the ideological tone in the absence of Andrei Zhdanov, the true inspirer of the meeting, who was ill. Picasso made what was described as the first public address of his life (in favor of Pablo Neruda, then facing persecution in Chile). And Fadeiev denounced Sartre, who had not been invited because *Les Mains sales* was taken as an attack on Communist methods (Zhdanov had also vetoed invitations to Malraux and Camus). The attack on Sartre as a hyena and a jackal was not to everyone's taste, and the British delegates Julian Huxley and Richard Hughes protested against the one-sided nature of the event. After telling the congress that culture did not necessarily have to be politicized — his UNESCO was proof of that —

Huxley left before the congress was over. (It was still possible in those days to say that about UNESCO.) Witnesses observed the healthy skepticism of Picasso through it all. He openly mocked Fadeiev for his attack on formalist art — modern art, in other words. When confronted with officially inspired anti-Semitism in Poland, Picasso let it be known that his own painting was "Jewish," that Eluard's poetry was "Jewish," as was that of Apollinaire (whose mother was of the Polish nobility). The congress was still in session when the news came that Zhdanov had died in Moscow. Fadeiev did not hide his despair. "What will we do without him?" he said. Fadeiev committed suicide after the revelation of Stalin's crimes by Khrushchev.

The next international event was a meeting in New York in March 1949, but Eluard and other French delegates were denied U.S. visas, so the National Committee of Writers called a rally in Paris to allow them to make the speeches they would have delivered at the Waldorf-Astoria Hotel. In April, in the Salle Pleyel in Paris, a World Congress of Partisans of Peace was conceived as a follow-up to the Wroclaw meeting. Fadeiev attended, and so did Ilya Ehrenburg (who had also been in Wroclaw). A permanent committee was founded with Frédéric Joliot-Curie as president, Aragon and Fadeiev as vice-presidents, and a Communist functionary as secretary-general. The Paris meeting is best remembered for its emblem, a dove drawn by Picasso (who privately observed that far from being a symbol of peace, the dove was an unusually aggressive bird). Then a meeting of the World Congress of Partisans of Peace in Sweden in March 1950 issued a Stockholm Appeal calling for a ban on atomic weapons: the United States had developed a hydrogen bomb, but the Soviets did not yet have one. The Appeal became the principal propaganda effort of Communists in the months that followed; Les Lettres Françaises gave it the front page week after week to report the growing number of signatures, citing prominent non-Communists who had lent their names, including Pierre Benoit, Marc Chagall, Gérard Philipe, Jacques Prévert, Pierre Renoir. When it was all over, the claim was that six hundred million signatures had been collected. This was the last Soviet-inspired peace effort on such a grandiose scale before hot war began in Korea in June. Then, in the year of Stalin's death, the Soviet Union proudly announced the testing of its own hydrogen bomb.

What troubled non-Communist intellectuals, and an increasing number of Communists as well, was the accumulation of evidence that Stalinist society was founded on a universe of camps, not the idealistically motivated penal rehabilitation colonies sung in Soviet fiction, where former criminals were making a useful contribution to society, but a system under which innocent victims were subjected to arbitrary arrest and indeterminate sentences, when they did not disappear outright. The Kravchenko case against *Les Lettres Françaises* had contained too many extraneous issues having to do with Kravchenko's character and career to affect opinion decisively. It would take a second trial, involving some of the same facts, to shake the Left Bank.

The instrument for a renewed attack on the camp system was David Rousset, a left-wing Socialist who had himself published his experiences as a concentration-camp prisoner of the Nazis. On the front page of *Le Figaro Littéraire*, on November 12, 1949, he addressed an appeal to former political prisoners of Germany to join an investigatory commission on the Soviet camps. On November 17, Pierre Daix, himself a former inmate of a Nazi camp, replied on the front page of *Les Lettres Françaises*, alleging that Rousset sought to make Nazi camp victims the allies of the Nazis themselves in a war against the Soviet Union. Daix accused him of falsifying documents, even of transposing testimony on Nazi camps so that it seemed to concern Soviet camps. To Daix, Stalin's camps were the "perfecting... of the complete suppression of the exploitation of man by man."

Rousset filed a complaint for libel. It was heard in the same court-room where Kravchenko's complaint against the same newspaper had been heard. This time the defendants were Claude Morgan, as director, and Daix, as author of the article. The trial began a year after Rousset's appeal was first published. Although Daix and Morgan relinquished their right to furnish proof of the truth of their charges, in the hope of avoiding the calling of witnesses to the reality of the Soviet camps, the court allowed evidence to be heard. So here was another trial in the spirit of the Kravchenko affair, with the same aggressive behavior by the defendants and their partisans, the same interruption of testimony; at one point Morgan was expelled from the courtroom for shouting at a witness.

This time the witnesses included Elinor Lipper, a German Communist who had taken refuge in the Soviet Union in 1937, at the height of the purges, and who had been a victim of arbitrary arrest followed by eleven years in Soviet camps; Jules Margoline, a Polish immigrant to Palestine who was caught by the war while visiting his parents in Poland, to become a Soviet prisoner for five years; Alexander Weissberg, an Austrian Jew and Communist arrested in 1937 while working in a Soviet scientific laboratory, falsely accused of espionage; Valentin Gonzales, known as El Campesino, a Spanish Communist and Civil War hero sent to a Soviet forced labor camp when he took refuge in the USSR after the victory of Franco; and Margarete Buber-Neumann, heroine of the Kravchenko trial. In the verdict, announced in January 1951, Morgan and Daix were fined, Rousset receiving damages. In a joint letter to *The New York Times*, Arthur Koestler, Arthur Schlesinger, Jr., Reinhold Niebuhr, Norman Thomas, Roger Baldwin, George S. Counts, and Sidney Hook declared that this "extraordinary" trial had been "nothing less than a full-dress indictment of the entire system of slave labor... of the Soviet Union... comparable in moral significance and surpassing in human scope the Dreyfus trial of a half-century ago."

But could any evidence affect those who continued to remain loyal to Stalinism? Dominique Desanti, for instance, did not accept Rousset's case against Soviet labor camps, although she had known Rousset as an anti-Fascist resistance militant, and admired his book on the Nazi camps. This new trial had taken place in a climate of heightened tension between the blocs, but hadn't the Rajk trial and even Tito's excommunication been swallowed by the faithful? There seemed to be still more vital issues now, such as the very real war in Korea, where the Communists were already engaged in a new propaganda campaign alleging that the United States was making use of bacteriological warfare there. Even Sartre was concerned about the benefits the American side would gain from the verdict against *Les Lettres Françaises*. Soon after Rousset's appeal was published by *Le Figaro Littéraire*, Sartre and Merleau-Ponty had come out with a long and curious essay in *Les Temps Modernes* conceding that the existence of camps in the USSR was established, and even estimating that these camps might hold as many as ten to fifteen million prisoners; it went so far as to assert that "there is no Socialism when one citizen in twenty is in a camp." Still, Sartre and Merleau-Ponty wished to place the Soviet camps in the context of the evils of capitalism. They also accused David Rousset of being indifferent to the existence of detention camps for political prisoners in Spain and Greece. The Communists read the statement in *Les Temps Modernes* in their own way; in *Les Lettres Françaises* a headline explained: SARTRE AND MERLEAU-PONTY REFUSE TO CHOOSE BUT FORMER CAMP INMATES TAKE THE SIDE OF PEACE.

In retrospect, Sartre wondered what else he might have done, torn between the revelations about the Soviet camps on one side, and the evils of capitalism on the other. "To strike out, on right and left, against two giants who wouldn't even feel our blows?"

★   ★   ★

In the face of the long experience of French and foreign Communists in mobilizing opinion and opinion-makers, and their ability to provide rank-and-file support through a network of mass-membership organizations, any ad hoc Western effort to stage similar psychological warfare could only seem feeble. Yet Malraux had warned from the beginning of the cold war that non-Communists would have to imitate the tactics of Communists. As chief propagandist in the Gaullist movement, he attempted to carry out his own campaign in the press and in public meetings, directed toward intellectuals. But the most significant cold-war effort of this kind on the Western side became the responsibility of a Congress for Cultural Freedom, founded in an atmosphere of tension in Berlin in June 1950; indeed, when the news of the Communist attack in Korea was announced, there were fears that the Soviet army would quickly take over West Berlin, making prisoners of the congress participants. Leading anti-Communists such as Sidney Hook, Arthur Schlesinger, Jr., James Burnham, and James T. Farrell had come to Berlin from the United States, with Arthur Koestler and Herbert Read from the United Kingdom, Ignazio Silone from Italy, Charles Plisnier from Belgium, and Carlo Schmid from Germany. From France there were David Rousset, Henri Frenay of the wartime Combat movement, and Jules Romains; Sartre and Merleau-Ponty refused to come. In all, over a hundred delegates from twenty nations heard accounts of Soviet abuses of human rights and joined in a message of solidarity for their colleagues in Eastern Europe. In a paper dealing with methods of action, Arthur Koestler argued that intellectuals had to commit themselves, going beyond the mere statement that they were neither Communists nor anti-Communists. An international committee was chosen to create a permanent organization to issue proof of violations of freedom in the Soviet bloc, as well as to provide assistance to fugitives from totalitarian countries.

In Paris, the organizers of the Congress for Cultural Freedom wanted to recreate the environment for free debate that had existed before the Second World War in Paul Desjardins's Union pour la Vérité. When the congress was formally launched in August 1950, it boasted some eminent libertarians among its honorary chairmen: Benedetto Croce, John Dewey, Karl Jaspers, Salvador de Madariaga, Jacques Maritain, and

Bertrand Russell. Denis de Rougemont was chairman of the executive board, Nicholas Nabokov president. Both the international headquarters and the offices of the French section were in Paris, and soon the organization was producing periodicals in English (*Encounter*), French (*Preuves*), and other languages, counterparts to the preexisting *Der Monat* published in German by Melvin Lasky. The permanent staff soon recruited independent leftists such as François Bondy, Manès Sperber, and René Tavernier, who refused both Stalinism and the new left school represented by the Sartrians, and who did not reject on principle the idea of American participation in an organization devoted to freedom.

Later it was learned that the essential financing for the Congress for Cultural Freedom came from the American government, via the Central Intelligence Agency; but the French participants knew nothing of that. Nor was the American connection the principal reason it was difficult to obtain the cooperation of non-Communist intellectuals; most had simply been burned too often, and no longer wished to join anything; they had to be won over one by one. It was easier to recruit rightwingers such as Thierry Maulnier, but they did not move the organization in the direction its sponsors wished it to go.

Arthur Koestler, who was then in France, was a ubiquitous presence. The most eminent recruit was Raymond Aron, who helped to keep the debate on a high level. But Aron himself realized that he was not a typical Left Bank intellectual, and he had been blackballed by many of his peers because of his "Atlantic" position — he favored cooperation between Europe and the United States. *Preuves*, the congress's French magazine, considered its target audience to be both the readers of Sartre's *Les Temps Modernes* and those of the left-Catholic and increasingly neutralist *Esprit*. Among members of the non-Communist left who cooperated with the congress were Jean Cassou, now thoroughly disillusioned with fellow-traveling, and Jean Guéhenno. André Gide issued a statement of support for the founding congress in Berlin, and the Congress for Cultural Freedom defended Gide's memory when the Communists attacked him after his death. Malraux was sympathetic to the congress, spoke at its first public meeting in France, and then participated in a cultural festival it held in Paris in April 1952, with eminent foreign guests such as William Faulkner, James T. Farrell, and Ignazio Silone.

The Congress for Cultural Freedom lasted a long time, but it was never a match for the Stalinist apparatus.

33   No Third Way

IN THE FACE OF the blocs drawing into their respective camps like magnets those who believed Stalin represented peace and brotherhood, and those who saw in alliance with the United States a guarantee of basic freedoms, was there a third solution? Some still felt there might be. As early as November 1947, Emmanuel Mounier's *Esprit* published a "First appeal to international opinion" signed by a group of Left Bank writers and other intellectuals — Camus, Sartre, Merleau-Ponty, Beauvoir; Mounier and Jean-Marie Domenach of *Esprit*; Georges Altman of the left-wing (but not Communist) daily *Franc-Tireur*; Claude Bourdet of *Combat*. The signers declared that "bloc politics," with its promise of a balance of power, did nothing to guarantee peace, for "armed peace is not peace." They warned that Europe was already a battlefield for the rival blocs, each seeking recruits and reducing the French to a state of servitude. "But if we consent, even through our inertia, to this servitude, we cease being victims to become accomplices." Hope lay in a united Europe equally independent of the United States and of the Soviet Union, a Europe whose member states would adopt Socialism and divest themselves of colonies. This appeal was to have been published in *Les Temps Modernes* as well as in *Esprit*, but at the last minute Maurice Merleau-Ponty, though a signer, refused to let it appear in the magazine he edited with Sartre, apparently to avoid offending the Communists.

Thus began the era of neutralism — of the third force, the third way. It was an attractive notion, that one could by one's own will turn away from the horrid world developing before one's eyes: from an expansionist Soviet Union annexing the smaller states on its borders, from an arms buildup in the West led by the United States. Claude

Bourdet, the veteran of the wartime *Combat* resistance movement and of a Nazi concentration camp, had taken over the editorship of *Combat* from Camus and the original group, and began using that paper as early as June 1947 to call for a Socialist Europe independent of the U.S. and the USSR both. On December 24, soon after the publication of the "First appeal," *Combat* published an "Appeal for the setting up of a Third Force," which once more demanded a Europe "independent of any 'bloc.' " This time the signatories included Henri Frenay, founder of the Combat resistance movement, and those veterans of the political wars, Jean Guéhenno and François Mauriac. An executive board was formed, a meeting held at the old Salle de Géographie on the Boulevard Saint-Germain. In an editorial in *Combat* on February 18, 1948, Claude Bourdet called for a coalition of "the most intelligent and energetic members of SFIO [the Socialist Party], left-wing Christians, non-Stalinist revolutionaries, progressive minds of all tendencies . . ."

In February 1950 the paper's owners forced Bourdet out of *Combat*. He soon joined Roger Stéphane and a young team of left-wing idealists who were producing a modest periodical modeled on British weeklies such as *The Economist* and *The New Statesman and Nation*. *L'Observateur Politique, Économique et Littéraire* it was called, until use of the title was challenged by another magazine and it became *France-Observateur*, prefiguring the mass-circulation *Nouvel Observateur*. Here, in a weekly editorial, Bourdet developed his favorite theme: a neutral Europe. *L'Observateur* even published a special issue, "Is Neutrality Possible?" on June 8, 1950, in which the staff joined with outside contributors to make a case for a third way. Jean Cassou, for example, warned that the Atlantic Pact and the Cominform increased the likelihood of war. Sartre described the Atlantic Pact as "a cold war operation." The result, he wrote, was that "half of the French consider the other half as traitors; the government considers the Communists traitors . . . But a very large minority accuses the government itself of treason, blaming it for its submission to the United States . . ."

L'Observateur's circulation, if influential, was tiny. But neutralism had the support of a far more powerful voice: *Le Monde*, printing over 150,000 copies daily, reached practically everyone in France with intellectual pretensions. Hubert Beuve-Méry, director of *Le Monde*, was an early advocate of a neutralist response to the rise of major powers in the East and West. Etienne Gilson, a specialist in medieval philosophy, a former professor at Harvard and a member of the Académie Française, published an article in *Le Monde* on March 2, 1949, entitled "L'Alternative." He expressed doubts about the sincerity of the Atlantic Pact, accusing the United States of hoping to buy Europe with its dollars. His "alternative" to alliance with the United States was armed European neutrality. Although Gilson's was not the first statement of this position in *Le Monde*, it represented the most energetic presentation of the case against Atlantic solidarity, and by one of the chief policy-makers of the newspaper. Before the conflict ended, two members of the board of *Le Monde* resigned in protest, one of them accusing the paper of violent anti-Americanism.

★   ★   ★

Bourdet's Third Force had not caught on. The next attempt to provide an organizational framework to advocate neutrality was the Rassemblement Démocratique Révolutionnaire (RDR), or Revolutionary Democratic Rally, founded in February 1948 a few months after the "First appeal to international opinion." RDR's inaugural manifesto denounced "the rot of capitalist democracy" on one side, "the limitation of Communism to its Stalinist form" on the other, and "the defects of a certain kind of Social Democracy" for good measure. The best-known supporter of the new movement was Jean-Paul Sartre, who collaborated with the left-wing Socialist David Rousset. Their first general assembly was held in March in the Sociétés Savantes on the Rue de l'Odéon. RDR was not meant to be a political party, and it even encouraged the active participation of disillusioned Socialists and Communists, although the Communist Party soon denounced this upstart movement that threatened to lure away some of its members. Raymond Aron, Sartre's comrade of prewar years, and now his adversary, dismissed the founders of the new movement as "the heirs of revolutionary romanticism."

The Sartre-Rousset movement began to publish a magazine called *La Gauche*, to which even Camus contributed. On December 13, 1948, it organized a rally that drew some four thousand people, with half again as many unable to find room in the hall. The meeting received enthusiastic support from the daily *Franc-Tireur* (whose director, Georges Altman, and editor, Charles Ronsac, were early converts to RDR) and a sharp denunciation from *L'Humanité*, as an "anti-Soviet meeting organized by a clique of intellectuals whose showy generalities and literary salon slogans scarcely veiled their acceptance of the capitalist regime." Camus spoke at the meeting:

> In an era when the conqueror, by the very logic of his attitude, becomes
> executioner and policeman, the artist is obliged to be insubordinate.
> Faced with contemporary political society, the only coherent attitude for
> the artist, if he is not to give up his art, is refusal without concession. Even
> if he should desire it, he cannot be an accomplice of those who employ the
> language or the tactics of contemporary ideologies.

Sartre, at the same meeting, called for European disarmament. "If the
people of Europe choose one of the 'two great' parties or one of the two
great nations for protection against the other one," he said, "they
contribute to the threat to the one from which they seek protection, and
thus bring war closer." Other speakers included André Breton, Bourdet,
Merleau-Ponty, Richard Wright (whose speech was translated by
Simone de Beauvoir), Theodore Plievier, Carlo Levi. Some of the same
personalities, like Camus and Breton, were also involved in public
meetings to support "citizen of the world" Garry Davis.

But RDR was not to last. Already at the December meeting, Rousset
angered Sartre by making what Beauvoir scornfully dismissed as "an anti-
Communist diatribe." For the Sartrians in RDR sought an alliance with
the Communist Party on social issues, while Rousset and his friends, in
Beauvoir's opinion, "were sliding to the right." Rousset and Altman, she
observed in her diary, were willing to accept financial support from
American trade unions, while the Sartrians did not trust even left-wing
Americans. The issue came to a head the following spring. RDR and
Franc-Tireur sponsored an International Day of Resistance to
Dictatorship and War on April 30, 1949, which comprised an afternoon
assembly in the Grand Amphitheater of the Sorbonne and an evening
rally in a sports arena. These events followed a Communist-sponsored
international peace meeting, the World Congress of Partisans of Peace,
which had opened in Paris ten days earlier, although the International
Day was not officially identified as a counterdemonstration for fear of
antagonizing part of its target audience.

But Sartre thought he detected the anti-Communist motivation
behind the International Day of Resistance, and he decided to oppose it.
Richard Wright apparently complained to him that he had been
pressured by the American Embassy to take part. They and Merleau-
Ponty decided to boycott the afternoon and evening events, and to issue
a statement condemning Soviet territorial annexations *and* the Atlantic
Pact in equally harsh language. Sartre then summoned an extraordinary

assembly of RDR and persuaded the membership to disavow Rousset. "We assassinated RDR and I left for Mexico, disappointed but serene," Sartre later recalled. When he returned to Paris that autumn, he told Merleau-Ponty, "No more active politics. The magazine, the magazine alone."

★   ★   ★

Sartre was not the only one who was disappointed. Its most fervent advocates soon agreed that the neutralist movement had failed. Etienne Gilson himself called it a defeat in the columns of Le Monde. "Between the two blocs," concluded Simone de Beauvoir, "there was definitely not a third way." Merleau-Ponty reacted to the Korean War, to the violation by the Communists of the image he had chosen to give them, by simply turning away from combat to apolitisme. "The guns are speaking," he told his comrades of Les Temps Modernes, "there is nothing left for us to do but to remain silent." The parliamentary elections of June 1951 seemed an opportunity for testing neutralism with the voters, but the neutralist candidates lost. Eternal optimists, Bourdet and like-minded militants pursued their campaign for a solitary France through movements such as La Nouvelle Gauche [The New Left], with some of the neutralists even turning to Charles de Gaulle when his politics of "national independence" seemed to encounter theirs. On their side, the Communists exploited neutralism as a weapon against the Atlantic Pact, while detesting the neutralists and letting them know it. Raymond Aron warned in Le Figaro in February 1950 that neutralization of Europe could only be "an encouragement for the aggressor."

Sartre was no longer neutralist, anyway. He had chosen his side and was constructing an ideology to justify it. Simone de Beauvoir found him different. Success had not changed him, but "he no longer set foot in the cafés that we used to love so much"; he had become a public figure, and she would complain, "Ah! Why aren't you just an obscure poet?" He spent his days studying politics. On the one hand, he rejected the Communist-sponsored Stockholm Appeal and attacked the Soviet camp system. On the other, he disagreed when Merleau-Ponty approved of the American intervention in Korea. His friend and biographer Francis Jeanson places Sartre's definitive acceptance of Stalinist Communism in 1951, the year he wrote the play Le Diable et le Bon Dieu, which represented his own rejection of neutralism. For one must choose, and he saw only one choice. "For the time being," he told an interviewer, "the [Communist] Party represents the proletariat for me... It is impossible to take an anti-Communist position without being against the proletariat." The fruit of his reflections, the logical result of his choice, was a long essay, "The Communists and Peace," the first section of which appeared in Les Temps Modernes in July 1952. In it he argued that the USSR did not want war, that the working class understood this, and so was unaffected by anti-Soviet propaganda. He now joined the Communist-inspired peace movement, proudly referring to himself as a fellow traveler. He became the hero of the next international peace congress organized by the Communists, in Vienna; and he chose to remain silent about the Stalinist terror that raged in the Soviet Union and its satellites during the last years of Stalin's life.

Meanwhile, Albert Camus had drawn quite the opposite conclusions. One might be neither victim nor executioner, but one had to choose all the same. While Sartre was studying to be a better Communist, Camus was composing — in silence, and often in pain, because of his recurring tuberculosis, far from the Paris crowd that asked only to worship him — the libertarian answer to Stalinism. In the long essay he called L'Homme révolté ("The Rebel"), he examined theories of revolt, seeking to discover how and why the revolutionary ideal was perverted by modern forms of totalitarianism that invoked doctrine to justify murder. His book satisfied revolutionary Socialists, militant trade unionists, even anarchists; but it could not please a fellow traveler, who in accepting Stalin was obliged to accept necessary murder.

Camus's book appeared in October 1951. Shortly before, a chapter on Nietzsche and nihilism had been published in Les Temps Modernes. But reviewing the complete book in Sartre's magazine was another story. The young team around Sartre was even more susceptible than their chief to the temptations of Stalinism, and if Sartre hoped for a charitable judgment on Camus's essay, he knew he would not get it from any of these angry young men and women. Finally he had his young disciple Francis Jeanson write the review, apparently expecting Jeanson to be gentle. It appeared in the May 1952 issue. Jeanson was hardly gentle, mocking what he called Camus's pseudophilosophy and pseudohistory. Camus reacted sharply; his reply appeared in the August issue, and he was no gentler than Jeanson had been:

I'm getting a bit tired of receiving, and of seeing veteran militants who never turned away from the struggles of their times receive, lessons in efficacy from critics who never placed anything other than their armchairs in the direction of history . . .

Jeanson published a rebuttal in the same issue, and so did Sartre himself. Indeed, Sartre's attack put an end to whatever remained of his relations with Camus. "Our friendship was not an easy one, but I shall miss it," Sartre began. "Many things kept us together, few separated us. But these few were still too many: friendship can also become totalitarian . . ." He accused Camus of having abandoned his "Trotskyism of the heart" in favor of moral law. "Your morality changed first into moralizing; today it is only literature, tomorrow perhaps it will become immorality."

A previous quarrel between Sartre and Camus had ended when Camus slammed the door; now it was Sartre's turn. This door was heard everywhere on the Left Bank and wherever Left Bank noises still counted. Even Right Bank readers of *Le Figaro Littéraire* heard about it, and so did the rank and file picking up a sensational weekly such as *Samedi-Soir*, which ran a three-column headline:

THE SARTRE-CAMUS BREAK IS CONSUMMATED

But no thinking person saw this ideological parting of ways as a personal quarrel between a M. Sartre and a M. Camus.

Epilogue

THERE MIGHT BE a sequel to this story. It would cover the final paroxysmal years of the reign of Joseph Stalin, at least until the first authorized exposé of his crimes by Nikita Khrushchev in 1956, or until Khrushchev's own crimes in Hungary later the same year; but would that change much? To follow the movements of Sartre around the Left Bank, for example, would not be very useful. Having offered himself to the Communist cause, he made only those moves the Communists required of him. Camus retreated to a silence he seldom abandoned; the brutality of the Sartrian offensive against *L'Homme révolté* was primarily responsible. One could indeed choose to be a pariah, as Camus had done, but then one could not expect to have any influence. Camus himself did not wish anyone to follow in his steps. He had been rejected by most of his peers of the literary Left Bank after the explosion in *Les Temps Modernes*; the realization that Camus had been right all along, that they had abandoned him to follow the herd, runs like a leitmotif through present-day reminiscences of that unhappy period. In an allegorical tale he called "Jonas," Camus drew the portrait of a successful artist, much like the successful author he was, who could no longer do his work because of his idolaters, and because of those who demanded that he speak out against injustice. Jonas ends up retreating to a makeshift loggia in a corner of his apartment, where a friend discovers him before an empty canvas on which only a single word is written, although no one can tell whether the word is *solitaire* or *solidaire*.

With France now a battlefield in the cold war, could anything anyone said matter? Simone de Beauvoir noted a change in behavior of the postliberation generation. "They are sufficiently interested in politics to discuss it in the bars of Saint-Germain-des-Prés, but not enough to use politics to find a manner or reasons for living," she recorded in her journal. "It wasn't their fault. What could they do? What could one do, at this time, in France?" André Breton, who for decades had called the shots with lucidity through all the twists and turns of his intellectual peers, told an interviewer in 1951: "The setting up of two antagonistic blocs, each of which dreams and plans only the annihilation of the other and the subordination of whatever remains to its own ends, leaves little room for free expression, in the sense it has always been understood." His own suggestion was that his fellows seek to avoid both the lies of Stalinism and the ideological response of the American side: to keep cold war out of the publishing houses, the magazines, and the art galleries of the Left Bank. But he himself agreed that this was a utopian desire. For Roger Stéphane, studying the cases in 1950 of three men he called adventurers — T.E. Lawrence, André Malraux, Ernst Von Salomon — it was the very dimension of world events that reduced his contemporaries to passivity, if not to helplessness. "The era of individual adventures is over," Stéphane proclaimed. "A man alone, today, no longer has a chance to make an imprint on history." Malraux, the only one of Stéphane's adventurers still living, was no longer his own man, but part of a political apparatus.

Clearly, it no longer mattered what the writers and artists of Paris thought about world affairs, let alone what they tried to do about them. One of the first of the engaged intellectuals of Popular Front days to realize what had happened was André Chamson. Early in the cold war, he published an essay in an anthology of left-wing manifestos called L'Heure du choix ("The Hour of Choice"). He could remember when "every gesture and every word from France had an influence on universal history," when intellectuals such as himself "had responsibility in every matter that concerned the destiny of mankind." It had been naïveté, he confessed, but a generous naïveté. The illusion was lost with the war, with the defeat of June 1940. Then, after the liberation, Chamson and his comrades thought for a while that they might once more sit atop history.

But today ... in this precarious peace and in this universal disorder, how can one still believe that the engagement of France might be one of the elements that will create the history of tomorrow? How can one still believe that we are in the center of this history and that what we do can have a decisive effect on the future?

With the atomic age, he discovered, "We have lost control of events, of the power to create them and to guide them when they become events capable of having significance for the whole world."

★ ★ ★

It was patently true that no French voice was then being heard outside France. Power was heard; guns were heard. Stalin's alleged remark mocking the power of the Catholic Church — "How many divisions does the Pope have?" — could also have been made about writers and artists of Paris: how many divisions did they have, now? But it also seemed as if these writers and artists were voluntarily divesting themselves of whatever power they might still exercise. By adopting neutralism, by looking for "third ways" out, they appeared to seek a withdrawal from the struggle. One could hardly expect to rouse an audience at the Palais de la Mutualité with a rallying cry to the effect that one intended to sit still and not to react to what was happening in the cruel world outside, as those who thought that they could launch a "third way" political movement discovered. Those who accepted the role of fellow-traveling (and they could be fellow travelers of the West as well as of the East) also surrendered the initiative to outside forces.

Raymond Aron, then and later one of the most acute observers of intellectual Paris, explained the situation in a report to Americans in 1950, when the cold war was becoming hot in Korea. "French writers, artists, and philosophers never doubted in the past that their work or thought, such as it was, had a universal significance," Aron wrote. "The course France elected to pursue, either in its domestic affairs or in the conduct of its foreign policy, was of immediate concern to the world." But now, France's intellectuals knew that their country was no longer a first-class power. French culture might still be prized, but "French policy and the political opinions of the French intellectuals no longer count for anything beyond the borders of the country." Aron recalled when a writer could influence his nation's policy; but now the "pacifism" of France's intellectuals reminded him of the situation of helpless Belgians or of the Dutch before World War II. "Citizens of a country wedged between great powers and sure to be occupied by one side or the other in case of war, they have good reason to dread its coming. But history hardly troubles itself about persons and peoples who let themselves be reduced to the role of objects."

For an object one was, when one was handed a plane ticket to

Wroclaw or Warsaw or Vienna or wherever one's Party guides chose to hold the next "peace congress," when one wrote for a newspaper or a magazine whose Communist sponsorship was scarcely concealed. Later the most lucid of them, or the most disillusioned, made public confession. Vercors, for one, admitted that he had been a figurehead, a decorative vase, for the past dozen years, from the time he emerged from occupied France as a hero of the resistance press, until the day came when "the vase is no longer presentable."

But during the dozen years when they made the rules for intellectual Paris, these decorative vases managed to intimidate many who did not share their views. Their mockery drove Camus to silence, branded as Fascist the wizened veterans of prewar Communism, like Arthur Koestler, who had made the mistake of becoming disillusioned a full generation too soon. And if one insisted stubbornly that one need not take sides, could one claim to be in the tradition of the intellectuals of the 1930s and 1940s, who had indeed taken sides?

★   ★   ★

Much later, in retrospect, Ilya Ehrenburg would comment on the declining importance of artists and writers and the rise of scientists, when the development of atomic energy made it a great deal more important to listen to scientists than to poets. In France the time approached when technocrats would take over the seats of power from philosophers, when the Ecole Nationale d'Administration, France's school for leadership training, replaced the faculties of literature and philosophy in the plans of the ambitious young, when — in the words of an observer of the new dispensation — "Jean-Paul Sartre can sign a thousand petitions a day, but he will remain, at best, respectably without influence."

Indeed, although this was not understood by even the most lucid observers while it was happening, and it remained for the sociologists and cultural historians to announce it, the decline of the impact of Parisian intellectuals coincided with the decline of Paris as capital of Europe, and intellectual capital of the world. It happened in the 1950s, when city planners gave priority to economic growth, at the expense of cultural institutions and of the cityscape itself. Automobiles took over a considerable portion of the sidewalks, occupying space that had formerly belonged to café tables, that had been reserved for strolling. Bistros, bookstores, artisans' shops gave way to boutiques born of prosperity and the tourist industry (many of the tourists at traditional Left Bank haunts had simply crossed the river from the dull Right Bank neighborhoods where they lived). Saint-Germain-des-Prés ceased to be a village. A famous café advertised itself as the "rendezvous of the intellectual elite," but the day the slogan was printed its claim was no longer true. Could an inhabitant of the literary Left Bank look out of a window to spot friends in a café across the boulevard, as Jean Cassou did in the 1930s? It would have taken keen eyesight, and patience, to penetrate the automobile traffic and the exhaust fumes. And even if one could see across the Place Saint-Germain-des-Prés, let alone make one's perilous way across it, one was unlikely to find a friendly face in the crowd at the café tables.

So they turned inward, and homeward. Nearly a decade passed before another generation of Left Bankers was heard from, and when they spoke out, it was over more sharply defined, national issues: the defense of the Republic against Charles de Gaulle (a lost cause), the independence of France's North African territories (a hard-won battle), and some very real threats to civil liberties that had been taken for granted during most of the present century. In the end, after token resistance, many succumbed to the temptations of Gaullist nationalism, just as they or their elders had been the captives of Stalinist internationalism.

But in the 1950s, as the present story comes to an end, the Left Bank was taking a long vacation from politics. One had been stung enough. "How can we forget the successive submissions and resignations, the explosive ruptures, the excommunications, the imprisonments, the suicides?" declared Alain Robbe-Grillet in 1957, when he was thirty-five years old and fully resolved as a writer not to repeat the errors of previous generations. "Let us give the notion of commitment the only meaning it can have for us," he concluded. "Instead of being political, commitment for the writer is the full consciousness of the current problems of his own language, the conviction of their importance, the will to resolve them from the inside."

"Mean something! You and I, mean something!" exclaims a character in Samuel Beckett's *Endgame*, to the accompaniment of an abrupt laugh. "Ah, that's a good one!"

Sources

IN THE PLACE OF standard footnotes, the following chapter-by-chapter list of references will serve as a thematic bibliography for readers who would like to investigate particular subjects or personalities in detail. Where not specified otherwise, books and periodicals were published in Paris.

CURTAIN RAISER
Interview with Jean Cassou.
André Breton, *Entretiens, 1913-1952* (1969); Eugène Dabit, *Journal intime, 1928-1936* (1939); Pierre Daix, *Aragon, une vie á changer* (1975); Ilya Ehrenburg, *Memoirs, 1921-1941* (New York, 1966); Ehrenburg, *Vus par un écrivain d'U.R.S.S.* (1934); Nino Frank, *Le Bruit parmi le vent*, vol. 2 of *Mémoire brisée* (1968); Lucie Mazauric, *Vive le Front populaire!* (1976); Maurice Nadeau, *Histoire du Surréalisme* (1964); Maria Van Rysselberghe, *Les Cahiers de la Petite Dame: Notes pour l'histoire authentique d'André Gide*, vol. 2, *1929-1937*, Cahiers André Gide no. 5 (1974).

Part I
CHAPTER 1 MOVING IN
Interviews with Jean Cassou, Pierre Daix.
Simone de Beauvoir, *La Force de l'âge* (1960; Emmanuel Berl, *Interrogatoire par Patrick Modiano* (1976); Arno Breker, *Paris, Hitler, et moi* (1970); André Breton, *Entretiens, 1913-1952* (1969); Pierre Daix, *La Vie de peintre de Pablo Picasso* (1977); Régis Debray, *Le Pouvoir intellectuel en France* (1979); Albert Demangeon, *Paris: La Ville et sa banlieue* (1939); Henri Dubief, *Le Déclin de la Troisième République, 1929-1938*, vol. 13 of *Nouvelle histoire de la France contemporaine* (1976); *Du côté de chez Lipp* (1963); Auguste Dupouy, *Géographie des lettres françaises* (1942); Léon-Paul Fargue, *Le Piéton de Paris* (1939); Jean-François Gravier, *Paris et le désert français en 1972* (1972); Jean Guéhenno, *La Foi difficile* (1957); Lucie Mazauric, *Ah Dieu! que la paix es jolie* (1972); Edmée de la Rochefoucauld, *Léon-Paul Fargue* (1959); Albert Thibaudet, *La République des professeurs* (1927).

Christophe Charle, "Situation sociale et position spatiale, essai de géographie sociale du champ littéraire à la fin du dix-neuvième siècle," *Actes de la Recherche en Sciences Sociales* (February 1977).

CHAPTER 2 MAKING FRIENDS
Interviews with Raymond Aron, Jean-François Sirinelli.

Simone de Beauvoir, *Mémoires d'une jeune fille rangée* (1958); Robert Brasillach, *Une Génération dans l'orage* (1968); Lucien Combelle, *Péché d'orgueil* (1978); Claude Jamet, *Notre Front populaire: Journal d'un militant, 1934-1939* (1977); Paul Nizan, *Aden-Arabie*, preface by Jean-Paul Sartre (1960); Nizan, *Les Chiens de garde*, 3rd ed. (1976); Alain Peyrefitte, *Rue d'Ulm: Chroniques de la vie normalienne* (1977); Henri Queffelec, *Un Breton bien tranquille* (1978).

Bernard Alliot, "Sartre à huis clos," *Le Monde* (April 20-21, 1980); Jean-Paul Sartre, "Merleau-Ponty vivant," *Les Temps Modernes*, nos. 184-185 (October 1961); Claude Willard, "Les Intellectuels français et le Front populaire," *Cahiers de l'Institut Maurice Thorez* (October 1966-March 1967).

CHAPTER 3 AT HOME
Interviews with Jean Cassou, André and Lucie Chamson, Clara Malraux, Manès Sperber.

Ilya Ehrenburg, *Memoirs, 1921-1941* (New York, 1966); Ehrenburg, *Vus par un écrivain d'U.R.S.S.* (1934); Nino Frank, *Le Bruit parmi le vent*, vol. 2 of *Mémoire brisée* (1968); André Gide, *Journal, 1889-1939* (1948); Gide, *Littérature engagée* (1950); Frédéric J. Grover, *Six entretiens avec André Malraux sur des écrivains de son temps, 1959-1975* (1978); Jean Guéhenno, *La Foi difficile* (1957); Louis Guilloux, *Carnets, 1921-1944* (1978); *L'Indépendance de l'esprit: Correspondance entre Jean Guéhenno et Romain Rolland, 1919-1944*, Cahiers Romain Rolland no. 23 (1975); Jean Lacouture, *André Malraux* (1973); Paul Léautaud, *Journal littéraire*, vol. 12, *mai 1937-février 1940* (1962).

Clara Malraux, *Voici que vient l'été* and *La Fin et le commencement*, vols. 4 and 5 of *Le Bruit de nos pas* (1973, 1976); Maurice Martin du Gard, *Les Mémorables*, vol. 3, *1930-1945* (1978); Claude Mauriac, *Conversations avec André Gide* (1951); Lucie Mazauric, *Ah Dieu! que la paix est jolie* (1972); Mazauric, *Le Louvre en voyage, ou Ma vie de châteaux, 1939-1945* (1978); Ernst Erich Noth, *Mémoires d'un Allemand* (1970); Maria Van Rysselberghe, *Les Cahiers de la Petite Dame*, vol. 2, *1929-1937*, vol. 3, *1937-1945*, and vol. 4, *1945-1951*, Cahiers André Gide nos. 5-7 (1974, 1975, 1977); Alain Silvera, *Daniel Halévy and His Times* (Ithaca, N.Y., 1966); Manès Sperber, *Au-delà de l'oubli*, vol. 3 of *Ces temps-là* (1979); André Thirion, *Révolutionnaires sans révolution* (1972).

Ramon Fernandez, "Littérature et politique," *La Nouvelle Revue Française* (February 1935); André Gide, "Pages de Journal," *La Nouvelle Revue Française* (July, September, and October 1932); Pierre Guiral, "Daniel Halévy, esquisse d'un itinéraire," *Contrepoint*, no. 20 (1976); "Interview avec André Malraux," *La Littérature Internationale*, nos. 5 and 6 (Moscow, 1934); Hélène G. Maire, "Sur Daniel Halévy," *Ecrits de Paris* (February 1975); Jean Schlumberger, "Gide Rue Visconti," *La Nouvelle Revue Française* (March 1935).

Gidés own file of press clippings, now in the Dossiers Gide at the Bibliothèque Jacques Doucet in Paris, also provided useful material.

CHAPTER 4 PLACE OF WORK, PLACE OF PLAY
Interviews with André and Lucie Chamson, Eugène Guillevic, Clara Malraux, Manès Sperber.

Julien Benda, Les Cahiers d'un clerc, 1939-1949 (1950); Simone de Beauvoir, La Force de l'âge (1960); Brassai, Conversations avec Picasso (1964); Suzanne Chantal, Le Coeur battant: Josette Clotis — André Malraux (1976); Eugène Dabit, Journal intime, 1928-1936 (1939); Ilya Ehrenburg, Memoirs, 1921-1941 (New York, 1966); Léon-Paul Fargue, Le Piéton de Paris (1939); Nino Frank, Le Bruit parmi le vent, vol. 2 of Mémoire brisée (1968); André Gide, Journal, 1889-1939 (1948); Anne Heurgon-Desjardins, ed., Paul Desjardins et les Décades de Pontigny: Etudes, témoignages et documents inédits (1964); Léo Larguier, Saint-Germain-des-Prés, mon village (1938); Maria Van Rysselberghe, Les Cahiers de la Petite Dame, vol. 2, 1929-1937, and vol. 3, 1937-1945, Cahiers André Gide nos. 5 and 6 (1974, 1975); André Thirion, Révolutionnaires sans révolution (1972).

Ramon Fernandez, "Littérature et politique," La Nouvelle Revue Française (February 1935).

CHAPTER 5 SMALLER WORLDS
Interview with Manès Sperber; correspondence with Miriam Chiaromonte.

Ilya Ehrenburg, Memoirs, 1921-1941 (New York, 1966); Arthur Koestler, The Invisible Writing (New York and London, 1954); Anaïs Nin, The Diary of Anaïs Nin, vol. 2, 1934-1939 (New York, 1971); Elliot Paul, The Last Time I Saw Paris (New York, 1942); Gustav Regler, The Owl of Minerva (New York, 1960); Manès Sperber, Au-delà de l'oubli, vol. 3 of Ces temps-là (1979); Georges Wickes, Americans in Paris (New York, 1969).

Cahier Arthur Koestler, Cahiers de l'Herne (1975); "Etre une Allemande sous le nazisme," interview with Irmgard Keun by Jean-Louis de Rambures, Le Monde (February 29, 1980).

Part II
CHAPTER 6 FOUNDING FATHERS
Julien Benda, The Treason of the Intellectuals (New York, 1928); Jean-Pierre A. Bernard, Le Parti communiste français et la question littéraire, 1921-1939 (Grenoble, France, 1972); Jean Cassou, preface to Louis de Villefosse, L'Oeuf de Wyasma (1962); L'Indépendance de l'esprit: Correspondance entre Jean Guéhenno et Romain Rolland, 1919-1944, Cahiers Romain Rolland no. 23 (1975); Fred Kupferman, Au pays des Soviets: Le voyage français en Union soviétique, 1917-1939 (1979); Herbert R. Lottman, Albert Camus (New York and London, 1979); Maurice Nadeau, Histoire du Surréalisme, 1964; Romain Rolland, Par la révolution, la paix (1935); Jean Touchard, La Gauche en France depuis 1900 (1977).

Front Mondial, monthly organ of the Comité mondiale contre la guerre impérialiste, issues 1-9 (1933); L'Humanité (May 29, June 4-9, 1933); Monde (June 24, 1933); Romain Rolland, "La Patrie est en danger!" L'Humanité (May 1, 1932); Claude Willard, "Les Intellectuels français et le Front populaire," Cahiers de l'Institut Maurice Thorez (October 1966-March 1967).

CHAPTER 7 ENGAGEMENT WITH MOSCOW
Interviews with Jean Cassou, André Chamson, Pierre Daix, Clara Malraux, Manès Sperber.

Pierre Andreu and Frédéric Grover, Drieu La Rochelle (1979); Association des Ecrivains et Artistes Révolutionnaires, Ceux qui ont choisi: Contre le fascisme en Allemagne, contre l'impérialisme français (1933); Dimitri T. Bratanov and Svetlomir D. Bratanov, Romain Rolland et la Bulgarie (Sofia, 1970); Jean-Paul Brunet, L'Enfance du parti communiste, 1920-1938 (1972); Pierre Daix, Aragon, une vie à changer (1975); Dominique Desanti, Les Staliniens: Une expérience politique, 1944-1956 (1975); André Gide, Littérature engagée (1950); Frédéric J. Grover, Drieu La Rochelle, 1893-1945 (1963); Arthur Koestler, The Invisible Writing (New York and London, 1954); Branko M. Lazitch, in collaboration with Milorad M. Drachkovitch, Biographical Dictionary of the Comintern (Stanford, Calif., 1973); Georges Lefranc, L'Expérience du Front populaire (1972); Lefranc, Histoire du Front populaire, 1934-1938 (1974); Herbert R. Lottman, Albert Camus (New York and London, 1979); André Malraux, Antimémoires (1967); Maurice Nadeau, Histoire du Surréalisme (1964); Gustav Regler, The Owl of Minerva (New York, 1960); Philippe Robrieux, Maurice Thorez (1975); Maria Van Rysselberghe, Les Cahiers de la Petite Dame, vol. 2, 1929-1937, Cahiers André Gide no. 5 (1974); Manès Sperber, Au-delà l'oubli, vol. 3 of Ces temps-là (1979); André Wurmser, Fidèlement vôtre: Soixante ans de vie littéraire et politique (1979).

Louis Aragon, "Avez-vous lu 'L'Aveu'?" Les Lettres Françaises (February 12, 1969); Aragon, "Vive Gorki!" Commune (April 1938); Commune (1933-1939, entire); L'Humanité (March 21 and 23, 1933); Littérature de la Révolution Mondiale and La Littérature Internationale (both Moscow), entire; Claude Willard, "Les Intellectuels français et le Front populaire," Cahiers de l'Institut Maurice Thorez (October 1966-March 1967).

CHAPTER 8 ENGAGEMENT IN MOSCOW
Interview with Clara Malraux.

Louis-Ferdinand Céline, Bagatelles pour un massacre (1937); Pierre Daix, Aragon, une vie à changer (1975); Ilya Ehrenburg, Memoirs, 1921-1941 (New York, 1966); André Gide, Littérature engagée (1950); Gide, Retouches à mon Retour de l'U.R.S.S. (1937); Fred Kupferman, Au pays des Soviets: Le Voyage français en Union soviétique, 1917-1939 (1979); Jean Lacouture, André Malraux (1973); Clara Malraux, Voici que vient l'été vol. 4 of Le Bruit de nos pas (1973); Nadezhda Mandelstam, Hope Against Hope (New York, 1970); Gustav Regler, The Owl of Minerva (New York, 1960); Maria Van Rysselberghe, Les Cahiers de la Petite Dame, vol. 2, 1929-1937, Cahiers André Gide no. 5 (1974).

Candide (January 10, 1935); Commune (September-October 1934); Jacqueline Leiner, "Autour d'un discours de Malraux: 'L'Art est une conquête,'" La Revue des Lettres Modernes, nos. 304-309 (1972); André Pulicani, "Chez Gen Paul, à Montmartre," L.-F. Céline, vol. 1, Les Cahiers de l'Herne no. 3 (1963).

Chapter 9 Right and Center
Interview with Raymond Aron.

Otto Abetz, *Histoire d'une politique franco-allemande, 1930-1950* (1953); Pierre Andreu and Frédéric Grover, *Drieu La Rochelle* (1979); Julien Benda, *Les Cahiers d'un clerc, 1939-1949* (1950); Jean-Pierre A. Bernard, *Le Parti communiste français et la question littéraire, 1921-1939* (Grenoble, France, 1972); Louis Bodin and Jean Touchard, *Front Populaire 1936* (1961); Robert Brasillach, *Une Génération dans l'orage* (1968); R. L. Bruckberger, *Tu finiras sur l'échafaud* (1978); Musée de l'Ancien Evêché de Lausanne, *Catalogue de l'exposition Céline* (Lausanne, Switzerland, 1977); Michèle Cotta, *La Collaboration, 1940-1944* (1964); Léon Daudet, *Paris Vécu: Rive Gauche* (1930); Pierre-Marie Dioudonnat, *Je Suis Partout, 1930-1944: Les Maurrassiens devant la tentation fasciste* (1973); Henri Dubief, *Le Déclin de la Troisième République, 1929-1938* (1976); Claude Estier, *La Gauche hebdomadaire, 1914-1962* (1962); Alfred Fabre-Luce, *L'Epreuve, 1939-1946*, vol. 2 of *Vingt-cinq années de liberté* (1963).

Jacques Isorni, *Le Procès de Robert Brasillach* (1946); Paul Léautaud, *Journal littéraire*, vol. 12, *mai 1937-février 1940* (1962); Jean-Louis Loubet del Bayle, *Les Non-conformistes des années 30* (1969); Maurice Martin du Gard, *Les Mémorables*, vol. 3, *1930-1945* (1978); Lucien Rebatet, *Les Décombres* (1942.); Claude Roy, *Moi je*, vol. 1 of *Somme toute* (1969); Frédéric Vitoux, *Céline* (1978); Eugen Weber, *Action Française: Royalism and Reaction in Twentieth-Century France* (Stanford, Calif., 1962); Michel Winock, *Histoire politique de la revue "Esprit," 1930-1950* (1975).

L.-F. Céline, vol. 1, *Les Cahiers de l'Herne* no. 3 (1963).

Chapter 10 Unity of Action
Interviews with Jean Cassou, André and Lucie Chamson.

Pierre Andreu and Frédéric Grover, *Drieu La Rochelle* (1979); Robert Brasillach, *Une Génération dans l'orage* (1968); André Breton, *Entretiens, 1913-1952* (1969); Jean-Paul Brunet, *L'Enfance du parti communiste, 1920-1938* (1972); Eugéne Dabit, *Journal intime, 1928-1936* (1939); Henri Dubief, *Le Déclin de la Troisième République, 1929-1938* (1976); Ilya Ehrenburg, *Memoirs, 1921-1941* (New York, 1966); Jean Guéhenno, *Journal d'une "revolution," 1937-1938* (1939); *L'Indépendance de l'esprit: Correspondance entre Jean Guéhenno et Romain Rolland, 1919-1944*, Cahiers Romain Rolland no. 23 (1975).

Georges Lefranc, *L'Expérience du Front populaire* (1972); Lefranc, *Histoire du Front populaire, 1934-1938* (1974); H.-R. Lenormand, *Les Confessions d'un auteur dramatique*, vol. 2 (1953); Clara Malraux, *Voici que vient l'été* vol. 4 of *Le Bruit de nos pas* (1973); Maurice Martin du Gard, *Les Mémorables*, vol. 3, *1930-1945* (1978); Lucie Mazauric, *Ah Dieu! que la paix est jolie* (1972); Mazauric, *Vive le Front populaire!* (1976); Lucien Rebatet, *Les Décombres* (1942); Maria Van Rysselbergbe, *Les Cahiers de la Petite Dame*, vol. 2, *1929-1937*, Cahiers André Gide no. 5 (1974); André Wurmser, *Fidèlement vôtre* (1979).

Commune (March-April 1934); *Europe* (April 15 and May 15, 1934); Claude Willard, "Les Intellectuels, français et le Front populaire," *Cahiers de l'Institut Maurice Thorez* (October 1966-March 1967).

CHAPTER 11 In Defense of Culture
Interviews with André and Lucie Chamson, Yves Lévy.

For background and texts of speeches in this and later chapters I have drawn
liberally from the files on the International Writers Congress compiled by Rose
Adler and preserved in the Bibliothèque Jacques Doucet. Among the periodical
sources are *Commune, Monde,* and *L'Humanité.* There is no complete
publication of the congress proceedings, the most formal effort being in Russian
(*Mezhdunarodni Kongres Pisateli v Zashchitu Kulturi,* Moscow, 1936), but it
omits many speeches, including those of dissenters. Other important accounts
appear in André Gide, *Journal, 1889-1939* (1948); Gide, *Littérature engagée*
(1950); Jean Guéhenno, *Journal d'une "révolution," 1937-1938* (1939); Maria
Van Rysselberghe, *Les Cahiers de la Petite Dame,* vol. 2, *1929-1937,* Cahiers
André Gide no. 5 (1974).

Other sources: André Breton, *Entretiens, 1913-1952* (1969); Robert
Conquest, *The Great Terror: Stalin's Purge of the Thirties* (New York and
London, 1968); Eugène Dabit, *Journal intime, 1928-1936* (1939); Ilya
Ehrenburg, *Memoirs, 1921-1941* (New York, 1966); Frédéric J. Grover, *Six
entretiens avec André Malraux sur des écrivains de son temps, 1959-1975* (1978);
Jean Guéhenno, *La Foi difficile* (1957); *L'Indépendance de l'esprit:
Correspondance entre Jean Guéhenno et Romain Rolland, 1919-1944,* Cahiers
Romain Rolland no. 23 (1975).

Arthur Koestler, *The Invisible Writing* (New York and London, 1954); Jean
Lacouture, *André Malraux* (1973); H.-R. Lenormand, *Les Confessions d'un
auteur dramatique,* vol. 2 (1953); Clara Malraux, *La Fin et le commencement,* vol.
5 of *Le Bruit de nos pas* (1976); Lucie Mazauric, *Vive le Front populaire!* (1976);
Maurice Nadeau, *Histoire du Surréalisme* (1964); Gustav Regler, *The Owl of
Minerva* (New York, 1960); Claude Roy, *Moi je,* vol. 1 of *Somme toute* (1969);
Victor Serge, *Mémoires d'un révolutionnaire, 1901-1941* (1978).

Louis Aragon, "Avez-vous lu 'L'Aveu'?" *Les Lettres Françaises* (February 19,
1969); Isaiah Berlin, "Conversations with Russian Poets," *The Times Literary
Supplement* (London, October 31, 1980); Denis de Rougemont, "Ni droite ni
gauche," *La Nouvelle Revue Française* (August 1935).

CHAPTER 12 Malraux and the Intellectuals' War
Interviews with Jean Cassou, André and Lucie Chamson.

Dossiers Gide; Dossier on the Second International Writers Congress,
compiled by Tristan Tzara. (Both in the Bibliothèque Jacques Doucet.)

Louis Bodin and Jean Touchard, *Front populaire 1936* (1961); Robert
Brasillach, *Une Génération dans l'orage* (1968); Louis-Ferdinand Céline,
Bagatelles pour un massacre (1937); Suzanne Chantal, *Le Coeur battant: Josette
Clotis — André Malraux* (1976); Ilya Ehrenburg, *Memoirs, 1921-1941* (New
York, 1966); André Gide, *Journal, 1889-1939* (1948); Gide, *Littérature engagée*
(1950); Frédéric J. Grover, *Six entretiens avec André Malraux sur des écrivains de
son temps, 1959-1975* (1978); *L'Indépendance de l'esprit: Correspondance entre
Jean Guéhenno et Romain Rolland, 1919-1944,* Cahiers Romain Rolland no. 23
(1975); Arthur Koestler, *The Invisible Writing* (New York and London, 1954);
Koestler, *The Yogi and the Commissar* (New York and London, 1945); Jean
Lacouture, *André Malraux* (1973); Georges Lefranc, *Histoire du Front populaire,*

1934-1938 (1974); H.-R. Lenormand, *Les Confessions d'un auteur dramatique,* vol. 2 (1953).

André Malraux, *Le Temps du mépris* (1935); Clara Malraux, *Voici que vient l'été and La Fin et le commencement,* vols. 4 and 5 of Le Bruit de nos pas (1973, 1976); Lucie Mazauric, *Vive le Front populaire!* (1976); Lucien Rebatet, *Les Décombres* (1942); Gustav Regler, *The Owl of Minerva* (New York, 1960); Maria Van Rysselberghe, *Les Cahiers de la Petite Dame,* vol. 2, *1929-1937,* and vol. 3, *1937-1945,* Cahiers André Gide nos. 5 and 6 (1974, 1975); Manès Sperber, *Au-delà de l'oubli,* vol. 3 of Ces temps-là (1979); Michel Winock, *Histoire politique de la revue "Esprit," 1930-1950* (1975).

Commune (December 1936, May and August 1937, and particularly the article "Revues étrangères" in the May issue); Walter G. Langlois, "André Malraux, 1939-1942, d'après une correspondance inédite," *La Revue des Lettres Modernes,* nos. 304-309 (1972); *Littérature Internationale,* no. 9 (Moscow, 1973); *Vendredi* (1936-1937).

CHAPTER 13 GIDE'S RETURN
Interviews with Jean Cassou, André and Lucie Chamson.
Dossiers Gide, Bibliothèque Jacques Doucet.

Eugéne Dabit, *Journal intime, 1928-1936* (1939); Ilya Ehrenburg, *Memoirs, 1921-1941* (New York, 1966); André Gide, *Journal, 1889-1939* (1948); Gide, *Littérature engagée* (1950); Gide, *Retour de l'U.R.S.S.* (1936); Gide, *Retouches à mon Retour de l'U.R.S.S.* (1937); Jean Guéhenno, *Journal d'une "révolution," 1937-1938* (1939); Louis Guilloux, *Carnets, 1921-1944* (1978); Fred Kupferman, *Au Pays des Soviets: Le Voyage français en Union soviétique, 1917-1939* (1979); Lucie Mazauric, *Vive le Front populaire!* (1976); Gustav Regler, *The Owl of Minerva* (New York, 1960); Maria Van Rysselberghe, *Les Cahiers de la Petite Dame,* vol. 2, *1929-1937,* and vol. 3, *1937-1945,* Cahiers André Gide nos. 5 and 6 (1974, 1975); Victor Serge, *Mémoires d'un révolutionnaire, 1901-1941* (1978); André Wurmser, *Fidèlement vôtre* (1979).

Victor Serge, "Pages de journal," *Les Temps Modernes* (June 1949); *Vendredi* (1936-1937).

CHAPTER 14 PLUNGING INTO BARBARITY
Interviews with Raymond Aron, Jean Cassou, André and Lucie Chamson.

Association Internationale des Ecrivains, *Conférence du 25 juillet 1938* (1938); Simone de Beauvoir, *La Force de l'âge* (1960); Suzanne Chantal, *Le Coeur battant: Josette Clotis-André Malraux* (1976); Lucien Combelle, *Péché d'orgueil* (1978); Stéphane Courtois, *Le PCF dans la guerre* (1980); Ilya Ehrenburg, *Memoirs, 1921-1941* (New York, 1966); André Gide, *Journal, 1889-1939* (1948); Gide, *Pages de journal, 1939-1941* (Algiers, 1944); Jean Guéhenno, *Journal d'une "révolution," 1937-1938* (1939); Anne Heurgeon-Desjardins, ed., *Paul Desjardins et les Décades de Pontigny* (1964).

Jean Lacouture, *André Malraux* (1973); Alain Laubreaux, *Ecrit pendant la guerre* (1944); Paul Léautaud, *Journal littéraire,* vol. 12, *mai 1937-février 1940* (1962); Clara Malraux, *Voici que vient l'été* vol. 4 of Le Bruit de nos pas (1973); Claude Mauriac, *Conversations avec André Gide* (1951); Lucie Mazauric, *Vive le*

Front populaire! (1976); Roy Medvedev, *Let History Judge* (New York, 1971); Paul Nizan, *Aden-Arabie*, preface by Jean-Paul Sartre (1960); Jean-Jacques Brochier, ed., *Paul Nizan, intellectuel communiste*, vol. 1, *Articles et correspondance, 1928-1939* (2nd ed., 1970); Gustav Regler, *The Owl of Minerva* (New York, 1960); Maria Van Rysselberghe, *Les Cahiers de la Petite Dame*, vol. 3, *1937-1945*, Cahiers André Gide no. 6 (1975); Manès Sperber, *Au-delà de l'oubli*, vol. 3 of *Ces temps-là* (1979); Jean Touchard, *La Gauche en France depuis 1900* (1977); Michel Winock, *Histoire politique de la revue "Esprit," 1930-1950* (1975); André Wurmser, *Fidèlement vôtre* (1979).

Commune (September-October 1938, June 1939); Walter G. Langlois, "André Malraux, d'après une correspondance inédite," *La Revue des Lettres Modernes*, nos. 304-309 (1972); "Jean Paulhan 1884-1968," *La Nouvelle Revue Française* (May 1, 1969); Vendredi (March 25 and October 7, 1938).

CHAPTER 15 FLEEING THE LEFT BANK
Interview with Jean Cassou.

Simone de Beauvoir, *La Force de l'âge* (1960); Emmanuel Berl, *Interrogatoire par Patrick Modiano* (1976); Martin Blumenson, *The Vildé Affair: Beginnings of the French Resistance* (Boston, 1977); Suzanne Chantal, *Le Coeur battant: Josette Clotis-André Malraux* (1976); Michèle Cotta, *La Collaboration, 1940-1944* (1964); Pierre Daix, *Aragon, une vie à changer* (1975); Ilya Ehrenburg, *Memoirs, 1921-1941* (New York, 1966); André Gide, *Attendu que . . .* (Algiers, 1943); Gide, *Pages de Journal, 1939-1941* (Algiers, 1944); Jean Guéhenno, *Journal des années noires, 1940-1944* (1947); Sacha Guitry, *Quatre ans d'occupations* (1947).

Arthur Koestler, *The Invisible Writing* (New York and London, 1954); Paul Léautaud, *Journal littéraire*, vol. 13, *février 1940-juin 1941* (1962); Clara Malraux, *La Fin et le commencement*, vol. 5 of *Le Bruit de nos pas* (1976); Maurice Martin du Gard, *La Chronique de Vichy, 1940-1944* (1975); Claude Mauriac, *Conversations avec André Gide* (1951); Paul Nizan, *Aden-Arabie*, preface by Jean-Paul Sartre (1960); Claude Roy, *Moi je*, vol. 1 of *Somme toute* (1969); Maria Van Rysselberghe, *Les Cahiers de la Petite Dame*, vol. 3, *1937-1945*, Cahiers André Gide no. 6 (1975); Jean-Paul Sartre, *Situations*, vol. 10, *Politique et autobiographie* (1976); Manès Sperber, *Au-delà de l'oubli*, vol. 3 of *Ces temps-là* (1979); Roger Stéphane, *Toutes choses ont leur saison* (1979); Vercors, *La Bataille du silence* (1970).

Cahier Arthur Koestler, Cahiers de l'Herne (1975); André Gide, "Feuillets," *La Nouvelle Revue Française* (February 1941); Walter G. Langlois, "André Malraux, 1939-1942, d'après une correspondance inédite," *La Revue des Lettres Modernes*, nos. 304-309 (1972); Jean-Paul Sartre, "Merleau-Ponty vivant," *Les Temps Modernes*, nos. 184-185 (October 1961).

Part III
CHAPTER 16 CAPTURING THE N.R.F.
Interviews with Eugène Guillevic, Gerhard Heller.
Jean Paulhan archives, courtesy of Mme Jacqueline Paulhan.

Otto Abetz, *Histoire d'une politique franco-allemande, 1930-1950* (1953);

Pierre Andreu and Frédéric Grover, *Drieu La Rochelle* (1979); *Aragon parle avec Dominique Arban* (1968); Marcel Arland, *Ce fut ainsi* (1979); Emmanuel Berl, *Interrogatoire par Patrick Modiano* (1976); Centre d'Etudes Gidiennes (Université de Lyon II), *La Nouvelle Revue Française, 1940-1943* (Lyon, 1975); Chancellerie de l'Ordre de la Libération, *Exposition Résistance-Déportation*, catalogue (1980); Jacques Chardonne, *Chronique privée de l'an 1940* (1940); Michèle Cotta, *La Collaboration, 1940-1944* (1964); Dominique Desanti, *Les Staliniens* (1976); Pierre Drieu La Rochelle, *Récit secret: Journal d'exode, 1944-1945* (1961).

Jean Guéhenno, *Journal des années noires, 1940-1944* (1973); Louis Guilloux, *Carnets, 1921-1944* (1978); Gerhard Heller, "Bribes d'un journal perdu," unpublished manuscript; Centre Culturel International de Cerisy-la-Salle, *Jean Paulhan le souterrain* (1976); Paul Léautaud, *Journal littéraire*, vol. 13, *février 1940-juin 1941*, vol. 14, *juillet 1941-novembre 1942*, and vol. 15, *novembre 1942-juin 1944* (1962, 1963, 1963); Maurice Martin du Gard, *La Chronique de Vichy, 1940-1944* (1975); Henry de Montherlant, *Le Solstice de juin* (1941); Henry Muller, *Retours de mémoire* (1979); Maria Van Rysselberghe, *Les Cahiers de la Petite Dame*, vol. 3, *1937-1945*, Cahiers André Gide no. 6 (1975); Pierre Seghers, *La Résistance et ses poètes* (1974).

Les Lettres Françaises, clandestine distribution, reproduced after the war in facsimile (1942-1944); *La Nouvelle Revue Française* (December 1940-June 1943); "Jean Paulhan 1884-1968," *La Nouvelle Revue Français* (May 1, 1969).

CHAPTER 17 PARIS VS. VICHY
Interviews with Gerhard Heller, Lucien Scheler.

Otto Abetz, *Histoire d'une politique franco-allemande, 1930-1950* (1953); Simone de Beauvoir, *La Force de l'âge* (1960); Joseph Billig, *Le Commissariat Général aux études juives*, vol. 1, *1941-1944* (1955); UNESCO, *Book Production 1937-1954 and Translations 1950-1954* (1957); Syndicat des Editeurs, *Convention sur la censure des livres* (September 28, 1940); Alfred Fabre-Luce, *L'Epreuve, 1939-1946* (1963); Gerhard Heller, "Bribes d'un journal perdu," unpublished manuscript; Paul Léautaud, *Journal littéraire*, vol. 13, *février 1940-juin 1941*, vol. 14, *juillet 1941-novembre 1942*, and vol. 15, *novembre 1942-juin 1944* (1962., 1963, 1963); H.-R. Lenormand, *Les Confessions d'un auteur dramatique*, vol. 2 (1953); *Liste Otto: Ouvrages retirés de la vente par les éditeurs ou interdits par les autorités allemandes* (September 1940).

Maurice Martin du Gard, *La Chronique de Vichy, 1940-1944* (1975); Henry de Montherlant, *Le Solstice de juin* (1941); Pascal Ory, *Les Collaborateurs, 1940-1945* (1977); Syndicat des Editeurs, *Ouvrages littéraires français non désirables* (July 8, 1942, revised May 10, 1943); *Production et mouvements des imprimés d'ordre intellectuel et commercial* (1946); Maria Van Rysselberghe, *Les Cahiers de la Petite Dame*, vol. 3, *1937-1945*, Cahiers André Gide no. 6 (1975); André Thérive, *L'Envers du décor, 1940-1944* (1948); Eugen Weber, *Action Française: Royalism and Reaction in Twentieth-Century France* (Stanford, Calif., 1962); Jean Zay, *Souvenirs et solitude* (1945).

Philippe Bourdrel, "Le Gouvernement de Vichy et les juifs de France," *Le*

Monde (February 20, 1979); Luc Estang, "A travers la presse littéraire," *Poésie 44* (November-December 1944); Armand Robin, "Domaine terrestre," *La Nouvelle Revue Française* (January 1941).

CHAPTER 18 THE STRUCTURES OF COLLABORATION
Interview and correspondence with Gerhard Heller. Jean Paulhan archives.

Otto Abetz, *Histoire d'une politique franco-allemande, 1930-1950* (1953); Robert Aron, *Histoire de l'épuration*, vol. 2 (1975); Simone de Beauvoir, *La Force de l'âge* (1960); Robert Brasillach, *Une Génération dans l'orage* (1968); Comité d'Action de la Résistance, *L'Affaire Grasset*, Les Cahiers de la Résistance no. 1 (1949); Michèle Cotta, *La Collaboration, 1940-1944* (1964); Pierre Daix, *Aragon, une vie à changer* (1975); Karl Epting, *Réflexions d'un vaincu: Au Cherche-Midi à l'heure française* (Bourg, France, 1953); Alfred Fabre-Luce, *L'Epreuve, 1939-1946* (1963); Jacques Isorni, *Le Procès de Robert Brasillach* (1946).

Ernst Jünger, *Journal*, vol. 2, *1943-1945* (1953, revised as Second journal parisien, 1980); Paul Léautaud, *Journal littéraire*, vol. 13, *février 1940-juin 1941*, vol. 14, *juillet 1941-novembre 1942*, and vol. 15, *novembre 1942-juin 1944* (1962, 1963, 1963); Herbert R. Lottman, *Albert Camus* (New York and London, 1979); Maurice Martin du Gard, *La Chronique de Vichy, 1940-1944* (1975); Henry de Montherlant, *Textes sous une occupation, 1940-1944* (1953); Henry Muller, *Retours de mémoire* (1979); Claude Roy, *Moi je*, vol. 1 of *Somme toute* (1969); Pierre Seghers, *La Résistance et ses poètes, 1940-1945* (1974); André Thérive, *L' Envers du décor, 1940-1944* (1948).

La Gerbe (August 6 and 13, 1942); *Je Suis Partout* (1941-1944, entire); *Les Lettres Françaises*, clandestine (November 1943, February 1944).

CHAPTER 19 EVERYBODY COLLABORATED
Interviews with Pierre Daix, Gerhard Heller, Claude Roy.

Robert Aron, *Histoire de Vichy, 1940-1944* (1954); Maurice Bardèche, *Lettre à François Mauriac* (1947); Simone de Beauvoir, *La Force de l'âge* (1960); Emmanuel Berl, *Interrogatoire par Patrick Modiano* (1976); Robert Brasillach, *Une Génération dans l'orage* (1968); Brassai, *Conversations avec Picasso* (1969); Arno Breker, *Paris, Hitler, et moi* (1970); Michel-Antoine Burnier, *Les Existentialistes et la politique* (1966); Louis-Ferdinand Céline, *Les Beaux Draps* (1941); Céline, *Bagatelles pour un massacre* (1937); Michèle Cotta, *La Collaboration, 1940-1944* (1964); Stéphane Courtois, *Le PCF dans la guerre* (1980).

André-Louis Dubois, *Sous le signe de l'amitié* vol. 1 of *A travers trois républiques* (1972); Jean Galtier-Boissière, *Mon journal pendant l'occupation* (Garas, France, 1944); Galtier-Boissière, *Mon journal depuis la libération* (1945); Galtier-Boissière, *Mon journal dans la grande pagaïe* (1950); Sacha Guitry, *Quatre ans d'occupations* (1947); Guillaume Hanoteau, *L'Age d'or de Saint-Germain-des-Prés* (1965); Jacques Isorni, *Le Procès de Robert Brasillach* (1946).

Ernst Jünger, *Journal*, vol. 1, *1941-1943*, and vol. 2, *1943-1945* (1951, 1953, revised as *Premier journal parisien* and *Second journal parisien*, 1980); Paul

Léautaud, *Journal littéraire*, vol. 13, *février 1940-juin 1941*, and vol. 14, *juillet 1941-novembre 1942* (1962, 1963); Maurice Martin du Gard, *La Chronique de Vichy, 1940-1944* (1975); Robert 0. Paxton, *Vichy France: Old Guard and New Order, 1940-1944* (New York, 1972); Claude Roy, *Moi je*, vol. 1 of *Somme toute* (1969); Charles Tillon, *On chantait rouge* (1977); Frédéric Vitoux, *Céline* (1978).

Georges Blond, "Les Repos de Weimar — Choses vues au Congrès des Ecrivains d'Europe," *Je Suis Partout* (October 23, 1942); *Les Cahiers du Communisme* (May 1980); *L.-F. Céline*, vols. 1 and 2, Les Cahiers de l'Herne nos. 3 and 5 (1963, 1965); *Les Lettres Françaises*, clandestine (December 1942 and April 1944); "Paris 40-44," *Les Dossiers du Clan* (May 1967).

CHAPTER 20 THE RESISTANCE, THROUGH THE LOOKING GLASS
Interview and correspondence with Gerhard Heller.

Otto Abetz, *Histoire d'une politique franco-allemande, 1930-1950* (1953); Jacques Debû-Bridel, *La Résistance intellectuelle* (1970); Jean Guéhenno, *Journal des années noires, 1940-1944* (1947); Gerhard Heller, "Bribes d'un journal perdu," unpublished manuscript; Marcel Jouhandeau, *Journal sous l'occupation* (1980); Paul Léautaud, *Journal littéraire*, vol. 16, *juillet 1944 — août 1946* (1964); Lucien Rebatet, *Les Décombres* (1942).

Les Lettres Françaises, (June 7, 1946).

CHAPTER 21 MIDNIGHT PRESSES
Interviews with Jean Bruller ("Vercors"), Edmond Charlot, Lucien Scheler. Correspondence with Claude Morgan.

Club des amis du livre progressiste, *Mille neuf cent quarante quatre*, preface by Lucien Scheler (1964); Jacques Debû-Bridel, *Les Editions de Minuit* (1945); Paul Léautaud, *Journal littéraire*, vol. 15, *novembre 1942-juin 1944* (1963); Claude Morgan, *Les Don Quichotte et les autres* (1979); Jean Paulhan, *Oeuvres complètes*, vol. 5 (1970); Jean Paulhan and Dominique Aury, *La Patrie se fait tous les jours* (1947); Vercors, *La Bataille du silence* (1970).

Les Lettres Françaises, clandestine (September 1942-August 1944).

CHAPTER 22 CNE AND COMPANY
Interviews with Lucien Scheler, René Tavernier.

Louis Aragon, *Le Crève-Coeur et Les Yeux d'Elsa* (London, La France Libre, 1944); Simone de Beauvoir, *La Force de l'âge* (1960); Club des amis du livre progressiste, *Mille neuf cent quarante quatre*, preface by Lucien Scheler (1964); Michèle Cotta, *La Collaboration, 1940-1944* (1964); Pierre Daix, *Aragon, une vie à changer* (1975); Jacques Debû-Bridel, *La Résistance intellectuelle* (1970); Ecrivains en prison (1945); Max-Pol Fouchet, *Un jour, je m'en souviens . . .* (1969).

Jean Galtier-Boissière, *Mon journal dans la drôle de paix* (1947); Galtier-Boissière, *Mon journal dans la grande pagaïe* (1950); Jean Guéhenno, *Journal des années noires, 1940-1944* (1947); Gerhard Heller, "Bribes d'un journal perdu," unpublished manuscript; Jean Lacouture, *François Mauriac* (1980); Herbert R. Lottman, *Albert Camus* (New York and London, 1979); Claude Morgan, *Les Don Quichotte et les autres* (1979); Jean Paulhan and Dominique Aury, *La Patrie se fait tous les jours* (1947); Claude Roy, *Moi je and Nous*, vols. 1 and 2 of *Somme toute* (1969, 1972); Pierre Seghers, *La Résistance et ses poètes* (1974).

Le Magazine Littéraire, interviews with Max-Pol Fouchet and Claude Roy (June 1973).

CHAPTER 23 TOPOGRAPHY OF GERMAN PARIS
Interviews with Marguerite Duras, Gerbard Heller, Dionys Mascolo, Claude Roy.

Sylvia Beach, *Shakespeare and Company* (New York, 1959); Simone de Beauvoir, *La Force de l'âge* (1960); Martin Blumenson, *The Vildé Affair: Beginnings of the French Resistance* (Boston, 1977); Brassai, *Conversations avec Picasso* (1969); Pierre Daix, *La Vie de peintre de Pablo Picasso* (1977); Dominique Desanti, *Les Staliniens* (1975); Alfred Fabre-Luce, *L'Epreuve, 1939-1946* (1963); Fabre-Luce, *Journal de la France, 1939-1944* (Geneva, 1946); Jean Galtier-Boissière, *Mon journal pendant l'occupation* (Garas, France, 1944); Galtier-Boissière, *Mon journal depuis la libération* (1945); Jean Guéhenno, *Journal des années noires, 1940-1944* (1947).

Hommage à Yvonne Zervos (1970); Jacques Isorni, *Le Procès de Robert Brasillach* (1946); Ernst Jünger, *Journal*, vol. 1, *1941-1943*, and vol. 2, *1943-1945* (1951, 1953, revised as *Premier journal parisien* and *Second journal parisien*, 1980); Paul Léautaud, *Journal littéraire*, vol. 13, *février 1940-juin 1941*, vol. 14, *juillet 1941-novembre 1942*, and vol. 16, *juillet 1944-août 1946* (1962, 1963, 1964); Maurice Martin du Gard, *La Chronique de Vichy, 1940-1944* (1975); Adrienne Monnier, *Les Gazettes d'Adrienne Monnier, 1925-1945* (1953); Claude Morgan, *Les Don Quichotte et les autres* (1979); Claude Roy, *Moi je and Nous*, vols. 1 and 2 of *Somme toute* (1969, 1972); Roy, *Les Yeux ouverts dans Paris insurgé* (1944); Vercors, *La Bataille du silence* (1970).

Les Lettres Françaises (September 9, 1944).

CHAPTER 24 PARISIANS FAR FROM PARIS
Interviews with Mme Julien Benda, Jean Cassou, Edmond Charlot, Max-Pol Fouchet, Gerhard Heller, Claude Roy, René Tavernier.

Dossiers Gide, Bibliothèque Jacques Doucet.

Pierre Andreu and Frédéric Grover, *Drieu La Rochelle* (1979); Julien Benda, *Les Cahiers d'un clerc, 1939-1949* (1950); Emmanuel Berl, *Interrogatoire par Patrick Modiano* (1976); André Breton, *Entretiens, 1913-1952* (1969); Suzanne Chantal, *Le Coeur battant: Josette Clotis — André Malraux* (1976); Alfred Fabre-Luce, *Journal de la France*, vol. 1, *mars 1939-juillet 1940* (1941); Max-Pol Fouchet, *Un jour, je m'en souviens . . .* (1968); Jean Galtier-Boissière, *Mon journal pendant l'occupation* (Garas, France, 1944); Galtier-Boissière, *Mon journal depuis la libération* (1945); André Gide, *Attendu que . . .* (Algiers, 1943); Gide, *Pages de journal, 1939-1941* (Algiers, 1944); Gide, *Journal, 1942-1949* (1950).

Paul Léautaud, *Journal littéraire*, vol. 15, *novembre 1942-juin 1944* (1963); Alain Malraux, *Les Marronniers de Boulogne* (1978); Clara Malraux, *La Fin et le commencement and Et pourtant j'étais libre*, vols. 5 and 6 of *Le Bruit de nos pas* (1976, 1979); Maurice Martin du Gard, *Les Chroniques de Vichy, 1940-1944* (1975); *Paris — New York: Echanges littéraires au vingtième siècle, exposition catalogue* (1977); Maria Van Rysselberghe, *Les Cahiers de la Petite Dame*, vol. 3, 1937-1945, Cahiers André Gide no. 6 (1975); Antoine de Saint-Exupéry, *Lettre à un otage* (1944); Pierre Seghers, *La Résistance et ses poètes* (1974); Manès Sperber, *Au-delà de l'oubli*, vol. 3 of *Ces temps-là* (1979); Vercors, *La Bataille du silence* (1970).

Confluences (Lyon, 1941-1944); Pierre Drieu La Rochelle, "La Fin des Haricots," *La Nouvelle Revue Française* (December 1942); Luc Estang, "A travers la presse littéraire," *Poésie 44* (November-December 1944); Frédéric J. Grover, "Malraux et Drieu La Rochelle," La Revue des Lettres Modernes, nos. 304-309 (1972); Walter G. Langlois, "André Malraux 1939-1942, d'après une correspondance inédite," *La Revue des Lettres Modernes*, nos. 304-309 (1972); "Les Poètes de la revue Fontaine," *Poésie* (September-November 1978).

CHAPTER 25 LIBERATION
Interviews with André and Lucie Chamson, Gerhard Heller; correspondence with Heller.

Victor Barthélemy, *Du communisme au fascisme* (1978); Sylvia Beach, *Shakespeare and Company* (New York, 1959); Simone de Beauvoir, *La Force de l'âge* (1960); Brassai, *Conversations avec Picasso* (1969); Lucien Combelle, *Péché d'orgueil* (1978); Jean Galtier-Boissière, *Mon journal pendant l'occupation* (Garas, France, 1944); Gerhard Heller, "Bribes d'un journal perdu," unpublished manuscript; Ernst Jünger, *Journal*, vol. 2, *1943-1945* (1953); Herbert R. Lottman, *Albert Camus* (New York and London, 1979); Maurice Martin du Gard, *Les Mémorables*, vol. 3, *1930-1945* (1978); Lucie Mazauric, *Le Louvre en voyage, 1939-1945* (1978); Claude Roy, *Nous*, vol. 2 of *Somme toute* (1972); Pierre Seghers, *La Résistance et ses poètes* (1974).

Combat, August-December 1944, particularly the article by Jean-Paul Sartre, "Toute la ville tire," in the August 31 issue.

Part IV
CHAPTER 26 PICKING UP THE PIECES
Interviews with Jean Bruller ("Vercors"), Jean Cassou, Pierre Daix, Eugène Guillevic, Lucien Scheler. Jean Paulhan archives.

Simone de Beauvoir, *La Force des choses* (1963); Julien Benda, *Les Cahiers d'un clerc, 1939-1949* (1950); Laurent Casanova, *Le Parti communiste, les intellectuels, et la nation*, 2nd ed. (1950); Jean Galtier-Boissière, *Mon journal pendant l'occupation* (Garas, France, 1944); Galtier-Boissière, *Mon journal depuis la libération* (1945); Galtier-Boissière, *Mon journal dans la grande pagaïe* (1950); Jean Guéhenno, *La Foi difficile* (1957).

Jean Lacouture, *François Mauriac* (1980); Paul Léautaud, *Journal littéraire*, vol. 16, *juillet 1944-août 1946* (1964); Herbert R. Lottman, *Albert Camus* (New York and London, 1979); Claude Mauriac, *Un autre de Gaulle: Journal, 1944-1954* (1971); Jean Paulhan, *Lettre aux directeurs de la résistance* (1951), *suivie des répliques et des contre-repliques* (1968); Paulhan, *Oeuvres complètes*, vol. 5 (1970); Maria Van Rysselberghe, *Les Cahiers de la Petite Dame*, vol. 3, *1937-1945*, Cahiers André Gide no. 6 (1975); Vercors, *La Bataille du silence* (1970).

Julien Benda, "Un Fossoyeur de la France: Jean Paulhan," *Europe* (September 1948); *Cahiers de la Pléiade* (April 1947); "Jean Paulhan 1884-1968," *La Nouvelle Revue Française* (May 1, 1969); *Les Lettres Françaises* (1944-1945); Emmanuel Mounier, "Y a-t-il une justice politique?" *Esprit* (August 1947); Roger Secrétain, "Echec de la résistance," *Esprit* (June 1945).

CHAPTER 27 CONSEQUENCES
Interviews with Jean Bruller ("Vercors"), Jean Cassou, André Chamson, Eugène Guillevic, Gerhard Heller. Jean Paulhan archives.
Pierre Andreu, *Le Rouge et le blanc, 1928-1944* (1977); Pierre Andreu and Frédéric Grover, *Drieu La Rochelle* (1979); Robert Aron, *Histoire de l'épuration*, vol. 2 (1975); Victor Barthélemy, *Du communisme au fascisme* (1978); Emmanuel Berl, *Présence des morts* (1956); Robert Brasillach, *Une Génération dans l'orage* (1968); Lucien Combelle, *Péché d'orgueil* (1978); Comité d'Action de la Résistance, *L'Affaire Grasset*, Les Cahiers de la Résistance no. 1 (1949); Charles de Gaulle, *Mémoires de guerre*, vol. 3, *Le Salut, 1944-1946* (1959); Pierre Drieu La Rochelle, *Récit secret: Journal d'exode, 1944-1945* (1961).
Jean Galtier-Boissière, *Mon journal pendant l'occupation* (Garas, France, 1944); Galtier-Boissière, *Mon journal depuis la libération* (1945); Galtier-Boissière, *Mon journal dans la grande pagaïe* (1950); André Gide, *Journal 1942-1949* (1950); Frédéric J. Grover, *Drieu La Rochelle, 1893-1945* (1979); Grover, *Six entretiens avec André Malraux* (1978); Sacha Guitry, *Quatre ans d'occupations* (1947); Jacques Isorni, *Le Procès de Robert Brasillach* (1946); Herbert R. Lottman, *Albert Camus* (New York and London, 1979).
Maurice Martin du Gard, La Chronique de Vichy, 1940-1944 (1975); Claude Mauriac, *Conversations avec André Gide* (195 I); Mauriac, *Un autre de Gaulle: Journal, 1944-1954* (1971); Henry Muller, *Retours de mémoire* (1979); *Le Procès de Charles Maurras* (1946); Claude Roy, *Moi je*, vol. 1 of *Somme toute* (1969); Maria Van Rysselberghe, *Les Cahiers de la Petite Dame*, vol. 3 *1937-1945*, and vol. 4, *1945-1951*, Cahiers André Gide nos. 6 and 7 (1976, 1977); Frédéric Vitoux, *Céline* (1978); Eugen Weber, *Action Française: Royalism and Reaction in Twentieth-Century France* (Stanford, Calif., 1962).
Bibliographie de la France (December 22-29, 1944); Frédéric Grover, "Malraux et Drieu La Rochelle," *La Revue des Lettres Modernes*, nos. 304-309 (1972); *Les Lettres Françaises*, clandestine (August 1944) and postliberation (1944-1950).

CHAPTER 28 NEW FACES AND OLD
Interviews with Jean Bruller ("Vercors"), Lucien Scheler.
Simone de Beauvoir, *La Force des choses* (1963); Michel-Antoine Burnier, *Les Existentialistes et la politique* (1966); Jean Galtier-Boissière, *Mon journal dans la grande pagaïe* (1950); Roger Garaudy, *Une littérature des fossoyeurs* (1947); Guillaume Hanoteau, *L'Age d'or de Saint-Germain-des-Prés* (1965); Francis Jeanson, *Sartre dans sa vie* (1974); Jean Kanapa, *L'Existentialisme n'est pas un humanisme* (1947); Herbert R. Lottman, *Albert Camus* (New York and London, 1979); Henri Mougin, *La Sainte Famille existentialiste* (1947); Jean Paulhan and Dominique Aury, *La Patrie se fait tous les jours* (1947); Jean-Jacques Brochier, ed., *Paul Nizan, intellectuel communiste*, vol. 1, *Articles et*

correspondance, 1928-1939, 2nd ed. (1970); Jean-Paul Sartre, *Qu'est-ce que la littérature?* (1976).

"Jean Paulhan 1884-1968," *La Nouvelle Revue Française* (May 1, 1969); Jean Kanapa, "Les Mots ou le métier de l'écrivain," *Poésie 47* (August-September 1947); *Les Lettres Françaises* (1944-1949, especially December 3, 1944); "La Résistance et la politique," *Combat* (September i, 1944); Jean-Paul Sartre, "Merleau-Ponty vivant," *Les Temps Modernes,* nos. 184-185 (October 1961); Les Temps Modernes (October 1945, July 1947).

CHAPTER 29 CHANGING SAINT-GERMAIN-DES-PRÉS

Interviews with Jorge Amado, Marguerite Duras, Dionys Mascolo.

Simone de Beauvoir, *La Force des choses* (1963); Jean Daniel, *Le Temps qui reste* (1973); Michel Fabre, *The Unfinished Quest of Richard Wright* (New York, 1973); Herbert R. Lottman, *Albert Camus* (New York and London, 1979); Claude Mauriac, *Une Amitié contrariée,* vol. 1 of *Le Temps immobile* (1970); Edgar Morin, *Autocritique* (1959); Claude Roy, *Nous,* vol. 2. of *Somme toute* (1972); Maria Van Rysselberghe, *Les Cahiers de la Petite Dame,* vol. 4, *1945-1951,* Cahiers André Gide no. 7 (1977); William Gardner Smith, *Return to Black America* (Englewood Cliffs, N.J., 1970); *Sur le Seuil, 1935-1979,* history of Seuil publishing house (1979).

Herbert R. Lottman, "The Action Is Everywhere the Black Man Goes," *The New York Times Book Review* (April 21, 1968); Jean-Paul Sartre, "Gide vivant," *Les Temps Modernes* (March 1951); Sartre, "Merleau-Ponty vivant," *Les Temps Modernes,* nos. 184-185 (October 1961).

CHAPTER 30 THE PARTING OF WAYS

Interviews with Jean Bruller ("Vercors"), Jean Cassou, Pierre Daix, Marguerite Duras, Eugéne Guillevic, Dionys Mascolo, Charles Ronsac.

Nello Ajello, *Intellettuali e PCI, 1944-1958* (Bari, Italy, 1979); Laurent Casanova, *Le Parti communiste, les intellectuels, et la nation* (1951); Pierre Daix, *J'ai cru au matin* (1976); Charles de Gaulle, *Mémoires de guerre,* vol. 3, *Le Salut, 1944-1946* (1959); Dominique Desanti, *Les Staliniens* (1975); Jean-Marie Domenach, *Ce que je crois* (1978); Roger Garaudy, *Une littérature de fossoyeurs* (1947); Claude Morgan, *Les Don Quichotte et les autres* (1979); Edgar Morin, *Autocritique* (1959); Claude Roy, *Nous,* vol. 2 of *Somme toute* (1972); André Stil, *L'Optimisme librement consenti* (1979); Roger Vailland, *Le Surréalisme contre la révolution* (1948); Elio Vittorini, *Gli Anni del "Politecnico": Lettere, 1945-1948* (Turin, Italy, 1977).

Guy Besse, "L'Expansionisme idéologique des Yankees," *La Démocratie Nouvelle,* no. 2 (1948); *Esprit* (December 1949); René Etiemble, "De deux ou trois nom de dieu d'intellectuels," *Les Temps Modernes* (November 1946); Jean Gratien and Edgar Morin, "Une Interview d'Elio Vittorini," *Les Lettres Françaises* (June 27, 1947); Jean Kanapa, "Les Mots ou le métier d'écrivain," *Poésie 47* (August-September 1947); *Les Lettres Françaises* (February 10, 1949); Elio Vittorini, "Politique et culture," *Esprit* (January 1948).

CHAPTER 31 COMMUNISTS AND ANTI-COMMUNISTS

Interviews with Raymond Aron, Pierre Daix, Max-Pol Fouchet, Manès Sperber, René Tavernier.

André Siegfried, Roger Seydoux, Edouard Bonnefous, eds., *L'Année politique: Revue chronologique des principaux faits politiques, economiques, et sociaux de la France de la Libération de Paris au 31 Décembre 1945* (1946); Louis Aragon, *La Lumière et la paix: Discours prononcé au Congrès National de l'Union Nationale des Intellectuels, le 29 avril 1950* (1950); Marcel Arland, *Ce fut ainsi* (1979); Simone de Beauvoir, *La Force des choses* (1963); André Breton, *Entretiens, 1913-1952* (1969); Laurent Casanova, *Le Parti communiste, les intellectuels, et la nation* (1951).

Pierre Daix, *Aragon, une vie à changer* (1975); Daix, *J'ai cru au matin* (1976); Daix, *La vie de peintre de Pablo Picasso* (1977); Charles de Gaulle, *Mémoires de guerre*, vol. 3, *Le Salut, 1944-1946* (1959); Dominique Desanti, *Les Staliniens* (1975); *L'Heure du choix* (1947); Jean Kanapa, *Le Traître et le prolétaire ou l'entreprise Koestler and co. ltd.* (1950); Arthur Koestler, *The Invisible Writing* (New York and London, 1954); Herbert R. Lottman, *Albert Camus* (New York and London, 1979).

Alain Malraux, *Les Marronniers de Boulogne* (1978); André Malraux, *Antimémoires* (1967); Malraux, *Les Conquérants*, including his speech of March 5, 1948 (1959); Claude Mauriac, *Un autre de Gaulle: Journal, 1944-1954* (1971); Claude Morgan, *Les Don Quichotte et les autres* (1979); Edgar Morin, *Autocritique* (1959); Claude Roy, *Moi je and Nous*, vols. 1 and 2 of *Somme toute* (1969, 1972); Maria Van Rysselberghe, *Les Cahiers de la Petite Dame*, vol. 4, *1945-1951*, Cahiers André Gide no. 7 (1977); Manès Sperber, *Au-delà de l'oubli*, vol. 3 of *Ces temps-là* (1979).

Cahier Arthur Koestler, Cahiers de l'Herne (1975); *Les Lettres Françaises* (January 17, 1947); *Liberté de l'Esprit* (1949-1950); André Malraux and James Burnham, "The Double Crisis," *Partisan Review* (New York, April 1948); Claude Morgan, "Nettoyer devant sa porte," *Les Lettres Françaises* (February 1, 1946).

CHAPTER 32 COLD WARFARE
Interviews with Raymond Aron, François Bondy, Pierre Daix, Manès Sperber, René Tavernier.

Marcel Arland, *Ce fut ainsi* (1979); Simone de Beauvoir, *La Force des choses* (1963); Claude Bourdet, *L'Europe truquée: Supranationalité pacte atlantique, force de frappe* (1977); Pierre Daix, *Aragon, une vie à changer* (1975); Daix, *J'ai cru au matin* (1976); Daix, *La Vie de peintre de Pablo Picasso* (1977); Dominique Desanti, *Les Staliniens* (1975); Jean Galtier-Boissière, *Mon journal dans la grande pagaïe* (1950); Pierre and Renée Gosset, *Le Procès Kravchenko contre "Les Lettres Françaises"* (1949); Francis Jeanson, *Sartre dans sa vie* (1974); V. A. Kravchenko, *J'ai choisi la liberté* new edition with preface by Pierre Daix (1980); Claude Morgan, *Les Don Quichotte et les autres* (1979); Edgar Morin, *Autocritique* (1959); *Le Procès des Camps de Concentration Soviétiques* (1951); Jean-Paul Sartre, David Rousset, and Gérard Rosenthal, *Entretiens sur la politique* (1949); Roger Stéphane, *Toutes choses ont leur saison* (1979); Michel Winock, *Histoire politique de la revue "Esprit," 1930-1950* (1975); André Wurmser, *Fidèlement vôtre* (1979).

Michèle Barat, "K.K.K.K. le 'Koestler's congress' à Berlin," *L'Observateur* (July 6, 1950); *Carrefour* (October 20 and 27, November 3 and 9, 1948); Henri

Guillemin, "Les Mémoires du R. P. Bruck," *Le Monde* (December 15, 1978); Sidney Hook, "The Berlin Congress for Cultural Freedom," *Partisan Review* (New York, September-October 1950); "Letters to the Times," *The New York Times* (February 15, 1951); *Les Lettres Françaises* (1947-1950); Maurice Merleau-Ponty and Jean-Paul Sartre, "Les Jours de notre vie," *Les Temps Modernes* (January 1950); *Preuves* (1951); David Rousset, "Au Secours des déportés," *Le Figaro Littéraire* (November 12, 1949); Jean-Paul Sartre, "Merleau-Ponty vivant," *Les Temps Modernes*, nos. 184-185 (October 1961).

CHAPTER 33 NO THIRD WAY
Interviews with Claude Bourdet, Pierre Daix, Roger Stéphane.
Simone de Beauvoir, *La Force des choses* (1963); Michel-Antoine Burnier, *Les Existentialistes et la politique* (1966); Abel Chatelain, *Le Monde et ses lecteurs sous la IVe République* (1962); Claude Estier, *La Gauche hebdomadaire, 1914-1962* (1962); René Etiemble, *Littérature dégagée, 1942-1953* (1955); Michel Fabre, *The Unfinished Quest of Richard Wright* (New York, 1973); Jean-Noël Jeanneney and Jacques Julliard, *Le Monde de Beuve-Méry* (1979); Francis Jeanson, *Sartre dans sa vie* (1974); Herbert R. Lottman, *Albert Camus* (New York and London, 1979); Jean-Paul Sartre, David Rousset, and Gérard Rosenthal, *Entretiens sur la politique* (1949); Roger Stéphane, *Toutes choses ont leur saison* (1979); Michel Winock, *Histoire politique de la revue "Esprit," 1930-1950* (1975).
Combat (1947-1948); *Esprit* (1949-1951); Sidney Hook, "Report on the International Day Against Dictatorship and War," *Partisan Review* (New York, July 1949); Francis Jeanson, "Albert Camus ou l'âme révoltée," with reply by Camus and further texts by Sartre and Jeanson, *Les Temps Modernes* (May and August 1952); *L'Observateur* (1950); Jean-Paul Sartre, "Merleau-Ponty vivant," *Les Temps Modernes*, nos. 184-185 (October 1961).

EPILOGUE
Interviews with Raymond Aron, Jérôme Lindon.
Simone de Beauvoir, *La Force des choses* (1963); André Breton, *Entretiens, 1913-1952* (1969); Ilya Ehrenburg, *Memoirs, 1921-1941* (New York, 1966); René Etiemble, *Littérature dégagée, 1942-1953* (1955); *L'Heure du choix* (1947); *Paris Ville Internationale*, Travaux et Recherches de Prospective no. 39 (1973).
Raymond Aron, "Politics and the French Intellectuals," *Partisan Review* (New York, July-August, 1950); Claude Jeantet, "Quand l'ENA chasse la Sorbonne," *Le Monde* (April 24, 1979); Jean-Paul Sartre, "Merleau-Ponty vivant," *Les Temps Modernes*, nos. 184-185 (October 1961).

Index